AF764661

Calendar

OF

SELECT PLEAS AND MEMORANDA
OF THE CITY OF LONDON

Calendar

OF

SELECT PLEAS AND MEMORANDA OF THE CITY OF LONDON

Preserved among the ARCHIVES of the CORPORATION of the CITY OF LONDON at the GUILDHALL

A.D. 1381–1412

Edited by

A. H. THOMAS, M.A.

LATE OF ST CATHARINE'S COLLEGE, CAMBRIDGE
DEPUTY-KEEPER OF THE CITY RECORDS

PRINTED BY ORDER OF THE CORPORATION UNDER THE DIRECTION OF THE LIBRARY COMMITTEE

CAMBRIDGE : AT THE UNIVERSITY PRESS
MCMXXXII

CAMBRIDGE
UNIVERSITY PRESS

University Printing House, Cambridge CB2 8BS, United Kingdom

Cambridge University Press is part of the University of Cambridge.

It furthers the University's mission by disseminating knowledge in the pursuit of education, learning and research at the highest international levels of excellence.

www.cambridge.org
Information on this title: www.cambridge.org/9781107463974

© Cambridge University Press 1932

This publication is in copyright. Subject to statutory exception and to the provisions of relevant collective licensing agreements, no reproduction of any part may take place without the written permission of Cambridge University Press.

First published 1932
First paperback edition 2014

A catalogue record for this publication is available from the British Library

ISBN 978-1-107-46397-4 Paperback

Cambridge University Press has no responsibility for the persistence or accuracy of URLs for external or third-party internet websites referred to in this publication, and does not guarantee that any content on such websites is, or will remain, accurate or appropriate.

CONTENTS

CORRIGENDA

p. 86, line 32, *to read* Walter "Hervylle."
p. 237, line 17, *to read* "William" More.

INTRODUCTION

THE present volume, unlike its predecessors, is described as a calendar of *select* pleas and memoranda, because a somewhat larger number of formal entries and records of small debt actions have been omitted. Care has been taken, however, to include all passages which seem to add in any way to our knowledge of the times, and especially those which may throw light on the civic disturbances regarded by historians as a struggle between the victualling and non-victualling guilds. In this connection, attention may be drawn to an interesting correspondence with John of Gaunt, who interceded on behalf of John Norhampton, the banished ex-mayor[1]. Certain English enrolments, including two letters of Sir John Hawkwood, the famous leader of the White Company, are also worthy of note, and are reproduced *verbatim*[2]. For the rest, among other matters illustrating London life, the editor has set out fully the numerous inventories of household goods, plate, jewels and textile fabrics, which give information on domestic conditions and the trade and manufactures of the period.

THE LAW MERCHANT

On reference to the subject-index, it will be noticed that in many of the actions which came up for trial the proceedings are said to be according to the law merchant. There are similar mentions of this law, though not so numerous, in earlier calendars. But on a comparison of such actions with others of a commercial nature, not so described, it is obvious that the causes of action, the manner in which they were pleaded, the proofs which were accepted and the remedies provided were the same. This is especially the case in the early Mayor's Court rolls, 1298–1307, in which the law merchant is only twice mentioned[3]. Many of the actions there

[1] Below, pp. 109–13. [2] Below, pp. 279–81, 308–10, 313.

[3] Holdsworth, *Law Quarterly Review*, CLXII, p. 223. "It was regarded as pre-eminently the court for the settlement of the disputes of foreign merchants, and therefore as a court in which the law merchant was

came on appeal from the Sheriffs' *curia de forinsecis*; others were initiated on bills and verbal complaints put in by merchants. Though there is no direct reference to the law merchant, there can be no doubt that these are law merchant actions and that the authorities were dealing with commercial causes in the manner prescribed by the king in 1285[1], when he took the city into his hand. In such matters the "custom of the city" and the "law merchant" appear to be almost convertible terms; and no real distinction can be drawn between them[2].

Law merchant records in England

Hitherto, owing to the lack of printed records, it has been difficult to estimate how far the mercantile rules of the Italian cities and the great continental fairs were adopted in England. Pollock and Maitland were inclined to think that the English law merchant consisted mainly of rules of evidence, proof of sales and other contracts and the legal value of the tally and the God's penny, and that if it were possible to recover them, we might find some which had their origin on the coasts of the Mediterranean[3]. Miss Bateson was struck by the fact that merchant law was merely a subsection, chiefly concerned with procedure, in the borough custumals, which had little to tell us of "the rules of hosting and brokerage, the beginnings of the negotiable instrument or the responsibilities of partnership, the delivery of goods, owner's risk, negligence, covenant and account[4]." But as the custumals, whatever their date, are mainly compilations of ancient customs of the 12th and early 13th centuries, before there was any large commercial intercourse with the continent, their silence is not unnatural[5]. Unfortunately the only English treatise on the subject in the

administered; and, in fact, there are more cases on these rolls, which raise important questions of maritime and commercial law than on any of the rolls of fair courts and borough courts already in print." Cf. *Ricart's Kalendar* (Camd. Soc.), p. 95.

[1] *Munimenta Gildhallae Londoniensis* (Rolls Series), I, p. 295.

[2] The Staple Court at Westminster frequently remitted actions to the Mayor's Court, where they were tried "by the custom of the city and the law merchant." *Cal. Plea & Mem. Rolls*, 1364–1381, pp. 277, 283. See also below, pp. 27, 33, 162, etc.

[3] Pollock and Maitland, *Hist. Eng. Law*, I, p. 467.

[4] Mary Bateson, *Borough Customs* (Seld. Soc.), II, p. lxxxiv.

[5] The Liber Albus of London, compiled in 1419, contains many rules which were obsolete more than a century before.

Middle Ages is also of comparatively early date. The section on the Lex Mercatoria in the Little Red Book of Bristol[1], written probably soon after 1280[2], has much to say about procedure, but can only point out three particulars in which the law merchant differed from the common law—its curtailment of delays, the responsibility of a defendant's pledges, and the onus laid upon a plaintiff to prove his claim. Little further help was afforded by the publication of the records of the court of St Ives Fair. The disputes concerned petty amounts and the primitive rules for solving difficulties cannot be said to have affected the development of commercial law[3].

In recent years, however, more material has become available. The select cases extracted by Dr Hubert Hall from the records of central courts and his later studies of statutory recognisances reveal that the law merchant was dealing with intricate commercial disputes, for which the common law could give no remedy[4]. Similar evidence is afforded by our London rolls. It may be seen from actions in which considerable amounts of money were at stake that the London courts in the later 14th century were doing justice between great merchants and financiers, as well as between small traders. They show further that Englishmen travelled widely and were in constant business relations with foreign merchants both at home and abroad. Such traffic could only be carried on if there were some common agreement as to rights and duties. And although it has been said that any great absorption of the Italian law merchant in England is unlikely before the 16th century, it would appear that the many travelling English merchants could hardly remain ignorant of the legal rules observed in foreign fairs and centres of commerce. To what extent this traffic in ideas was reflected in the practice of English local courts is a question which can only be answered as the archives of important English towns are brought to light and more thoroughly examined.

[1] F. B. Bickley, *Little Red Book of Bristol*, I, p. 58.

[2] H. G. Richardson, *Eng. Hist. Rev.* XXXVII, p. 243, n. 2.

[3] C. Gross, *Select Cases on the Law Merchant*, I (Seld. Soc.); Holdsworth, *Hist. Eng. Law*, V, p. 113.

[4] Hubert Hall, *Select Cases on the Law Merchant*, II (Seld. Soc.). I have to thank Dr Hall for allowing me to read in proof his further volume.

Nature of the law merchant

Whatever be the exact nature of the English law merchant, it was regarded some time before the end of the 13th century as a distinct body of rules apart from the common law[1], applicable to the affairs of merchants and commonly used in fairs and merchant-towns. On occasion these rules could be followed in the king's central courts and both there and in the local courts it was recognised as international in its scope. In 1291 the barons of the Exchequer were ordered to hear an action of account between Gettus Honesti of Lucca and Peregrin son of Gerardin of Chartres, in which a sum of 50,000 marks was involved[2]. The defendant pleaded that in the transaction under review he was not a factor of the plaintiff but a partner of the society of which both were members. This was a plea, says the record, of which the truth could not be investigated by the common law. Later, when books of accounts were produced, the barons confessed that they did not understand their idiom and that the laws and customs used between merchants were unknown to them. A jury drawn from the greater societies of merchants in London was twice called upon to give verdicts on facts, after which the matter was submitted to two successive boards of auditors who struggled with a complicated mass of accounts before retiring in favour of arbitrators, by whom, after prolonged and difficult labour, a final award was given. The majority of the merchants who helped to solve the problem, as jurors, auditors or arbitrators, were Italians, but German and French merchants and at least one Englishman took part. Doubtless the barons of the Exchequer had learnt something of the law merchant before the case ended.

This was not an isolated case. The king's justices were ordered in 1313 to deal, according to the law merchant, with piracy claims by Flemings[3], in 1320 with a dispute between England and Flanders as to spoil[4], and in 1321 the itinerant

[1] Charter of Henry III to London, 1268, W. de G. Birch, *Historical Charters of the City of London*, p. 38.

[2] Hall, *Law Merchant*, II, pp. 53–4.

[3] R. G. Marsden, *Select Pleas in the Court of Admiralty* (Seld. Soc.), I, p. xix; *Foedera*, II (1), p. 210.

[4] Marsden, *op. cit.* p. xxii; *Rot. Parl.* I, pp. 356–9.

justices in London were directed to try an action by the law and custom of the realm or by the law merchant[1].

In all the above cases it seems to have been assumed that the law merchant was understood by, and essentially the same for, merchants of every country. The same assumption underlies the correspondence between important towns, which freely called upon each other to supply information under seal upon mercantile matters[2], to entertain the actions of their merchants[3], and to enforce the judgments of their courts[4]. Such judgments by the law merchant were recognised everywhere as valid, and it was a good defence in an English court to plead that the plaintiff had already obtained recovery in a merchant court abroad[5]. A marked feature of the correspondence was a plea for such reasonable and fair treatment as the authorities would wish their own merchants to receive elsewhere.

Law merchant as jus gentium

It was doubtless this insistence on a common sense of fairness, together with the international character of the law merchant and the fact that the legal ideas of many nations were brought into contribution, which led to its definition as a *jus gentium* or *lex naturae*. In the 15th-century custumals of Rye, Winchelsea and Fordwich, the judges were instructed "to have recourse to the laws of nature, on which are founded and whence proceed all written laws[6]." A similar definition was given by the Chancellor before the King's Council in the Star Chamber in 1473. In his view a plea by foreign merchants as to the breaking of bulk by a carrier should not be tried by statute, but by the law of nature, "which is called by some the law merchant and which is law universal throughout the world," and he infers that such law is proper

[1] Richardson, *E.H.R.* XXXVII, p. 244, n. 1, quoting Assize Roll 546 m. 47 d.

[2] *Cal. P. & M. Rolls*, II, pp. 166–7; below, pp. 42–3, 82–3, 128, 140–2, 165, 314.

[3] *Cal. P. & M. Rolls*, I, pp. 10, 56, 89, 131, 172, 215, etc.

[4] R. R. Sharpe, *Cal. of Letters*, p. 143.

[5] Bickley, *Little Red Book*, I, pp. 80–1; *Cal. P. & M. Rolls*, II, p. 136, where John de Stodeye, vintner, who had been arrested as a surety for debt, was discharged because his principal had already been condemned in Bayonne and had paid his debt.

[6] Bateson, *Borough Customs*, II, p. 59.

to the chancery[1]. As will be noticed later, alike in its procedure and its ideas, the law merchant had close resemblances to equity.

Early mercantile courts in London

London, owing to its situation and natural advantages, was early marked out to be a great commercial centre and a resort for foreign merchants. In the laws of Ethelred II are regulations for traders from Flanders, Ponthieu, Normandy, France and the towns of Rouen, Huy, Liége and Nivelles[2], and about a hundred and thirty years later rules were put on record concerning the Lorrainers, the men of the Emperor, the Danes and the Norse[3]. That there was trade with Italy in the 12th century may be inferred from the settlement of Italian families in the city[4]. The itinerant justices in 1220 were informed that passing merchants called "pepoudrous" could already sue for debt and torts in the Husting, but that the mayor and sheriffs were willing, with the assistance of two or three aldermen, to do speedy justice to them day by day outside the Husting[5].

The Sheriffs' Court for foreigners

Apparently the mayor and sheriffs acted separately. The sheriffs already exercised jurisdiction over citizens in an ancient court, which now took cognisance of foreign pleas[6]. So numerous were the latter, that about 1230 complaint was made that the pleas of citizens were being delayed[7]. Fifty years later it was the only court of this nature known to the Bristol author of the Lex Mercatoria, from which it may be inferred that it was far more frequented than the Mayor's Court[8]. However, the jurisdiction of both courts was recognised by the constitutions issued by Edward I, when he took the city into his hand and appointed a warden. In order that foreign merchants should not be delayed by long drawn out pleas, the warden and sheriffs were enjoined to hold pleas day by

1 Hall, *Law Merchant*, II, p. lxxxv; Holdsworth, *Hist. Eng. Law*, V, p. 116.

2 Liebermann, *Gesetze der Angelsachsen*, I, p. 232.

3 Add. MS. 14, 252, fos. 99 *b*–100 *b*; Bateson, *E.H.R.* XVII, pp. 499–502. Höhlbaum suggests c. 1130 for the date of these regulations.

4 W. Page, *London, its origin and early development*, pp. 236, 239.

5 *Munim. Gild. Lond.* (R.S.), I, p. 67.

6 *Cal. of Early Mayor's Court Rolls*, pp. xiv–xv.

7 Liber Ordinacionum, fo. 173.

8 Bickley, *Little Red Book*, I, p. 59, which says that a merchant would find pledges for prosecution, if he were in London, before the Sheriff.

day for foreigners, appointing someone in their places if they were unable to attend[1]. Unfortunately only one roll of the Sheriffs' Court survives, namely that of the year 1320–21, when the popularity of the court seems to have been on the wane. However, in the period 1300–1307, some sixteen actions terminated in the Sheriffs' Court were taken on appeal to the Mayor's Court[2] on the ground of partiality, or of error in the record and process or the giving of judgment; and in thirteen of these appeals a copy of the record in the former court is preserved in the file. They concern debt, detinue of pledges after repayment, covenant, trespass, account, partnership, guarantee and contract of affreightment, and were obviously pleaded by the law merchant.

The Sheriffs' Court appears to have preserved a concurrent jurisdiction with the Mayor's Court in law merchant cases until the latter part of the 14th century[3]. Possibly the Statute of the Staple, which drew a distinction between the law merchant and the customs of cities and boroughs[4], may have resulted in a loss of litigants. Whereas in 1344 the court was ordered by writ to do justice between a citizen and a Hanse merchant[5], in 1355 the Sheriff was called to account for the arrest of a debtor in a mercantile action, the debtor having already been admitted to bail in another action before the Staple Court of Westminster[6]. In the present calendar are recorded several mercantile actions begun in the Sheriffs' Court, which were called into the Mayor's Court before judgment had been rendered. The ordinary reason for this course lay in the custom that where a satisfactory trial was unlikely because of maintenance, intimidation, delay of justice

[1] Liber Ordinacionum, fos. 197–202 b. The so-called *Statuta Civitatis Londoniarum*, printed in *Statutes of the Realm*, I, pp. 102–4, as from a *cedula* in the Statute Roll, and dated 1285, are in fact a later confirmation and correspond with the text given in Letter Book C, fo. 15 b, among other enrolments of 1294.

[2] *Cal. of E.M.C. Rolls*, pp. 69, 98, 101–2, 110, 117–18, 118, 120, 121, 128–9, 129–30, 131–3, 133–4, 135, 135–6, 140–1, 143, 144–5, 166–7, 168–9, 181–2, 202, 242–3, 243–5, 261, 262–3.

[3] Richardson, *E.H.R.* XXXVII, p. 244 and n. 3.

[4] 27 Edw. III, Stat. 2, c. 8.

[5] *Cal. P. & M. Rolls*, I, p. 213. The alderman of the Hanse claimed and was allowed his court.

[6] Chancery, Extents on Debts, file 9.

and the like[1], the Mayor could take the action before himself, on request of either party. But in 1383 the reasons given were favouritism and the fact that the action concerned the law merchant[2]. In 1390 an action was removed from the Sheriffs' Court on the application of the parties because "the plaint touches the law merchant and such an action touching the said law and especially between foreigners is not wont to be terminated before the Sheriff but according to the custom of the city it ought to be finished and terminated in the Chamber (i.e. the Inner Chamber of the Guildhall) before the Mayor and Aldermen having knowledge of the law merchant[3]." The same reason was given in 1398 in an action of debt on account made[4] and in several subsequent actions. Nevertheless the Sheriffs' "foreign courts" continued to be held, and actions between foreign merchants were terminated there[5]. Possibly these were simple, straightforward actions in which the parties were content to abide by the common law, and as the foreign courts would be held from day to day, the procedure was as expeditious as that of the Mayor's Court.

The Mayor's Court

As we have seen, both in 1220 and 1285[6] the mayor was charged with the duty of giving justice day by day to foreign merchants, and there is little doubt this jurisdiction was one of the causes which led to the formation of the Mayor's Court. In accordance with the city's charters[7], the Husting Court could only be held on Monday and by adjournment on Tuesday[8], and consequently any meeting for judicial purposes on other days must be regarded as a separate court. Meanwhile other business was transferred from the overburdened Husting. In 1263, when no Husting was held, we find the Mayor and Aldermen dealing with offences against the assizes, i.e., the city ordinances relating to victuals, public order and the regulation of trade[9]. It is clear also that by

[1] Below, pp. 115, 242. [2] Below, pp. 42–3.
[3] Liber Dunthorn, fo. 68; Richardson, *E.H.R.* XXXVII, p. 244 and n. 3.
[4] Below, pp. 251–3.
[5] Below, pp. 263 (1399), 300 (1409), 303 (1411).
[6] *Munim. Gild. Lond.* (R.S.), II, p. 67; Liber Ordinacionum, fo. 173.
[7] Charter of Henry I. See Page, *London*, p. 276.
[8] Charter of Henry III, 1268. Birch, *Historical Charters*, p. 40.
[9] *Liber de Antiquis Legibus* (Camd. Soc.), p. 70. *Cal. of E.M.C. Rolls*, p. xviii.

1272 actions between citizens begun by the ancient procedure of bills of complaint had been crowded out of the Husting of Common Pleas[1]. Thus the Mayor's Court had become a resort both for foreigners and citizens. From an 18th century list of records it appears that there were then extant Mayor's Court rolls of 1277–8 and 1290–1. In other city books there are references to proceedings in 1280 and succeeding years[2].

The earliest record, however, of an action between foreign merchants comes from the year 1292, when the warden, Ralph de Sandwich, in obedience to a writ of *certiorari*, sent a transcript of an action pleaded before him[3]. A German merchant sued an Englishman, who was not a citizen and therefore ranked as a foreigner, for debt incurred at the Fair of St Ives, alleging that the latter had absconded. The warden entertained the action because the defendant was found in London and because his conduct, possibly owing to his being mistaken for a citizen, had gravely affected the commercial credit of the city. Interesting features of the action are the fact that the warden took counsel with the aldermen on a point of law, in the same way as merchants were consulted in other mercantile courts, and that the defendant was condemned because he was unwilling to submit himself to a jury of merchants frequenting the fair of St Ives.

In the period between 1298–1307, covered by the nine extant Mayor's Court rolls[4], there is an abundance of actions concerning foreign merchants, pleaded according to typical law merchant rules. They deal with a wide variety of causes—detinue of unredeemed pledges, proof of tallies, account, agency, covenant, debt, deceit and trespass; and while, as in almost all law merchant cases, they mainly illustrate procedure, they show also what the court considered to be the competence of the law merchant and the remedies allowed by it.

The absence of records between 1307 and 1323, the date of the first Plea and Memoranda roll, is to some extent relieved

[1] *Cal. of E.M.C. Rolls*, p. xix.

[2] *Ibid.* p. xx; *Cal. of Letter Book* B, pp. 10–12, 13–14; *Cal. of Letter Book* A, pp. 64, 120–1, 213; *Munim. Gild. Lond.* (R.S.), II (1), pp. 282–3.

[3] Richardson, *E.H.R.* XXXVII, pp. 242–9; Chancery Miscellanea, bundle 109, file 1.

[4] *Cal. of E.M.C. Rolls.*

by the account of the London law courts preserved in Ricart's Kalendar[1]. This was borrowed, so the compiler tells us, "oute of a boke that was maistir Henry Daarcy sometyme recorder of London in kinge Edward the thirdes daies." Darcy was mayor, not recorder, in 1337–9, and his book almost certainly owed its origin to the inquiries made by the itinerant justices in 1321[2]. The Mayor's Court, it appears, was held before the Mayor and Aldermen in the Chamber or the Husting, and this from day to day at their will. They were accustomed there, with other jurisdiction, to hold pleas of debt and other actions personal whatsoever by bill, as well between merchants and merchants by law merchant as between others that would plead by process made against the parties, and it was customary that no error should be sued of judgments given before the Mayor and Aldermen in the Chamber of the Guildhall according to the law merchant.

The Staple Courts

No small number of the merchants whose actions were heard in the Mayor's Court were connected with the staple exports of wool, woolfells, hides and tin, and London from 1326 onwards was one of the English Staple towns[3]. A change of policy in 1353 relegated the city to the position of a port for Westminster, to which the Staple was transferred, a change which Dr Tout regarded as an intentional blow to London[4]. The Statute of the Staple laid down that the mayors and constables of the Staple should have jurisdiction and cognisance within their towns of all Staple merchants, their servants and households by the law merchant and not by common law nor by usage of cities, boroughs and other towns, and that this cognisance should extend to contracts and covenants arising both within the Staple and without, saving to a plaintiff the right to sue in other place of the common law if he wished[5]. Actually its economic effect on London was short-lived. The custom-house was in London. It was only Londoners who could supply the cash and goods for the

[1] L. Toulmin Smith, *Ricart's Kalendar* (Camd. Soc.), pp. 20, 95–113.
[2] Richardson, *E.H.R.* XXXVII, p. 243, n. 6.
[3] E. Lipson, *Econ. Hist.* I, pp. 476–9; *Cal. Pat. Rolls*, 1324–7, p. 269; *Ibid.* 1327–30, pp. 98–9.
[4] T. F. Tout, *Beginnings of a Modern Capital* (Raleigh Lecture, 1923), p. 19.
[5] 27 Edw. III, Stat. 2, c. 8; *Statutes of the Realm*, I, p. 336.

Westminster Staple[1], and the mayoralty of the Staple was usually held by a London citizen[2].

In the legal sphere, however, the Statute, with its reference to the custom of boroughs, seems to have led the city clerks to emphasise that the procedure of the Mayor's Court was a true law merchant procedure, and especially in cases where the Staple Court at Westminster was unable to do justice because the defendant had no goods in the Staple, whereby he could be attached to answer. In 1362 an action between Lombards, which involved partnership accounts, was sent under the seal of the Staple to the mayor and recorder for the above reason and because the mayor of the Staple wished to safeguard the liberties of London. It was pleaded by the law merchant, and after an attempt to empanel a jury of the moiety, was finally submitted to the arbitration of four Lombards[3]. Next year four cases relating to debt, partnership, and the liability of executors were dealt with in the same way[4], and other actions were remitted to London in following years[5]. In one action the mayor of the Staple himself appears as plaintiff. In Blakeney *v.* Jacob in 1378 the record runs "and because the plaint concerned merchandise the mayor fixed a day for hearing in a private room at Guildhall before himself and the other aldermen, so that the action might be terminated according to the law merchant[6]." The competence of the court is stressed in two actions in 1380, where the mayor informed the parties that he was mayor of the Staple of Westminster as well as mayor of London, and that the law merchant was pleadable before him both in the Staple and the Chamber of the Guildhall[7]. In both cases the litigants exercised the right of deciding whether they would plead by the law merchant or not.

The Inner Chamber

The above reference to a private room bears witness to a separation between the ordinary business of the Mayor's Court, which was held in the Chamber proper, and the

[1] Tout, *op. cit.*

[2] E.g. Pye, *Cal. P. & M. Rolls*, II, p. 25; Walworth, p. 277; below, p. 72; Hadley, below, p. 312.

[3] Gascoigne *v.* Gysane, *Cal. P. & M. Rolls*, I, pp. 258–9.

[4] *Ibid.* pp. 261–3.

[5] *Cal. P. & M. Rolls*, II, pp. 9, 25.

[6] *Ibid.* p. 248.

[7] *Ibid.* pp. 277, 283.

mercantile actions, which were heard in the Inner Chamber, where the administrative Court of Aldermen usually met. The reason for this change no doubt lay in the intimate nature of the proceedings, which, beginning with pleading, often developed into an audit and examination of accounts and documents, in which the plaintiff and defendant took part, questions being put to them and to all who could throw light on the transactions under review[1]. From this time forward the Inner Chamber seems to have taken on the character of a separate court, so separate in fact as not to preclude proceedings elsewhere. In 1407 a complainant obtained an order in the Inner Chamber for specific performance, and that proving ineffective, a month later he entered an ordinary action of detinue on the civic side of the court, where he had judgment for specific performance of the contract, if possible, but otherwise for damages[2].

It was in the Inner Chamber again that the important case of Burton *v.* Derby on non-payment of a bill of exchange was heard in 1436, when the mayor, in answer to a *certiorari* from the Court of Common Pleas, returned a description of law merchant procedure in the Mayor's Court. He claimed that the city of London from time immemorial had been one of the ancient and notable towns and merchant Staples of the whole realm of England, and that according to the custom of the city and the law merchant the Mayor and Aldermen had the power of hearing and considering causes of visiting and resident merchants as to all manner of loans, barretries, exchanges, letters of payment and other mercantile matters and contracts entered into at fairs and market-towns outside the realm of England. Such actions could be tried by juries of merchants passing between foreign places where such actions arose and the city, or if this form of trial were not adopted, then by the examinations and confessions of the parties, witnesses, letters, instruments or other suitable kinds of proof, according to the law merchant and the custom of the

[1] Below, pp. 171–2; see also pp. 31–5 for an action necessitating examination of documents.

[2] Below, pp. 285–6, 287–8.

city. The court gave remedies agreeable to good faith and consonant with reason[1].

Law merchant and equity

In this reference to equity lies the difficulty of deducing principles. There would be the same difficulty in attempting to systematise the considerations which may have moved the Chancellor in the 15th century when he was called upon to deal with grievances for which the common law afforded no alleviation. The city authorities acted according to their sense of fairness[2], guided by the common conscience of men of business. We may say that the law merchant recognised commercial rights and duties of which the common law took no cognisance, that its aim was to do substantial justice, and that its procedure was designed to meet the needs of busy men. The principles of the law merchant are to be found in the customs of commercial intercourse, to which the courts gave sanction from time to time.

Competence of law merchant

The competence of merchant courts was wide. All pleas except those of land, says the treatise in the Little Red Book, naturally belong to those laws[3]. Felony of course must be excepted. In addition to the common actions of debt and contract, the London records show that detinue, apprenticeship, the liabilities of executors, deceit, and miscellaneous torts were entertained[4]. The same is true of the Fair Court of St Ives, which, in many of its actions, appears to be rather a court for merchants than a special law merchant tribunal. In course of time the tendency was to restrict the law merchant to cases of exceptional difficulty, and to leave those actions which could be sued at common law to the king's courts or to the ordinary local courts[5].

[1] Liber Dunthorn, fos. 68 b–69 b, and Letter Book K, fo. 163 b, for the writ and return of 3 Nov. 1437. The preliminary proceedings are given in the return to a *certiorari* of 14 Feb. 1437. The justices remitted the action to the Mayor's Court, where, after examination of the parties and their factors on oath, and other numerous forms of proof, judgment was given on a bill of exchange of £30 with 20*s*. damages.

[2] Below, p. 301, *consultum fuit ulterius per curiam per eorum conscienciam quod....*

[3] Bickley, *Little Red Book*, I, p. 57.

[4] *Cal. of P. & M. Rolls*, I, p. 263; *Cal. of P. & M. Rolls*, II, pp. 75–6; below, pp. 33, 89–90, 140, 163.

[5] The Lex Mercatoria says that merchants could forgo the law merchant and sue at common law, which happened more frequently than otherwise. Bickley, *op. cit.* p. 57.

There was no limitation as to amount. The custumal of Torksey claimed that in its piepowder court, covenants, contracts, trespasses and debts both above and below the sum of forty shillings could be tried[1]. To judge from an action which was taken on appeal from the Fair Court of Stamford to the Court of Common Pleas, in which the defendant pleaded that the court could not adjudicate in a claim of over twenty shillings without the king's writ, this custom was not disputed by the justices[2]. The Mayor's Court, both on its civic and its mercantile side, dealt with claims of any amount, and this privilege, though now restricted to actions where the whole cause arises within the city, still obtains to-day[3].

Origin and venue of actions

In earlier days the Mayor's Court appears to have been stricter than other courts in confining its attention to pleas connected in some way with the city. The Lex Mercatoria declares that where a plaintiff was able to prove his plea by a deed or by a suit of proper witnesses, there was nothing to hinder the court from discussing an action, the origin of which lay outside the market[4]. It was usually the duty of proof which deterred the city authorities. In dealing with the case of the debtor who absconded from Lynn in 1292, the warden thought it necessary to excuse his action on the ground that the credit of London was involved and the debtor had been run to earth in the city[5]. In 1300, when a knight who had gone on expedition to Scotland in the retinue of another knight, sued the latter for the loss of three horses, alleging that the agreement made in Norfolk had been confirmed in London, the Sheriffs' Court told the parties to sue at common law, because the contract was a foreign one, the horses were not merchandise, and the court could not call a jury of the venue[6]. However, in another case of 1305, where a contract of affreightment was made in Bordeaux for carriage of wine to London, the same court admitted the action and allowed the defendant to clear himself by compurgation of a

[1] Gross, *Law Merchant*, I, p. xxxvii.
[2] Hall, *Law Merchant*, II, p. 42.
[3] *Corporation Statement*, 1893, p. 80.
[4] Bickley, *op. cit.* p. 70.
[5] Richardson, *op. cit.* p. 248.
[6] *Cal. of E.M.C. Rolls*, pp. 69–70.

charge of wilful delay, apparently on the ground that the wine had actually been delivered in London[1]. Again in 1299, when the wardens of the Fair of Champenoise Brie urged the warden of London to compel a number of foreigners to satisfy other foreigners on a contract made at the Fair in 1292, he summoned the defendants and accepted as exoneration an acquittance of 1293 under the seal of the then wardens[2]. About 1321 rules were set down for guidance in the matter. The Sheriffs' Court (and no doubt the Mayor's Court) was regarded as competent to deal with actions between merchants on contracts made in other mercantile towns, at home or abroad, so long as there was an express condition that the debt should be repaid, or the goods delivered or account made in London[3]. Returns made in 1390[4] and 1436[5] suggest that the court was then admitting any actions arising in fairs and market-towns abroad, provided that the parties either resided or continually resorted to the city. In the 16th and 17th centuries the fiction was adopted that the venue of such actions lay in the parish of St Helen's, London, and therefore fell within the cognisance of the court.

Merchants as givers of judgments

In the Mayor's Court merchants do not appear to have co-operated in the work of the court to the same extent as elsewhere. In every court of a market, says the Lex Mercatoria, judgments ought to be rendered by the merchants of the same court and not by the mayor or the steward of the court[6]. In case of false judgments, the suitors of the court, who included residents of the town or fair and merchants actually present at the time, were liable to penalties, because they, and not the lords of the fairs, were bound to render judgments. This was in accordance with the ancient customs whereby

[1] *Cal. of E.M.C. Rolls*, pp. 168–9.

[2] Letter Book C, fo. 44 b. Sharpe mistakenly called the action an inquiry.

[3] *Munim. Gild. Lond.* I, p. 215. 17 Edw. IV, c. 2 limited the jurisdiction of Fair Courts to contracts, deeds and trespasses made and committed within and during the fair.

[4] Matuleano *v.* Conago, below, pp. 171–2.

[5] Burton *v.* Derby, Liber Dunthorn, fos. 68b–9.

[6] Bickley, *op. cit.* I, pp. 70–1; Gross, *Law Merchant*, I, p. xxv, quotes Year Book, 6 Edw. IV, f. 3 for a decision of the justices that the steward or chief officer of the court was the judge. Cf. *ibid.* p. xxxv.

the suitors of a court were the doomsmen, the men who gave judgments. At least as late as the time of Edward I the suitors are acting in this way in the county courts and continued to do so in manorial courts till modern times[1]. But it must be remembered that judgment was a word of wide applications. There might be several judgments in an action, both as to fact and as to law. Where the suitors in the court of St Ives speak on facts, it would be more proper to call them a jury; in the cases where they give "judgments" on law they appear either to have been deciding on the form of proof admissible or giving information on merchant custom[2]. Probably it is true to say that though they gave judgments, they were not judges.

There are several traces of the suitors as doomsmen in the city records. In 1230 and again in 1246 it was necessary to prevent advocates and those concerned in actions from joining in the forming of judgments[3]—a fact which indicates that in the Husting others than the mayor and sheriffs co-operated. Representatives from the wards were summoned to the court[4] and it was doubtless these suitors, described as "assessors," who sat upon the Four Benches of the Husting in the 12th century, and of the Sheriffs' Court in 1291[5]. Nevertheless towards the end of the 13th century the giving of final judgment belonged to the mayor and sheriffs, while the aldermen had taken over the consultative duties of the suitors at large[6]. In the law merchant prosecution heard by the warden in 1292, the latter took counsel with the aldermen on a point of law[7]. It was the Mayor's Court with the mayor or warden as

[1] P. and M., *Hist. Eng. Law*, I, pp. 548–53, 592–4.

[2] Gross, *Law Merchant*, I, pp. xxxv, 17, 18, 24–30, 33–5, 50, 76, 90.

[3] Liber Ordinacionum, fo. 173 b; Iter Roll AA, m. 6.

[4] Husting Pleas of Land, Roll 2, m. 5 (A.D. 1274); Common Pleas, Roll 2, m. 1.

[5] Add. MSS. 14,252, fo. 98; Letter Book A, fo. 96; H. T. Riley, *Memorials of London*, pp. 27–8.

[6] Husting of Common Pleas, Roll 24 Interlocutoria. Cf. Letter Book C, fo. viii; *Munim. Gild. Lond.* I, p. 403. In 1303 each of the aldermen was called upon to give his judgment on a question of inheritance. They did so on extra-curial days, and final judgment was given by the mayor and sheriffs on the actual court days. Letter Book C, fo. 96.

[7] Richardson, *op. cit.* p. 249. *Et loquendum est cum aldermannis et consulendum super huiusmodi verificacione.*

judge which dealt with law merchant actions between 1298 and 1307. But soon afterwards the aldermen began to assume the nature of associate judges. It may be that they were called in as merchants and that the court was approximating its procedure to that of other merchant courts. About 1321 the court is said to be held before the Mayor and Aldermen[1] and the latter are invariably mentioned in the reasons given for judgments. As we have seen, in later law merchant proceedings special emphasis is laid upon the fact that the aldermen were merchants and had knowledge of the law merchant[2].

Counsel not admitted

Dr Holdsworth has pointed out in connection with the Italian law merchant that many of the city statutes prohibited the employment of lawyers except in special cases...the lawyers, it was thought, should be employed to settle points of law and not to argue matters of fact and to put a good face on a bad cause[3]. In this matter the court of London followed the Italian custom rather than the practise of English Fair Courts[4]. Counsel might be and frequently were employed on the ordinary side of the court and even in the Sheriffs' Courts for foreigners[5], but it is quite clear that they were forbidden in law merchant cases. In answer to a writ on behalf of a merchant, who complained that he was not allowed to plead his case by competent counsel, return was made that it was immemorial custom to terminate such pleas by examination on oath and other means of eliciting the truth without any counsel or other form of plea[6].

Summons and attachment

The process by which defendants were brought to answer was more favourable to citizens than to foreigners. In case of the former, summons was issued to appear on the next court day, and on default, his house was sequestrated by way of distress with increasing severity until, after four defaults, the goods and chattels of the debtor were appraised and delivered to the creditor, under pledge to answer therefor if the debtor should appear within a year and a day to disprove the debt. Thus on a bill presented on Thursday 14 Jan. 1389,

[1] *Ricart's Kalendar*, p. 95. [2] Liber Dunthorn, fos. 68, 68 b–69 b.
[3] Holdsworth, *Hist. Eng. Law*, v, p. 83.
[4] F. W. Maitland, *Select Pleas in Manorial Courts* (Seld. Soc.), p. 135. Gross, *Law Merchant*, I, p. xxxiv.
[5] Below, p. 115. [6] Below, pp. 171–2.

a citizen was summoned to appear on Saturday, sequestrated to appear on Monday, Tuesday and Wednesday, on which latter day judgment would have been given, but for a writ of *supersedeatis*[1]. If, however, the plaintiff brought six, four or two freemen to bear witness that the debtor was likely to abscond, he might be arrested by his goods or by his body[2]. On the other hand, a foreigner was not entitled to a summons, but immediately on a plaint being affirmed by pledges he might be attached by his goods or, if he had none in the city, by his person[3]. Nevertheless the courtesy of a summons appears to have been extended on occasion to foreigners, doubtless when they were well known as men of substance[4]. By city custom attachments, both on citizens and foreigners, might be made on debts owed or goods belonging to defendants. In other words, where a third person owed money or goods to a defendant, these might be attached as a foreign attachment[5]. By an extension of the custom, where a creditor had goods of a debtor as pledges for a loan, he might have formal delivery of these goods[6]. This latter custom amounted to pawning, the goods being redeemable only within a year and a day.

As will be seen from the instance of sequestration given above, the law merchant court was held daily, and the procedure afforded a speedy remedy to litigants. This was in accordance with the constitutions of 1285, which insisted on "*hastif remedie*" for travelling merchants—a phrase repeated in the regulations of 1321 and 1364, the latter of which runs: "*et le Mair lour fra hastive droiture, de jour en autre, sans nulle delay, solonc la ley marchaunt*[7]." In the rules of the Italian law merchant, the same stress was laid upon speedy justice, and as Dr Holdsworth has pointed out, the influence of the canon law worked strongly in the same direction[8]. The

[1] Plea & Mem. Rolls, A 29, m. 12. See below, pp. 165–6.

[2] *Munim. Gild. Lond.* I, p. 213. See below, p. 187.

[3] Below, pp. 113, 250.

[4] Plea & Mem. Rolls, A 28, m. 3; A 32, m. 1 b. Cf. Bickley, *Little Red Book*, p. 62; Hall, *Law Merchant*, II, p. 31.

[5] *Munim. Gild. Lond.* I, pp. 207–9; below p. 10, n. 2. Attachments could also be made on rents, below, pp. 26, 31, 131.

[6] *Cal. of P. & M. Rolls*, II, p. 231.

[7] Letter Book G, fo. 165.

[8] Holdsworth, *Hist. Eng. Law*, V, pp. 81–2, 82, n. 2.

Decretal *Saepe contingit* contains several features common to the Mayor's Court—the repressing of delays, the oath that the proceedings were in good faith[1], the examination of parties and the definitive judgment in writing[2].

Proof by documents

An action could be begun by ordinary bill with pledges for prosecution, by petition[3] or even by verbal complaint[4]. When the question of proof arose, writings, tallies, witnesses, juries and compurgation were admissible in the order given. In actions of covenant and debt, such writings would take the form of recognisances, statutory and civic, obligations or bonds, and in the latter half of the 14th century, if not earlier, bills of exchange or letters of payment. It was probably in reference to the latter that the Mayor and Aldermen in the Inner Chamber in 1439 gave a definite ruling that by the ancient custom of the city a schedule of parchment or paper written by the hand of a debtor or other person whatsoever, and sealed and delivered by the debtor himself, debarred him from making his law, i.e. clearing himself by compurgation[5]. But it was possible to plead against all such specialties that they were not the deed of the defendant, in which case proof might either take the form of witnesses or a jury. The same pleading was open to a plaintiff, when the defendant produced an acquittance. We learn from an interesting appeal in 1278 that a mere collation of seals was not regarded by the law merchant as sufficient proof of the genuineness of a deed[6].

It frequently happened in law merchant actions that a defendant pleaded that his documents were elsewhere or that he could produce authentic letters under the seal of a merchant town to prove that he had already sustained judgment or was quit of the debt claimed[7]. He was required to take an oath to that effect and to find pledges before being allowed an adjournment. Occasionally the court itself wrote for in-

[1] Below, pp. 134, 172, 252, 296, 317; *Munim. Gild. Lond.* I, p. 200.
[2] *Cal. of E.M.C. Rolls*, pp. 183–4.
[3] *Cal. of P. & M. Rolls*, II, pp. 88, 212; below, p. 176.
[4] Below, p. 287.
[5] Letter Book K, fo. 177 b.
[6] Hall, *Law Merchant*, II, p. 21.
[7] *Munim. Gild. Lond.* I, pp. 212–13.

formation, not only as to acquittances[1] but on special matters arising out of the pleadings[2].

Tallies In the city a sealed tally was regarded as having the same validity as a written obligation and debarred a defendant from his law[3]. He could, however, allege that the date of payment was other than the plaintiff declared or deny that the tally was genuine. The burden of proof was thus thrown upon the plaintiff and it was a principle of the law merchant that he must prove his tally by good and loyal citizens or merchants and not by men of low condition (*ribauz*)[4].

Witnesses As regards witnesses, the mercantile actions in which they are mentioned show that there was a distinct movement away from earlier formalism towards more modern methods. The Sheriffs' Court in 1302 gave judgment for a creditor even though his witnesses proved a debt less than he claimed and did not agree as to the source of indebtedness, and in spite of the fact that the aldermen who examined them did not put the proceedings on record. The Mayor's Court reversed the judgment[5]. But they themselves in a civic case, where a defendant put himself on a jury and at the same time offered four witnesses, summoned the jury and added the four witnesses to give them information[6], thus giving a striking forecast of modern actions with judge, jury and witnesses. As time went on, the success of a case no longer depended on the exact agreement of witnesses. Mercantile actions, especially where partnership accounts were involved, in which bonds had been drawn and sales made by agents and where debts were assigned in settlement of claims, became so intricate that, though a debt was clearly owed, neither the plaintiff nor defendant might know the extent of it, and no one witness could be conversant with all the circumstances. In the returns made as to law merchant procedure it is clear that witnesses

[1] See Sharpe, *Cal. of Letters*; *Cal. of P. & M. Rolls*, I, under "letters"; *ibid.* II, pp. 129, 136.

[2] *Cal. of E.M.C. Rolls*, pp. 132, 142; below, pp. 43, 140–2.

[3] *Munim. Gild. Lond.* I, p. 214. Cf. Hall, *Law Merchant*, II, pp. lxxxi–lxxxv, 40.

[4] *Munim. Gild. Lond.* I, p. 294.

[5] *Cal. of E.M.C. Rolls*, pp. 183–4.

[6] *Ibid.* p. 58. Cf. below, p. 42, where two informers were added to a jury.

were only part of the means whereby the facts were elicited and that the court, anxious to arrive at an equitable solution, had passed the stage when a victory could be snatched on a legal quibble[1] or a minute divergence of testimony.

The jury

All through our period the jury was closely akin to a body of witnesses[2], and this was especially the case in mercantile actions. In the law merchant the jury was always in a sense a special jury, chosen either as likely to be cognisant of the facts or in a position to discover them. In purely mercantile actions, juries of merchants were impanelled, but if more technical knowledge were required, travellers, masters of ships, sailors and tradesmen might be selected[3]. Connected with this desire for special knowledge was the institution of "the jury of the moiety." Edward I in 1285 enjoined that where denizen and foreigner were at issue, one half of the jury should be of denizens, the other of foreigners visiting the city, if it were an action of contract or debt of which foreign merchants could have cognisance[4]. A slightly different procedure is described by the Carta Mercatoria of 1303[5]. Half of the jury were to be of merchants of other places and half of other good and lawful men of the place where the plea was heard, and this apparently was to obtain in all actions, whether between denizen and foreigner or foreigner and foreigner. The latter was the custom observed in London[6]. If it proved impossible to find a moiety of foreigners, a jury of citizens was impanelled[7].

Wager of law

The last and least satisfactory form of proof was that of wager of law or compurgation. By the end of the 13th century it was no longer applicable in violent forms of trespass[8], though it continued as a proof *faute de mieux* in the other civil

[1] But two instances of judgment on errors of proceeding, rather than the merits of the case, must be noted. In 1364 a defendant appears to have lost his case because he offered wager of law and then proffered an acquittance, refusing to make his law. *Cal. of P. & M. Rolls*, II, pp. 261–2. In 1392, a plaintiff failed because of an omission in his bill, though the co-defendant admitted the truth of the bill. Both were law merchant actions.

[2] *Cal. of E.M.C. Rolls*, pp. xlii–xliii; Maitland, *Social England*, I, p. 291.

[3] *Cal. of E.M.C. Rolls*, pp. 21, 39, 119, 193, 221.

[4] *Munim. Gild. Lond.* I, p. 292.

[5] *Ibid.* II (1), pp. 207–8.

[6] *Cal. of P. & M. Rolls*, II, pp. 52, 272.

[7] *Ibid.* p. 278.

[8] *Munim. Gild. Lond.* I, pp. 294–5.

wrongs grouped under that term[1]. Its principal use was in actions of debt, detinue and contract, where the plaintiff had no writing or tally and could call no witnesses, or where a jury could not be expected to elicit the facts. In law merchant actions it took two forms, the sevenfold oath and the peremptory or decisory single oath.

In the former, the party took an oath that he owed no debt or made no contract and produced six others to swear, not as to the facts, but as to the credibility of his oath. Though the Liber Albus tells us that this form of oath applied to foreigners as well as to citizens[2], the only instance in which a foreigner is recorded as clearing himself with the seventh hand occurred in 1300. In the few subsequent actions where foreigners waged their law, the number of compurgators is not mentioned.

The more usual form of wager of law was the peremptory oath, sworn either by plaintiff or defendant. The latter might challenge his opponent to swear that his suit was true, and if the plaintiff refused, the defendant went quit. He could also, with the consent of the plaintiff, take an oath that his defence was true, with the same result[3]; or the plaintiff, where a matter was alleged in bar of action, or a dilatory exception was raised, could put the defendant on his oath, winning his action if he refused, or being ousted himself, if the defendant took the oath[4]. It is possible that some of the instances of compurgation by foreigners, where no number of oath helpers was stated, were in fact peremptory oaths. In all cases where foreigners waged their law, the oaths were taken *incontinenti*, doubtless in accordance with the necessity for *hastif droiture*.

[1] *Cal. of E.M.C. Rolls*, pp. 73, 98, 147, 235; *Cal. of P. & M. Rolls*, I, p. 210; *Ibid.* II, pp. 56–7, 224, 266–7.

[2] *Munim. Gild. Lond.* I, pp. 294–5. The Liber Albus (*Ibid.* p. 203) also mentions a threefold oath for foreigners, which Miss Bateson regarded as a mistake, arising from the name of the oath—"Lex Tertia." *E.H.R.* XVII, p. 490. There is no instance of a foreigner taking an oath with the third hand. But on one occasion a citizen was allowed to put himself voluntarily on a threefold oath. *Cal. P. & M. Rolls*, II, p. 42. In the present calendar there are two instances of threefold oaths, pp. 15, 252–3, and another of a fivefold oath, p. 44. They appear to have been merely challenges, which the other party might refuse, whereas, in the peremptory oath, a refusal meant losing the action.

[3] *Ibid.* pp. 217–18.

[4] *Ibid.* p. 521.

As may be imagined, compurgation is rarely found in any commercial action of importance. It was more suitable for disputes concerning petty amounts than for claims arising out of the transactions of financiers and merchants.

Arbitration

Arbitration in law merchant actions appears early, especially among foreigners[1], and towards the end of our period became the favourite method of settling disputes. It was usual for each of the parties to choose two arbitrators, with an umpire to make the award if the four failed to agree. The advantages were obvious. Foreign arbitrators understood the speech and book-keeping of their fellow-countrymen, and it is interesting to notice that in certain actions, where a plaintiff or a defendant seemed, from the pleadings, to have no case at all, the award went in his favour[2]. The parties undertook openly in court, or entered into mutual bonds, to accept the award, a day being given for its production[3]. In either case, if one party refused, the other could sue on the bond or the covenant witnessed by the court[4]. Sometimes the mayor ordered the enrolment of the award[5], and at other times it was enrolled at the request of one of the parties[6]. There are instances of judgments given in the terms of the award[7], and if the award contemplated duties to be performed by the parties, the court would examine the arbitrators and give judgment that the award had been fulfilled and that bonds be returned[8]. The mayor himself or the recorder might consent to act as umpire[9]. At other times the mayor appointed arbitrators, in accordance with the law merchant[10], and in one instance a jury, which had been elected and tried, chose four arbitrators to examine the matter on their behalf[11]. In all these cases it is important to notice that arbitration was an integral part of the court proceedings, that awards had the force of formal judgments and were solemnly recited in court.

In another class of actions the court itself acted as a body

[1] *Cal. of E.M.C. Rolls*, pp. 43, 50; Hall, *Law Merchant*, II, pp. 53–4.
[2] *Cal. of P. & M. Rolls*, II, pp. 75–6.
[3] Below, pp. 140, 198, 207.
[4] Below, p. 192. [5] Below, p. 307. [6] Below, p. 142.
[7] Below, pp. 77–8, 162–3. [8] P. & M. Rolls, A 24, m. 4 b.
[9] *Cal. of P. & M. Rolls*, II, pp. 86, 158.
[10] Below, pp. 127, 136, 207. [11] Below, p. 314.

of referees. Where persons out of court entered into arbitration and deposited mutual bonds in the hands of a third person, the latter allowed himself to be summoned for detinue by one of the parties, pleaded that he had no knowledge whether the award had been fulfilled, and prayed the court to summon the parties to interplead, thus securing official recognition and a final judgment on the matter at issue[1]. A variant of this action occurred when the bailee of a bond for conditional payment was sued and prayed for interpleader and judgment[2].

Liability of master and servant, merchant and factor

It has been suggested above that the principles of the law merchant, as understood in London, must be sought in the mercantile customs revealed in pleadings rather than in the judgments recorded. A frequent cause concerned the liabilities of principals and agents in trading. Much business was done at home and abroad for considerable amounts by apprentices, or by time-expired apprentices variously described as servants, merchants or attorneys of their masters.

The Lex Mercatoria rules that where apprentices and under-merchants, publicly known to be trading for their masters, procured merchandise to be lent to them to the use of their masters, the masters were responsible[3]. The London rules of 1285 say that the master was responsible if the merchant creditor can prove that the servant or apprentice, who bought goods for him, was with his master at the time and carried the goods to his master's house or brought them into his power; and this rule was made because masters sometimes disavowed their servants while retaining the goods[4]. Its effect seems to have been to throw the onus of proof upon the creditor. In 1345 a merchant sued a pepperer for money lent to his attorney in Bruges, and the defence was made that the alleged attorney was only a learner and not an attorney, factor or apprentice[5]. In another action where a principal was sued, he admitted that the apprentice was his agent, but denied that the loan was taken for his use or came into his possession. The parties having agreed to put themselves on

[1] *Cal. of P. & M. Rolls*, II, p. 278; below, pp. 239, 245–6.
[2] *Cal. of P. & M. Rolls*, II, pp. 97–8, 110, 281–2; below, pp. 218, 241.
[3] Bickley, *Little Red Book*, I, p. 66.
[4] *Munim. Gild. Lond.* I, p. 286.
[5] *Cal. of P. & M. Rolls*, I, p. 217.

the evidence of the apprentice, the latter confessed that he had borrowed the money for his own use[1]. Such actions as these would bring home to merchants the necessity of safeguarding themselves. Apprentices and servants were often provided with letters of attorney, and creditors before parting with money or goods required bonds for payment. In the latter case they sued the agent. Thus in 1389 an apprentice suffered judgment for debt and then sued his master, who was adjudged to pay the debt for him, because the latter had approved the transaction and the wine had been bought for his use and profit[2]. However, such actions were rare. To judge from a number of cases, principals appear to have paid the creditors, and to have sued the apprentices or their sureties, where the apprentices' conduct of trading amounted to "wasting his master's goods[3]."

The liability of agents to principals naturally depended on the conditions imposed by the latter. According to the Lex Mercatoria an apprentice who lent his master's goods, or in other words gave credit, was responsible only if he did so against the forms and conditions stipulated by his master[4]. A common custom was to deposit goods or a sum of money in an apprentice's hands to trade therewith for the benefit of his master under definite instructions. In such an arrangement the apprentice was bound to render account after a given interval, and to restore the deposited sum or goods *in toto*[5]. Or he might be sent abroad with money or goods to deal according to his discretion for his master's advantage[6]. In the latter case, his liability would only extend to wrongdoing or reckless conduct. In one case an apprentice's sureties maintained successfully that the master had no claim because the boy was too young to be allowed to trade[7].

[1] Below, p. 177.
[2] Below, pp. 162–3.
[3] *Cal. of P. & M. Rolls*, I, p. 268; *Ibid.* II, pp. 86–7; below, pp. 127–8, 221–2.
[4] Bickley, *Little Red Book*, I, p. 78.
[5] Below, pp. 140–2.
[6] Below, pp. 89–90.
[7] *Cal. of E.M.C. Rolls*, p. 158. But see *ibid*, pp. 237–8, where an apprentice loses money in trade through falling ill, and is condemned to pay. London apprenticeship actions do not support Malynes in saying that "a factor is bound to answer the losse which happeneth by overpassing or exceeding his commission, whereas a servant is not, but may incurre his master's displeasure." Malynes, *Lex Mercatoria*, 1622, p. 111.

The commenda Arrangements of this kind shade imperceptibly into those contracts known to the Italian law merchant as *commenda*[1], where the travelling merchant was rewarded with a fixed salary or a proportion of the profits[2], and the home-merchant must be prepared to suffer risk as well as receive profit[3]. As an apprentice received no pay, his trading contract can only be considered a *commenda* in so far as experience is regarded as an emolument. But the time-expired apprentice or servant was undoubtedly paid either by salary or profits. Where he received instructions, he was liable for losses incurred by breach of them. An undermerchant in 1380 was condemned for 4000 woolfells or their value, £60, because he undertook to account either for the goods or the money, and a bond from the purchaser was not accepted as an equivalent[4]. In another case, where the undermerchant had sold the goods, he was sued either to repay their value or to obtain from the purchaser satisfactory security, as he had promised. Here the parties chose six Lombard merchants to assist and inform the mayor, and to examine papers and hear evidence with him, in order that he might be able to render a better and juster judgment according to the law merchant[5].

The societas There are many references to partnership in the rolls, both in particular adventures and in general trading. In one instance a merchant is sued to render account for the time when he was the plaintiff's receiver and traded for their common profit[6]. This appears to be akin to the arrangement known as the *collegantia*, where the travelling merchant contributed a portion of the capital and shared in risk and profit. The defendant claimed that he merely received a sum of money, to trade therewith to the profit and at the risk of the plaintiff. Full partnership, corresponding to the modern

[1] Ashley, *Econ. Hist.* I, pp. 412–14. Holdsworth, *Hist. Eng. Law*, VIII, pp. 195–7.

[2] Often one fourth. See below, p. 28. Holdsworth, VIII, p. 195.

[3] *Cal. of E.M.C. Rolls*, pp. 104–5. It was the element of risk which distinguished the *commenda* from usury. See *Munim. Gild. Lond.* I, p. 400; Holdsworth, VIII, p. 104.

[4] *Cal. of P. & M. Rolls*, II, pp. 276–7.

[5] *Ibid.*. pp. 283–4. Both these cases resemble brokerage rather than *commenda*.

[6] *Cal. of E.M.C. Rolls*, pp. 104–5.

English business partnership, is found in earlier days mainly among Italians and German merchants. But in 1363 unlimited liability, the test of such partnership, is pleaded in an action between English merchants of the Staple[1]. In several later actions the liability of a *societas*, or of one member of it, for the transactions of the other members, was recognised and enforced by the Mayor's Court. In 1373 an Englishman, on behalf of his partner, meets a bill of exchange effected with Italian merchants at Bruges, apparently by an English partner[2].

Credit and financial instruments

Another class of transactions illustrates the use of credit in medieval London, and the financial instruments by which it was effected. In spite of the assertion that dealing for credit was little developed and dealing in credit was unknown[3], all the evidence goes to show that both were far more general than was previously supposed. In London the formal documents witnessing the duty of repaying loans or of making future payments for goods supplied were as follows: (1) Recognisances made before the city chamberlain and one or two aldermen or before the Sheriffs[4], in which the debtor acknowledged a debt payable to the creditor or his certain attorney. Sometimes to attorney is added "bearing the writing of this obligation" or "the letter of this debt," or even "a tally of this debt[5]." The debtor agreed that in case of non-payment the debt should be levied from his lands, rents and goods. A large number of these recognisances are recorded between 1274 and 1312 in Letter Books A and B. They were not superseded by the statutory recognisances set up by the Statute of Acton Burnel, for on 13 Dec. 1383 a city ordinance directed that they should continue to be taken before the chamberlain notwithstanding the act[6]. The city custom was recorded before the itinerant justices in 1321[7] and occasional

[1] *Cal. of P. & M. Rolls*, I, pp. 262–3. Below, pp. 83, 194–7, 304.
[2] *Cal. of P. & M. Rolls*, II, p. 127.
[3] Cunningham, *Growth of English Industry and Commerce*, I, p. 362.
[4] *Munim. Gild. Lond.* I, p. 215.
[5] Letter Book A, fos. 41, 42 b.
[6] *Cal. of Letter Book A*, p. 79.
[7] *Munim. Gild. Lond.* II (1), pp. 322–4. Cf. K.B. 27/262. Probably the recognisance mentioned below (p. 293) as being made before an alderman was a recognisance of this kind.

enrolments are found throughout the next two centuries[1]. (2) The statutory recognisances of the above-mentioned act and of the Statute of Merchants, 13 Edw. I, known as statutes merchant[2]. Rolls of the latter are preserved among the city records, beginning in 1285 and continuing till 1392. They were taken before the Mayor and a clerk, and provided for payment to be made to the creditor *vel suo certo nuncio scriptum inde obligatorium deferenti*, or on default to be levied in accordance with the act. (3) The Statute Staples set up by 27 Edw. III stat. 2 c. 9[3]. (4) Obligations or bonds, which, the Liber Albus tells us, might be simple, endorsed or by indentures[4]. The simple bond was equivalent to a civic recognisance, though there was not the same provision for automatic recovery in case of default. The endorsed bonds or bonds by indentures contemplated payment on certain conditions. We meet also with the penal bond, in which a debtor binds himself to pay a certain sum, usually twice what is owed, if he fails to pay his debt by a certain date[5]. None of these instruments, it must be noted, contained a pure bearer clause, as was often the case with similar foreign documents[6]. The bearer clause was very rare in England in the 14th century, if it existed at all. "Payment to an attorney bearing the document" is a mixed clause, as restricted in its operation as an order clause[7].

Transfer and negotiation of obligations

All these documents were enforceable both by the common law and the law merchant. To a certain extent they were by their nature transferable. The certain attorney or messenger

[1] *Cal. of P. & M. Rolls*, I, pp. 106, 121–2, 264; *ibid.* II, pp. 117, 251; below, pp. 82, 130, 155, 191, 197, 199, 224, 302.

[2] *Statutes of the Realm*, I, pp. 53, 98.

[3] *Ibid.* p. 337.

[4] *Munim. Gild. Lond.* I, p. 209.

[5] But in the city a creditor suing on a penal bond could recover only what was due. *Ibid.* p. 211.

[6] P. & M. Rolls, A 38, m. 3, *a rendre e paier au dit monsieur Pierre a son comand ou au portour de ces lettres.*

[7] The only instance of a pure bearer clause known to the editor among some hundreds of recognisances and bonds occurs in a penal bond. See below, p. 107, *aut latori presencium* twice repeated. The instance quoted by Dr Holdsworth (*Hist. Eng. Law*, V, p. 113) from Maitland, *Select Pleas in Manorial Courts*, p. 152—*vel cuicunque de suis scriptum inter ipsos confectum portanti*—is a mixed clause and the bearer must prove that he is "*de suis*." So too in *Cal. of Letter Book A*, p. 3, the payee must bring letters of the creditor.

might be merely an agent collecting a debt for his principal, but he might also be the purchaser of the writing armed with a power of attorney or a letter of recommendation. In the latter case it has been considered that the consent of the debtor was necessary to the assignment, but this was probably intended not so much to safeguard the interest of the debtor as of the assignee, and was not invariable[1]. It would appear to have been easy to transfer a debt once, for the appointment of an attorney was a simple matter in the city and did not require a royal writ[2]. Moreover, in certain letters of attorney, power was given to appoint a further attorney[3]. But the transferable instrument could hardly become a fully negotiable instrument without a series of such letters depending one upon another.

When we turn, however, from the formal difficulties of transfer to the records of actual occurrences, there is reason to believe that bonds were regarded in law merchant courts as objects of value in themselves, which the holder, whoever he might be, could realise. In a curious action in the Sheriffs' Court for foreigners in 1320 a chaplain was sued by the executors of William Servat for having broken into the testator's boxes, and for having carried away, sold and disposed of two statute merchants of £115, which had been entrusted to the testator under certain conditions, an Exchequer bill of 5 marks from the king to the said William, two sealed indentures of the testator, an obligation of £96 from the Archbishop of Canterbury to Reginald de Brandon, which Richard de Honewik had pledged to the testator for £40, and a bond of 200 marks from Sir Henry de Beaumont to the Earl of Hereford, which the latter had pledged for £110. The defendant pleaded that the testator had given him the two statutes and the Exchequer bill in recompense for services rendered when he was the testator's receiver of customs at Lynn and other places. He produced an acquit-

[1] See M. M. Postan, *Private Financial Instruments in Medieval England*, in *Vierteljahrschrift für Sozial- und Wirtschaftsgeschichte*, XXIII (1), pp. 48–51.

[2] Letters of attorney were common documents and, on presentation, were copied into the records. Letter Book A, fo. 41 b; B, fo. 122 b and many other instances in the rolls.

[3] P. & M. Rolls, A 38, m. 3.

tance. A jury found him guilty and the acquittance not the deed of the testator[1].

Assignment of debts

The assignment of debts in satisfaction of claims is illustrated by many instances in the city records. While some of these were small book debts, commonly proved, according to the Lex Mercatoria, by the evidence of tradesmen and their servants[2], the majority were duly secured by documents, which were handed over for execution[3]. In the same way tallies passed from hand to hand[4]. All these arrangements were not only recognised as a matter of course, but might even be ordered by the court, in accordance with the law merchant[5]. In the 15th century we hear of a "common buyer of debts" and of the sale of bonds[6]. The common law courts would by then recognise an assignment if it could be proved that the assignor and assignee had a common interest such as the settlement of debts, but a common interest could not be proved if it appeared that the assignee had merely purchased the deed from the assignor without any particular reason for doing so[7]. But what the common law would not sanction was admitted by the law merchant. If the latter did not make the transferable instrument fully negotiable, it made it as negotiable as was necessary for ordinary business purposes.

Bills of exchange

A distinctive feature of the law merchant in London was its recognition and enforcement of the contracts created by

[1] Sheriffs' Court Roll, m. 26. Cf. *Cal. of E.M.C. Rolls*, p. 172, where Reginald de Thunderle in 1305 buys two bills of £70 15s 11d from William Foundepe, and the latter's messenger fails to deliver them.

[2] Bickley, *Little Red Book*, I, p. 63. P. & M. Rolls, A 36, m. 3, a grant of goods, chattels and debts, *debitos tam per scripta obligatoria et evidencia quam sine*....

[3] *Cal. P. & M. Rolls*, II, pp. 75–6, 91, 111–12, 168–9, 211; below, pp. 27, 43, 225, 227, 274–5. In Roll A 39, m. 12 b is a bond in £40, *solvendis eisdem Johanni Sadelere, executoribus vel assignatis*. See also *ibid.* A 57, m. 1 b, A 59, m. 6.

[4] *Cal. of P. & M. Rolls*, II, pp. 89–90.

[5] Below, p. 231, P. & M. Rolls, A 56, m. 2 (1427), where two recognisances are handed over to satisfy a debt, the balance to be returned; *ibid.* A 67, m. 7 b, bond handed over in payment of a debt, the balance to be used in paying another debtor. M. M. Postan, *op. cit.* p. 47, where instances are cited from Early Chancery Proceedings.

[6] M. M. Postan, *op. cit.* p. 49.

[7] Holdsworth, *Hist. Eng. Law*, V, p. 535.

bills of exchange or letters of payment. The transaction covered by these documents may be stated as follows. *A*, the drawer, a merchant trading in a foreign country, obtains a sum in local currency from *B*, the creditor, and gives to him a letter addressed to *D*, his master or partner at home, the drawee, asking him to pay the amount, which either *B* or *C*, the bearer of the letter, may present. The business of supplying ready money for a consideration appears to have been in use among Italian and continental merchants before it was taken up by English merchants. But the latter were well acquainted with its advantages, of which they availed themselves from the beginning of the 14th century onwards.

One form of the bill of exchange was that later known as a letter of credit, or to-day as a traveller's cheque. It was a true bill of exchange, with the difference that the drawer, and not the creditor, derived profit. Thus an English rector in 1300, who had stolen £17 and was intending to flee abroad, took it to the house of a member of the Italian company of Pulci, receiving from him a letter of payment addressed to a branch of the company in Paris. The Italian gave evidence that the letter had not been cashed in London or Paris, from which latter place a warning had gone out to other places to withhold payment, but he did not know whether payment had already been made elsewhere[1]. Five years later an English purchaser of a bill of exchange, which his brother had presented at Anvers (Antwerp) in Brabant, sued the company of Peruzzi, the drawers, for non-payment[2]. The company acknowledged the facts and agreed to pay on production of the bill and proof that it had not been honoured. As a rule there was little complaint as to non-payment and on more than one occasion Italian societies met claims even when the letters of payment were lost[3]. The advantages to merchants, pilgrims and travelling clergy are obvious. All the traveller's cheques noted in these Calendars were issued by Italians[4]. As they were

[1] *Cal. of E.M.C. Rolls*, p. 94. See Holdsworth's comment on these actions, *op. cit.* VIII, pp. 130–1, and remarks on the connection between exchange and banking, *ibid.* pp. 128–30.

[2] *Cal. of E.M.C. Rolls*, p. 200.

[3] Below, pp. 241, 287.

[4] *Cal. of P. & M. Rolls*, II, pp. 10, 77–8, 115, 122; below, pp. 200, 223, 250, 304, 315.

usually banded together in financial and trading companies, with branches in large cities, they were peculiarly fitted for business of this kind. There is no evidence to show that the transactions mentioned above were secured by bonds or obligations or by any other documents than the order to pay.

Ordinary bills of exchange are mentioned in a number of cases in our rolls. In 1345 two German merchants advance money in Bruges to an Englishman, whose letter of payment was not honoured in England on the ground that he had no authority to draw it[1]. In 1373 an Englishman in partnership with an Italian, Matthew Johan, paid the sum of £100 drawn upon the latter on an exchange made at Bruges with Reyner Domenyk of Florence by William Agland, servant of Roger Morton of York. In this case the drawee had nothing before him but a mere order to pay, and the payee, Peter Mark, agreed to reimburse him, if the letter proved to be false[2].

English merchants and credit

The present calendar shows that in the last twenty years of the 14th century Englishmen had begun to take a definite part in issuing money abroad against bills of exchange. In 1381 a time-expired apprentice, John Colshull, sued his former master, Thomas Gisors, for repayment of three several sums of money which he had paid to his master's creditors[3]. He had effected exchanges at Bruges with William Ancroft, attorney of Adam Fraunceys of London, for a supply of Flemish crowns and had entered into bonds, which he had subsequently discharged from his own monies. His master in defence pleaded that the plaintiff in the course of trading had drawn bills of exchange on him to the amount of £5954 5s 5d, which he had honoured, and the plaintiff had not rendered account. In proof he put in a schedule of these bills, and notes that he did not include an amount of £309 18s 4d because he had lost the letters of payment[4]. The list is noteworthy as showing that the merchants who supplied the plaintiff with money for trading were no longer exclusively Italians. Of the fifty-four persons named at least fifteen were

[1] *Cal. of P. & M. Rolls*, I, p. 217.

[2] *Cal. of P. & M. Rolls*, II, p. 154.

[3] Below, pp. 31–5.

[4] A 25, m. 22. *De qele darrein somme lez lettres de paiementz ne purroms unqore trover mes mostroms par escriptz qe le ditz John ad resceu lez sommes.* Unfortunately omitted from the précis below.

well-known English merchants, while of the remainder, Flemings and Germans outnumbered the Italians. It is clear that English merchants were taking a far larger share in financial and commercial transactions abroad than is usually credited to them—a fact which is evidenced by many actions in the present calendar[1].

Negotiable bills

Of course in bills of exchange, where four or more persons might be involved, their relations to each other might be governed by obligations and authorities. Sometimes powers of attorney might bind the drawer and drawee, the creditor and payee[2]. But there is no need to suppose that the drawee demanded and received on every occasion confirmatory documents beyond the letters of payment themselves. The Mayor's Court Rolls of the 14th century do not decide for us whether bills of exchange ordered payment only to a named person or his attorney, or were payable to bearer. The example of a bill of exchange of 1472 among the Cely Papers has a bearer clause[3] and probably such a clause was usual in that century. In any case, bills of exchange passed freely and were the subject of sale. In an action of 1414 Richard Ikelington, who had acquired a bill of exchange after it had gone through other hands, sued for payment and only failed because the original contract was conditional[4]. It would appear that the drawee sometimes protected himself by demanding that the payee should warrant him against any other claims. On the same membrane a drawee in England, who felt doubts, entered into a bond to meet the letters of payment if it were proved that payment had not already been made at Middelburg. Proof was forthcoming and he paid. In another case, where money was borrowed from the mayor of the Staple of Calais, the drawee, a Florentine merchant in England, who paid a certain John Wandesford the sum of £130 on the letter of payment, required in addition a bond to indemnify him against the creditor or any other claimant[5]. A further need for caution on the part of drawee might arise from the fact that occasionally

[1] See below, pp. 125, 176, 241, for other instances of English merchants advancing foreign currency against bills.

[2] Below, pp. 32, 43, 146.

[3] M. M. Postan, *op. cit.* p. 65.

[4] P. & M. Rolls, A 43, m. 7 b.

[5] *Ibid.* A 74, m. 2.

the creditor abroad obtained from the drawer a bond as well as a bill of exchange, and recovered on the former[1].

Market overt Among minor matters of mercantile interest are several entries relating to market overt, which show this custom in an intermediate state of development. The person who bought goods in London, which was a perpetual market, secured a title rather to the value of his purchase than to the purchase itself. In 1377 William Bardolf, lord of Wermegeye, sued for the return of four escutcheons of his arms found in the possession of a goldsmith. The latter pleaded that they had been openly exposed for sale in the city and that a certain foreign minstrel had bought them from other foreigners. The plaintiff replied that the foreigners had no title to them. To this the defendant said that he was not bound to answer because he could verify his own purchase. As the plaintiff did not dispute the open purchase, judgment was given for the defendant, because "the aforesaid verification was a complete bar to the plaintiff's action[2]." But there is little doubt that Bardolf might have recovered the escutcheons if he had proffered their value. The cases which suggest this are bound up with a question of pledging.

In 1365 Mary Convers, to whom the count of Harecourt had pledged jewels for a loan, herself raised money on them. The person who took the jewels sold them and they came into the hands of a certain Gillemyn de Nerny. The count was allowed to have his jewels on repayment of the loan to the last-named, while Mary Convers, who had wrongfully parted with the jewels, not only had to make up his purchase-price to Nerny but also recompense him for the profit he had expected to make[3]. In a similar action in 1377 the person who had originally pledged two silver-gilt basins received them back on repayment of the loan, while satisfaction was made in the same way to the purchaser for what he had paid, with an additional amount for his lost profit[4]. Apparently so long as the purchase took place openly in London, the buyer acquired a title to value. The title to property, and the

[1] Below, p. 125.
[2] *Cal. of P. & M. Rolls*, II, pp. 255–6.
[3] *Ibid.* pp. 30, 35.
[4] Below, pp. 290–1.

restriction of the custom to sale in a shop by shopkeepers of articles in which they usually dealt, were developments of the 16th century[1].

Among other law merchant rules illustrated by the rolls are those relating to withernam, the God's penny[2], and sea carriage of goods. As regards the latter the Mayor's Court exercised an admiralty jurisdiction, which was not seriously challenged until the 16th century[3], and dealt with matters of affreightment[4], liability in collision[5], jettison[6], arrest of cargo[7] and warranty of a ship and tackle[8].

The large questions as to the absorption of the law merchant, as understood in England, by the common law, and the effect of the former on later maritime and commercial law, lie outside the scope of this introduction, which is intended only to draw attention to the customs of merchants recognised by the city courts. But the brief summaries of actions in this series of calendars may serve to show that English merchants were far more busily engaged in international commerce than is generally allowed, and that the methods of business and the rules and obligations of contracts observed abroad were well known to them and in constant use in England. And it is possible, as further material becomes available, that long-established native practice will be found to have influenced the development of commercial law as fully as did the continental law merchant.

[1] See Holdsworth, *Hist. Eng. Law*, v, pp. 105, and n. 4, 110–11.

[2] The God's penny was regarded by the Carta Mercatoria (*Munim. Gild. Lond.* II (1), p. 266) as clinching a bargain among merchants. Its use in the city was confined to small trading and agreements for leases. In an action below (p. 290), where a usurious bargain by pawning was made with the God's penny, the court held that it gave no sanction and its use in such a transaction was against custom and conscience.

[3] Holdsworth, *op. cit.* I, p. 530.

[4] *Cal. of E.M.C. Rolls*, pp. 123, 168–9, 192–3, 243–4; *Cal. of P. & M. Rolls*, II, pp. 120, 138–9, 246; below, pp. 133–4, 194–7, 199–200.

[5] *Cal. of E.M.C. Rolls*, pp. 223–4.

[6] *Cal. of P. & M. Rolls*, II, p. 118.

[7] *Cal. of E.M.C. Rolls*, p. 221; below, p. 284.

[8] Below, p. 234.

CALENDAR OF SELECT PLEAS *and* MEMORANDA *of the* CITY OF LONDON

ROLL A 25

[*John Norhampton, mayor*]

Theodoric Van Sylen and Baldewyn Claysson, merchants of Flanders, by their bill exhibited before the Mayor and Aldermen in the Chamber of the Guildhall according to the custom of the city, demanded against Allard Smyth of Rye[1], mariner, £179 10s due for merchandise bought from them. The said Allard came in his proper person and acknowledged the debt. Therefore it is considered that the said Theodoric and Baldewyn shall recover against him their said debt. And they freely remitted their damages. And nothing of mercy[2] because the same Allard came the first day. And for default of payment the same Allard is committed to prison until *etc.* Afterwards on 4 May the same year William Brampton, attorney of the said Theodoric and Baldewyn, as appears by the deed next following, came before the mayor and granted that he was satisfied of the sum aforesaid and prays that the same Allard be delivered from prison, on whose petition the same Allard is delivered, and thus the court and the sheriff are quit thereof. Membrane 1 *20 March 1382*

A power of attorney from the above Theodoric Van Sylen and Baldewyn Claisson to William Brampton, citizen of London, to exact and receive the above sum of money. Given under their seals on 25 March 1382. *26 March 1382*

Luke Cosyn was committed to prison for vilifying William Fulbourne and other jurors in a suit between himself and James Rameseye before John Hende, one of the sheriffs of London. *7 March 1382*

William Swalewe, servant of Nicholas Cordewaner of Estchepe, Henry Clemme, servant of William Mildenhale, *28 April 1382*

[1] Allard Smyth of Rye *alias* le Fevre with his accomplices had captured a cargo of wheat belonging to merchants of Bruges and had afterwards agreed to pay the price of the wheat. The present action appears to have been sued in order to put the matter on record. See p. 5. For a previous capture of wheat from Bruges by Athelard Smith see *Cal. Close Rolls*, 1377–81, p. 262.

[2] No amercement.

cordwainer, and John Medelond were committed to prison because they went wandering by night in the ward of Billyngesgate about the eleventh hour of the clock, in a suspicious manner and against the ordinance of the Mayor and Aldermen[1]. Next day they were mainprised under penalty of £20 each not to make any covin or assembly nor to wander about in a suspicious fashion either by night or at any other time, but to comport themselves well and loyally towards the officers of the city and the rest of the king's people.

Membr. 1 *b*

...was committed to prison because, when he was indicted in the ward of Billyngesgate, where he dwelt, as a man of ill fame and condition, he obtained in the Court Christian a mandate of excommunication against the good men of the said ward on the pretext that they had maliciously defamed him[2], and also because he threatened to burn down the whole ward and especially the house of John Blak. Afterwards on 17 May he was sworn to keep the peace under penalty of £40.

Membr. 2
29 Nov. 1381

Gilbert Maunfeld undertook in court that 9 casks of wine, belonging to a certain John Mayton of Sandwich and then lying in a ship of Sandwich in *le Pole* of the Thames, should be conveyed to Sandwich; and the said John Mayton shall bring testimonial letters thereof under the seal of the mayor or bailiff of Sandwich this side of Christmas.

William Stokesby, William Sharpyng, Geoffrey Grigge, John Wakele, Peter atte Pole, Thomas Heyward, Richard Sprot and Nicholas Rote, vintners, were sworn for the scrutiny of wines and to prevent new wines being placed in cellars where there were old wines[3].

[1] The Court of Aldermen.

[2] At this time and for long afterwards there was no action for defamation in the common law courts, and a remedy was usually sought in the ecclesiastical courts, though actions for defamation were common in manorial and borough courts. In London recourse to the ecclesiastical courts was punishable when a remedy could be had in the Mayor's Court. See Pollock and Maitland, *Hist. Eng. Law*, II, pp. 536–8.

[3] On 4 Dec. 1370 proclamation was made that after new wine had been placed in a taverner's cellar, it was not to be sold until the old wine had been removed to another place. See Letter Book G, fos. 244 *b*, 260.

Inquest held before John Norhampton, mayor of the city of London, and John Rote and John Hende, sheriffs, at Guildhall to inquire what evildoer or evildoers by night tore away and threw down certain shields, on which were painted the arms of the king and the emperor together, and another shield bearing the arms of the king alone, which shields had been erected round the Conduit in honour of the king and Anne the queen-consort on the occasion of their passing through the city to Westminster for their wedding ceremonies on Monday before the feast of St Agnes [21 Jan.][1]— by oath of Richard Goudchild and twenty-three others. The jurors say that about midnight on the Monday aforesaid three shields, each bearing the arms of the king and emperor together, and another shield of the arms of the king alone were violently and maliciously pulled down to the grave dishonour and scandal of the king and queen and to the manifest danger and damage of the city, and that afterwards, when similar shields were painted and set up by precept of the mayor on the following day, a certain Godescalkus of Westfal in Duchesland[2], servant of John Porter, goldsmith, came about midnight the same day to the Conduit and began to hack down a newly-painted shield with a knife called a "*baselard*," and before he could succeed in so doing he was taken with the knife in his hand. They say further that the same Godescalcus tore away and threw down the four shields on the previous night, as they were given to understand; that he had resided in London for the last ten years and more; and that his master, John Porter, was a native of France and was born in the

Membr. 2 *b*
28 Jan. 1382

20 Jan. 1382

[1] *Scutis... circa conductum in honore ipsius domini Regis & Anne Regine consortis sue tempore adventus ipsius Regine per medium civitatis ad sponsalia inter dictum dominum Regem & ipsam apud Westmonasterium facienda die lune proximo ante festum sancte Agnetis virginis anno supradicto appositis.* This gives the day of the marriage as 20 Jan. 1382, though it is not clear whether Anne passed through the city on that day or earlier. Sir J. H. Ramsay, *Genesis of Lancaster*, II, p. 182, follows John Malverne's continuation of Higden (R.S. 41 (9)), p. 11, in saying that Anne was received with the greatest honour by the citizens of London on 18 Jan. and was married on 12 Kalends of February (20 Jan.). The same date for the marriage is given in the *Grey Friars Chron.* (Camd. Soc. O.S. 53), p. 7 and *A short English Chronicle* (Camd. Soc. N.S. 28), p. 25. The writer in the *Dict. Nat. Biog.* says the marriage was on 14 Jan., no doubt on Froissart's authority.

[2] Westphalia in Germany.

allegiance of the king of France. Being asked if the said John or any one else was a confederate or consented to the abovementioned acts, they answered—no, so far as they could find out among themselves.

27 *Nov. 1381* *Pleas before the Mayor and Aldermen in the Chamber of the Guildhall on Wednesday before the feast of St Andrew* [30 *Nov.*] *Aº* 5 *Ric. II* [1381]

Floria, widow of Andrew de Shaldeford, brought a bill of complaint against John de Donyngton for having taken Maude, widow of Simon atte Grene, aunt on the father's side of the above Andrew, out of her custody together with two messuages in the parish of St John Walbrook, in which the said Andrew, by his will enrolled in the Husting[1], had given to the said Maude a life interest, with remainder to the complainant. The said Maude, she alleged, was now very aged and had little sense or discretion to look after herself; and the said John de Donyngton was not maintaining or providing for her in a manner befitting her position and means, wherefore the complainant prayed the court to summon the said John to explain how he came to assume the guardianship of the said Maude. [*French*]

The said John appeared on summons on the Monday following and asked leave to consider the matter till Wednesday, when he would answer the complainant "peremptorily," but failed to appear on that day. Thereupon came John Huwet and Denise his wife, a kinswoman of the said Maude, having no interest in the property, and asked the court to grant to them the guardianship of the said Maude together with her rents and tenements, which were of the annual value of 100s. And because both Floria and John were claiming the reversion of the property after Maude's death, it was considered that the guardianship be delivered to John Huwet and Denise his wife, who found sufficient security, *viz.* Michael Trenthennek and John Ruggele, skinner, that they would maintain the said Maude well and honestly according to her condition;

[1] Husting Rolls of Deeds and Wills, 106 (128).

and the serjeant of the Chamber, Robert Markele, was ordered to execute the judgment.

Thiery van Zilen came before the Mayor and Aldermen and prayed that the following letter might be enrolled: *12 Feb. 1382*

Testimonial letters from the burgomasters, echevins and council of the town of Bruges certifying that Louys de Zeeland, Jehan Cornet, Nychaises van den Bussche, Victor Dongheres and Johan Zuernic, burgesses of Bruges, had appeared before them and had appointed Thiery van Zilen and Jaquemon Scoetelare, bearers of these letters, their general proctors and special messengers, with full power jointly and severally to demand restitution of a cargo of wheat in a ship captured by Alaerd le Fevre[1] and his accomplices about the middle of May last past, which was taken into the port of Rye under the jurisdiction of the constable of Dover, and also of other cargoes of wheat carried in four ships, which were captured in the week before Midlent by Jacque le Moer of Hithe (*del Yde*). Agreements having been made as regards the restitution of the said wheat, the said Thiery and Jaquemon were empowered to levy, receive and give acquittances for moneys due in lieu of it. Given under the seal of the town of Bruges 1 Dec. 1381. [*French*]

Adam Ryebred of Spalding was brought before the Mayor and Aldermen on a charge of wandering through the city begging and pretending that he was unfit for work, whereas, upon examination of his body, it was manifest that he was strong and lusty, capable of labour and able to earn his food and clothing and a reasonable wage in any part of the kingdom, and thus he was defrauding genuine beggars and poor people, and deceiving the public. The said Adam did not deny it. Accordingly he was sworn not to beg within the liberty of the city henceforth, under penalty of the pillory if he were convicted thereof. Membr. 3 *22 Nov. 1381*

Afterwards Geoffrey Auncel from Ireland, Simon Crockere from Somerset, John Sperlyng of Hoddesdon, Patrick the

[1] Cf. Allard Smyth of Rye; above, p. 1.

Irishman, Thomas Potager of Bristol, John Gurdelere and other "*faitours*[1]" were similarly sworn.

Writ to the mayor, the keepers of the pleas of the crown and the sheriffs of London reciting that a writ of exigent had been sent to Walter Doget and William Knyghtcote, sheriffs, ordering them to exact Simon Dyere of Colchester and Hugh Spryngafeld from Husting to Husting until, according to the law and custom of the realm of England, they were outlawed if they did not appear, and if they appeared they were to be brought before the king's justices at Westminster to answer John Hadlee, grocer, in pleas of debt of £10 17s 1d and 100s respectively, which writ ought to have been returned before the justices at Westminster on the octave of St Michael last past. Nevertheless the said Walter and William had failed to return the writ in contempt of the king's court. The mayor *etc.* are commanded to search the rolls, writs and memoranda in their custody and to send before the justices on the octave of the Purification [2 Feb.] all records relating to the above outlawry[2]. Witness, R Bealknapp at Westminster 20 Oct. A° 5 Ric. II [1381].

Return of John Norhampton, mayor, Richard Odyham, chamberlain and keeper of the pleas of the crown, John Rote and John Hende, sheriffs, giving extracts from the Husting Rolls of Common Pleas, to the effect that Simon Dyere and Hugh Spryngafeld were exacted on the Mondays, 19 Nov.

[1] Impostors, cheats, see *Statutes of the Realm*, 7 Ric. II, c. 5.

[2] Outlawry in the city had by this time become merely a process for compelling a defendant to appear to answer a plaintiff. Its use originally was in appeals or indictments for felony. There is some confusion as to the number of exactions. At the *Iter* of 1244 the citizens said that a man suspected of felony should be exacted three times, which was considered too little by the justices. *Munim. Gild. Lond.* (R.S.), I, p. 86. At the *Iter* of 1276 they declared that an Englishman was exacted three times and an alien four. *Ibid.* II (1), pp. 333–8. Commenting on this, Pollock and Maitland say that "what is in substance the same procedure may be said to involve three, four or five exactions; for we may or may not count what happens at the first or what happens at the last court as an exaction." *Hist. Eng. Law*, II, p. 581, n. 2. From the early 14th century the procedure was five exactions, following on a writ of *exigent*, and outlawry immediately after the last exaction. See the description of the city courts, *Munim. Gild. Lond.* I, p. 190 and Ricart's *Kalendar* (Camd. Soc. N.S. 5), pp. xx, 94.

and 3 Dec. 1381; 20 Jan., 27 Jan. and 10 Feb. 1382, being outlawed on the last-mentioned date.

A bill[1] handed to the queen for the city's liberties: Membr. 3 *b* *Billa porrecta Regine pro libertate Civitatis*

To the most excellent and most noble lady, Queen of England and France, your faithful subjects and very humble servitors the mayor, aldermen and the whole commonalty of the city of London make supplication that, whereas you are their supreme and natural liege lady, and whereas it pertains to your most benign piety, as well by right of your imperial majesty, of which you are possessed by birth, as of your royal dignity, by the emblems of which your position is made more resplendent, to assume, with bowels of compassion, the office of a mediatrix with that most excellent prince and puissant lord, our lord the king, your lord and ours, and in the exercise of your magnificence to recommend your subjects to our very noble lord aforesaid, as did other our queens, who preceded your most excellent highness in your realm of England—may it please your most clement and pre-eminent nobility thus to mediate by gracious words and deeds with our lord the king, so that he, in his royal munificence, may be willing to maintain and graciously to support and to confirm without diminution our liberties and privileges, granted by himself and his noble progenitors, kings of England, to us and our city, and confirmed during his time after deep deliberation with his council, since these liberties, being as it were our inheritance, afford to us, with the assistance of our labours, the means of our livelihood, and if they are withdrawn from us, we are thereby deprived of our very sustenance; and, may it be pleasing in your most gracious eyes, we submit that we have never knowingly in word or deed acted contrary to or offended against our said most illustrious lord or against your most noble ladyship, nor ever in future till the hour of death shall we so offend,

[1] This bill was probably handed to Anne of Bohemia when she passed through the city on the way to her *sponsalia* with Richard II. See above, p. 3, n. 1. There were doubtless some festivities, but the passage quoted from Herbert, *History of the twelve great livery companies*, II, p. 218, is dated A° 6 Ric. II. See *Dict. Nat. Biog.* Anne of Bohemia. The festivities described by Strickland, *Lives of the Queens*, I, p. 595, appear to have taken place in 1377.

but with all our powers so act as to serve your good pleasure and honour. These things, most excellent lady, we have boldly presumed to lay in your merciful hands, because our ladies, the queens of England, on their first arrivals, have been wont to afford to their subjects the like manifestations of their generosity, and it is the prerogative of your pre-eminence—a pre-eminence resting as well upon your natural birthright as upon moral education and the endowments of virtue—to do the same and even more.

26 Feb. 1382 Certificate of John de Norhampton, mayor, that on 26 Feb. 1381(2) he had inspected a letter of proxy on parchment sealed with the red seal of the most excellent and puissant prince, the King of Navarre, in the following terms:

Charles, King of Navarre, Count of Evreus, to all who shall see these letters, greeting. Whereas an agreement has been made between Thomas Trevet, knight, and Master Pascal Dylardye, clerk, acting on our behalf, Eneco de Sole and Johanco Dartasse, masters of Sir Olyver de Claekyn[1], of the second part, and Sir John Darondell, claiming the third part of the ransom of the said Sir Olyver, of the third part, in accordance with which we ought to have the third part of the ransom aforesaid, as appears by indentures sealed by the parties, which agreement we confirm by these presents, we acquit the said Eneco and Johanco as regards the value of the said ransom, and the said Sir Olyver, on condition that the latter pay us the third part of such reasonable amount as shall be determined between the said masters and Sir Thomas and Master Dylardye, and further we appoint the said Sir Thomas and Master Dylardye our general proctors to receive moneys due and to accord upon and perform all matters touching the said ransom. In witness whereof we have sealed these presents with our privy seal in the absence of the great seal. Given in our castle of Tassaille the last day of December 1379.

[1] Oliver du Clequin, Glequin, or Guesclin, brother of the famous warrior Bertrand du Guesclin. See *Cal. of Plea and Memoranda Rolls*, 1364–81, pp. 297–300, for earlier proceedings relating to his ransom, and Johnes' *Froissart* (1849), I, pp. 552–4, for the circumstances of his capture.

By virtue of the above proxy the said Pascal had appeared before the mayor and acknowledged receipt from Sir Oliver de Claekyn, knight, seigneur of La Roche Tesson, by the hands of Philepot de Hodant, esquire, of the sum of 2000 francs of the coinage of the king of France due at Christmas last in part payment of 7500 francs, for which payment the said Sir Oliver, Sir John de Vendosme, seigneur of Feuillet, Sir Alein de Beaumont, seigneur of Sainte Nomee, and others had entered into bond in Paris on 18 Aug. last, and the said Sir Oliver had delivered hostages at Calais, namely, Sir John de Beaumond, knight, and Piere de Vendosme and Bertram de Claekyn, esquires. In witness thereof the mayor had caused this present certificate to be sealed with the mayoralty seal of the city of London on the day and year abovementioned. [*French*]

7 March 1382

Memorandum that certain writings and deeds relating to lands in Strode[1] near Rochester co. Kent, which were entrusted to the chamberlain, John Cauntebrigge, at the instance of Henry Yevele and others, were delivered on 7 March 1382 to William Croydon and Henry Gellay, attorneys, at the request of the said Henry and by precept of the mayor.

Membr. 4

Copies of eleven deeds, dated between 1338 and 1345, between Henry atte Rothe, citizen and chandler of London, and Elias Chaunceler of Strode and Emma his wife.

Membr. 5
23 Feb. 1382

John Hende, draper, was summoned to answer Richard Burton and John Boys of co. Essex for detaining two documents which they had entrusted to him on the previous 18 Nov. The said John appeared and, without challenging the jurisdiction of the court, said that the documents had been delivered to him, as an impartial custodian, by the plaintiffs and a certain Sir Thomas Fastolf, knight, of co. Cambridge, in accordance with certain conditions contained therein, and as he was unaware whether the said Sir Thomas had fulfilled the conditions or not, he prayed that he be summoned to show cause *etc.*

The deeds, which were produced in court, consisted of a

[1] Strood co. Kent.

statute merchant, whereby the said Sir Thomas bound himself to pay £200 to the plaintiffs for merchandise bought from them in the Staple of Westminster, and a bill of defeasance attached thereto, providing that the statute merchant should be of no effect if the said Sir Thomas carried out the following agreements: that he would give them within six days a sure title in the manor of Gilden Morden, called "Bonesbury[1]," which he had sold to them in fee simple, cause all persons who had acquired any estate in the manor from himself or his late wife Johane to release their interest, and would obtain a sure title in the manor of Irchestre, co. Northampton, by release of those having interest therein. On the other hand, if the plaintiffs were ousted from the first-mentioned manor by Margaret, the present wife of Sir Thomas, after his death, or by the heirs of the aforesaid Johane, or by anyone acting on behalf of the chief lords of the fee, or if the plaintiffs became responsible to the king for any debts owed by the said Sir Thomas, or were vexed by any annuities or other burdens charged on the manor by him, or were called upon to pay any fine for purchase and were not reimbursed, then these documents should be returned to the plaintiffs and the money due on the statute merchant should be payable. [*French*]

The parties appeared on 28 March, when Robert Markele, serjeant of the Chamber, reported that the said Sir Thomas could not be found within the liberties of the city and had no possessions within the same liberties whereby he might be summoned to attend. Accordingly the statute merchant and bill were delivered to the plaintiffs.

Membr. 5 *b*
27 Feb. 1382

At the court held before John Hende and John Rote, sheriffs of London, William Waleworth, citizen of London, plaintiff, offered himself against John Salman, burgess of Bruges, in a plea of debt upon demand of £100, for which the debtor had been attached by foreign attachment[2] and

[1] Bondesbury, one of several small manors in Guilden Morden co. Cambs.

[2] By the custom of foreign attachment a debtor could be attached to appear by goods in the hands of a third person, called the garnishee, and if he made four defaults the goods were delivered to the plaintiff,

now made default for the fourth time. The plaintiff prayed that the attachment be valued and delivered to him in accordance with the custom of the city. Thereupon a valuation was made by Thomas Rolf and Richard Marleburgh, *stacyneres*, and Thomas Bonauntre and John Wych, tapicers, as follows: a book of Romance of King Alexander in verse (*rimiatus*), well and curiously illuminated, value £10; and a *dorser* of Arras work representing the coronation of King Arthur, 9 yards long and 3 yards wide, value £6. The attachment was handed over to the plaintiff in part satisfaction of his debt under security of John Whiteheved and William Askham to answer therefor, or for the value, if the said John Salman should submit himself to justice within a year and a day.

Power of Attorney from Peter Bragadyn, merchant of Venice, to Hugelin Gerard and Thomas Lippy of Bologna (*Bononia Crassa*). Dated 24 March 1382. *29 March 1382*

Richard Waldegrave, knight, certified before the Mayor and Aldermen that on 8 May he and his household with their horses and divers goods had taken lodging with Thomas Taillour at the *Swerd on the hoop*[1] in Fleet Street, and the same day two coffers, called "*trussyngcofres*," had been stolen, one of which contained his seal and articles of jewellery of the value of 40 marks. In order that he might not be responsible for any document sealed with his seal after the date of the theft, he prayed that the facts might be entered on the rolls. William Wynkefeld, knight, attended the court and testified to the same effect on his behalf. Membr. 6 *10 May 1382*

John Stockyngbury was brought before the Mayor and *13 May 1382*

becoming his property if the defendant did not submit himself to justice within a year and a day. A garnishee or any other could come forward to prove that the goods, supposed to belong to the debtor, were his own property and that the debtor had no part in them to the value of 4d or more. By an extension of the custom, a defendant could be attached by goods in the hands of the plaintiff as garnishee. In this case the goods were generally pledges for money borrowed, and the plaintiff, who could not get his debt paid, acquired a legal right to the unredeemed pledges.

[1] For a previous theft at this inn, for which the innkeeper was made liable, see *Cal. of Plea and Mem. Rolls*, 1364–81, p. 260. Possibly the inn gave its name to Hanging-Sword Alley.

Aldermen for having a large dung heap on the banks of the Thames next to his house at Billingsgate, to the detriment of the Thames water, the damage of the commonalty and the disgrace of the city. He prayed for a reasonable time to remove it and cleanse the place, and agreed of his own free will to pay the chamberlain, Richard Odyham, the sum of £10, if this were not done before the feast of the Nativity of St John the Baptist [24 June]. He undertook further to construct a wharf on the site before Michaelmas under penalty of £20.

Membr. 6 *b*
24 April 1382

Hugh Adam of Derby, who was one of the bailiffs of that town during the last year, was brought before the Mayor and Aldermen on a charge that, by his officials at Derby[1], he had taken from a certain John Deysterre, butcher or drover, of London, the sum of 40d as custom on his merchandise, against the liberty of the city of London, granted and confirmed by the king and his predecessors, whereby the citizens of London are quit of toll and lastage and every other custom throughout the king's dominions on either side of the seas and at all the king's ports at home and abroad. The said Hugh was not able to deny the charge. Accordingly it was considered that he repay the 40d unjustly taken, which he agreed to do. And further he found mainprise, *viz.* Thomas Maunfeld, glasier, of Fleet Street and William Pouns of Derby, who undertook that he would in future behave peaceably towards all citizens of London, and especially the said John, and that he would neither do nor cause to be done any damage or oppression to any of them, under penalty of £40 payable to the chamberlain or his successors in case he were convicted thereof.

Membr. 7
2 May 1382

John Lancastre of Hatfeldbrodook[2] was attached to answer John Organ, citizen and mercer, in a plea of trespass, wherein the latter complained that on 14 June 1381 the defendant

[1] The common procedure in *withernam* was to attach men of the offending town to make good the loss of the aggrieved citizen; here the actual offender was caught. Cf. *Cal. of Early Mayor's Court Rolls*, p. 115; *Cal. of Letter Book E*, pp. 33, 42; Mary Bateson, *Borough Customs* (Seld. Soc.), I, pp. 119–25.

[2] Hatfield-Broad-Oak co. Essex.

with other evildoers unknown, who were then in insurrection against the king[1], came with swords and poleaxes against the king's peace, seeking for the plaintiff and threatening to destroy his houses and kill him, so that he from fear of death took flight, and in alarm for his goods carried them away from his houses and buried them in the parish of St Olave in Old Jewry, to wit, cloths of gold, velvets, *baudekyns*[2] of silk, linen cloths and other valuable articles (*jocalia*) of mercery worth £200, which goods thus concealed deteriorated and decayed, against the peace and to the plaintiff's damage £500. And thereof by his bill exhibited before the Mayor and Aldermen according to the custom of the city he produced suit *etc.*

The defendant pleaded not guilty and offered to verify his plea, wherein he prayed judgment. The plaintiff said that the defendant was guilty as alleged in the declaration and put himself on the country; and the defendant did likewise. But after the jury was tried and sworn and charged to render their verdict, the defendant demanded, in order to have a final issue of the matter, that the plaintiff should be put on his oath to say whether his action was a true one or not[3]. The plaintiff, in accordance with the custom of the city, accepted the oath and said he was willing to swear that the action was a true one, as set out in his bill and declaration, except as regards the amount of damages sustained by him, and he took the oath to that effect. Thereupon the jury, being sworn to assess the damages, fixed the amount at £40. Accordingly it was considered that the plaintiff recover his taxed damages, and for default of payment the defendant was committed to prison.

Richard Norbury, mercer, sued John Courtray for detinue of chattels, under the following circumstances. When the *17 May 1382*

[1] During the Peasants' Revolt. The men of Essex and Kent had effected an entrance into the city on 12 June.

[2] A rich silk material, embroidered, brocaded, and sometimes interwoven with gold thread.

[3] This was the "peremptory oath" admissible in actions of debt and covenant, and here extended to trespass. See *Munim. Gild. Lond.* (R.S.), I, pp. 217, 521; *Cal. of Letter Book G*, p. 73; Letter Book H, fo. 286 *b*; *Cal. of Early Mayor's Court Rolls*, pp. xxxv–xxxvi, and numerous instances in this volume.

count of St Pol[1] was in England he bought from the plaintiff between Easter and Michaelmas, 1378, certain velvet cloths and beds to the value of £40. As he failed to pay for them, the plaintiff in the Sheriffs' Court obtained the arrest of a quantity of pearls belonging to the count, which were in the hands of the defendant, in order that his debt might be paid. Thereupon the count told his servant, John Brayles, to satisfy the plaintiff out of the value of the pearls, but in spite of their being under arrest and notwithstanding the count's orders, the defendant refused to give them up; wherefore the plaintiff brings his bill of complaint in accordance with the law merchant and the custom of the city.

The defendant, after pleading that he had no knowledge that the pearls were the property of the count, said that they were entrusted to him by a certain Caulus, a knight of the count's household, to be set, and that he was to have £4 for his workmanship. He was willing to give them up, if the court so directed, on condition that he received the £4 due to him. The pearls, which he produced in court, were valued by oath of Richard Whityngton and John Wodecok, mercers, as follows: 424 pearls at 1½d each, 53s; 294 at 2½d each, £3 1s 3d; 180 at 1¼d each, 18s 9d; 1½ oz. 3¾ dwt. at 16s 8d the ounce, 28s 1d; 1⅛ ounces[2] at 10s the ounce, 11s 3d; sum total £8 12s 4d. The pearls were delivered to the plaintiff under security to save the court and the defendant harmless against the count, Caulus or any other person, and the plaintiff then paid the defendant £4 for his work.

Membr. 7 *b* William Morton brought a bill against Robert de Eye, cutler, in which he complained that there had been a negotiation between them as to his becoming apprentice to the said Robert, after which the latter had caused a scrivener to draw up indentures according to his own wishes, whereby the complainant was to pay 4 marks to him at Michaelmas, to provide for himself during the first year of the apprenticeship and to pay a penalty of £40 if he broke the conditions. He had never agreed to these terms and refused to do so without

[1] Walerand, count of St Pol, then a prisoner in England. *Cal. Close Rolls*, 1377–81, p. 324.

[2] *Una unc. di. qua.*

the consent of his parents and his friends. Thereupon Robert had agreed that he should go to his parents and friends to learn their wishes. And because his father and his other friends were unwilling to give their consent to the indentures, the said Robert had sued him in the Sheriffs' Court, as though he were a hired labourer, and had caused him to be arrested.

On 19 June, when the said Robert appeared on summons, the complainant offered that if the said Robert, together with Martin Godard and John Morton[1], would swear that there was a covenant between them that he should provide for himself during the first year, then he would be ready to serve as his apprentice for seven years. Thereupon Robert, Martin and John took an oath on the book that there was such an agreement. Accordingly it was considered that the complainant should serve the said Robert as his apprentice, and the latter was enjoined to provide for him and teach him and not to treat him unjustly or maliciously under penalty of losing him. As regards the bond in £40, it seemed to the court, in view of the fact that the plaintiff was under age, to be against all reason and it was therefore cancelled. The said Robert was then told to take his apprentice away with him. But instead, he took him immediately to the Sheriffs' compter in Milk Street and there without any reason unjustly caused him to be imprisoned till 21 June, making no provision for his sustenance. On that day the said Robert *19 June 1382*

[1] The only threefold oath in the city was in the verification of goods, being similar to the oath used in identifying waifs and strays. See Mary Bateson, *Borough Customs* (Seld. Soc.), II, pp. 163–4. In foreign attachment, the garnishee could swear with the third hand that the goods attached were his own, *Cal. of Early Mayor's Court Rolls*, pp. xxxvi, 17, and he could also prove that goods attached by error in other courts were his own, *Ibid.* p. 68. The present instance has similarities with the "peremptory oath," where a defendant could put himself on the oath of a plaintiff or *vice versa*, but whereas the peremptory oath was a single oath and refusal to accept it meant losing the case (*Munim. Gild. Lond.* I, pp. 217, 521), here it was plainly a case of a challenge which might be refused without penalty. There was a similar challenge in 1365, *Cal. of Plea and Mem. Rolls*, 1364–81, p. 42, and in 1383, see below, p. 44, where the defendant offered to stand by the oath of the plaintiff and two others. The plaintiff *gratis acceptavit* and produced four others. As there was no compulsion, such challenges cannot be regarded as regular "wagers of law."

was brought before the Mayor, Recorder and Aldermen and as he could give no reason or excuse for the imprisonment of his apprentice, which was directly contrary to the injunction and judgment of the court and brought disgrace and opprobrium on the city, it was considered that the complainant be exonerated, and the said Robert was ordered to bring the indentures into court for cancellation, which was done the same day.

Membr. 8
14 March 1382

Ralph Strode[1] was summoned to answer William Temple, Robert Rotherham, Walter Barkeswell, Thomas Cruche, Thomas Beneyt, John Payn, Thomas Sulhill, Thomas Bole, John Marram and John Carbrok, *bladsmythes*[2], in a plea of deceit, wherein they complained that on 17 Nov. 1376 he had advised them in the Guildhall to move the Mayor and Aldermen to have certain articles touching their mistery granted and enrolled in the Chamber, telling them that these articles would be of great profit to the city and themselves. Accordingly he had been retained to be of their counsel for making this suit and received from them 40d the same day, and acting on his advice they had prayed the Mayor and Aldermen from day to day to grant the articles, until the defendant, plotting to annul and destroy their suit, on 26 Jan. 1377 deceitfully informed the mistery of Cutlers of the matter, and took the part of Simon atte Nax, Henry Blakwyne, Robert Austyn and others of that mistery against his own employers in praying the Mayor and Aldermen not to grant or enrol the aforesaid articles, whereupon the said Cutlers, solely by his advice and counsel, prayed the Mayor and Aldermen that the Bladesmiths should not have their purpose and desire, and this the said Ralph did unjustly and to their damage £100. *Note* that the Bladesmiths' bill is in the file of bills terminated between Easter and the feast of St John

[1] He was appointed common pleader or counter (*communis narrator*) of the city in 1373. *Cal. of Letter Book G*, p. 317. Also described as "common serjeant" (*communis serviens*). See *Cal. of Plea and Mem. Rolls*, 1364–81, p. 186. Apparently he was allowed to practise privately. In the 16th century the two offices became distinct and the common serjeant is now a judge.

[2] See proceedings of 1408 relating to these two misteries, H. T. Riley, *Memorials of London*, pp. 567–8, and the ordinances of the Bladesmiths, *Cal. of Letter Book L*, pp. 25–8.

the Baptist, together with the ordinances proposed by the Bladesmiths.

The defendant pleaded not guilty and offered to defend himself by his law[1] as a freeman in accordance with the custom of the city, and thereof he prayed judgment. The plaintiffs pleaded that in such a case he was not entitled to his law and also prayed for judgment. In order that the court might be advised, the action was adjourned until 14 June 1382. On that day both parties renounced their pleading to judgment and willingly put themselves on an examination of the Cutlers mentioned in the bill and agreed to stand by it. Thereupon the Cutlers, being separately examined on oath, swore that the defendant had not been retained or paid by them, that he was not of their counsel and had given them no information, whereby the Bladesmiths' articles were rejected. Accordingly it was considered that the Bladesmiths take nothing by their bill, but be in mercy.

Peter Serdau of Genoa, who was arrested by Nicholas Exton, alderman of Billingsgate, on suspicion of being of the allegiance of the king's enemies and of having come to these parts in order to spy on the realm of England, being hostile to the same, was sent to the mayor and questioned by him on 30 June. He declared that he belonged to Genoa and was not an enemy nor a spy. At the same time Cosma Dorea and Lodewyc Malbek swore on the book that as an honest mariner he came in a ship called a "*karik*[2]" to Southampton and was intending, with the favour of God, to sail thence with his merchandise for Lombardy. *30 June 1382*

Robert Joynour, servant of Robert Wydmere, joiner, was found by a jury not guilty of a charge brought against him by William Causby, chaplain, of having taken and carried away from the plaintiff's house in the parish of St Mary *12 June 1382*

[1] By the sevenfold oath, himself and six oath-helpers. The plaintiffs objected, doubtless on the ground that they had writings or other satisfactory evidence. The "law" was now regarded as a proof *faute de mieux*. See *Munim. Gild. Lond.* (R.S.), I, p. 294.

[2] Carrack.

Magdalene near Oldefysshstrete the following goods: £30 in gold and silver, a psalter of the value of 6s 8d, another large book containing several grammatical treatises of the value of 33s 4d and 5 yards of linen cloth, value 8s.

It was afterwards reported to the Mayor and Aldermen that the plaintiff had called the jurors false and perjured. When he was questioned on the point on 26 June he spoke maliciously in court and was thereupon sent to prison. Next day he was bound over in £20 that he would neither speak ill of the jurors nor begin proceedings against any of them in any court.

Membr. 8 *b*
10 July 1382

A certain physician (*fisicus*) to the queen came before the Mayor and Aldermen and said that he had paid John Blake, goldsmith, the sum of 5 nobles for a silver cup and covercle which he had purchased, but that the said John refused to deliver them. Thereupon came the said John and said that he had only been paid 3 nobles, and this he was prepared to prove by six men, as a freeman of the city. The plaintiff consenting, the defendant together with six others swore that he had only received 3 nobles from the physician.

9 July 1382

Thomas Norwich, chaplain, was attached to answer Henry de Wilton in a plea of trespass, wherein the latter complained that the defendant on divers occasions between 1 Aug. 1381 and 8 July 1382 by force and arms and against the peace had eloigned and carried away the plaintiff's wife Joan, woollen and linen cloths, silver plate, dishes, pewter saltcellars and iron and brass pots and pans.

A jury brought in a verdict that as regards the wife, she was nothing but a common strumpet, and so there was no eloigning[1], but the defendant was in possession of certain goods belonging to the plaintiff of the value of 60s, some of which Joan had brought to him and the rest he had himself

[1] I.e. no force, fraud or persuasion was used. See Blackstone's *Commentaries*, III, p. 131. The remedy provided by statute Westminster I, 3 Edw. I, c. 13 was rarely used by aggrieved husbands in London, who usually preferred to sue for the value of goods, clothes etc., "asported," receiving judgment for damages and the committal of the offender to a debtor's prison.

taken. It was considered that the defendant pay 60s damages and restore the goods, in default of which he was committed to prison.

Margery, living at the Coppedhalle[1] near the Herber[2] in London, was summoned for refusing to give up to Richard Coventre, clerk, the following goods entrusted to her, *viz.* a locked chest containing a complete *Corpus Legis Canoni* (*sic*) of the value of £10, a coverlet (*superlectulum*) with a basin and ewer of the value of 13s 4d and other goods worth 20s, and also a bundle containing a box of deeds relating to the plaintiff's lands in co. Warwick, a basin and ewer of the value of 6s 8d, a pitcher (*urciolus*) worth 2s, and two brass pans and one of iron of the value of 4s.

The defendant appeared and said that she was ready to defend herself by her law as a freewoman of the city, whereupon the plaintiff prayed that she might be examined on oath and offered to stand peremptorily by the examination. As the result of the examination it appeared to the court that she had received no goods and chattels as alleged, and accordingly it was considered that the plaintiff take nothing by his bill, but be in mercy.

Membr. 9
2 March 1382

William Grenyngham was summoned to answer John Yerdele in a plea that he render account of 13 woollen cloths of the assize of length and width and of the value of 102 marks, received from the plaintiff on 22 May 1374 by the hands of Simon Gardiner, fuller, to trade therewith and to render account when required, which he refused to do, to the plaintiff's damage £40.

The defendant, while protesting[3] that he did not acknowledge either the quantity or the value of the cloth, pleaded

[1] A messuage and shops in Dowgate Hill in the parish of St John Walbrook. See Harbin's *Dictionary of London*; C. L. Kingsford's ed. of *Stow's Survey*, II, p. 318.

[2] A mansion on the east side of Dowgate. *Ibid.*

[3] *Facit protestacionem.* The *protestando* was a word made use of to avoid double pleading in actions. The defendant brushes aside certain allegations of the plaintiff and then *pro placito dicit* that on which he is willing to take issue. See Jacob's *Law Dictionary*; Tidd's *Practice* (1821), pp. 717–18.

that Isabella, wife of the plaintiff, was a common maker of woollen cloth[1], and that she delivered the said cloths to the said Simon to be fulled and after they were fulled she ordered him to take them to the defendant, which he did. He pleaded further that by the custom of the city[2] contracts made by married women engaged in a mercantile art were as effectual as contracts made by their husbands, that Isabella had always used the art of making woollen cloths and sold the same as a *feme sole*, and that on 20 May 1374 she came to his house in Lothbury and told him that she had sold the cloth to William Sutton and others for 102 marks, and he was to deliver the cloth to the said William, taking a bond from the said William, Geoffrey Sutton, William Chaloner and Thomas de Angyr, cordwainer, in the sum of 204 marks as security for the payment of the aforesaid 102 marks, and this was done because he was an officer of the city and better able to enforce payment than either Isabella or her husband. He said further that he had never received any part of the purchase-money for the cloth, and that on 24 June 1378 the said John Yerdele came to his house and asked him for the above bond, which was given up to him; nevertheless he, the defendant, had always been and was still willing to sue the debtors on the bond at the plaintiff's expense, and to give security that he would do nothing to prevent the money being recovered. Accordingly he prayed judgment whether any action lay against him.

The plaintiff pleaded that he had no knowledge of any such custom in the city as alleged, that he was himself continuously in possession of the cloth until William Grenyngham received it, and that even if there had been a contract [between the defendant and his wife] on Saturday 20 May, which he did not acknowledge, nevertheless the contract which he himself made with the defendant on Monday 22 May could not be less effectual. Since the defendant did not deny

[1] *Communis factrix et operatrix.*

[2] This was a correct citation of city custom, see *Munim. Gild. Lond.* (R.S.), I, p. 204; *Laws and Customs of London* (1765), p. 111. "If a *feme covert*, the wife of a freeman, trades by herself in a trade, with which her husband does not intermeddle, she may sue and be sued as a *feme sole*, and the husband shall be named only for conformity."

receiving the cloth, he prayed judgment and that auditors of an account be appointed.

Afterwards, on 17 July, the plaintiff, on being called, failed to appear. Accordingly it was considered that he take nothing by his bill, but be in mercy.

Bond of Gilbert Bene, cordwainer, of the parish of Sordiche, John Hidyngham and William Chaloner to Nicholas Burle in 26s 8d. Membr. 9 *b* *7 Aug. 1382*

Be it remembered that good men of the mistery of Goldsmiths[1] came before John Norhampton, mayor, complaining that a certain Robert Betoyne, goldsmith, had made two hafts (*manubria*) of latten and gilded them so that they appeared to be all of gold, in deception of the people and to the scandal of the mistery. The said Robert, being questioned, admitted that the hafts were deceptive and said that a certain John Twyford, cutler, had asked him to make them in this manner for the use of the earl of Buckingham. William Tyngewyk, John Carbonel, Thomas Davy and John Bulstrode, wardens of the aforesaid mistery, together with Adam Bamme, John Fraunceys and John Forster, good men of the same, gave evidence that they had discussed the matter with the earl, who agreed that the hafts, being deceptively made, should be handed over to them for destruction. The court allowed the hafts to be delivered to the wardens, but as they had no knowledge of the matter beyond the wardens' evidence, the latter were warned not to break or part with the hafts without the earl's permission. The above-mentioned Robert was then sworn not to make any hafts of this kind or any deceptive work in future. *4 Aug. 1382*

An inquest was taken before the Mayor and Aldermen to discover what evildoers and disturbers of the peace had molested foreigners bringing fish to the city for the use of the king, his magnates and commonalty, or what other persons had been molested on account of these foreigners, contrary to the ordinance made and proclaimed by the Mayor, *8 Aug. 1382*

[1] Acting under their charter of 16 March 1327. See *Cal. of Plea and Mem. Rolls*, 1323–64, p. 61; Letter Book G, fo. 104.

Aldermen and Common Council[1]. The jury said on oath that a certain Robert atte Wode, fishmonger, on Wednesday last struck a certain Alice Yonge on Cornhill, because she was talking there with a foreigner belonging to her own district, who had brought fish for sale, and because she brought water for him to wash his hands and invited him to come and have a drink with her. They said further that John Ditton, fishmonger, aided and abetted the said Robert.

When charged before the Mayor and Aldermen, the latter admitted his offence and put himself on the favour of the court. He was sent to prison until the court should be advised as to their judgment. The said John Ditton pleaded not guilty and put himself on the country. A jury was summoned for the following Saturday, on which day they found him not guilty. But since he was a man of bad character, as was testified by many persons of credit, he was committed to prison until further order. Afterwards on 10 Aug., on the ground that the offence confessed by Robert atte Wode was a great and enormous trespass against the king, his magnates and commonalty, and brought shame upon the Mayor and Aldermen and their ordinance, and in order that others might be prevented from committing similar offences, it was considered that the said Robert be imprisoned for a year and a day, to date from the eighth day of August, unless meanwhile he obtain the indulgence of the court.

Membr. 10

John Hankyn, fishmonger, was attached to answer Richard Elme, baker, in a plea of trespass, wherein the latter complained that on 30 Sept. 1381 the defendant by force and arms[2], to wit swords, had taken, abducted and carried away the plaintiff's wife Alice, together with 6 woollen cloths of blanket worth £40, 4 mazers with silver bands worth 12 marks, 2 pieces of silver worth 30s and 8 gold rings worth 10 marks.

The defendant pleaded not guilty and put himself on the

[1] See *Cal. of Letter Book H*, pp. xxvii–xxxi, 192–4. The case arose out of the attempt of the non-victualling parties in the city to curtail the monopoly of the freemen-fishmongers and to enable non-citizens to engage in retail trade.

[2] The law supposed force and restraint because the wife had no power to consent. Blackstone's *Commentaries*, III, p. 131.

country. On 8 Aug. a jury of St Botolph's Bishopsgate found that as regards the mazers, silver pieces and rings he was not guilty, but guilty of eloigning the wife and carrying away the woollen cloths, to the plaintiff's damage 200 marks. Accordingly it was considered that the plaintiff recover the damages taxed by the jury, but that he be in mercy for his false claim concerning the mazers *etc.* *8 Aug. 1382*

A foreign attachment of cloth valued at £17 6s 8d was delivered to John Gena, merchant of Dinant (*Dynand*) in Almaine, plaintiff in an action of debt against William Spicer of Shrewsbury. *8 Sept. 1382*

Robert Denton, chaplain, was summoned to answer Richard Stacener, chaplain, in a plea of deceit, wherein he complained that when he (the plaintiff) and others were intending to buy certain rents to the value of 17 marks for the purpose of founding a house of charity to receive persons who had lost their memory [*existentes extra memoriam suam*] and especially priests, the defendant came to him and gave him to understand that he had a good plot of ground in the parish of All Hallows, Berkyngcherche, which he was willing to devote to the purpose. Thereupon, on Monday before Christmas 1371, the defendant was paid £28, but he afterwards sold the ground, while retaining the £28, thus deceiving the plaintiff and causing him damage to the extent of £40. *10 May 1382*

The defendant appeared and prayed leave to imparl[1] till Monday the 12th, which was granted to him peremptorily. On that day he did not come but left the court. Therefore it was considered that the said Richard recover the said £28 against him and that he be taken to satisfy the plaintiff thereof.

Writ of protection in favour of Robert Aleyn of London, knight, *alias* Robert Aleyn of London, fishmonger, who was then on the king's service in Portugal in the company of John Fernande[2], knight. Dated at Westminster 23 Feb. 1382. Membr. 10 *b* *23 Feb. 1382*

[1] An imparlance was an extension of time to consider of an answer to a plaintiff's declaration. It was granted *peremptorie*, i.e. he must either appear to plead on the given day or lose the action by default.

[2] Cf. *Cal. Close Rolls*, 1381–5, p. 112.

Membr. 11
8 July 1382

Custance Somerset, prioress of the house of St Helen, London, was summoned to answer John Chamberleyn, chaplain, and John Norffolk, executors of the will of Cecilia, widow of Thomas Rose, clerk, on a demand for payment of arrears of rent, they saying that a certain Elianora de Wyncestre, prioress of the said house before Custance, had by deed granted to the late John de Shene, saddler, certain rents in Ivylane in the parish of St Faith for a term of 400 years, that the said John did afterwards bequeath the same to Alice his wife, who afterwards married Richard de Kyghtele of Kersaultone[1], cook, and they granted the same to the above Cecilia, and that as executors they had frequently applied to the said Custance for payment of the arrears of rent, but in vain, to their damage 100s. They produced in court the deed of the said Elianora, which also contained a lease of premises in Philippeslane charged with quitrents to the prior of Newerk by Rippele and the heirs of Robert Fouke, the deed of the said Richard de Kyghtele and Alice his wife, and the will of the said Cecilia.

The prioress by her attorney, Gilbert Meldebourne, pleaded that her predecessor Elianora had nothing in demesne or in reversion in the above-mentioned tenements except an annual quitrent of 40s which had always belonged to the convent, that the tenants after the supposed grant had not attorned[2] to John de Shene, and further that the annual payment was only a pension chargeable on the person of the late prioress and was not by law chargeable on the person of the present prioress. She prayed judgment. The executors pleaded that the grant by Elianora had been made by consent of the convent and that the defendant had not denied that John, Alice, Richard and Cecilia had afterwards successively had seisin of the rent, and they prayed judgment thereon.

A day was given that the court might be advised as to their judgment, when the prioress made default, and though order was given to distrain her for a further day to hear judgment, she again made default. Therefore it was considered that the

[1] Carshalton co. Surrey.

[2] *Attornment* signifies the tenant's acknowledgment of a new lord, on the sale of lands etc.

executors recover the arrears and that the prioress be in mercy.

Henry Cauntebrigge brought a bill before the Mayor and Aldermen to the following effect: In the year 1364 he had borrowed, by way of chevisance[1], from Geoffrey Puppe and William Brampton a quantity of merchandise, *viz.* stockfish called "*gricoks*," saltfish, tables[2], pitch and tar amounting to £26, the loan being effected by a broker. As security he had given a bond for a sum of money and an annuity of £10 for eight years on property in the parish of St Christopher on Cornhill, and furthermore he had entered into a recognisance of £88 12s 8d in the Chancery. It was agreed that for every year the creditors held the above property they should allow a rebate of £10 on the debt. They had actually held the property for four and a half years, when the plaintiff repaid the debt of £26 and a further sum of 20 marks. But the creditors would only allow him a rebate of 10 marks (£6 13s 4d) each year for the four and a half years, so that in addition to the repayment of their debt, they obtained from him £15 (the difference between the £10 and 10 marks per annum) and the above-mentioned 20 marks (£13 6s 8d), making £28 6s 8d. The creditors had given him back his deeds but had not cancelled the recognisance in Chancery, which he was afraid might cause loss to himself or his executors. [*French*] Membr. 11 *b* *8 Nov. 1382*

The defendants pleaded that the plaintiff had given them an acquittance on condition that the recognisance should be withdrawn and they had in fact immediately afterwards withdrawn it. Thereupon the mayor took the parties into the Inner Chamber of Guildhall, where the defendants agreed to return the recognisance to the plaintiff and give him an acquittance.

John Mountagu, *alias* Hatfeld, was summoned to answer Thomas Hatfeld his brother for payment of the sum of £40 Membr. 12 *26 July 1382*

[1] A bargain whereby a man bought a quantity of goods, entering into a recognisance to pay a certain amount, which goods were then sold to a confederate for a smaller sum. It was an attempt to evade the ecclesiastical laws against usury, by cloaking the transaction under the guise of legitimate bargain and sale.

[2] *Tables piche & tar.* Possibly the meaning is cakes of pitch and tar.

under a bond. He made four defaults and it was reported to the court that he had fled to the priory of St Mary Southwark outside the liberty of the city and that he had no goods and chattels in the city, but only tenements and rents in the parishes of All Hallows Graschirchestret and St Margaret Patyns. The plaintiff prayed that these might be assigned to him by way of foreign attachment until his claims were satisfied, in accordance with the custom of the city observed in the like case from of old. The court consented and after summoning the tenants inquired from them what rents were in arrear and warned them not to pay any moneys to the defendant until the plaintiff had been fully satisfied. One of the tenants, Robert Broud, who was rented at 14 marks, informed the court that the defendant had undertaken to keep the tenement in repair against wind and rain and until this was done he could make no profit from it. The court then ordered a report from the sworn masons and carpenters of the city[1], who certified that the necessary repairs could be made for 40s, which the plaintiff was told to charge against the arrears due from that tenement. But the tenant refused to pay the workmen more than 2 marks or to pay the plaintiff anything, contrary to the order of the court. He was committed to prison till he should pay and find security for future payments of rent.

Membr. 13
8 June 1382

Luke Bragadyn, merchant of Venice, was summoned to answer Richard Morell and Henry Pensehurst, partners and merchants of London, in a plea for the payment of the sums of £566 15s and £341 9s, on the ground, as set forth in two bills, that by the immemorial custom of London and the law merchant a principal was bound to satisfy debts incurred by his recognised agent for merchandise bought on his behalf, where such merchandise accrued to his use and profit, and

[1] The sworn masons and carpenters were officials, usually four in number, who advised the mayor and aldermen in disputes relating to party-walls, encroachments and other matters arising under Fitz Aylwin's Assize of Building. For their oath, A.D. 1301, see *Munim. Gild. Lond.* (R.S.), II, p. 100; *Cal. of Letter Book C*, p. 86. References to them and to their reports continue throughout the Middle Ages, until their office was absorbed into that of the Sworn Viewers after the Fire of London. They are represented to-day by the surveyors and inspectors of the city.

that the said Luke at Calais on 1 Jan. 1380(1) in the house of Paul Fraunceys, a common broker of the Staple there, inquired from the plaintiff Henry as to divers sorts of Coteswold wool which he and his partner had in Calais, and then showed him his signet and requested him, when his son Nicholas or some other agent should arrive bearing the signet, to deliver the wool to him and to take from him bonds for payment under the said signet, and that on 8 Jan. the said Nicholas arrived and took delivery of the wool, giving bonds for payment of the above amounts on 7 March 1381 and 12 Jan. 1382, and that afterwards the said wool accrued to the use and profit of the defendant at Bruges, a merchant town in Flanders, but nevertheless the defendant refused to pay the above sums, to the plaintiffs' damage £1000.

After process continued, the defendant appeared on 8 July and admitted the debt. He informed the court that he had sued a certain Peter Gracian to render account of business dealings between them, including the matter of the wool, on which the present claim was being made. He was willing, if the auditors found that he had not paid to Peter the above-mentioned sums of money, that he would himself pay them immediately to Nicholas Brembre, knight and merchant, to whom they had been assigned by the plaintiffs in satisfaction for debts owed by them to Nicholas. But even if it were found that he had paid the money to Peter, he was willing to satisfy the said Nicholas, on condition that he received acquittances for the bonds and was not troubled as regards any other debts of Peter, and on condition that the latter remained in prison until he (Peter) had reimbursed him.

Thereupon the court appointed Walter Silyle and John Shadeworth, Englishmen, and Gulstan Pynel or Gerard Bek and Gautron de Bardes, Lombards, as auditors, who on 19 Aug. produced the account. They found that Luke owed Peter £91 12s 8d, and that Peter ought to perform the following matters, *viz.* deliver to Luke a barrel of *Inde Bakade*[1], pay him 103s on behalf of John Swyft, mercer, deliver two

[1] Possibly Indian spice or dye, *bakade* being derived from *baca* or *baccar*, a berry.

sarplers[1] of wool, which he had arrested at Calais, or £40, pay £161 5s due from certain Brabantine merchants for the wool of William Grevel, deliver a quantity of goods belonging to Matthew Dony which he had pledged with the company of Arige[2] of Bologna for £150 *gros*[3], give him a fourth part of the profits on 73 sarplers of wool on a bargain made with William Grevel, account for the sum of £26 19s paid as costs to Henry Pensehurst on the wool, and withdraw an action for £1800 which he had brought against Luke in the Sheriffs' Court. [*French*]

On this the court committed Luke to prison for his debt of £91 12s 8d and ordered that Peter be confined in fetters in the *Bocardo*[4] of Newgate till he had satisfied Luke on his claims. The latter then, in accordance with his undertaking, agreed to pay Nicholas Brembre the sum of £908 4s claimed and a further sum of £341 16s, and he and Peter were committed to prison.

Finally on 2 July 1385, Nicholas Brembre, who was then mayor, appeared in court with Luke and Peter, who were both at large, and announced that they had come to an agreement. All parties prayed that each might be exonerated against the others. And thus the court was quit of the matter.

Membr. 13 *b*
31 Oct. 1382

Mandate under the privy seal, informing the mayor and sheriffs that the king had pardoned Reginald Neuport *alias* Reginald de la Chambre for certain words which he was alleged to have spoken against the king's person and other trespasses and misprisions for which he had been committed to Newgate. Whereas the said Reginald was indebted in divers sums of money on loan at the Receipt of the Exchequer, the mayor and sheriffs were commanded to send him before the treasurer and barons of the Exchequer with the causes

[1] Bales, said to contain 80 tods of wool, each tod weighing 28 lbs. and consisting of three or four fleeces. See *N.E.D.*

[2] The Arigi, an Italian banking and trading company.

[3] Flemish denomination.

[4] *Bocardo* was one of the syllogisms in logic. The name was applied to a room in Newgate, and there was also a *bocardo* in the north gate of Oxford. Possibly, as a *bocardo* was an argument in logic from which one could not escape, some lettered prisoner used the word to describe humorously what was evidently a particularly secure prison-room.

of his detaining, in order that they might deal with him according to the laws and usages of the realm. [*French*]

Return of the mayor and sheriffs that long before the receipt of the mandate, the said Reginald had been arrested for trespasses and misprisions touching the king and the city, likewise for a debt of £16 which John Bonne, saddler, recovered against him for detinue of a horse, and another debt of 18s 6d claimed against him by John Kendale, tailor, and further, that he might render account to the Mayor and Aldermen[1] of £72 and other goods and chattels received by him for the use of Walter, John and Jacomina, orphans of Giles de Melyn, late citizen, the Mayor and Aldermen by the custom of the city having the custody of the goods and chattels of orphans. Nevertheless they would send the said Reginald before the barons of the Exchequer as demanded, praying that after satisfaction had been made to the king he might be returned to prison according to ancient custom.

Duplicate entries in Morell and Pensehurst *v.* Bragadyn. Membr. 14 and 15

Names of the good men of the divers misteries (49) elected for the Common Council in the time of John Norhampton, mayor, A° 5 Ric. II. Membr. 16 and 17 *1381–2*

Draperes: Robert Boxford, Thomas Noket, John Pounchon, Robert Somersete, Geoffrey Walderne, John Vyner.

Merceres: William Hawe, John Loveye, John More, Thomas Austyn, Salman Salman, John Dane.

Grocers: Richard Hatfeld, Thomas Wyght, John Wiltshire, John Bradfeld, William Culham, Richard Loseye.

Aurifabri (goldsmiths): Thomas Hay, Thomas Paunton, Thomas Polle, Drew Barantyn, John Luton, John Carbonel.

Vynters: Henry Vannere, William More, John Tilneye, Richard Sprot, Henry Herbury, John Colshull.

Piscenarii (fishmongers): Thomas Lyncolle, John Rydere, Henry Morton, John Poynaunt, John Burwell, William Brampton.

Pelliparii (skinners): Walter Pykenham, Thomas Duc, William Frenyngham, Richard Dawe.

[1] Sitting as a court of orphanage.

Taillours: Walter Ewayn, Robert Lyndeseye, John Northfolk, Richard Spencer, William Denton, Thomas Bridlyngton.

Brouderers: Robert Ascombe, John Cretyng.

Sadeleres: John Pounfret, Walter Yonge, Thomas Soys, William Shirewode.

Wexchaundeleres: John Pope, Richard Saveray.

Breweres: John Waldegrave, John Bysshop, John Hore, John Cook of Cornhull.

Allutarii (cordwainers): Nicholas Snypston, Bartholomew Mildenhale, John Longe, senior, Robert de York.

Armurers: William Trippelowe, Robert Sendale.

Talughchaundelers: Richard Manhale, Robert Kyng, John Brokholl, Richard Breyngwayn.

Bochers: Roger Crips, William Gilot, Elias Weston, John Dorsete, Thomas Clerk, John Creek.

Ismongeres: Robert Parys, Reginald Coleman.

Salteres: Thomas Walpole, John Codonore(?).

Shermen: John Lacy, John Ellyngham.

Webbes: John Bathe, William Goryng, John Bisshop.

Digheres: Nicholas Maynard, Walter Anne.

Cotellers: Robert Austyn, Richard Shirbourne.

Gurdeleres: John Lewyn, Thomas Fissh.

Curreours: Richard Serle, Thomas Willyngham.

Fulleres: Richard Skeet, William Stoket.

Foundours: Adam Holt, Stephen Godefrey.

Haberdassheres: Richard Chiryngton, John Bristowe, John Pountfreit, Richard Romeney.

Fustours: John Burdevile, John Philip.

Peautrers: Walter Hervyle, Gavyn Kentys.

Wodemongers: John Asshurst, Thomas Freke.

Plomers: John Daundeseye, William Horewode.

Bakeres: Gilbert Lyrp, Simon Frenssh.

Tapicers: John Dig, Thomas Bonauntre.

Lethersellers: William Belhomme, John Swanton.

Peyntours: William Larke, John Lynk.

Tanneres: (blank).

Hureres: Nicholas Andevere, Ralph Bristowe.

Joynours: Laurence Joynour, John Wydemere.

Whittawyeres: John Whitbred, Richard Maynolf.

Lorymers: John Mymmes, Nicholas Petit.
Bowyeres: John Derneford, Thomas Coton.
Fleccheres: John Orchard, John Shordich.
Horneres: Henry Hogeston, John Chechely.
Smythes: Robert Malteby, Walter Houpere, Roger Mark, William Albon.
Masouns: Nicholas Petyt.
Hatteres: (blank).
Sporieres: Roger Payn, John Dene.
Pouchemakers: Thomas Fulbourne, William Furneux.
Pynneres: Hugh Bromhull, William Coventre.

Pleas held in the Chamber of the Guildhall of the city of London before John Norhampton, Mayor, and the Aldermen according to the custom of the city and the law merchant Membr. 18

John Jewell, attorney of Thomas Gisors, merchant, made a complaint as follows: On 27 Nov. 1381 a certain John Colshull, late servant and attorney of Thomas Gisors, brought an action for debt against his late master in the Sheriffs' Court before John Hende, sheriff, claiming from him three several sums of £105, £165 and £110 8s 8d, and the said Thomas having made default, his lands, tenements and rents in the city were delivered to the plaintiff as a foreign attachment until his claims should be satisfied, unless the said Thomas should submit himself to justice within a year and a day. Afterwards the said Thomas appeared before John Sely, sheriff, and prayed that John Colshull be summoned to appear on 5 Nov. 1382 to show cause why the lands and tenements should not be restored to him, since he was now ready to submit himself to justice and to prove that he owed nothing. Nevertheless, the plea had for a long time been left pending, neither discussed nor terminated, because the sheriff favoured John Colshull; for which reason, and because the matter concerned the law merchant, the attorney now prayed the Mayor and Aldermen to cause the record and process of the action to come before them, in order that they might make an end of the matter. *10 Feb. 1383*

The Mayor and Aldermen granted the request and ordered the parties to appear and the sheriff to bring the record and process on 27 Feb. 1383, on which day the sheriff brought the record and process of the proceedings held before John Hende, sheriff, on 27 Nov. 1381, and before John Sely, sheriff, on 5 Nov. 1382 [as summarised above in the attorney's complaint].

Thereupon John Jewell, on behalf of Thomas Gisors, prayed that John Colshull make his declaration against the said John Jewell.

The said John Colshull, after citing a power of attorney of 24 Aug. 1372, whereby his master empowered him to receive debts, give acquittances, trade with his goods and enter into bonds for payments, declared that afterwards his master wrote to him at Bruges, asking him to pay 1000 crowns[1], at the rate of £105 sterling, to a creditor named John van Putten, *Esterlyng*, which payment the plaintiff made out of his own money, and so, by the law merchant, an action accrued to him to demand that amount from his master in reimburse-
Membr. 18 *b* ment. As regards the sum of £165 claimed, he declared that he made an exchange with William Ancroft, attorney of Adam Fraunceys of London, of 1500 crowns, at the rate of £165 sterling, for his master's use, and therewith he paid divers sums to his master's creditors, *viz.* £100 Flemish *gros*[2] to John Fermer and £49 17s 6d Flemish *gros* to John van Assen, making a total of 1500 crowns[3]. In order to raise this money he had entered into a personal bond to the said William Ancroft and a certain John Ussher, and he had subsequently redeemed his bond by paying the amount due out of his own moneys. And as regards the sum of £110 8s 8d, he declared that he had made another exchange with William Ancroft of 1000 crowns, at the rate of £110 8s 8d sterling, and had paid that sum to a creditor of his master, Peter Arnauld of Vines, Gascon[4], and that he had afterwards redeemed his bond out of his own moneys.

[1] *De m. scutis.* [2] *Grossorum de moneta Flandrie.*

[3] In this transaction the Flemish £ was worth a fraction over £1 2s sterling.

[4] *De Vines gascoign.* It is not impossible that this means "for Gascon wines," though the pleading is in Latin.

The said Thomas Gisors, while not acknowledging the above allegations, pleaded that the plaintiff, at the time when he alleged these payments to have been made, was under obligation to render account to his master for certain sums of money, as set forth in a roll produced in court; and by the custom of the city and the law merchant, if any servant or agent made payments on behalf of his master, he had no right of action against him for reimbursement, so long as he had in his hands moneys of his master sufficient to cover those payments, which moneys the plaintiff at that time had. Wherefore he prayed restitution of his lands and tenements.

The plaintiff, in reply, produced a quitclaim, dated 6 July 1373, whereby the defendant had released him, under the name of "John Colshull, late apprentice of Thomas Gisors," of all claims, debts, accounts and trespasses, subsequent to which he had received no moneys from his master save a free gift of £10.

The defendant prayed judgment on the ground that the plaintiff had not denied having received the moneys set forth in the roll produced, while the plaintiff likewise prayed judgment because his quitclaim freed him from the necessity of answering to the roll.

After process continued, on 23 Oct. 1383 it was considered by the court that John Colshull recover his debts, and that the execution of the judgment in the Sheriffs' Court stand, in accordance with the custom of the city and the law merchant.

Record and process in the Sheriffs' Court 18 Dec. 1381, Membr. 19
when Thomas Gisors made his fourth default, having fled to sanctuary at Westminster, and on 4 Nov. 1382 when the said Thomas appeared in court and prayed that John Colshull be summoned to show cause why the lands and tenements of the said Thomas should not be restored to him, as set forth in the court.

[The property, of an annual value of £44 12s 8d, consisted of cellars, apartments (*mansiones*), wharves, shops, chambers, a brewhouse and a *stuhous*[1] in Grantham Lane, an inn in

[1] Stewhouse or bath-house.

the Ryole and a quitrent in Grenewichlane. Among the tenants were William van Hulst, Lucebet Frowe, John Walworth, William Strangsell, John Peres, Geoffrey Waldern, John Hane, William, servant of Thomas Moreaux, knight, Thomas Feltwell, John Salkyner, Thomas Symbleby, Richard North, Peter Berynge, Roger Ronner, Richard Garlond, Laurence van Hulst, Giles van the Brok, Geoffrey Maynard, Nicholas Thame, Richard Herlegh, Thomas Sypsey, Gilbert Bonet and Reginald atte Pole.]

Membr. 20 Formal entry of affirmation on 25 Nov. 1381 by John Colshull of his plaints against Thomas Gisors.

Membr. 21 Duplicate list of rents as above, as certified by Richard Walden, the mayor's serjeant.

Membr. 22 Particulars of the exchanges belonging to the charge of Janekyn Colshull towards Thomas Gysors from 17 Sept. 1369 until his departure for Brittany.

[According to this list, John Colshull, while trading for his master, had received £5954 5s 5d, which had been exchanged for Flemish crowns at rates varying from 2s 1d to 2s 7d the crown and for nobles at par, i.e. 6s 8d the noble. The names of the money-changers were as follows: Philip Lose, Lombard, Gerwyn Smythous, *Esterlyng*, Bertyn Rest, Silvester Nicholas, Michel Scrose, Tideman Skof, *Esterlyng*, Herman Lange, Nicholas Mundel, William Anecroft, Reyner Domynyk, Christopher Fidelis, Anselyn Scrose, Matthew Vyleyn, Lambright Bosworth, Simond Reynes, Fraunceys Daffiano, Segher Onyn, John Welde, attorney of Richard Norton, Thomas Wight, John Priour, Conrod Bosworth, Henry Whitstrate, Nicholas Amenate, Robert Peper, Gregory de Feat, Dyne Blanchard, William Wyght, John Brisele, Peter Rundenell, Gerwyn Trappe, Everard Whitstrate, John Wale, John Shadeworth, Huberd Andrewe, Lawrence Frose, Robert Perham, Symkyn Syryngham, Thomas Stokton, Antoigne Raimonde, Sesar Hinkestebergh, Henry Whitstrate, John Hedyngham, Edmond Halsted and Dyne Sanouche.]

Membr. 23–5 Pleadings in the above action as entered on the file.

Writ of *certiorari* as to the above, 1 March 1385. Membr. 26

Copies of the pleadings, apparently as returned with the writ. Membr. 27–9

A further list of the exchanges as set out on membr. 22, with notes of additional sums paid to the said John Colshull on a voyage to Flanders in the 43rd year of Edw. III, and at Durdreght[1] in the same year, at St Edmundsbury for another voyage to Flanders the next year, on a third voyage to Flanders and on a voyage to Brittany in the company of Sir Robert Nevyll, together with divers tuns of wine received by him in the ships of Henry Wankynthorpe and Herman Tidemanson and in the cog of Clays van Saunten, of all of which Thomas Gisors prayed that an account be rendered. Membr. 30

[1] Dordrecht.

ROLL A 26

Further, of the time of John Norhampton, mayor

Membr. 1
31 May 1383

Thomas Depham of co. Norfolk was committed to prison for saying that the news of the war[1] which the lord bishop of Norwich began in Flanders and other previous news from those parts were false.

Membr. 1 *b*
6 Dec. 1382

John Filiol, fishmonger, who had been committed to prison for opprobrious words against the mayor, as recorded in Letter Book H, fo. 157[2], was set free at the instance of his friends, by mainprise of William Naffertone, John Norwych, John Southam and John Enemeth for his good behaviour towards the officers of the city under penalty of £100.

12 June 1383

William Sherere was mainprised for his good behaviour by John Charney and Richard Serle and sworn to set out immediately to join the bishop of Norwich in Flanders.

25 June 1383

John Hood, armourer, was mainprised to appear before the Mayor and Aldermen when summoned, and further sworn not to sell any *bassynet*[3] of Flanders as of London manufacture nor to place the mark of any London man upon any such basinet or any other armour of the same country.

The same day Thomas Hogecote was sworn to be obedient to the surveyors of the mistery of Armourers.

30 June 1383

Richard Leukenore, *corsour*[4], was mainprised to keep the peace and not to use shameful, indecent or evil words to

[1] This so-called "crusade" against the French, as the followers of the Pope of Avignon, ended in complete failure, and Flanders, the best market for English wool, fell under the control of France. For an account of this campaign and the siege of Ypres, see Major A. F. Becke, R.A. Jour. LIII, 3.

[2] Filiol, a fishmonger, had said that John Norhampton the mayor had maliciously deprived the freemen-fishmongers of their living. In the course of conversation he declared that he would willingly call the mayor a *falsus scurro vel harelot* and fight him at Horsedoune. As a matter of fact, the decision to admit non-citizen fishmongers to trade retail was made not by the mayor alone but by the Common Council.

[3] A light steel headpiece.

[4] Horse-dealer.

any stranger or freeman whereby the city of London might be defamed.

Quitclaim from Augustine Damasce, merchant of Lucca, executor of Master Laurence de Nigris, to Bartholomew de Bosano, merchant of Lucca. Membr. 2 *20 Nov. 1382*

Nigel Taillour of Holbourne produced before the Mayor and Aldermen a bill of complaint addressed to the King of Castile and Lyons[1], duke of Lancaster, to the effect that Roger Gailer of Holbourne, at the time of the rising, was a leader of the rioters and rode with a great rabble to the Savoy and St John's[2], for which he had purchased a charter of pardon, and nevertheless he and his wife said openly to their neighbours that they would willingly spend £100 of the money he had gained at the Savoy and St John's in order to be revenged on their poor and loyal neighbours. [*French*] *14 Nov. 1382*

Thereupon an inquest was summoned from the neighbourhood to make inquiry. The jurors, being sworn, said that the above-mentioned Roger Gailer was not one of the principal captains at the time of the rising, nor did he ride with the mob to the Savoy, as alleged, but he rode with other evildoers to the house of St John at Clerkenwell and there feloniously stole certain goods, *viz.* a book called "a missal" and a small side of bacon, of the value of 100s, and also certain bulls sealed with lead, all of which he afterwards restored to the officials of the house.

Memorandum that on 22 Dec. 1380 Guy de Port, Lombard, brought a bill demanding from William Gappe, William Ode and Custaunce Beamond, executors of Thomas Beamond, the sum of £11 for two cloths of silk *engreyn*[3] supplied by him to the said Thomas on 30 Oct. 1376. After the latter's death in Lombardy, the executors had declared that during *5 Dec. 1382*

[1] John of Gaunt, king of Castile and Leon, whose palace of the Savoy was sacked by the rioters during the Peasants' Revolt.

[2] The house of the Knights Hospitallers of St John of Jerusalem at Clerkenwell, which was also sacked.

[3] Dyed with the *kermes* or *scarlet grain*, a name applied to cochineal under the idea that the cochineal insect was a grain or berry. Afterwards the sense of "grain" altered, and to dye in grain signified to dye into the fibre, to dye fast.

his lifetime he had paid the amount to a merchant in Lombardy for the complainant and offered to bring proof of the fact, meanwhile depositing £11 in court. As they had failed to bring proof, he prayed that the money be delivered to him.

Though the defendants, on being summoned, had made four defaults, the money still remained in court[1]. Accordingly on 5 Dec. 1382 it was delivered to the plaintiff under security to answer therefor if the defendants should submit themselves to justice within a year and a day.

13 Dec. 1382 Nicholas Darel, hostiller, was summoned to answer Tidemann Wauschede for a debt of £22 10s, the balance due on the purchase of two hogsheads of steel in 1377, the price being £28 10s, of which the defendant had paid £6 on account at the time of sale.

The defendant pleaded that the only debt he owed was one of £22 10s due on a bond, and he was willing to make his law that he owed no other debt[2], and as the plaintiff had not produced any bond for the £22 10s, he prayed judgment as to whether any action lay against him. The plaintiff then acknowledged that there was no other debt than the £22 10s, but as the bond was lost he could not produce it. If the defendant would pay this debt, he would give him a general acquittance or enter into any security the court might require that he would not sue the defendant on the bond, if he found it. He prayed that the defendant answer further. The latter said he did not wish to make any further answer. Accordingly, in default of an answer, it was considered that the said Tidemann recover the said £22 10s, that the defendant be committed to prison and that the plaintiff give him an acquittance on his leaving prison or paying the debt. Afterwards on 13 May 1384 the plaintiff came into court and asked that the defendant be released from prison since they had come to an agreement.

Membr. 2 *b*
15 Dec. 1382 Hugh de Ware, fishmonger, was attached to answer Robert

[1] I.e. the money paid into court was treated as a foreign attachment and the court was in the position of a garnishee. See above, p. 10, n. 2.

[2] A "law" was permissible in an action of debt where there was no writing or tally. See *Munim. Gild. Lond.* (R.S.), I, p. 294.

Aleyn, knight, in a plea of trespass, wherein the latter complained that at Michaelmas 1361 he leased to a certain John Blake, cornmonger, a messuage, shop, cellar and ten solars in Thames Street by Billingsgate for 10 years at 17 marks annual rent and afterwards assigned this rent to Ralph de Mordon, who in turn assigned it to the above Hugh, which assignment the plaintiff ratified, further granting to him to hold the premises for two further years after the expiration of the lease, and nevertheless the defendant forcibly retained the premises for another year still, to the plaintiff's damage 20 marks.

The defendant pleaded that a certain John Bethewode, *tymbermonger* and citizen, had sued the plaintiff for a debt of £36 before the justices of the Bench at Westminster in Michaelmas term 1378, as the result of which the plaintiff had been put in exigent and outlawed, and that therefore the present action, being a personal action and originating from a time long before the outlawry, was extinguished.

To this the plaintiff replied that the king by a charter, which he produced, had pardoned him the outlawry, that he had made suit by *scire facias* against the aforesaid party according to the form of the statute[1] upon which his pardon was allowed to him, and that inasmuch as the defendant did not deny his allegations he prayed judgment and damages.

Process being continued, the parties appeared on 12 Feb. 1383, when it was considered that the plaintiff take nothing by his bill, but be in mercy, and that the defendant go quit thereof.

Afterwards on 25 Feb. the king by a writ of *certiorari* ordered that the tenor of the record and process be returned to Chancery, which was done.

Writ of protection in favour of John Gemel, esquire, then about to cross the sea in the company of Betrucat de Lebret in the king's service. *13 Dec. 1382*

[1] See Stat. 5 Edw. III, cc. 12, 13. It was a principle of law that by outlawry a man was disabled to sue, of which all might take advantage in pleading, until the outlawry was reversed. Apparently the court gave judgment on the ground that the action was extinguished by the outlawry.

Membr. 3
29 Jan. 1383

Memorandum that the king sent to the mayor a letter sealed with his signet charging him to arrest Ogolyne Gerard, Lombard[1], and to deliver him to Sir Thomas Morrieux, constable of the Tower, to await the king's pleasure. The prisoner's goods and chattels, with all his papers and letters found in his lodging, were to be delivered under the mayor's seal to the king's *continuel conseil* in London. Given under the signet at the manor of Sheen, 29 Jan. 1383. [*French*]

After the above orders had been carried out the king sent a writ to the effect that since Hugh (*sic*) Gerard was prepared to answer any charge, and Peter Marke, Nicholas Luke, Galadine de Reest, Angel Cristofre, Bernard George and Thomas Lyppe had entered into security in Chancery to produce him when required and to account for his goods under a penalty of 1000 marks above their value, the king ordered that the said Hugh and his goods be delivered from arrest and prison. Dated at Westminster 13 Feb. 1383.

26 Feb. 1383

Writ of protection in favour of John Cristian of Salisbury, then about to cross to foreign parts in the company of Henry, bishop of Norwich.

19 March 1383

William Spaldyng, tailor, was brought before the Mayor and Aldermen in the Chamber of the Guildhall for speaking evil and shameful words against Robert Croule, tawyer, whence discord might have arisen between the two misteries of Tailors and Tawyers. He put himself on the mercy of the Mayor and Aldermen and was sentenced to prison for forty days. Afterwards on the same day, at the request of the aldermen and of the good men of the mistery of Tawyers, he was set free, being bound over to keep the peace under penalty of 100 marks payable to the chamberlain if he were again convicted.

Membr. 3 *b*
2 March 1383

Writ of *corpus cum causa* to the mayor ordering him to send Peter Gracyan, Lombard, then a prisoner in Newgate, before the council at Westminster on the Wednesday following with the cause of his taking and detaining.

[1] He was charged, as agent of Peter de Matmano, merchant of Bologna, with having concealed and not paid the custom and subsidy on precious stones and other goods brought to England and exposed for sale. See *Cal. Close Rolls*, 1381–5, pp. 288, 419.

Return that on 19 Aug. 1382 the said Peter, in a plea of account between himself and Luke Bragadyn, merchant of Venice, was adjudged to prison until he had made satisfaction for a debt of £383 8s and other goods. Also on 15 Dec. following the said Peter had undertaken to pay, on behalf of the said Luke, the sum of £1250 to Nicholas Brembre, knight, in case the said Luke, who was then in prison, failed to pay that amount. Since the said Peter had failed to make either of these payments, he was detained in prison, in accordance with the custom of the city and the law merchant. While obeying the king's command, the mayor prays that the prisoner may be returned to custody according to custom.

William Thornhill, armourer, was committed to prison for selling wine in Fleet Street at 8d the gallon, instead of 6d, as laid down in the statute[1]. Two days later he was bound over to obey the statute and to indemnify the mayor and other officials of the city against the king and the city. *25 April 1383*

The same day William atte Sele, baker of tourte-bread[2], was bound over to make his bread of the correct weight, under penalty of £40.

Letter of attorney from Jerome Arigi of Boloigne le Crasse (Bologna) to Saint de Bartilmeu de Saint[3] of Bologna to receive and sue for debts due to him and to transact business on his behalf. Membr. 4 *9 June 1383*

Similar letter from Thomasin Lippy, merchant of Bologna.

An inquest of office before John Norhampton, mayor, and William Cheyne, recorder, to inquire whether a messuage in the parish of St Martin Ludgate, late belonging to Thomas atte Crouche, was entailed so as to descend to Roger, son *7 May 1383*

[1] Stat. 5 Ric. II, c. 4. Proclamation was made on the previous day, 24 April 1383, in accordance with the statute. *Cal. of Letter Book H*, p. 214.

[2] A coarse brown bread, the price and weight of which was regulated from time to time. At the Assize of Bread of 7 Dec. 1369 the penny tourte-loaf was fixed at the weight of 56s 8d. Sele had already been twice condemned to be dragged through the city on a hurdle with his short-weight loaf hanging from his neck. City's *Liber de Assisa Panis*, fos. 119, 123, 125 *b*.

[3] See below, p. 82, n. 2.

of William, son of the said Thomas, or could be alienated by the said William—by oath of twelve jurors and two informers, William Norton and John Willughby. A verdict was given that Thomas atte Crouche had been seised of the messuage in his demesne as of fee and right and had granted it by charter to Thomas Lemynstre, parson of the aforesaid church, and Henry Aldryngton, their heirs and assigns, which Thomas and Henry had thereupon reconveyed it by feoffment to Thomas atte Crouche and Agatha his wife for the term of their lives with remainder to William, his heirs and assigns, and that on the death of the said Agatha, William had sold the reversion (*sic*) to a certain Richard Pulle, to whom Thomas atte Crouche had attorned, and who now, after the deaths of Thomas and William, occupied and held the messuage in his own right as he was well entitled to do; and further, that the said messuage was not entailed.

17 June 1383 Grant from William Bartelot, son and one of the heirs of Thomas Bartelot, to Thomas Elys of Sandwich in fee simple of lands *etc.* in Kent and the Isle of Thanet, and letter of attorney to Thomas Rollyng, chaplain, of Sandwich, to deliver seisin.

Membr. 5
12 May 1383 Memorandum that Robert Kydenot had recently sued Richard Horewode, mercer, for a debt of £4 due in part payment of a larger sum owed to himself and a certain Robert Colyn, and that in the course of the proceedings a certain Henry Permay came and said that the above claim was in respect of a quantity of linen cloth sold, and since Robert Colyn was indebted to himself in a far larger sum he prayed that the money paid by Richard Horewode should be retained and paid over to himself. As the money had been lying for a long time in the Sheriffs' Court without any discussion or judgment, the said Robert Kydenot prayed the mayor to summon the action into the Chamber of the Guildhall and there deal with it according to the law merchant.

Accordingly the mayor gave the parties a day on 12 May 1383, when Richard Horewode gave evidence on oath as to purchasing the linen, but said he did not know whether it belonged to Robert Kydenot or Robert Colyn. Thereupon

Robert Kydenot asked for and obtained fifteen days adjournment in order that Robert Colyn, who was in Calais, might be examined in the presence of the mayor of the Staple of Calais or his lieutenant and constables. After that interval he produced in court a certificate [*French*] dated 14 April 1383 from the lieutenant and constables of Calais, to the effect that Robert Colyn had appeared before them and had informed them that the linen belonged to himself alone and that he had assigned the money due for it to Robert Kydenot because he was indebted to him in a larger sum of money, and that he owed nothing to Henry Permay.

This document having been read by the court, it was considered that the £4 should be delivered to Robert Kydenot under security that, if the said Henry Permay or Robert Colyn should appear within a year and a day and prove reasonably that it belonged to them or either of them, the said Robert should repay it.

In an action by Joan, wife and attorney of John Olney, woolmonger, against Richard Scotard for a debt of £17, the latter's attorney, John Merssh, produced a writ of protection dated 13 July in favour of the above Richard, who was then about to cross the sea with Thomas Fychet to join the company of Henry, bishop of Norwich. By which writ the said action remains without a day. *24 July 1383*

Letter of attorney from Cosmas de Aurea, merchant of Genoa, to John de Carlo, merchant of Genoa, to receive all sums due to him, both from his debtors and by way of exchange, and to transmit them to Genoa, and further to charge him with the payment of sums received on exchange, but this power of attorney was not to extend to binding the said Cosmas by obligations or making further payments than as expressed above. Membr. 5 *b* *2 July 1383*

William Brikles, pepperer, executor of the will of Sabina Yerdele[1], brought a bill of complaint before the Mayor and Aldermen showing that the said Sabina six years before her Membr. 6 *24 July 1383*

[1] Widow of Henry de Yerdelee, a wealthy fellmonger. R. R. Sharpe, *Cal. of Wills enrolled in the Court of Husting*, II, p. 131; *Cal. of Letter Book H*, pp. 179, 319.

death had set apart and specified in her will a sum of £100 for the support of a chaplain to celebrate divine service in the church of All Hallows the Great for her wellbeing in life and for her soul after death, the said chaplain to receive an annual salary of 10 marks. She had appointed Walter Lyndon as chaplain and had placed the money in the hands of Robert Corn on account of the trust and affection she felt for him. The said Robert had paid the chaplain £40 for the six years before her death and 33s 4d for the first quarter of the year afterwards. But though the chaplain had celebrated for three further years, the said Robert would neither pay him the £20 thus due nor appoint another chaplain.

The said Robert appeared on summons on 27 July and said that Sabina at the time of her death had acquitted him of all that remained of the £100, i.e. £60, and that he had paid 33s 4d more to the chaplain of his own free will, and that therefore he need not answer further, nor pay more to the chaplain, nor appoint another one. The plaintiff answered that so far as his own knowledge went Sabina had never acquitted him. Thereupon the defendant offered to pay the £20 in arrears of the chaplain's salary, if the plaintiff together with two other good men would swear that he had no knowledge that Sabina had remitted the £60[1]. The plaintiff accepted this offer and produced four men, *viz.* Roger Carneford, Henry Baret, John Romeseye and William Campyon, who, after he had taken the oath, swore that his oath, so far as they knew, was a true one.

Accordingly it was considered that the defendant pay the £20 in arrears to the chaplain, and as the latter had received no notice about seeking other work, that the defendant pay him 10 marks for the coming year. And since the will produced in court showed that the testator wished the defendant to be exonerated from finding a chaplain if he fell into poverty through misfortune or any other cause, the question of continuing the chaplain's services was respited until the court should have information as to the defendant's means. The defendant then paid £20 arrears of salary and afterwards

[1] This was a challenge, not a compulsory wager of law. See above, p. 15, n. 1.

on 30 Nov. the instalment of the present year's salary due at Michaelmas.

Richard Fodringay and John Godard, esquires, exhibited to the Mayor and Aldermen an indenture and an obligation. They prayed that, although no payment had been made to them at the date specified in these documents, the Mayor and Aldermen would bear witness, if necessary, that they were willing to fulfil their own undertakings in the matter: *21 Aug. 1383*

Covenant reciting that John Northebury, Richard Foudringay and John Godard had bought a barge of Bristol, with all its goods and gear, which had belonged to John Poculchurch, Thomas Martyn, Geoffrey Martin, William Stephens, John Bradewey and Ralph Welles, burgesses of Bristol, and John Weneton, citizen of London, from Pascual Miglice, John de Lano and other Spaniards, John Pulmic and several other Bretons and Frenchmen, enemies of the king of England. They now agree to sell the barge again to John Poculchurch and his companions for £800 payable on 15 Aug. in the house of Robert Boxeford in Cheap. The said Poculchurch and his companions agree to purchase the barge; and if they fail to pay the above amount, a bond of £183 6s 8d shall remain of full force and effect and the barge shall remain with the said John, Richard and John to do with as they will. But if they shall pay the said sum of £800, the bond shall be of no effect and the barge shall come into their possession. For their part the said John, Richard and John promise to deliver the barge as soon as a message shall arrive at Brest that the money has been paid. Dated 2 June 1383. [*French*]

Obligation from John Pokelcherche and his companions to Janekyn Northbury, Richard Foudringey and John Godard to pay £366 13s 4d[1] at the above date and place by reason of a pure and loyal loan made to them by the said Janekyn, Richard and John, in deliverance of their bodies from the hands and prison of Pascoual Miglice, Johan de Lano and other Spaniards and Frenchmen their enemies. Dated 1 June 1383. [*French*]

[1] This document appears to be incomplete. To judge from the amounts, it seems to be the bond referred to in the covenant, being in a double penalty, defeasible on payment of £183 6s 8d, but the defeasance is omitted.

Membr. 6 *b*
24 Sept. 1383

Nicholas Stoke of co. Southampton, who had been detained in prison for a year on a charge of violent behaviour and for having threatened to burn divers houses, and who had nearly died there, was liberated with the consent of the sheriff, on taking an oath for his good behaviour.

Membr. 7
10 Nov. 1383

Writ of *habeas corpus* directed to the sheriffs and coroner[1] of London. Whereas of late the king had ordered them to send under their seals to Chancery the tenor of an appeal which Leticia, widow of John Cryel, knight, had made before them without writ against Richard Boydon, late servant of John Cornewaille, knight, for robbery and breach of the peace, which order they had obeyed, and whereas the king had caused the tenor of the appeal to come before him (*coram nobis*)[2] for the due execution of the appeal, and because it is expedient and necessary that the court should be informed as to that appeal with all its circumstances before proceeding to execution thereof, accordingly the sheriffs and coroner are ordered to send the appeal with all matters relating thereto under their seals before the king at Westminster on 16 Nov., and further the sheriffs are ordered to have the body of the said Richard, then detained in Newgate, before the king on the above day, and to warn the said Leticia to sue her appeal against him. Witness R. Tresilian at Westminster 10 Nov. 1383.

Membr. 7 *b*
25 Oct. 1383

James le Brauwere, attorney of James le Grave of Bruges, having sued Richard Aylesbury of London for the sum of £21 4s 6d *gros* of Flanders, being the balance due of a sum of £45 12s 5d *gros turnois* of Flanders of which £26 7s 5d sterling had been paid[3], obtained judgment. On 3 Dec. 1383 he prayed that execution of the judgment cease, as he had come to an agreement with the debtor.

[1] The coroner was a king's officer and combined with his coronership the offices of king's chamberlain of the city and king's butler. The system by which the sheriffs and coroner or chamberlain held inquests as to deaths by misadventure and received appeals was an ancient one, being certified to the justices at the *Iter* of 1244. See *Munim. Gild. Lond.* (R.S.), I, pp. 77, 81, 82; II, p. 296; R. R. Sharpe, *Cal. Coroner's Rolls*, p. 1.

[2] Into the court of King's Bench.

[3] Giving a value of a fraction over £1 0s 9d sterling for the Flemish £.

Philip Fretheby brought a bill of complaint against Andrew Sewardby, tailor, as follows: Whereas the said Andrew had in his charge the sum of £12 belonging to the plaintiff and conceived a plot to compass the death of the plaintiff in order to possess that money, he requested him on 8 March to take with him the defendant's servant, Walter, and show him the way to Bridlington in the county of York and promised him 6s 8d for so doing, of which he paid him 3s 4d, and on the same day he procured and hired the said Walter to kill the plaintiff on the way. When the plaintiff and the servant reached a valley five leagues from Lincoln, the said servant drew his baselard and struck the plaintiff suddenly and then beat and illtreated him and left him for dead, to the damage of the plaintiff £100; wherefore he prayed redress and asked the Mayor and Aldermen to note the fact that the defendant told friends of the plaintiff that he had paid the money to the plaintiff, who had been robbed and killed by thieves on the way. [*French*] *2 Oct. 1383*

John Botkisham, the serjeant of the Chamber, was ordered to summon the parties for 6 Oct. On that day the defendant produced a quitclaim of all actions, real and personal, made to him by Simon Swan and the plaintiff, which was dated 20 Aug., subsequent to the trespass alleged in the bill. The plaintiff acknowledged the quitclaim. Therefore it was considered that he take nothing by his bill, but be in mercy, and that the said Andrew go thereof without a day. And because the plaintiff prosecuted contrary to his own deed, it was considered that he be committed to prison and pay a fine at the mayor's discretion. Afterwards on 1 Feb. 1384 he was released on payment of a fine of 40d.

Robert Aleyn, knight, was summoned on a bill exhibited to the Mayor and Aldermen to answer William, prior of the hospital of the Blessed Mary without Bishopsgate, in a plea of debt. Gilbert Meldebourne, the plaintiff's attorney, declared the amount as £19, i.e. £15[1] for bread, beer, meat, Membr. 8 *21 July 1383*

[1] The declaration appears to have been copied incorrectly. Omitting the loans and the sum of 18s, mentioned though not included in the total, the claim for board and lodging amounted to £15 6s 8d, for which judgment was obtained.

fish and other victuals bought by Matilda, the defendant's wife, for herself and her two servants when she was in the hospital, to wit, 18s thereof for two loaves, two gallons of beer and two dishes of cookery every day from 11 July to 22 Aug. 1378, in the time of John Lyndeseye then prior; 66s 8d which she borrowed from the prior through Robert Salisbury, canon of the hospital, on 20 July 1376; £8 6s 8d for other victuals supplied to her for 50 weeks from 22 Aug. 1378 at 40d a week in the time of Robert Salisbury, who was sub-prior during the vacancy; £7 for other victuals during the time of the present prior from 5 Aug. 1379 for 42 weeks at 40d a week; and 6s 8d borrowed from the prior on 15 June 1381 through Thomas Tomme, chaplain; all of which sums the defendant refused to pay, to the plaintiff's damage £20.

The defendant denied the debt, excepting the loan of £3 6s 8d, and put himself on the country. As regards the loan he said that his wife gave as security a locked and sealed forcer containing goods of the same value, which forcer still remained in the prior's hands. Thereupon the prior's attorney was ordered to bring the forcer to court on 28 July.

Process was continued till 8 Oct., when the attorney brought into court one large and six small buttons, made of silver pennies, together with the forcer. In the absence of the said Matilda, who had the key, the forcer was opened and found to contain nothing of any value. It was sealed again with the seal of John Charneye, coroner of London, and returned to the prior. The defendant's attorney then produced a writ of protection in favour of the defendant, running from 29 Aug. for one year, and prayed that the action might be adjourned without a day. The court allowed the protection as regards the two debts for money borrowed. But, since by the custom of the city a protection was not valid in a plea concerning victuals, a jury was chosen, tried and sworn. They found for the plaintiff as regards the claim for £15 6s 8d and taxed the damages at 10 marks. Therefore it was considered that the plaintiff recover these sums.

Afterwards on 29 Oct. the prior came into court before Nicholas Brembre, Mayor, and the Aldermen, with a writ of the king annulling the protection, and prayed that the defendant might be summoned to answer for the loans. The latter made four defaults, whereupon it was considered that the said £3 13s 4d should be arrested and remain in the prior's hands and be allowed to him as a deduction from a larger sum of money which Robert Aleyn had recovered against him in an Assize of Freshforce heard before the sheriffs, unless the defendant appeared within a year and a day.

ROLL A 27

[*Nicholas Brembre, knight, mayor*]

Membr. 1
18 May 1384

William Mayhew, grocer, was charged before the Mayor and Aldermen with having said that their judgments were unjust, that the city was badly governed and that John Costantyn, cordwainer[1], who was recently beheaded in Cheap for the insurrection of 11 Feb., made by him and his accomplices to the terror of the city and the suburbs, was falsely and iniquitously condemned to death by them. The said William acknowledged having spoken these words and put himself on the mercy of the court. He was committed to prison until the Mayor and Aldermen should be advised as to rendering judgment upon him.

Afterwards on 26 May he was brought into court. And because the aforesaid words had been spoken falsely and maliciously and expressly redounded to the shame and dishonour of the mayor and other governors of the city, and in order that others might be prevented from speaking like words, it was considered and adjudged, as had previously been done in like cases according to the custom of the city on many other occasions, that the said William should have a year's imprisonment from 18 May and then pay a fine for his contempt according to the discretion of the Mayor and Aldermen for the time being, unless further indulgence should be granted to him in the meantime. Afterwards on the same day, by the mayor's favour and at the request of several aldermen and other good men, he was mainprised by Adam de St Ives and Henry Perot for his good behaviour towards the king and his people and all the officers of the city, and not to speak such words again under penalty of £40, and he was sworn to fulfil the above undertakings and to save his mainpernors harmless. Thereupon he was allowed

[1] See *Cal. Pat. Rolls*, 1381–5, p. 391; *Cal. of Letter Book H*, p. 231 for a ratification, on the petition of the mayor, sheriffs and aldermen, of judicial proceedings in the Guildhall resulting in the execution of John Costantyn for having attempted to raise a riot. The mayor, sheriffs and aldermen acted in their capacity as justices of the peace, in accordance with the city's jurisdiction in this respect. See Introduction to *Cal. of Plea and Mem. Rolls*, 1323–64.

to make fine with half a mark to the chamberlain and was released.

Matilda, widow of Hugh Holbech and executrix of his will, was summoned to answer William Croydon in a plea of detinue of goods and chattels worth £10 5s 10d, *viz.* 2 vats of lead and one *ledtrogh*, £6; one *mokestunne*[1], 13s 4d; one *yeltunne*[2], 10s; 12 *kemelyns*[3], 13s 4d; 6 barrels, 4s; one *altunne*, 2s; 2 *algistes*[4], 3s 4d; one *clensyngtunne*, 6s 8d; 2 *watertunes*, 3s 4d; one *worttyne*[5] and one *watertyne*, 2s 8d; one bucket with an iron chain and cord, 4s; one *clensyngsyve*, 3s; one *clensyngtonge*[6], 4d; one *vanne*[7], 12d; one half-bushel and one peck measure, 8d; one pottle and one quart measure, 6d; 6 racks for a stable, 10s; two *dressyngbordes*[8] and one *stok*[9], 6s 8d; and three pairs of handmills, 20s; all of which the plaintiff declared that he had placed in the custody of the above Hugh on 23 Aug. 1367 in the parish of St Athelburga[10] within Bishopsgate. On the death of Hugh, they came into the possession of the defendant, who refused to restore them, to the plaintiff's damage £20. *23 May 1384*

The defendant appeared and denied having received the goods as declared by the plaintiff and offered to defend herself by her law as a freewoman of the city, to which the plaintiff assented. A day was given her on 26 May to make her law with six other women according to the custom of the city, and she was mainprised meanwhile by John Clee and Stephen Spilleman. On the day aforesaid the parties appeared and the defendant made her law with six other women that she had not received the said goods. Therefore it was considered that the said William take nothing by his bill, but be in mercy for a false claim, and that the said Matilda go thereof quit.

1 Possibly a mash-tun.
2 Ale-tun.
3 *sc. kimnel*, a tub.
4 Ale-joist, a barrel-stand.
5 A *tine* or tub for wort, the infusion of malt before fermentation.
6 Cleansing-tongs.
7 *Sc.* fan, a winnowing-basket for separating chaff from grain.
8 A table for dressing meat.
9 A wooden block for chopping meat or fish.
10 St Ethelburga.

Membr. 1 *b* Mainprises of divers persons for keeping the peace: 3 Nov. 1383, Richard Leukenore, *corsour*, by Henry King, *corsour*, and John Staunton; Robert Brampton, *corsour*, by Richard Forster and John Staunton; Richard Waltham by Robert Austyn and Thomas Cotone; 26 Jan. 1384, Simon Frensshe, baker, by Edmund Horton, Walter Parker and Thomas Fraunkeleyn; John Hatfeld, *squyer*, by Gilbert Meldebourne, John Kelsey and John Dyke towards John Creke, *corsour*; 3 Feb. 1384, John Abraham, chaplain, by John Abraham and Ralph Abraham; 9 May 1384, Robert Goldryng, gardener, and John Baroun, miller, by Thomas Horsman, Roger Parys, Robert Torkeseye and John Seman, dyer, to answer David Man, cordwainer, and Here Nichol, chaplain, and their companions for a trespass and to keep the peace; 10 May 1384, William Mileward by John Walworth, vintner, and Richard Merlawe, ironmonger, on the same conditions; 25 May 1384, John Hillyng, paviour, by John Holbech, Nicholas Maynard, John Seman, John Norfolke, Nicholas Yvyngho, Thomas Hert, John Coventre and Roger Carpenter; 13 May 1384, Richard Leukenore, *corsour*, by Henry King and John Salisbury.

25 March 1384, John Neweman of co. Kent by Peter Persholt and William Neweman, weaver, towards John Scot, *ripiere*[1].

20 April 1385, Robert Gandrey, esquire, by Adam Kirkham and Walter Pek, tailors, William Whetele, cordwainer, and William Osebarn, goldsmith, towards John Walworth, vintner; 5 May 1385, Walter Cole, *bedemaker*, by Thomas Clement, brewer, William Fychet, goldsmith, William Swaynlond, pewterer, and Robert Person, taverner, towards ThomasRolf, *lumynour*[2]; 9 May, Thomas Prentyz of Sudbury by Robert Haule, draper, John Rouhed and John Portrose of Sudbury and Edmund Heryng of Bury towards John Clenaunt of London; David Morys, *dauber*, by John Pally and John Goudman, weavers, to obey the officers of the city.

[1] Cf. *Cal. of Letter Book H*, p. 234. A name given to foreigners bringing fish to the city, who were now occupying the Stocks Market. Letter Book H, fo. 257 *b*, *les Ripieres qi amesnent pessoun del mier a la cite a vendre*. Supposed to be derived from *ripa*, a bank, shore.

[2] Illuminator.

Memorandum that at a congregation of the mayor, aldermen, and commoners summoned from the wards of the city as a Common Council on 11 June 1384 there were present Sir Nicholas Brembre, mayor, Sir William Walworth, John Hadle, Thomas Cornwaleys, John Hende, John Sely, Adam Bamme, Hugh Fastolf, John Chircheman, John Organ, Richard Preston, William Staundon, Adam de Seint Ive, Geoffrey Cremelford, William More, Thomas Welford, John Eston, William Ancroft and Roger Elys, aldermen, and the following commoners from the wards: Membr. 2 *11 June 1384*

Tour, William Tonge, Hugh Boys, Thomas Evesham.

Billyngesgate, John Beaufrount, John Wade, Thomas Girdlere.

Algate, Richard Morell.

Lymstret, John Clapshethe.

Langebourne, Thomas Bonaunter, John Dyke, William FitzHugh, John Studley.

Bisshopesgate, Henry Herbury, Peter Torold, John Sibyle, Adam Ratteseye.

Cornhull, Walter Pykenham, Thomas Irlond.

Bridge, Walter Sibyle, Robert Little, John Pountfreyt.

Douegate, William Wotton, Ralph Lubenham, John Wiltshyre.

Vinetrie, John Colshull, Thomas Medlane, John Tilneye, William Sharpyng.

Walbroke, Reginald Aleyn, John Basse, William Sudbury.

Cordwanerstret, William Pountfreyt, Geoffrey Walderne.

Bradstret, William Wodehous, Adam Karlill.

Colmanstret, William Kyng, Robert Havelok.

Chepe, John Fraunkeleyn, Geoffrey Grigge, Thomas Mak William.

Farndon, Elis Weston, Roger Excestre, Simon atte Nax.

Crepulgate, John Forster, Gilbert Prynce, John Higyn.

Aldrichesgate, Thomas Exton, John Dancastre, John Bathe, John Bokkyng.

Bredstret, Thomas Rolf, John Ragenel, John Scorfeyn.

Quenehithe, John Trigge.

Chastel Baynard, John Redyng, John Vautort, John Asshurst.

Candelwykstret, James Snow, William Ivory.

Portsokne, William Burford.

Whereas divers rumours, covins, congregations and affrays had taken place in the city since the time when Sir Nicholas Brembre was chosen to the office of the mayoralty, for which divers reasons had been given, some saying that the fault lay in one person, and others in another, and in order that there might be full knowledge and testimony of the truth, it was demanded of each of the abovenamed persons, by the faith which he owed to God and the king and by the oath which he had taken to the city, to declare on his conscience by whom and in default of whom these disturbances had been made and who was the cause of them, sparing none, and the abovenamed persons severally declared on their faith and oath that the said disturbances had taken place by default of John Norhampton, late mayor of the city, and had been made by him ever since he had been discharged from his office and Sir Nicholas Brembre had been chosen to that office, and that the said John Norhampton was the cause of all the disturbances. [*French*]

22 March 1385 Memorandum that at a congregation of the mayor, aldermen and several good men chosen from the wisest and most discreet men of the wards summoned and assembled in the Chamber of the Guildhall on 22 March 1385 there were present Sir Nicholas Brembre, mayor, William Cheyne, recorder, John Hadle, John Boseham, Robert Warbulton, Henry Vannere, John Hende, Adam de Seint Ive, William More, Nicholas Exston, John Fressh, John Rote, Roger Elys, John Fraunceis, Thomas Welford, William Staundon and Simon Wynchecombe, aldermen, and the following persons from the wards:

Billyngesgate, John Wade, Thomas Girdelere, John Beaufront.

Douegate, William Wotton.

Langebourne, Thomas Bonaunter, John Dyke, William FitzHugh, John Studeley.

Lymstret, Richard Clapschethe and Richard Gregori.

Bredestret, Thomas Rolf, John Scorfeyn.

Farndon, Thomas Panton, John Hille, John Dorsete, William Pershore.

Crepulgate, John Furneux, John Loveye, Robert Asshcombe, John Forster, Gilbert Prynce, John Hugyn.

Bradstret, William Wodehous, Adam Karlill, Richard Willesdon, Beneit Cornewaille.

Aldrichesgate, Thomas Reynham, John Bockyng.

Castel Baynard, John Vatoft, John Asshurst, William Shrympelmerssh.

Cornhill, Walter Pykenham, Richard Manhale.

Walbrok, William Olyver, Reginald Aleyn, William Sudbury.

Vinetrie, John Colshill, Thomas Medelane, John Tilneye, William Sharpyng.

Bisshopesgate, Henry Herburi, Peter Torold.

Candilwykstret, William Horston, William Giles, Roger Mordon, William Spaldyng.

Queenhithe, Robert Parys, John Trig.

Tour, William Tonge, Hugh Sprot, Hugh Boys, Thomas Evesham.

Cordewanerstret, Robert Lyndeseye, William Pountfreit, Geoffrey Walderne, Robert Dane, Richard Hatfeld, John Hoo.

Chepe, Geoffrey Crymelford, Thomas Austyn, Thomas Vynent, John Fraunkeleyn, Geoffrey Grigge, Thomas Mak William.

Portsokne, William Wodeward.

Colemanstret, John Eston.

Bridge, John Pountfreit, Robert Lytle, John Mockyng, Richard Blomville.

Whereas there had long been dissension and division in the city between divers men of the same, whereby great evil and peril might arise, to the destruction and loss both of the city and of the whole realm, unless remedy were found by the aid of God, and the said mayor and aldermen and other wise men desiring peace, tranquillity, accord, unity and quiet among the people, and wishing to be informed and certified, as far as possible, as to the cause and root of the said dissension and division and how they might be ousted, and unity and accord be made and kept among the people, demand was made of every person, alderman and commoner, by the faith which he owed to God and our lord the king and the oath which he had made to the city, to declare and say openly on his conscience and as he would answer before God, sparing none, what was the cause and root of such dissension and division, whereupon all said severally that it was the life of John Norhampton, for so long as he remained alive all those that were of his covin hoped that he would return to the city and by this hope they comforted others, whereby dissension arose and would always continue so long as he lived. And further, each of them said on his conscience that the thing which would most easily engender unity and accord, and would oust all dissensions and divisions and, in their opinion, would bring the matter to a good end, would be to require and pray our said lord the king in his high and royal majesty that execution of the judgment of law given on the said John Norhampton in the Tower of London should be done, for so long as he lived the said people of his covin and lovers of his opinions would hope for his return to the city as aforesaid, which would be to the utter confusion and destruction of the city, which God forbid. And upon this, with one accord, it was agreed that it would be well for the mayor to take with him certain aldermen and commoners, such as seemed to him good, and to approach our lord the king, petitioning him in the manner and form abovesaid.

And also because the mayor and commoners were advised that for the safeguarding of the city and suburbs against any peril that might arise, it would be necessary that a good ditch and a pale above it should be made around all the suburbs of the city for its defence in case need should arise, which God forbid, and because it would take too long to settle the question as to how and in what manner it should be done, since many matters and arguments would be raised among so many men and peradventure no conclusion would be made, it was agreed by everyone that the mayor and aldermen on the morrow should choose from among themselves twelve aldermen and twelve commoners of the most sufficient and discreet men in the city to ordain and treat by what means and how the said matter should be brought into effect, and in what manner the costs which would be needed might be levied, and to do all other things which appertained to the said matter. And all the aldermen and commoners agreed to hold as firm and established whatever the said twenty-four thus elected should do in the matter, and on the morrow the said mayor and aldermen chose the persons underwritten to carry out and perform the said matter, to wit, Sir William Walworth, John Hadle, John Boseham, John Orgon, John Shadworth, Nicholas Exton, Henry Vannere, William Staundon, William More, Robert Warbulton, Thomas Welford and John Fraunceys, aldermen, William Tonge, Adam Karlill, Thomas Rolf, Thomas Girdelere, Henry Herbury, Richard Hatfeld, Thomas Exton, John Loveye, Geoffrey Walderne, John Kirketon, Thomas MakWilliam and Adam Bamme, commoners. [*French*]

In the presence of Nicholas Brembre, knight, mayor, in the mayor's house in the parish of St Michael Paternosterchirche, John Norhampton, citizen and draper, was mainprised by John More and Simon Wynchecombe, sheriffs, and John Toures, William Eriote, Thomas Lyncolln, Richard Brendewode and William Rule, drapers, to bear himself peaceably towards the king and his people and the officers of the city, to preserve the king's peace within the liberty of the city and without, to be obedient to the officers of the city for the time being and to be, and not to make or cause to be made any covin, conventicle, league or congregation openly or secretly by himself or by means of others, or any other thing by his means or speech, whereby rumour, disturbance, commotion or affray might in any way arise within the liberty of the city to the disturbance of the peace, and if he should discover any such covin, to reveal the same to the mayor for the time being and to prevent it, and to be ready, whenever warned, to appear before the said Mayor and Aldermen, and this under penalty of £5000, which the said John Norhampton and his mainpernors agreed, severally and together, to pay to the king and his heirs immediately the said John Norhampton should do anything contrary to any of the above articles or should offend or default in any of them. Membr. 3 *22 Jan. 1384*

22 Feb. 1384 William Norton, saddler, was mainprised by Roger Excestre, Walter Yonge, Thomas Kirewode and Thomas Soys, saddlers, and Gilbert Meldebourne, as above, under penalty of £100.

23 Feb. 1384 William Bowyere, skinner, in the presence of the Mayor, Recorder and Aldermen in the Chamber of the Guildhall, was mainprised by Robert Haringeie, mercer, Robert Lyndesey and John Maudeleyn, as above, under penalty of £100. He was also sworn to keep the above articles and to save his mainpernors harmless.

John Gest, skinner, was mainprised by John Bredestret, armourer, Stephen Frith, armourer, John Brundyssh, tailor, and Robert Vygerous, draper, and sworn as above, under penalty of £100.

William Valdrean, saddler, was mainprised by Richard Brok, Roger Excestre, Walter Yonge and Thomas Soys, saddlers, as above, under penalty of £100.

Robert Riseby, draper, was mainprised by John Hende, draper, Geoffrey Walderne, draper, Thomas Welford, fishmonger, Robert Somersete, draper, Richard Knouslee, draper, John Bottesham, goldsmith, Andrew Vyne, draper, and Robert Hunden, draper, as above, under penalty of £300.

25 Feb. 1384 William Watesham, cutler, was mainprised by Robert Eye, Richard Ledyate, John Wodhall and Martin Godard, cutlers, as above, under penalty of £40.

8 March 1384 John Muntham, joiner, was mainprised by Henry Goudchep, John Squyer, John Curson, Robert Norton of the Earl of Warwick's retinue[1], William Shirebourne, cutler, William Stanes, cutler, John Bussh, tallowchandler, and Hugh Avenell, as above, under penalty of £200.

14 March 1384 John Bussh, goldsmith, was mainprised by Henry Bamme and John Coraunt, goldsmiths, as above, under penalty of £40.

Membr. 3 *b*
26 April 1384 Gilbert Malenay, saddler, was delivered under bail to his master, John de Excestre, to bring him up before the Mayor and Aldermen when required, and the same John main-

[1] *Commorantem cum comite Warr'.*

prised him to observe the articles in the mainprise of John Norhampton under penalty of £100.

John Bere, haberdasher, was similarly delivered under bail to John Maymond, mercer, William Denton, tailor, William Talbot, tailor, John Kent, tailor, Roger Stapulhurst, mercer, and Thomas Soys, saddler. He was also mainprised as above under penalty of £100 and imprisonment, and was further sworn to obey the said articles, to save his mainpernors harmless and to keep his tongue from speaking evil or scandal of any of the officers of the city for the time being and to be hereafter. *28 June 1384*

John Der, cordwainer, was similarly mainprised by John Long, senior, Robert Sutton, Walter Gyngyvere and William Hare, cordwainers, under penalty of £100, and sworn to obey the articles and save his mainpernors harmless. *30 June 1384*

John More, mercer, in the presence of Sir Nicholas Brembre, knight, Mayor, and the Aldermen was mainprised by John Boseham, Robert Warbulton, John Shadeworth and William Shiryngham, mercers, until 1 Nov. to keep the peace towards the king and his people and the officers of the city, to obey the latter, not to make or cause to be made any congregation *etc.*, either openly or secretly, whereby any disturbance of the peace might take place, to warn the mayor of any such congregation *etc.*, to do his best to allay any disturbance and to appear on summons before the Mayor and Aldermen, under penalty of £4000, of which each of his mainpernors should be liable for £1000, if he failed to observe any of the above conditions. *13 Aug. 1384*

Richard Yoman was mainprised by John Groos, baker, Andrew Sywardby, tailor, William Arundel, cordwainer, and William Placidas, currier, to fulfil all the conditions in the mainprise of John More, under penalty of £40. *10 Sept. 1384*

William atte Hulle, cordwainer, was delivered under bail to Clement Kirketon, tailor, William Cosyn, hostiller, Ralph Elleswyk, tailor, and Roger Lilye, tailor, body for body, to bring him up when required. He was further mainprised to *14 Sept. 1384* observe the conditions of the mainprise of John Norhampton, under penalty of £400.

John Picot, cordwainer, was delivered under bail to William Cosyn, hostiller, John atte Hull and Edmund Romeseye, cordwainers, and Nicholas Walton, saddler, under penalty of £400.

1 Oct. 1384 John Bacon, tailor, was mainprised by Thomas Sibsay, Thomas Bridlyngton, John Byfeld and John Grosmond, tailors, and Dunstan Harcherigge, draper, as above, under penalty of £100. He was also sworn not to speak scandalously of the mayor, aldermen, or other officers of the city or of their government, and further to save his mainpernors harmless.

Membr. 4
10 Oct. 1384 William Bradestret, saddler, was mainprised by John Pountfret, Roger Excestre, Walter Yonge and Richard Peterburgh.

Further concerning the names of those who were mainprised or delivered under bail for the rumour and affray made in the Guildhall on the day of the mayor's election in the eighth year of Richard the Second

2 March 1385 John Remes, cordwainer, who acknowledged that at the last parliament held at Westminster he had publicly said that there would never be any quiet or rest in the city until an end had been made of Nicholas Brembre, now mayor, was nevertheless by the mayor's favour delivered under bail to Nicholas Bosebury, John Fery, Robert York, William Robyn, Robert Sutton and Walter Gyngyvere, cordwainers, body for body, to fulfil in their entirety the points and conditions in the mainprise of William Bradestret, under penalty of £100, and he was sworn to the same.

6 March 1385 Michael Hakeneye was mainprised by John Swanton, Adam Bridbroke, John Welles, fellmonger, and John Hakeneye, as above, under penalty of £40, and was further sworn to the same.

8 March 1385 John Lyncolle, goldsmith, who acknowledged before the Mayor and Aldermen that he had often been disobedient and had borne himself improperly towards the mayor and other officers of the city and, together with other evildoers, had made divers prosecutions, as well in parliament and before the magnates as before many others, against the mayor in particular and other governors of the city, and had reprobated and retarded their government to the utmost of his power, in disturbance of the king's peace and against his oath, prayed that the favour of the Mayor and Aldermen be granted to him. By the favour of the mayor he was delivered under bail to Henry Bamme, John Botisham, William de Louthe, Thomas Polle and William Stamynden, goldsmiths, as above, under penalty of £200, and was sworn to the same.

Robert Fraunceys, goldsmith, who made the same confession as John Lyncolle, was delivered under bail to John Luton, William Stamelden, William de Louthe, Henry Rokhawe, Roger Ryot and Richard Weston, as above, under penalty of £200, and was sworn to the same. *20 March 1385*

John Remes, cordwainer, who on the suggestion of the masters of his mistery was committed to prison for rebellion against them and for having spoken indecent words against the government of the city and for other evildoing, was mainprised by John Longe, senior, Robert York and Thomas Pountfreyt, cordwainers, as above, under penalty of £200, and sworn to the same. *1 Aug. 1385*

Nicholas Pound, tailor, was delivered under bail to Thomas Barton, goldsmith, William Skendelby, brewer, Richard Tutford, horner, John Newby, smith, John Gace, tiler, John Flemyng, horner, and Richard Bene, tailor, as above, under penalty of £100, and sworn to the same. *17 Aug. 1385*

Thomas Knape, tailor, was delivered in bail to the same under penalty of £100.

William Frere, barber, who was taken and committed to prison for having lied falsely and maliciously, saying that John Norhampton had arrived in London and that he had seen him, which words might have resulted in an affray, was liberated by the mayor's favour without mainprise, since he could not find mainpernors. He was sworn as above. *27 Sept. 1385*

11 Oct. 1385 Richard Molle, grocer, was mainprised by John Hokkele, grocer, John Curson, John Bussh, Nicholas Wyght, Alexander Pulter and Robert Hubert, *plomer*, for his good behaviour, as above, under penalty of £100, and sworn to the same.

30 March 1386 William Costantyn—concerning whom David, keeper of the gaol of Newgate, gave evidence that he was so ill that his life was despaired of—was delivered under bail to John Doget, currier, Walter Trote, cordwainer, William Spaldyng, tailor, and John Botkisham, serjeant, body for body, and was also mainprised to fulfil all the conditions of the mainprise of William de Bredstret under penalty of £100.

For the same reason Thomas Wakfeld was delivered under bail to Michael de Lenne, chandler, John Witby, weaver, John Slougter, armourer, and John Colney, glover, under penalty of £100.

Membr. 4 *b*
13 Oct. 1384 Whereas on the eve of the Translation of St Edward King (13 Oct.) A° 8 Ric. II (1384) proclamation was made throughout the liberty of the city of London, as well on behalf of the king by virtue of his writ, as on behalf of the mayor and aldermen, that no one of whatsoever rank or condition should go armed or wearing breastplate or jack, or should lead an armed force against the king's peace, nor that any one should go to the election of the mayor and sheriffs, except the mayor, aldermen, sheriffs and good men of the wards summoned thereto, under penalty of imprisonment and forfeiture of all that he might forfeit to the king, and under penalty of losing the freedom of the city, as is more fully contained in Letter Book H, fo. [182]; and whereas the mayor, aldermen, sheriffs and good men of the wards being summoned were present on the above feast in the Guildhall for the election of the mayor, and there were present Lord de Nevyll, Lord Fitz Wauter and Thomas Moreux, knights, who were sent by order of the king and his council, there came also certain persons of the middle sort belonging to divers misteries, who, forgetting themselves and having no respect for or fear of the proclamation, and being banded together in a great congregation and assembled in Guildhall, made a great clamour

and outcry to the great affray of the mayor, aldermen and commonalty and against the proclamation made in the city. Whereupon, these offences having been committed as well against the king as the mayor, aldermen and sheriffs, divers good men of several misteries made inquiries as to the same evildoers, and afterwards brought the names of certain men of their misteries who were suspected, while others of the guilty persons were taken and others again surrendered themselves, of whom some were mainprised and others delivered under bail, as follows:

The good men of the mistery of Armourers brought before Sir Nicholas Brembre, Mayor, and the Aldermen and Sheriffs, the names and bodies of the following persons: John Hood, William Randulf, Robert Wormewell, William Pountfreyt, Richard Pecok and John Shirewode, who were all delivered under bail to Simon Wynchecoumbe, John Scorfeyn, John Grove and Peter atte Hethe, armourers, who entered into mainprise for their appearance when summoned, their good behaviour and obedience to the officers of the city, and that they would take no part in covins, conventicles, plots or congregations against the peace, under penalty of £1000. They were further sworn to save harmless those to whom they were delivered under bail. *19 Oct. 1384*

Robert Betoyne, goldsmith, was mainprised by Richard Betoyne his father and John Clerke, poulterer, as above, under penalty of £100.

John Daventre, pinner, was mainprised by John Lorymer, *bukelsmyth*, Walter Berkeswell, bladesmith, and William Coventre, pinner, as above, under penalty of £100. *21 Oct. 1384*

Marginal note: divers tailors imprisoned and mainprised because they made an uproar at the election of the mayor

William Rule, tailor, and his companions, masters of the mistery of Tailors, showed to the Mayor and Aldermen the names of divers men of their mistery who, as they under- *21 Oct. 1384* stood, took part in an assembly of men of several misteries in St Paul's Church on the day of the mayor's election and went thence to the Guildhall to make an uproar, in disturbance of the peace and against the proclamation.

John Hastynge, tailor, who confessed, was delivered under bail to John Heydon, barber, and John Middleton, tailor, under the above conditions and under penalty of £100.

John Heyward, tailor, similarly bailed by Robert Holm, *steynour*, Adam Millyng, tailor, and Nicholas Symond, spurrier; Roger Lilye, tailor, by Adam Millyng, tailor, and Roger March, tailor; Richard atte Wode, tailor, by John Creke, tailor, and Adam Lady, tailor; Richard Chilterne, tailor, by Adam Bury, cordwainer, John Davy, *peyntour*, John Phelip, fuster, and Roger Laurens; Thomas Grisele, tailor, by Thomas
Membr. 5 Pope, shearman, and John Marchal, brewer; Henry Henle, tailor, by Thomas Pope and John Marchal; Roger Mordon, tailor, by Clement Kirketon and John Creke, tailors; Robert Ascow, tailor, who did not confess, by John Dymmoke and Clement Kirketon, tailors; William Hill, tailor, by John Grigge, William Holyn and Richard Cornewaill, tailors;
22 Oct. 1384 Peter Fykelden, tailor, by John Sewale, mercer, Robert Paunton, girdler, William Shirewode, saddler, and Henry Payn, fuster; Robert Crokehorn, tailor, who did not confess, by John Wilby, William Spaldyng, Thomas Bridlyngton, John Burwell, John Donyngton and John Sheldon, tailors; Thomas Mynde, who did not confess, by the same; all under penalty of £100.

John Boseham and others, masters of the mistery of Mercers, brought before the Mayor and Aldermen the following mercers: John Feraunt, John Chedder, Richard Guy, John Vyne, Thomas Everard, William Willesdon and John Toke, as men accustomed to speak maliciously of the Mayor and Aldermen and their government. They were delivered under bail to the said John Boseham, Robert Warbulton, John Organ, John Eston and John Shadeworth, on the above conditions and under penalty of £40 each.

Reymund Standulf, goldsmith, who admitted being at Guildhall, was delivered under bail to John Botisham, Thomas

Davy and John Frensshe, goldsmiths, and Gilbert Meldebourne, under penalty of £200.

Edmund Wodhull, cutler, for divers malicious words spoken against the mayor, was mainprised by Richard Goudchyld, John Salle, Walter Kynton and Martin Godard, cutlers, and Richard Betoygne, goldsmith, under penalty of £100.

Edmund Clay, cordwainer, who admitted being at Guildhall against the proclamation, was delivered under bail to Thomas Pope, shearman, Nicholas Bosbury, cordwainer, and William Morys and Walter Peryndon, armourers, under penalty of £100.

John Coraunt and John Somervyll, masters of the mistery of Goldsmiths, brought before the Mayor and Aldermen the following goldsmiths, Hugh Wetherby, Roger Broun, William Lucas, Andrew Stamelden, Stephen Walpol, John Walyngford, Robert Willy, John Welford, William Stamelden, Henry atte Grene and William Lyncoll, as suspected persons, who were accustomed to speak ill of the mayor and aldermen and their government, and as being of perverse and evil condition. Nevertheless by favour of the mayor all of them were delivered under bail to the said John Coraunt, John Somervyll, John Forster and John Botisham, goldsmiths, under penalty of £100.

John Smyth, armourer, bailed by Roger atte Hacche, girdler, John Whyte, goldsmith, Robert Knyght, armourer, and John Halyngbury, under penalty of £100. Membr. 5 *b* *24 Oct. 1384*

John Couewell, bailed by William Sallowe, junior, John Glosse, skinner, William atte Halle, hostiller, and Simon Berthorpe, saddler, under penalty of £100.

Stephen atte Frithe, armourer, bailed by Simon Wynchecoumbe, John Scorfeyn and John Grove, armourers, and Robert Asshcoumbe, *brodurer*, under penalty of £1000. *25 Oct. 1384*

Robert Arderne, *brodurer*, bailed by Robert Asshcoumbe, William Sauston and Elias Mympe, *brodurers*, and John Creek, tailor, under penalty of £1000.

William Hotte, tailor, bailed by William Spaldyng, draper, John Scorfeyn, armourer, and John Creek and John Kynne, tailors, under penalty of £1000.

Thomas Mynton, tailor, bailed by Robert Asshcoumbe, *brodurer*, Henry Payn, fuster, Nicholas Whitlock, *lorymer*, and Robert de Holdernesse, cutler, under penalty of £1000.

5 Nov. 1384 John Grene, servant of Edmund Wodhull, cutler, bailed by Walter Kynton, John Essex, Robert de Eye and Martin Godard, cutlers, under penalty of £100.

John Raulyn, John Wylde, Richard Kenyngton, Gerard Furbour, John Albon and Nicholas Doby, armourers, were mainprised by William Thornhull, William Trippelowe, John Shirewode, John Whyte, John Henham, John Herman, Michael Dundalk and John Grove, armourers, under penalty of £200, to fulfil the condition set forth in the bail of Roger Mordon.

William Brandon, servant of William de Thorpe, tailor, mainprised by Roger Elys as above.

William Salkyn, fuller, mainprised by Peter Persolte, Thomas Heed and Thomas Yonge, fullers, and John Maryner, brewer, as above, under penalty of £40.

18 Nov. 1384 Thomas Hogecot, Philip Chipstowe and John Parfay, armourers, were delivered under bail to John Scorfeyn, Peter atte Hethe, Richard Yernemouthe, John Grove, Robert Wormell and William Pountfreyt, as above, under penalty of £100.

24 Nov. 1384 William Kirkeby, tailor, who came to the Guildhall at the mayor's election contrary to the proclamation, was delivered under bail to Robert Ashcoumbe, *brodurer*, William Spaldyng, John Wilby, Thomas Multon, John Wyght and Clement Kirton, tailors, as above, under penalty of £200.

John Coraunt, goldsmith, who was held in great suspicion concerning the assembly of his mistery and other misteries at St Paul's Church on election day, which came to Guildhall to make an uproar, and who afterwards in the presence of the mayor, John Fraunceys, alderman, and others said that Robert Somersete and John Maudeleyn, tailors, had told him on the day before the election that Lord de Nevyll, Lord Fitzwauter and other lords ought to be present at the election, and that it was their wish as well as the wish of the Mayor and Aldermen that the men of the misteries ought to come there in their liveries for the election of the mayor, which words both he and Robert Somersete denied having spoken, was nevertheless by the favour of the mayor delivered under bail to Thomas Exton, John Forster, Bartholomew Castre and Thomas Hay, goldsmiths, as above, under penalty of £500.

William Wodecok, tailor, who came to the Guildhall on election day contrary to the proclamation, and went thence to his shop and fetched a sword, buckler and poleaxe, hoping that a riot would arise, was nevertheless by favour of the mayor delivered under bail to John Tilneye, Thomas Brakkele and Matthew Angelseye, tailors, and Thomas Beneyt, smith, as above, under penalty of £100. *6 Feb. 1385*

Henry Walsale, tailor, was also delivered under bail to Robert Shirwode, saddler, Henry Pye, William Goudman and William atte Halle, tailors, Thomas Rakeswell, *bokeler-maker*, and Robert Horham, blacksmith, under the above conditions.

William Mauncell was mainprised by Henry Goudchepe, Robert Malteby, Richard Biernes, cordwainer, and John Haringeye, saddler, to keep the peace, obey the officers of the city, not to engage in any covin *etc.* and to warn the Mayor and Aldermen thereof, under penalty of £100. Membr. 6 *3 June 1385*

William Fyssh, tailor, was similarly mainprised by William Russell, John Grigge and John Cornewaille, tailors, Walter Rous, mercer, and Robert Sutton, *brodurer*, under penalty of £100. *10 Nov. 1385*

John Whyte was mainprised by Geoffrey Walderne, John Rede, Richard Clophull, William Longisdon and William *11 Feb. 1386*

Doncastre, smiths, Thomas Curch and Robert Thorseby, *marchall*[1], as above.

4 April 1386 William Belhomme was delivered under bail to Robert Buxton, Richard Storteford, John de Swanton, Peter atte Hethe, John Lake and Roger atte Hacche, body for body, to fulfil all the conditions in the mainprise of William Mauncel, under penalty of £500, and to be ready and prepared to appear before the Mayor and Aldermen or before the king's justices when summoned. And further the above mainpernors undertook that the said William Belhomme would neither do nor cause to be done any injury to Agnes Caly in her person or her goods by act or word, under the said penalty.

Afterwards on 26 Jan. 1390 the Mayor and Aldermen granted that the above recognisance should be obliterated and held to be null and void, and that William Belhomme and his mainpernors should be exonerated, and so by precept of William Venour, mayor, the record was obliterated.

19 July 1386 William Stanes, cutler, was mainprised by Richard Goodchyld, Richard Waltham, Richard Shirebourne, John Salle, John Twyford and Robert Austyn, cutlers, to fulfil the conditions as in the mainprise of William Mauncell, under penalty of £200.

Thomas Kynggesbrugge, cordwainer, was mainprised by John Waleworth, vintner, Nicholas Bosbury, William Randolf, Robert Sutton, Robert Norton, cordwainers, and John Curson, as above.

John Lyndeseye, cutler, was mainprised by William Barnabe, John Curson, Robert Norton, William Trymenell, John Deux and Robert Hanslap, as above.

Richard Gibbes, cordwainer, was mainprised by John Walworth, Robert Bryan, Robert Mauncel, Thomas Duke, Thomas Pountfreyt, William Hare, Nicholas Bosebury and Nicholas Loseye, as above.

Richard Little, haberdasher, was mainprised by Robert Norton, John Curson, John Haryngeye, John Barbour, William Randolf and Nicholas Whitele, as above.

[1] Farrier.

Richard Sturdy, skinner, was sworn before the Mayor and Aldermen to be good and faithful to the king and his heirs, to behave peaceably towards the king and his people, to be obedient to the mayor, sheriffs and other officers, to be tractable and justiciable to the king's peace and to preserve it faithfully to the best of his power, to be ready to appear before the Mayor and Aldermen when warned, to engage in no congregation, covin *etc.*, which might lead to insurrection, the harm of the people, or injury to the government of the city, but to hinder such congregations and to warn the mayor and other officers of the city of them, and further to bear himself peaceably to the masters of his mistery for the time being and to be, and not to do or cause to be done any harm or injury to them, under penalty of £200. *29 Aug. 1386*

John Penreth brought a bill of complaint to the effect that he had been apprenticed to William Paston, *alias* Reynald, mercer, who was bound by the terms of the covenant to provide him with food, clothing and instruction, and that now his master had been imprisoned in Calais for debt more than eight weeks and his shop in London had been sealed up, with the result that the petitioner was wasting his time treading the streets (*batant les ruwes*). He prayed to be discharged of his apprenticeship and to be allowed to seek a livelihood where he could. [*French*] Membr. 7 *5 Nov. 1383*

Testimony was given by Robert Warbelton, John Shadeworth, John Eston and John Loveye, masters of the mistery of Mercers, that the said William was in prison in Calais, that his shop in London was sequestrated and that his wife had no means of providing for the apprentice. Thereupon, according to the custom, the said John was exonerated from his apprenticeship, on condition that he made no claim on his master for the unexpired portion.

John Bohoun, knight, demanded by bill against John Davy, goldsmith, divers charters, fines, writings and muniments touching his inheritance of manors, lands and tenements in Essex, Bucks and Sussex, which deeds came into Davy's hands on 11 Aug. 1382. *19 Nov. 1383*

The latter produced them in court in a sealed forcer, which was opened and by judgment of the court delivered to the plaintiff, who gave an acquittance for the same.

6 Dec. 1383 Nicholas Rote, John Waleworth, John Wakele, William Wallere, Thomas Say and John Andreu, vintners of the east part (of Walbrook), John Goldryng, chandler, and Geoffrey Haket, John Heyward, John Grantam, William Succh, William Cornhull and Paul Gisors, vintners of the west part, and Richard Manhale, chandler, were sworn for the scrutiny of wines in cellars and other places where wines were sold and to pour out into the kennel all such as were found unhealthy and corrupt, to prevent old wines from being stored with new, and, together with the chandlers, to survey vinegar and sauces kept in the shops and cellars of chandlers and to pour out *etc.*

Membr. 7 *b*
26 Nov. 1383 Writ to the mayor and sheriffs that, whereas John Yorke of London, brewer, had prayed the king that he was in danger of life and mutilation of his limbs by John Norhampton, draper, and John Bleton, they were to summon the said John and John and put them to mainprise under reasonable penalty not to do or cause to be done any harm or evil to the said John Yorke, and if the said John and John refused, they were to commit them to gaol until they were willing to find such mainprise. Dated at Westminster 26 Nov. 1383.

21 Dec. 1383 Quitclaim from John Culham, armourer, to John Freman of Foulmere[1] co. Cambridge. Witnesses, Simon Wynchecombe, sheriff, William Wyrcestre, keeper of Ludgate, Walter Chyld and Robert Foulmere, clerks, and Thomas de Lincoln.

11 Jan. 1384 Peter de Dalby, servant of John, lord of Welles[2], came into the Mayor's Court and proffered 40 marks owed by his lord to Hugh Fastolf and prayed that the matter be put on record.

15 Jan. 1384 Quitclaim from Hugelin Gerrard, merchant of Bologna (*Boloigne de Crace*), to Roger Excestre, saddler, and John Bradeley, tailor.

[1] Foulmire.

[2] John de Welles, Lord Welles, summoned to parliament from 20 Jan. 1376 to 26 Feb. 1421.

Richard Mayllour, *rakyere*[1] of Chepe ward, entered into a bond of 20s to the chamberlain not to cast or cause to be cast any dung or other ordure belonging to his own ward into the ward of Colmanstrete, or to throw such ordure into the kennels during rainy weather in order that the force of the water might carry it into Colmanstrete ward, and further to lead away and remove all ordure belonging to Chepe ward which was then in Colmanstrete ward. *14 Jan. 1384*

John Marchaunt, *rakyere* of Bassyeshawe ward, entered into a similar bond.

Whereas many men of divers places around London use nets of which the mesh is too close and take and destroy every kind of minute fishes called "*fry*" in the Thames, so that fish of any size or value can hardly arise or be found therein, to the grave damage of the whole city and other places adjacent to the river and against the ancient custom of the city, according to which the mesh of small nets used for fishing should be two inches wide at least, so that little fishes can easily pass through them, and in order to put an end to this loss, Nicholas Brembre, knight, mayor[2], summoned before him the good men of the following places, *viz.*, from the vill of Chesewyk[3], William Grene and John Wille; the vill of Fulham, John Hamond and John Broun; the vill of Wandesworth, John Coche; the vill of Batrycheseye[4], Thomas Fynch and John Bukke; and the vill of Stebbenhithe[5], Roger Sket and John Pynnok. Membr. 8 *15 Jan. 1384*

The above persons were sworn not to fish or cause any other person to fish with nets of which the mesh was closer than two inches, and if they found anyone else so doing,

[1] The rakyers were street-cleaners, paid out of sums levied from the wards. *Cal. of Plea and Mem. Rolls*, 1364–81, pp. 85, 150; *Munim. Gild. Lond.* (R.S.), I, p. 335.

[2] As conservator of the Thames in accordance with the city's charters, 8 Ric. I, 1 John, 11 Henry III and 1 Edw. III. Though the statute of 17 Ric. II, c. 9 enacted that the mayor for the time being should have the conservation of the statutes 13 Edw. I, c. 47 and 13 Ric. II, c. 19, the jurisdiction of the city over the Thames and Medway in the matter of weirs, stakenets and drawnets had been exercised continuously from 1237 onwards. See *Munim. Gild. Lond.* (R.S.), II (1), pp. 42, 116, (2), p. 543; *Cal. of Letter Book A*, pp. 185–8; *C*, p. 144; *E*, pp. 237–8; *F*, p. 111.

[3] Chiswick.

[4] Battersea.

[5] Stepney.

to take his net and bring it before the mayor, and in case they were forcibly prevented from performing their office, they should certify to the mayor the names of those who resisted them.

25 Jan. 1384 Memorandum that Katherine, widow of Adam Stable, mercer, appeared by her attorney before the Mayor and Aldermen and informed them that her late husband had bought a house near Sopereslane from Robert Marny, knight, and Alice his wife, and had bound himself by a statute before William Waleworth, then mayor of the Staple of Westminster, to pay 500 marks for it at certain terms, the last payment of 25 marks being due on 8 Jan. 1376 in the church of St Mary le Bow. Since no one appeared to receive it, he had brought it to Guildhall next day, but as the chamberlain was not there, he had taken it home again. On many occasions since then he had offered the money to Robert, who refused to accept it. Her husband having died, she now hands it over to Richard Odyham, chamberlain, for payment to Robert and Alice in return for an acquittance. The chamberlain received the money and then returned it to Katherine's attorney, John Chircheman, grocer, taking a bond from him on 3 Feb. that he would be prepared to pay it whenever Robert and Alice should appear to claim it.

Memorandum that in 1372 the wardship of Walter, son of Adam Glendon, together with £80, was committed to John Blakeney, mercer, as appears in Letter Book G, fo. 286, which John died leaving no goods or chattels to satisfy the orphan's claim, as was testified in court on 12 Jan. 1384, when the orphan, being of age, sued for his money. Thereupon, the sureties becoming liable, Walter Blankeney, mercer, and John Blakeney, fishmonger, appeared together with Robert de Louthe, tenant of the lands and tenements formerly belonging to the third surety John Mitford, and paid £41 4s. The fourth surety, John Stoke, did not appear and had no goods in the city whereby he might be distrained to come, but on 27 Jan., when he arrived in London, the said Walter, John and Robert de Louthe claimed against him the sum of

£10 6s, his share of the above £41 4s. Judgment was given against him for that amount and he was committed to prison, being released on 15 Feb., when payment was made. The balance of the inheritance, *viz.* £38 14s, which had been deposited in the hands of Adam Stable, was repaid by the latter's executors.

At a court held in the Chamber of the Guildhall according to the custom of the city before the Mayor and Aldermen, Walter Morton, fishmonger, offered himself against William Hert, baker, who had a day by foreign attachment in a plea of debt of 1250 marks. As the defendant made four defaults, the said Walter prayed that the attachment be valued according to the custom and delivered to him. The attachment was appraised by oath of John Calthorp, Robert Charwell and John Leyton as follows: Membr. 8 *b* *11 March 1384*

2 *troghes* for paste and one *moldyngburd*[1], 8s; 2 *bultynge-chestes*[2], 3s; one *brake*[3] and one *tubbe*, 2s; 10 quarters of meal (*farina*) and 2 quarters of flour, £3 12s; 2 pairs of bolting-sieves (*bultell'*), 12d; 3 *quartrons*[4] of wood, 4s; one *scaldyng-panne*, 3s; 3 *tubbes*, one *tyne*[5] and 2 *treyes*[6], 18d; one tankard bound with iron, 12d; one *dosser*[7], 3 *bankers*[8] and 3 *quissyns*, 18d; 5 *fates*[9] and 2 quarts, 10s; 2 quarters of *bren*, 18d; one chest, 12d; 6 quarters of grain, 36s; one table, 12d; one chair, 8d; one table and one bench, 6d; sum total, £7 7s 8d. Delivery was made to the plaintiff on security of John Mordon, fuller, and Robert Morton, fishmonger, to answer for the attachment if the defendant should appear within a year and a day. As the defendant had no other goods and chattels, his rents and tenements in the parish of Holy Trinity the Less in Vintry ward, valued at 6 marks per annum, were delivered to the plaintiff until he should be satisfied of his debt, under the above security.

William atte March, cordwainer, was charged at the suit Membr. 9 *12 May 1384*

[1] Moulding-board.
[2] Bolting-chest, a chest for coarse meal or bran bolted or sifted from the fine flour. [3] A baker's kneading-machine.
[4] Quarterns, quarters of a hundredweight. [5] A tub. [6] Trays.
[7] Or dorser, an ornamental cloth covering the back of a seat.
[8] A covering for a bench or chair. [9] Vats.

of the surveyors of the mistery of Cordwainers with having made shoes of oxhide and calfhide mixed, against the ordinance of his mistery[1], and also with having refused to allow them to survey his work and with resisting them rebelliously, against the common ordinance of the city. The defendant put himself on the favour of the court. It was considered that he be committed to prison for 10 days and pay 10s on his release, in accordance with the ordinance.

26 March 1384 Peter de Alemayne of Iscelworth[2], Robert Grey of Kyngeston[3] and John Walsshe of Shene, each having a pannier of small fish called "*fry*," and Hugh Daye of Shene with a *trogh*[4] of the same, were brought before the Mayor and Aldermen and charged with having caught the fish with nets and other engines of too narrow a mesh, to the destruction of the fish in the Thames and against the ordinance thereon made and enrolled. All of them admitted the charge and put themselves on the favour of the court. Thereupon, because this was their first offence and conviction, and because they confessed and bore themselves humbly, and in order to encourage them to come to the city with victuals, the panniers, *trogh* and fish were restored to them. They were forbidden, under penalty of the pillory, to use such nets or engines in future, and they promised not to do so.

Membr. 9 *b*
29 Feb. 1384 Memorandum that on 29 Feb. 1384 in the presence of the Mayor and Aldermen the following good men: John Wilton, John Fraunkeleyn, John Barry and John Pyion were sworn to oversee that all the foreigners bringing fresh fish from the sea to the city for sale, and taking their stand at or near the Stocks or in Chepe, should neither sell nor expose for sale any fish, which was putrid, stinking or unhealthy for man's body, and if they found any such fish to arrest it and carry it before the Mayor and Aldermen to do therewith as reason demands; and also that no *birlestere*[5] buy any sea fish or freshwater fish before 10 o'clock nor stand in any certain

[1] City's Liber Horn, fos. 339–40; *Munim. Gild. Lond.* (R.S.), II, p. 83 and *Calendars of Letter Books, passim.*
[2] Isleworth.
[3] Kingston-upon-Thames.
[4] *Sc.* trough, a wooden box-like receptacle.
[5] Hawker.

place at the Stocks or elsewhere but that they go from place to place within the liberty to serve the commonalty, and that they sell the same day all fresh fish which they buy after 10 o'clock and do not keep it for sale thereafter; and if the said surveyors found any birlster acting against any of the points abovesaid that they arrest him together with his fish and take them before the Mayor and Aldermen to receive such judgment as seems to them reasonable in such case; and also that all the *peteres*[1] who take fresh fish in the Thames east of the Bridge and bring it to the city for sale stand in Cornhill and nowhere else under pain of forfeiting their fish; and those who take fish west of the Bridge stand in Chepe and nowhere else. [*French*]

Memorandum that Peter Gracyan and Barthelmeu Seint, Lombards, chose Gautron de Bardes and Baltasar Obryache[2] to be arbitrators in all plaints and actions between them, and that the latter, with their consent, chose Amflion Pynel, Daniel de la Mer and Nicholas de Luk to be umpires to settle all points on which the said Peter and Barthelmeu could not agree, for the faithful performance of which the said Amfilon (*sic*), Daniel and Nicholas were sworn before the Mayor, Recorder and Aldermen. [*French*] *12 July 1384*

Adam Brikedon, mercer, who was summoned in a plea of account to answer Thomas Cornewaill, tailor, for the sum of £35 entrusted to him to trade therewith, pleaded that the plaintiff had no action against him because he had rendered account at Makynes wharf[3] in the parish of All Hallows Berkyng in the presence of Peter Oxenford and Roger Fuller, auditors. This the plaintiff denied. A jury of the venue found for the defendant. *4 July 1384*

Membr. 10

Matthew Passelewe was summoned to answer John Hende and John Rote, late sheriffs of London, in a plea of debt of £64 due on a bond of 1 Oct. 1381, wherein the plaintiffs *20 March 1383*

[1] Petermen, a common term in London for fishermen. The word is supposed to refer to the occupation of Simon Peter. Cf. peterboat.

[2] See below, p. 82, "Umbryak."

[3] See Husting Rolls of Deeds and Wills, 89 (52). This wharf lay east of the Woolwharf, being separated from it by the Stonewharf and a water-gate, and west of the wharves later known as "Marowe's New Quay."

by the custom of London produced suit[1] by their bill exhibited before the Mayor and Aldermen.

The defendant pleaded that the bond [French], which was in the names of John Chircheman, himself and Stephen Brown, was security for the payment by the said Stephen of £64 by quarterly portions, that being the amount for which he purchased the bailiwick of the Thames at Billingsgate for the year Michaelmas 1381 to Michaelmas 1382, and that Stephen had paid £32 for the first two quarters. The holders of the bailiwick had always been entitled to such wines and merchandise coming by water to Billingsgate as were forfeited by reason of their having been sold without payment of custom or toll. During Stephen's tenure of the bailiwick a quantity of Rhenish wine and other goods to the value of £100 were forfeited for this reason, but the sheriffs had wrongfully taken the forfeiture, so that the said Stephen was unable to pay the £32 due for the other two quarters. The defendant prayed judgment whether under these circumstances the plaintiffs could maintain their action against him.

The plaintiffs protested that they did not acknowledge any such custom as regards forfeitures, and moreover certain forfeitures were reserved to themselves in the agreement. During the time mentioned the only forfeiture was that of certain wines found in the possession of William Sharpyng, vintner, the quantity and value of which they did not know. These wines they had claimed as forfeit on the bailiff's suggestion, and with the latter's consent the question of their value had been settled in the house of John Hende in St Nicholas Lane near Candelwykstrete, where William Sharpyng agreed to pay £10. They were willing to account for this sum to the bailiff.

The defendant pleaded that the settlement was made without the bailiff's consent and prevented the bailiff from claiming anything against the said William on account of the forfeiture. On this question of consent a jury was summoned between the parties for the Wednesday following, on which day the

[1] By this time the suit of witnesses was a mere formality and apparently the putting in and affirming of a bill was regarded as the production of suit. In such bills the only names given were those of the pledges for prosecution. As regards suit, see Holdsworth, *Hist. Eng. Law*, I, pp. 300–1.

defendant offered that if the sheriffs would swear that the agreement was made by consent and in the presence of the bailiff he would admit the debt. The plaintiff John Hende agreed but as the co-plaintiff John Rote was absent from ill-health, a day was given on Saturday. In the meantime, by consent of the parties, William Cheyne, recorder, with Roger Elys, alderman, went on Friday to John Rote's house, where both plaintiffs took the oath. Next day it was considered that the plaintiffs recover £32 against the defendant and 40s damages taxed by the court, and that the said Matthew be in mercy.

John Aunger, *boteller*, was summoned to answer William Wyndesore, knight, in a plea of debt. The plaintiff's attorney, Richard Forster, declared that on 18 June 1380 in the parish of St Martin Ludgate the defendant had sold to the plaintiff bottles for carrying his wine on the king's service in France and Brittany in the company of the earl of Buckingham, which bottles, though guaranteed as sound, proved to be defective, so that 180 gallons of wine were lost, and afterwards on 14 Sept. 1383 in the church of the Friars Preachers, the parties had put themselves on the arbitration of William Carlil and Thomas Torold, masters of the mistery of Botellers, on the advice of the whole mistery, and the arbitrators found that the bottles were false and awarded that the said John Aunger should repay the cost of the bottles, *viz.* £18 6s 8d, together with £10 damages to the said William Wyndesore, both of which sums the defendant had refused to pay.

Membr. 10 *b*
16 Dec. 1383

The defendant, after protesting that he did not acknowledge any warranty or that the bottles were defective, pleaded that there had been a quarrel between himself and William Carlill, Thomas Torold and John Shadwell, who envied him and wanted to drive him out of the liberty of the city, because he exercised the same trade as themselves. These persons had instigated the plaintiff to bring an action against him in the Sheriffs' Court and afterwards he and the plaintiff had put themselves on the arbitration of Robert Ikford, William Poule, John Goldfynch and Philip de Wodestrete, on condition that none of the three above-mentioned persons should intermeddle therein. As regards the alleged award by

William Carlil and Thomas Torold, he maintained that it was contrary to this condition and therefore he prayed judgment as to whether any action lay against him.

The plaintiff repeated that the defendant put himself on the award of the above William and Thomas.

Process being continued, a jury on 6 July 1384 found that the parties put themselves, as the defendant alleged, on the arbitration of Robert Ikford, William Poule, John Goldfynch and Philip de Wodestrete, who said they could not make an end of the matter unless they had the advice of William Carlill and Thomas Torold, masters of the mistery, and thereupon, by consent of the parties, they were chosen to be in the arbitration, and the whole six of them then made the award in the terms declared by the plaintiff; and the jury assessed the damages, additional to the award, at 40d.

The action was adjourned till 21 July that the court might consult as to their judgment, and the defendant was committed to Ludgate for lack of mainprise. As the court wished further inquiry to be made, the jury were summoned again and after being sworn were asked whether William Carlill and Thomas Torold were afterwards elected as arbitrators or merely to advise and inform the arbitrators. The answer was, as arbitrators. Being asked further if the arbitration was made by assent of the mistery of Botellers, the jury replied that it was by assent of six men of the mistery and that there was only one other person belonging to the mistery and he was present when the arbitration was made. Accordingly it was considered, on the whole verdict, that William Wyndesore recover £28 6s 8d, as awarded by the arbitrators, and the damages taxed by the jury at 40d, and that the defendant be in mercy. And for default of payment the defendant was committed to Ludgate until he paid.

Membr. 11–11 *b*
10 June 1384

Whereas larcenies and divers evil deeds are commonly perpetrated more openly, notoriously and frequently in this present than in past times in the city of London, its suburbs and neighbourhood, which would not have been possible, if the thieves and evildoers had not been maintained and harboured by persons dwelling in the city and suburbs and residing with innkeepers, who cared little what kind of men they received, to the great damage of the citizens of the city and those repairing there and to the great disgrace and scandal of the same, and in order to prevent such damage and scandal, it was agreed by Sir Nicholas Brembre, Mayor, and the Aldermen[1] that all innkeepers within the liberty should be sworn to harbour no one longer than a day and night, unless they were willing to answer for them and their acts, nor to receive to their tables any strangers called "*travaillyngmen*[2]" or others, unless they had good and sufficient surety from them for their good and loyal behaviour, under penalty of answering for their actions and paying £100 to the Chamber for the use of the commonalty, if they were convicted of offending in either of the two above-mentioned points, and further that the said innkeepers should be sworn to inform the mayor if they had knowledge of any innkeeper or others harbouring men of ill fame or persons suspected of larceny.

[*French*]

[List of innkeepers of the several wards, with the names of their mainpernors: Langebourne, 13; Tower, 3; Bradstret, 2; Queenhithe, 3; Vinetrie, 2; Algate, 6; Bredstret, 22; Douegate, 5; Chepe, 4; Candelwykstret, 1; Lymstret, 1; Aldrichesgate, 6; Cordwanerstret, 1; Crepulgate Within, 7, including Richard Stom at the "*Saresineshed*"; Crepulgate Without, 7; Castle Baynard, 9; Billingesgate, 4; Farndon Without, under the following subdivisions: Holbourne, 25; Smythfeld, 20; Fletstret, 50, including the innkeepers of the "*Lyon*," the "*Sadel*," the "*Tabard*" and the "*Boor*," total, 95; Farndon Within, 6; Bassyeshaw, Colmanstret and Cornhull, none; grand total, excluding Walbrook, Bishopsgate, Bridge and Portsoken, for which no figures are given, 197.]

John Bacon, dean, and the chapter of St Martin le Grand brought a bill that, whereas St Martin le Grand was a free chapel of the king and possessed, by right of its first foundation, of a messuage in the parish of St Nicholas Flesshameles adjoining a little lane called "the Rydye[3]," which had been Membr. 12 *25 June 1384*

[1] As the Court of Aldermen. [2] Travelling-men, wayfarers.

[3] See Husting Roll, 169 (19); the lane was bounded on the north by the king's highway and on the south by a garden of St Paul's church.

a common lane and used by his predecessor, Walter Skirlowe, and the chapter, and their predecessors and tenants time out of mind for the carriage of their baggage from the highway to the house, nevertheless, when John de Norhampton was mayor, Edmund Yernemouthe and John Muntham, joiners, and William Essex, draper, had falsely given the mayor and Common Council to understand that the said lane was the private ground of the mayor and commonalty, so that by their agency the lane was closed and the dean and chapter and their tenants were not allowed to use it, whereby they had lost the greater part of their profit from the messuage—in consideration of which the Mayor and Aldermen were prayed to view the premises and grant a remedy. [*French*]

The said Edmund, John and William were summoned to appear in the Chamber on 27 June and made default. They were distrained by the closing and sealing of certain of their doors. On a second default other doors were closed, and on a third, all their doors. On a fourth default the mayor, recorder and aldermen viewed the lane and examined the good men of the neighbourhood, and as it seemed to them that the dean and chapter had always had free entrance and exit to and from the lane, as testified by the neighbours, until in the time of John Norhampton a gate had been built and kept closed at the entrance of the lane, it was considered that the dean and chapter and their tenants should have free entrance and exit at all fit times, on condition that the gate be kept closed at night. Thereupon the custody of the gate was committed to John Pyion, tenant of the messuage, saving to the mayor and commonalty the ownership of the lane.

30 July 1384 William Baret, merchant, offered himself against Sir Florimund de la Sparre, knight, in a plea of debt of 100 marks. As the defendant made four defaults, the plaintiff prayed that the foreign attachment be valued and delivered to him. The valuation was made by oath of John Coraunt, John Forster, Conerode Shillyng and Roland atte Bushe, goldsmiths, as follows: one large silver cup called "*Rose*," £7; one other cup with a base[1] of *treyfoyles*, 73s 4d; one *gobelet byker* of

[1] *Ciphus base cum treyfoyles.*

silvergilt, 66s; one ewer of silvergilt, 36s; one girdle of silvergilt with fifteen bars, £7; one gold *nouche*[1] with a stone called "*saphir*," 6 little sapphires, 6 stones called "*baleys*[2]," 6 *troches*, each *troche*[3] with 4 pearls and a stone called *dyamaund* in the middle, 40 marks; sum total, £48 15s 4d, which attachment was delivered to the plaintiff in part payment of his debt under security to answer *etc.*

Memorandum that John Calam, brewer, and John Person, cordwainer, appeared before John Bosham, *locum tenens* of the mayor, and divers good men, *locum tenentes* of the aldermen, and mainprised Thomas Cook, that he would, with the aid of God, carry 120 quarters of malt from the port of London in a *creyer*[4] called "*Seintemariebot*," of which John Lincoll was master, to the town of Calais and there discharge it, bringing back letters of discharge under the seal of the town-officials there between the present date and Christmas, under penalty of £40 payable to the chamberlain of London. [*French*] Membr. 12 *b* *20 Aug. 1384*

Writ of protection in favour of Richard Pecok, esquire, then about to set out for Portugal on the king's service in the company of the master of St James[5] of Portugal. Dated at Reading 17 Aug. 1384. *17 Aug. 1384*

Memorandum that a release and quitclaim, dated 12 Nov. 1371, from Margery, widow of John de Wycombe, mason, and daughter of William Coumbe, shearman, to John Turk, fishmonger, and Isabella his wife, of two tenements, with houses erected thereon, and two vacant plots in Haywharflane in the parish of All Hallows the Great, formerly belonging to John de la Rokele, son of Simon de la Rokele of Braugheng[6], had been handed in for enrolment about seven years previously, but had not been enrolled because no one appeared *4 Oct. 1384*

1 A clasp or brooch for holding together two sides of a garment.
2 *N.E.D.* a delicate rose-red variety of the spinel ruby, now called a balas ruby.
3 *N.E.D.* an ornamental button set with jewels in a bunch.
4 *Sc. crayer*, a small trading vessel.
5 Fernandus Alfons, master of the knightly order of St James, ambassador of the King of Portugal. See *Cal. Close Rolls*, 1381–5, pp. 549, 552, 635.
6 Braughing co. Herts.

to sue for enrolment. Since the quitclaim could not now be enrolled owing to the deaths of the said Margery and John, it was given back to the said Isabella in the presence of Richard Preston, alderman of Dowgate, who testified that she was the widow of John Turk.

3 Nov. 1384 Paul Gisors, Robert Harry, John Walworth, Richard Sprot, John Mockyng and Thomas Say, vintners, and John Goldryng, chandler, for the east part (of Walbrook), and John Edrop, John Andrew, Thomas Nel, Nicholas Rote, Geoffrey Haket and John Grantham, vintners, and Richard Manhale, chandler, for the west part, were sworn to the scrutiny of wines in cellars and other places, where they were sold, to pour out into the kennel all such as they found corrupt and unhealthy for man's body, and to certify to the Mayor and Aldermen how much old red and white wine there was in each place and to whom it belonged, and further to see that the vinegar and other sauces of the chandlers were sound.

Membr. 13
18 Nov. 1384 Bond of Baltazar Umbryak[1], James Fane, Andrew Michel and Francis de Mas before the mayor, recorder, aldermen and sheriffs in the Chamber of the Guildhall in 1000 marks to pay to Nicholas Brembre whatever sum should be charged against Sanctus Bartholomeo[2], Lombard, by the arbitrators appointed to settle disputes between the said Sanctus and Peter Gracian.

16 Dec. 1384 Thomas Wilyngham, *lethersellere*, acknowledged a debt of £17 5s 11d due to Matthew Passelewe, grocer, and payable on the feast of St Hilary next.

18 Jan. 1385 Mandamus, dated at Westminster 18 Jan. 1385, to the mayor and sheriffs, that they deliver John Nobelson[3], who had been taken and detained under arrest in the city on account of certain of the king's lieges having lately been taken on the Thames and carried to the town of Lescluse in

[1] Or Obryache, see above, p. 75.

[2] Otherwise Seint de Barthelmeu de Seint, Barthelmeu Seint *etc.*

[3] Nobelson, a Fleming, together with other seamen, had been arrested by the king's orders on an allegation by Richard Spicer that Nobelson's brother and the seamen had carried away Spicer's wife, servants and goods in a vessel on the Thames to Sluys. *Cal. Close Rolls*, 1381–5, pp. 467–8.

Flanders, who had afterwards been liberated, as the governor, constables and commonalty of the merchants of the Staple at Midelburgh had certified to the mayor by letter, if the said John Nobelson were detained under arrest for no other reason.

In accordance with the above the said John was delivered.

Robert Forster, senior, of Ancroft, acknowledged a deed whereby he granted, of his own pure and spontaneous wish, without fraud or guile, all his goods and chattels, alive and dead, to William Ancroft, citizen of London. Dated at London 1 Feb. 1384. Membr. 13 *b* *26 Jan. 1385*

Quitclaim from Peter Gracyan, merchant of Lucca, to Francis dil Masse of Siena and Sanctus, son of the late Bartholomew de Sancto, merchants of *Bononia Crassa* in Lombardy, and companions and attorneys of the society of Ieronimus Arigy of Bologna, of all actions arising from any debt, contract *etc.* between 8 March 1382 and the present day. Dated in London 25 Jan. 1384 according to the computation of the English Church [25 Jan. 1385].

Quitclaim from Nicholas Brembre, knight, to Francis dil Masse of Siena, Sanctus, son of Bartholomew de Sancto, and Ierolimus (*sic*) de Arregis, merchants of Bologna in Lombardy. Dated as above.

Quitclaim from Jakettus Dyne of Florence and Luke Bragadyn of Venice to Ieronimus Arigy of Bologna, Sanctus de Bartholomeo Sanctum, partner and attorney of the society of Ieronimus Arigy, and all their partners, of all actions against them for the sum of £75, which had been awarded to the said Jakettus by Galterus de Bardes, Andrew Michel and Galdinus Rest, arbitrators between him and Sanctus, on the ground that the said Sanctus had promised to pay that sum. Dated as above.

Bond from William Tedys, merchant of Florence, to Guilliam Miro, merchant of Cateloigne[1], for the payment of £47 2s 6½d in two portions at Christmas and Easter. Dated at London 8 Oct. 1384. [*French*]

[1] Catalonia.

Membr. 14
3 March 1385

Bond of Thomas Newton, William Swafham, clerk, and Robert Uppegate in 1000 marks to pay 500 marks in several portions at certain days in the church of St Botolph, Aldgate, to dame Margaret, widow of Thomas Graunson, knight, and Roger de Beauchamp, esquire, of co. Bedford. [*French*]

On 18 July 1387 the said Margaret and Roger acknowledged satisfaction.

4 March 1385

Memorandum that Thomas Gisors having demanded by bill from John Ware, son and executor of Margery de Croidon[1], divers charters and muniments relating to the inheritance of Agnes his wife due to her by the will of Richard de Croidon her father, the said John Ware on 15 July 1383 brought into court a charter of Edward III and forty-five other deeds in four boxes and a hamper. Thereupon John Philipot claimed the deeds on the ground that if Agnes died without issue the tenements devised would remain to him for life. The deeds were sealed by John Ware and kept in court. On the death of John Philipot, John and Agnes appeared in court and the deeds were delivered to the latter.

9 March 1385

John Lynford, esquire, and George Cressy, his brother, were mainprised to keep the peace with John Walworth, vintner, and Robert Shirwode.

Similar mainprise of the said John and Robert.

Membr. 14 *b*
1 March 1385

In an action for debt against Gilbert Lyrp, baker, and Alice his wife at the suit of Roger Elys and Alice his wife for the sum of 12s, a foreign attachment was valued and delivered to the plaintiffs, *viz.* a bed of "*blu*," 6s 8d, and half a dozen pewter vessels[2], 4s 7d, under security to answer therefor *etc.*

Membr. 15
[*13 Oct. 1384*]

The following[3] were summoned for the election of Nicholas Brembre, knight, mayor, A° 8 Ric. II (1384). [The occupa-

[1] See Husting Rolls, 103 (10), 106 (119). Margery, widow of William de Ware, married Richard de Croydone, fishmonger, who left to her by will a life-interest in certain tenements with remainder to his daughter Agnes, who married Thomas Gisors, and further remainder to his daughter Margaret, who married John Philipot.

[2] *Dimidia duodena vasi stannei.*

[3] In accordance with the Act of Common Council of 31 July 1384, laying down that the election of the mayor should take place annually

tions of the councilmen are added from the list on the *cedula*.]

TOWER: *Common Council*, William Tonge, vintner, Hugh Sprot, fishmonger, Hugh Boys, ironmonger, and Thomas Evesham, grocer.

John Northwick, Thomas Garnet, Richard Brangweyn, William Permay, Richard Haydok, Nicholas Wytele, Thomas Alleye, Richard Loseye, William Denton, John Pays, John Welde, John Mordon.

BILLINGSGATE: *Common Council*, Gilbert Maunfeld, ironmonger, John Wade, fishmonger, John Beaufront, woolman, and Thomas Girdelere, corder.

Thomas Lincolle, Simon Rous, John Claydon, John Claveryng, William Reynwell, John Vigerous, John Denner, Thomas Blosse.

ALDGATE: *Common Council*, William Cressewyk and Richard Morel, woolman.

William Badby, John Halstede, Roger Crede, Thomas atte Nasp, Thomas Clayman.

LIME STREET: *Common Council*, John Clapschethe, poulterer, and Richard Gregory, ironmonger.

John Bradle, John Plot.

CORDWAINER STREET: *Common Council*, Robert Lyndeseye, tailor, William Pountfret, skinner, Geoffrey Waldern, draper, Robert Harengeye, mercer, Richard Hatfeld, grocer, and John Hoo, grocer.

Henry Stacy, William Culham, Andrew Coggeshale, Thomas Sibsay, Thomas Heyward, John Bradfeld, Robert Dane, John Chyngford, John Sutton, John Wyncelowe, Simon Aylesham, Thomas atte Mille, Mark Ernele.

COLEMAN STREET: *Common Council*, William Kyng, draper, and Robert Havelok, ironmonger.

John Shelford, Richard Whityngton, Thomas Chapman, Richard Glemesford, Thomas Bigood.

on the feast of the Translation of S[t] Edward (13 Oct.), and that the mayor with the assent of sixteen aldermen at least should cause the Common Council to be summoned against that day, with others of the more sufficient men of the city, to make the same election *etc*. *Cal. of Letter Book H*, p. 241. For the development of the city electorate, see *The Times, City of London Book*, 1927, pp. 1–4.

CHEAP: *Common Council*, John Boseham, mercer, John Shadworth, mercer, John Fressh, mercer, John Frankeleyn, Geoffrey Grigge, vintner, Thomas Makwilliam, grocer.

Richard Russel, Richard Plot, Thomas Pope, William Potenham, Henry Godyn, John Sevesterre, John Pigeon, William Hide, William Chichely, John Viaunde, Richard Goodchild, Thomas Vynent, Thomas Ottelee, John Wyght, John Salle, Thomas Neel, Simon Wynchecombe, William Waddesworth, Thomas Austyn.

LANGBOURN: *Common Council*, Thomas Bonaunter, tapicer, John Dyk, tapicer, William Fizhugh, goldsmith, and John Studele, draper.

Richard Bengeo, John Hatfeld, Robert Honyford, Richard Estbrok, Richard Toky, Thomas Moraunt.

BISHOPSGATE: *Common Council*, Henry Herbury, vintner, John Sibile, woolman, Peter Torold, skinner, and Adam Ratteseye, hostiller.

Bartholomew Mildenale, John Cheverel, Thomas atte Swan, Godfrey Cost, Stephen Sewale, Bartholomew Berford.

CORNHILL: *Common Council*, Walter Pykenham, skinner, Richard Manhale, chandler, William Wangford, draper, and Thomas Irlond, skinner.

Robert Langeton, John Pynchon, Thomas Birch, Michael Trenthennek, Thomas Hardegray, Gilbert Hoo, John Barri, Richard Smyth, Thomas Leuesham, John Gofaire, John Cook, chandler, John Langhorn, John Claidich, pewterer.

BRIDGE: *Common Council*, Walter Doget, vintner, Walter Sibile, stockfishmonger, John Kirton, stockfishmonger, Robert Little, fishmonger, John Pountfreit, saddler, and John Sandhurst, chandler.

William atte Sele, Thomas Mallyng, Richard Radewell, William Radewell, John Bonet, Walter Hernylle, Thomas Haukere, John Burwell, Henry ȝevele, Henry Petipas, William Bys, William atte Lee, Richard Blomvile, Richard Grace, Robert Brabason, John Wapelode, Thomas Palmere, John Gatyn, Laurence Glovere, Peter Blak, Nicholas Bonet, Henry Norfolk, Thomas Gandre.

FARRINGDON WITHIN AND WITHOUT: *Common Council*, Nicholas Twyford, knight, goldsmith, John Rote, skinner,

John Carbonel, goldsmith, Elias de Weston, butcher, Roger Excestre, saddler, and Simon atte Nax, cutler.

John Longe, senior, Robert Boxford, Walter ʒonge, Philip atte Downe, William Lyncoll, John Wakele, Thomas Paunton, Roger Crane, Bartholomew de Castre, Robert Brian, William Pershore, William Thornhill, John Walworth, Adam atte Watre, Robert Lynne, Nicholas Rote, Nicholas Jurdan, Thomas Brompton, Thomas Duke, Thomas Polle, John Wilman, John Kantoys, John Staunton, Richard Storm, John Davy, William Sallowe, Henry Asselyn, Robert atte Shoppe.

BASSIESHAWE: *Common Council*, William Hawe, mercer.

Simon Worstede, John Bokelsmyth, John Seintmor, John Wodecok, John White.

CRIPPLEGATE: *Common Council*, John Loveye, mercer, John Foster, goldsmith, Robert Asshcoumbe, broderer, Gilbert Prince, painter, and John Hugyn, *fynour*.

Henry Bamme, John Maymond, Thomas Willyngham, William Larke, John Merssh, John Ottele, Richard Rose, John Steynton, John Hore, Richard Serle, John Furneux, John Toures, John Fifhide.

ALDERSGATE: *Common Council*, Thomas Exton, goldsmith, John Dancastre, coppersmith, John Bathe, weaver, and John Bockyng, weaver.

John Knotte, Thomas Reynham, John Luton, Philip atte Vyne, Henry Markeby.

DOWGATE: *Common Council*, William Wotton, woolman, William Wight, woolman, Ralph Lobenham, draper, and John Wiltshire, grocer.

William Smyth, Geoffrey Maynard, Nicholas Snypston, Thomas Wight, Edmund Olyver, John Bisshop, William Frith, Peter Persholte.

VINTRY: *Common Council*, John Colshull, vintner, Thomas Medelane, vintner, John Tilneye, vintner, and William Sharpyng, vintner.

Thomas Goodsire, John Roket, John Edrop, John Norfolk, John Andrew, John Mockyng, Henry Brounfeld, John Wydemere, Matthew Passelewe, William Venour, Richard Lytlyngton, Gilbert Merssh, Paul Gisors, Gilbert Bonet.

WALBROOK: *Common Council*, William Olyver, skinner, Reginald Aleyn, grocer, John Basse, draper, and William Sudbury, tailor.

William Knyght, Thomas Strode, Richard Spark, William Horscroft, Roger Abbot, Robert Reson, John Creek, Elys de Thorp, Richard Burton, William Fremyngham, Thomas Weylond.

BROAD STREET: *Common Council*, William Wodehous, skinner, Adam Karlill, grocer, Edmund Hoddesdon, mercer, and Richard Willesdon, chandler.

John Clee, Thomas Barton, Benedict Cornewaille, John Clenaunt, John Wilton.

BREAD STREET: *Common Council*, Thomas Rolf, skinner, William Shiringham, mercer, John Ragenel, fishmonger, and John Scorfeyn, armourer.

Thomas Erl, Michael Cornewaille, William Rothewelle, Robert Ivyngho, William Stapulte, John Goldryng, John Sexteyn, John Selverton, Henry Mordon, Roger Parys, John Poynaunt, Henry atte Wode, John Manyngton.

QUEENHITHE: *Common Council*, William Neuport, fishmonger, William Baret, grocer, John Trigge, fishmonger, and Robert Parys, ironmonger.

Thomas Horsman, Henry Grenecobbe, John Chipstede, Hugh de Ware, Thomas Chaundeler, John Waryner, Richard Sprot, William Wynter.

CASTLE BAYNARD: *Common Council*, John Redyngge, brewer, John Vautort, fishmonger, John Asshurst, woodmonger, and William Shrympelmerssh, woodmonger.

John Asshlee, Nicholas Symcok, John Reynold, Walter Pakwode, Thomas Freke, Gilbert Asshurst.

CANDLEWICK STREET: John Walcote, draper, John Brownesbury, butcher, James Snow, draper, and William Ivory, butcher.

William Spaldyng, John Grantham, William Horston, William Gilot, John Olneye, John Jurdon, John Pope.

PORTSOKEN: *Common Council*, William Burford, bellmaker, and William Wodeward, founder.

William Dawe, Nicholas Longe.

A list of the Common Council, by wards, corresponding to the above list, but containing the occupations of the councilmen. *Cedula*

John Colman, son of Reginald Colman late citizen of London, apprentice of Thomas Horsman, vintner, was attached to answer his master for conduct contrary to his indentures of apprenticeship, wherein he covenanted to serve for seven years from 24 June 1384 and to do no damage beyond 12d a year and not to waste his master's goods. And whereas the said master on 15 Sept. the same year in the parish of St Michael Queenhithe delivered to Nicholas Leykman, his apprentice, the sum of 205 marks in gold and sent him to travel with other merchants to Bordeaux in Gascony, to trade therewith to the best of his ability, as apprentices are bound to do according to the custom of the city, at the same time sending the said John with him to learn the business, when the apprentices arrived at Plymouth with the gold, which lay in a locked box in a London ship, of which Lawrence Ches was master, together with other goods of the complainant, the said John went aboard, at a time when the other apprentice was ashore, and broke into the box and carried away the 205 marks, to the complainant's damage £200, whereof he prayed a remedy according to the law merchant and the custom of the city. Membr. 16 *25 Jan. 1385*

The said John, who was present in court, being sworn and examined according to the custom as to the taking away of the money, admitted the greater part but said nothing about the rest, and in answer to matters put to him by the court continually varied his story. Thereupon in order to obtain the truth the two apprentices were examined separately. Both of them swore that the said John had eloigned the money, but the apprentice Nicholas acknowledged having received from John, by the hands of John Mersham, the sum of £40.

A day was given on 1 Feb. that the court might be advised as to giving judgment, and the said John was committed to Ludgate for lack of mainprise, on which day it was considered that the said Thomas recover £100 13s 4d and £10 damages, beyond the £40 already repaid and £20 received from the friends of the said John by reason of the apprenticeship, and for default of payment the said John was committed to prison.

Afterwards on 23 Sept. 1385 the master prayed that the apprentice might be released to him on bail until 28 Sept. as he was so sick that his life was despaired of. The boy was returned to prison on that day, but on 15 Dec. the same year the master again asked that the apprentice might be released on bail until 24 June 1386 for the same reason, which was allowed by the court on condition that he save the sheriffs harmless.

16 Dec. 1384 Henry Herbury sued Thomas Blount for the sum of £3 17s 6d due for the making of two gutters on the defendant's house in the parish of St Mildred in the Poultry. Walter Kynton, cutler, agreed on behalf of the defendant to pay whatever the court should adjudge as due from him. Thereupon the sworn masons and carpenters of the city, being ordered to investigate the matter, reported that the duty of making the gutters lay with the defendant. John Dudecote, carpenter, who had provided the timber and nails, swore that his costs amounted to 12s 6d, which the said Walter paid. As regards the rest of the claim it was agreed that he should pay the plaintiff £3 5s on condition that if the plumber, who asked that sum for five weys of lead (*pro quinque wagis*), would take less, the balance should be repaid to him.

Membr. 16 *b*
14 Feb. 1385 Writ *de minis* ordering the mayor to put Christian Kyllemere to mainprise for keeping the peace with Hermann Vynthorpe, John Clyppyng, William de Borne, Alevinus de Brake, John de Attenderne, Brounus Decuf, Frowyn de Oppenskede, Henry de Hethe, Frowyn Stupyng, Goscalcus de Broke, Nicholas de Lewere, John Poke, James de St George and Hildebrand Ispelyngrothe[1]. Dated 14 Feb. 1385.

Return giving the names of Thomas Rolf, William Oliver, Walter Pykenham and John Fremelyngham, skinners, as mainpernors, under penalty of £100.

Memorandum that a writ of *certiorari* was sent to the

[1] See below, pp. 100, 143, for variants of these names.

mayor and sheriffs demanding the cause of imprisonment of James Bynd.

Return to Chancery by the mayor and sheriffs that it had been reported to them by credible persons that the said James used to make lonely journeys to divers parts of France and so had fallen under suspicion of being a spy who carried news of the king's counsels to those parts, and for this reason he had been arrested and detained in the king's gaol of Newgate.

In an action for debt against John Waltham, skinner, at the suit of Hermann van Datel, merchant of Almaine, for the sum of £21 due on a bond, a foreign attachment was valued by oath of William Wiltshyre and Edward Caumber, skinners, and delivered to the plaintiff under security to answer therefor *etc.*, as follows: 22 *tymber*[1] of *herwerk*[2], at 8s 4d the *tymber*, total 13 marks 10s; 2 furs of *cristigray*[3], 32s; one fur of *stranglyng*[4], 6s; and half a fur of *ruskyns*[5], 2s. Membr. 17 *b* *16 March 1385*

The Common Council of the eighth year of Richard II by wards. *Cedula* *1384–5*

[As on membr. 15 and *cedula*, with the following changes.]

Billingsgate, William Ancroft, mercer, *vice* Gilbert Maunfeld, ironmonger.

Broad Street, Beneyt Cornewaille, draper, *vice* Edmund Hoddesdon, mercer.

Cornhill, John Pynchon, draper, *vice* Thomas Irlond, skinner.

Candlewick Street, William Horston, draper, William Giles, butcher, Roger Mordon, skinner, William Spaldyng, tailor,

[1] *Sc. timber*, a package of 40 skins (i.e. half skins, 20 pairs). See *N.E.D.*

[2] *Sc.* hare-work, dressed hare-skins.

[3] *Cristigray* was a variety of grey or *gris* fur, which, according to the Liber Horn, fo. 249 *b*, was the back of the squirrel in winter. "*Memorandum qe Gris et bis est le dos en yver desquirel.*" It may mean Christmas grey, or cresty grey, i.e. tufty, full-coated, the fur then being at its best. J. Hodgkin considered the word to be a repetition, *gris de grey*.

[4] Squirrel in autumn. *Strandling est Squirel contre le feste Seint Michel. Ibid.* Probably from late Latin, *stragulum, strangulum, stragulatus*, i.e. of varied colour. At this period the squirrel's winter coat of grey was coming through the summer coat of red.

[5] Squirrel in summer. *Roskyn est desquirel en este. Ibid.*

vice John Walcote, draper, John Brownesbury, butcher, James Snow, draper, William Ivory, butcher.

Bridge, John Burwell, fishmonger, John Mokkyng, vintner, Richard Blomvylle, fishmonger, *vice* Walter Doget, vintner, Walter Sibile, stockfishmonger, John Sandhurst, chandler.

Dowgate, Nicholas Snypston, cordwainer, *vice* Ralph Lobenham, draper.

Queenhithe, Thomas Fraunkeleyn, chandler, *vice* William Neuport, fishmonger.

Castle Baynard, less John Redyngge, brewer.

Farringdon, Thomas Panton, goldsmith, William Lyncolle, saddler, John Hill, mercer, John Dorsete, butcher, William Pershore, *chaloner*, *vice* Nicholas Twyford, goldsmith, John Rote, skinner, John Carbonel, goldsmith, Elias de Weston, butcher, Roger Excestre, saddler.

Cheap, Geoffrey Crymelford, grocer, Thomas Austyn, mercer, Thomas Vynent, mercer, *vice* John Boseham, mercer, John Shadworth, mercer, John Fressh, mercer.

Aldersgate, Sir Nichol Twyford, goldsmith, Thomas Reynham, goldsmith, *vice* Thomas Exton, goldsmith, John Dancastre, coppersmith.

Cripplegate, add John Furneux, draper.

Bread Street, less William Shiringham, mercer.

Cordwainer Street, Robert Dane, mercer, *vice* Robert Harengeye, mercer.

Coleman Street, John Eston, mercer, *vice* William Kyng, draper, Robert Havelok, ironmonger.

Bassieshawe, no names given.

Dorso Oath of the Common Council, and penalty of 40d for absence without reasonable excuse. [*French*]

Membr. 18 *21 July 1385* Simon Wynchecoumbe, late one of the sheriffs of London, brought a bill of complaint against Thomas Beton, baker, who had received from him the office of janitor of his compter[1] in Walbrook on 28 Sept. 1383 and had undertaken to guard all prisoners until Michaelmas following, saving the said Simon harmless, as appeared by his deed. Nevertheless a

[1] The sheriff's office, at which plaints were entered, also used as a place of detention for defendants arrested by their bodies to answer in pleas.

certain Simon Stacy, shipman, who had been arrested on 11 Jan. 1384 at the suit of John Brencheley, esquire, on a writ of *justicies* for detinue of chattels to the value of £200, escaped on 9 Feb. 1384. Thereupon John Brencheley sued the plaintiff by bill in the parliament[1] held at Salisbury after Easter, the bill being endorsed and sent to Chancery, whence a writ was issued summoning the plaintiff to answer John Brencheley there. Finally an award[2] was given that Simon Stacy had been delivered from prison without due process of law and the plaintiff was condemned in £200, for which John Brenchele was suing execution. Although the plaintiff had required the defendant to save him harmless, he had refused, to the plaintiff's damage £1000. [*French*]

The parties appeared on 24 July, when the plaintiff produced an agreement dated 28 Sept. 1383, whereby John Knesworth, John Bally, clerk, William Averey, clerk, Edmund Fraunceys, Bartholomew Berford, John Gravesende, Stephen Maynard, John Cook, *corsour*, Thomas Beton, baker, William Fader, carpenter, John Staunton, brewer, Robert Brampton, saddler, and John Groos, baker, received the office of janitor of the compter in Walbrook and custody of the prison for a year from Michaelmas 1383, covenanting to answer therefor and to save the sheriff harmless under penalty of the goods of each and all of them.

The defendant, after the bill and deed had been read, pleaded that in the record of Chancery between John Brenchelay and Simon Wynchecoumbe, the latter acknowledged that he had Simon Stacy in his custody at the time when John Brenchelay delivered to him the writ of *justicies*, and as the said John did not produce pledges for prosecution or begin or demand that process be made, the said Simon and his colleague John More had liberated Simon Stacy on 26 Jan. 1384, and between the reception of the writ and that

[1] I.e. by petition to parliament. For procedure on such petitions, see B. Wilkinson, *The Chancery under Edward III*, pp. xvii, 41, 81–3. A petition against a sheriff of London was a claim against the Crown, see Ehrlich, *Proceedings against the Crown* (*Oxford Studies in Social and Legal History*), p. 186; Holdsworth, *Hist. Eng. Law*, I, pp. 354–5, II, pp. 419–20.

[2] *Fuist agarde*. But notice that in the record of Chancery the ordinary phrase of judgment is used—*consideratum est*.

date there had been several Sheriffs' Courts. Further the defendant pleaded that after the 26 Jan., when, as the sheriff admitted in Chancery, the prisoner had been liberated, the latter had not been arrested or detained in his compter on account of any action of the said John Brenchelay. And accordingly, since the plaintiff and his colleague had voluntarily released Simon Stacy, the defendant prayed judgment whether the plaintiff could maintain his action against him contrary to the record in Chancery, of which the tenor was as follows:

Pleas before the lord king in his Chancery at Westminster on the octave of St Hilary A^{o} 8 *Ric. II* (20 *Jan.* 1385)

Writ reciting that John de Brencheleye had complained by a petition exhibited in the last parliament, that whereas Simon Stacy had been arrested by virtue of a writ of *justicies* and John de Brencheleye had subsequently gone abroad in the company of John, duke of Lancaster, a precept had been issued to the sheriffs to keep the said Simon in custody till a certain day, but the sheriff, Simon de Wynchecoumbe, by arrangement with the said Simon Stacy, had delivered him from prison long before the day mentioned in the precept, and that in cunning excuse for thus
Membr. 18 *b* liberating him, he had procured a writ in Chancery demanding the cause of the arrest of the said Simon, and that consequent upon the return of the writ, which was to the effect that the said Simon was detained in prison at the suit of Hugh de Brencheleye, a precept had been issued from Chancery ordering the delivery of the said Simon if he were detained for no other reason—although the said Simon had already been liberated—wherefore the said John de Brencheleye prayed the king in parliament for a remedy. Accordingly the sheriffs are now ordered to warn Simon de Wynchecoumble to appear in Chancery on the Thursday following to answer for his contempt and deceit and to show cause why he should not make satisfaction to John de Brencheleye to the value of the goods and chattels claimed. Dated at Westminster 8 Oct. 1384.

In obedience to the writ Simon de Wynchecoumbe appeared in Chancery and declared that there was no custom in the city with regard to a writ of *justicies* other than the common law. He pleaded that on 1 Jan. 1384 a plea of detinue of chattels had been affirmed at the suit of Hugh de Brencheleye, whereby Simon Stacy had been taken and detained in Newgate, that afterwards a writ of *justicies* on behalf of John de Brencheleye had been delivered to the sheriffs, upon which writ no pledges for prosecution were ever offered on the part of the plaintiff nor any process made or demanded, and that on 4 Jan. the king sent his writ under the privy seal directing that, whereas John de Brencheleye was departing for Calais to join the duke of Lancaster on the king's business, the sheriffs keep Simon Stacy under arrest until Easter or until John de Brencheleye returned, if this were consonant with the laws and customs of the city. Afterwards on 8 Jan. the king sent a writ of *certiorari* demanding the cause of the taking and detaining of Simon Stacy, to which it was returned that he was kept in prison at the suit of Hugh de Brencheleye, esquire. Thereupon friends of Simon Stacy moved the sheriff for his delivery, asserting that his detaining in prison was against the law, because John de Brencheleye did not find pledges for prosecution on the writ nor begin or continue process as he ought, nor did Hugh de Brencheleye prosecute his plaint after the above return. Accordingly the sheriffs, after taking the opinion of wise and discreet men of the city as to whether Simon Stacy could be legally detained, released him on 26 Jan., before which day and after the receipt of the writ of *justicies* divers Sheriffs' Courts had been held (at which process could have been made). Afterwards on 2 Feb. the king sent a writ ordering the release of Simon Stacy because divers men had mainprised him in Chancery; without that[1] Simon Stacy had been arrested for any other cause than here stated or that Simon de Wynchecoumbe had procured the writ of *certiorari*.

John de Brencheleye, while protesting that he did not acknowledge that no pledges for prosecution had been offered or process made, said that whereas Simon de Wynchecoumbe had admitted that the *justicies* had been received long before the precept (to detain Simon Stacy until Easter) and whereas it was clear from the return to the *certiorari* that the said Simon was detained in prison at the suit of both the said John de Brencheleye and Hugh de Brencheleye[2], and thus his arrest and detaining ought to be understood as having legally taken place at the suit of John

[1] *Absque hoc quod.* These words are difficult to construe in modern terms. According to Jacob, *Law Dictionary*, they are "words of exception made use of in a traverse"; as the defendant pleads that such a thing was done at B *etc.*, *absque hoc*, that it was done at *etc.* The French equivalent is *sans ceo*, and pleadings in English have "without that." It is a direct denial of a statement of fact made in a declaration or pleading, and it might be taken as an issue for the trial of the action. In later days *et non* could be used instead of *absque hoc*. See Tidd's *Practice* (1821 ed.), II, p. 714.

[2] Apparently the sheriff had misrepresented his return to the writ, see above.

de Brencheleye, he prayed judgment as to whether Simon de Wynchecoumbe ought to be admitted to verify his statement that Simon Stacy had been detained at the suit of Hugh alone.

Whereupon the pleadings having been heard, and it being understood that the Sheriffs' Courts were held on no fixed days but at the discretion of the sheriffs[1], and that no notice had been given to John de Brencheleye of the holding of any court, and the sheriff did not claim to have summoned him to any court, in consequence of which judgment might have been given against him for failure to attend, and without such judgment the other party, being attached to answer, ought not legally to have been acquitted, and also on the ground that Simon de Wynchecoumbe could not be admitted to verify that Simon Stacy had been arrested for some other reason than that stated on his own return to the writ, and further because it did not appear that there was any great need[2] for prosecutions on writs of *justicies* to be affirmed by pledges, for these and other reasons it seemed to the court that Simon de Wynchecoumbe had not said anything to clear himself. Accordingly it was considered that John de Brencheleye recover against him chattels to the value of £200, that being the amount claimed against Simon Stacy, and that the question of damages and the punishment of Simon de Wynchecoumbe for his deceit be left for further consideration[3].

Writ of *mittimus*, dated 3 May 1385, to the Mayor and Aldermen that the tenor of the proceedings in Chancery had been sent to them in order that they might proceed in the action of Simon de Wynchecoumbe against John Knesworth, Thomas Beton, baker, and others.

The plaintiff, Simon Wynchecoumbe, did not acknowledge the allegation of the defendant but said that Simon Stacy escaped and was delivered from prison without his assent and by default of the defendant, who was his servant and gaoler, and that the defendant ought not to be excused on the ground of allegations made against the plaintiff, because, although the defaults and actions of a sheriff's servant were the defaults of the sheriff as regards other

[1] See below, p. 114, n. 1, as to the days of the Sheriffs' Courts.

[2] *Non videtur quod multum indigeat quod....*

[3] This is an interesting and early instance of pleadings in Chancery according to common law. Though it is clear that the Chancery in early days exercised a common law as well as an equitable jurisdiction, actual records of such actions are very few. See *Select Cases in Chancery* (Seld. Soc.), pp. xv, 104; Holdsworth, *Hist. Eng. Law*, I, pp. 449–51, 450, n. 3.

parties, the servant was bound to answer the sheriff as between themselves. And whereas he said in Chancery that Simon Stacy was delivered (by the advice of wise and discreet men *etc.*), the truth was that he escaped by default of the defendant, and the wise and discreet men were the defendant and the others mentioned in the agreement. Accordingly, since the defendant did not deny that Simon Stacy did, in fact, escape, he prayed judgment. Membr. 19

The defendant denied that he advised the sheriff to liberate Simon Stacy, and he was prepared to verify his denial, if he could make it the issue of the action. Moreover he was willing to verify that Simon Stacy who was delivered on 26 Jan. was not arrested and detained in the compter after that date, and as regards any escape before that date he had no need to answer.

After further pleadings and adjournments, on 27 Feb. 1386 the parties appeared, when it seemed to the court that the defendant was bound to save the plaintiff harmless notwithstanding any answer the latter was alleged to have made, in case of any escape of the said Simon Stacy, and that the defendant did not keep his covenant. Therefore it was considered that the plaintiff recover against him the sum of £200 which John de Brencheley had recovered against the plaintiff in Chancery, and that the defendant be committed to prison, while the question of damages be left for further consideration.

Afterwards the king sent three writs, *primum*, *sicut alias* and *sicut pluries*, demanding the record and process of the above action to be returned to Chancery, and the Mayor and Aldermen returned the *sicut alias* with a roll attached thereto, containing the record and process.

Note that Thomas Beton afterwards prosecuted a writ of error before Robert Bealknap and his fellow-justices at St Martin le Grand, and on 6 Feb. 1388 Simon Wynchecoumbe reported that Thomas Beton had discontinued his action and was still at large, wherefore he prayed that he be arrested and again committed to prison, which was done. Membr. 19 *b*

Mittimus and copy proceedings sent by Chancery. *Cedule*

Membr. 20
18 May 1385

John Knesworth was summoned to answer Simon Wynchecombe, late sheriff, as above.

The defendant, while not acknowledging the date of the covenant or anything in it, pleaded that at the time when it was drawn up, he was a prisoner of the said sheriff in his compter in Walbrook and that under duress of imprisonment he was forced to make and seal the covenant. The plaintiff said that at the time mentioned the defendant was *sui juris* and at large. On this issue a jury found for the defendant. Therefore it was considered that the said Simon Wynchecombe take nothing by his bill but be in mercy.

7 March 1385

Mutual quitclaims of Luke Bragadyn, merchant of Venice, and Nicholas Brembre, knight.

Membr. 20 *b*
12 June 1385

Writ, dated 12 June 1385, to the mayor, directing that if William Coudeberk and Simon Brame of Ghent, who were before the king's council on matters concerning their town, should be willing to put on record before the mayor that William Matys (whom the mayor had lately arrested with his goods as an enemy of the king belonging to Bruges) was a native of Ghent and a loyal friend of Ghent, then the mayor was to deliver him and his goods from arrest and allow him to go where he would.

Return to the above in a *cedula* attached to the writ: The mayor had summoned William Coudeberk and Simon Brame, who testified as abovesaid, but did not know whether the goods arrested with William Matys were his own or not. Thereupon the mayor had summoned William Matys, who swore that all the goods were his own and none belonged to the king's enemies of Bruges. But previous to the receipt of the king's writs, Richard Odyham, Matthew Passelewe and John Sutton, citizens of London, had come and complained that the goods in question belonged not only to the said William but also to Wltre Gaffulkyn, one of the king's enemies of Bruges, the two being partners (*intermercatores*) in the goods, and that certain of the king's enemies belonging both to Bruges and Sluys, in time of truce between the king and France, had taken and carried away divers goods belonging to the complainants from a ship sailing from Zeeland to

London at a place called "Vergat[1]," contrary to the truce, *viz.* three bales of battery belonging to Richard of the value of £63, a hundred bales of *roche* alum belonging to Matthew of the value of £140 and a bale of Cyprus cotton belonging to John of the value of £8, wherefore they prayed that the goods of the said William Matys might be arrested, as being the goods both of William Matys and Wltre Gaffulkyn, and that the portion belonging to the latter be delivered to them as a reprisal in part satisfaction for their own goods. It was for this reason that the mayor had arrested the goods, which he could not disarrest till he had further command from the king, but he had liberated the said William Matys in obedience to the writ.

Thomas Wilyngham, leatherseller, was mainprised by Edmund Haringeye, John Swanton, William Belhomme and Richard Storteford to be obedient to the mayor and other officers of the city, to take no part in any congregation or covin which might lead to the harm of the people, and to keep the peace, under penalty of £100. *14 July 1385*

Richard Odyham, chamberlain of the city, brought a bill relating that the late John de Heylesdon, mercer, had left by will to his two orphan daughters the sum of £400, and whereas this money had not been paid to them, the petitioner by virtue of his office had on 13 Oct. 1384 arrested the sum of £178 16s ½d in the hands of Robert Harengeye, mercer, who owed that amount to the executors of the will in payment for 42 hundreds and 32½ ells of *Westvale large*[2] at 50s the hundred, total £105 13s 6½d, and 48 hundreds and 90 ells of *Pitlyng large*[3] at 30s the hundred,[4] total £73 2s 6d, Membr. 21 *16 June 1385*

[1] Veersche Gat (Walcheren, Holland). See *Cal. Close Rolls*, 1385–9, p. 2, for a writ following on this return and ordering that if Matys found security to answer the complainants, his goods were to be freed from arrest.

[2] Westwale is said by *N.E.D.* to be cloth of Westphalia in Germany, used for packing and for covering a table. *Earl of Derby's Expedition* (Camd. Soc.), pp. 35, 168.

[3] See Pickling, Picklin, Pyglyng, in *N.E.D.*, apparently a kind of canvas or coarse linen.

[4] The hundred of both cloths contained 120 ells at 5d and 3d the ell respectively. Cf. "1545 *Rates of Customs* cjb, Pyglyng the C. elles contey. xii score elles xxs." *N.E.D.*

which he had bought from them on 15 Aug. 1384, payment being due on 24 June 1385. The chamberlain prayed that the said Robert be summoned to find sufficient security for paying the money into the Chamber to the use of the orphans. [*French*]

The said Robert, appearing on summons on 16 June, acknowledged buying the cloth and said that the price was payable by certain portions, the first being due on 24 June. He entered into a recognisance for payment, and for greater security John Fressh became surety for him in all his goods and chattels. Afterwards full payment was made, £138 16s ½d being received by John Chircheman[1] and £40 by Thomas Rolf, skinner, on the said John's behalf.

And whereas the testator directed that if one of his daughters died under age £100 of her share should be paid to her sister, and since the said Margaret so died, John Gournay who had married Alice the other sister came before the Mayor and Aldermen on 27 Nov. 1392 and acknowledged receipt of £300 from John Chircheman.

31 July 1385 Letter of attorney from Luke Bragadyn, merchant of Venice, to James Dyne of Florence, to sue and defend on his behalf against Guydo de Port and Peter Gracyan, merchants of Lucca. Dated 29 July 1385.

Bond of Peter Gracian, merchant of Lucca, to James Dyne of Florence in £410 due on 1 April following, to pay that sum in the manner and form contained in an indenture enrolled in Guildhall, between Nicholas Brembre, knight, and the said Peter and Luke Bragadyn. Dated 29 July 1385.

Membr. 21 *b*
3 Aug. 1385 The following merchants of the Hanse of Almaine[2] came before the Mayor and Aldermen in the Chamber of the Guildhall: Henry Judex, Hermann Vyntthorp, John Clippyng, Alfunus Brake, Henry Wykethe, Henry de Heythe, Frowyn Stopyng, Andrew Kelmere, John Sachell, Hermann Datell, John Affelyng, John de Holthowse, "Autresward Magist9

[1] John Chircheman, alderman, acted as trustee for the orphans. *Cal. of Letter Book H*, p. 267.
[2] See above, pp. 90, 143.

del Nave[1]," who mainprised each other, under penalty of forfeiture of life and all their goods and chattels, not to leave the city without special permission of the mayor, and further that they would help by letters and all other means possible to secure the liberation of divers English merchants arrested with their goods in Prussia (*Pruys*).

Conrad Honterholp, Ellrand Yspelynthrode, Nicholas Lure, Tydemann van de Walde, Arnald Wandeler, John de Attenderne, Brunferner, John van Aake, Stradeo Platoun and Colardus le Cherpetire, merchants of the Hanse, were similarly sworn. *7 Aug. 1385*

John de Northwych, fletcher, was mainprised by William Waxwell and Saykyn Perkesdale, fletchers, under penalty of £40, to keep the peace and obey the officers of the city and the masters of his mistery, and to make good bolts (*petiliones*) and arrows. *15 Sept. 1385*

Membr. 22

Bond of Luke Bragadyn, Lombard, to Nicholas Brembre, knight, in £500, to perform covenants in a deed of equal date. Dated 1 April. [*Latin and French*] *10 July 1385*

Covenant, whereby Luke Bragadyn granted to Nicholas Brembre, knight, and Peter Gracyan, that he would not bring any action against the latter or cause him to be arrested within the term of seven years, unless the said Nicholas acknowledged that he had received satisfaction of his own claims against the said Peter. The other parties agreed that before 1 Aug. the said Peter should render account before arbitrators to the said Luke, and that the amount of any debt should be clearly stated, so that the said Luke might demand payment either after seven years, or before, if the said Nicholas had received satisfaction. Dated 1 April. [*French*]

Memorandum that Thomas Newton, William Swafham, clerk, and Robert Uppegate deposited in the hands of the chamberlain the sum of 100 marks in a sealed bag, that amount being due on 24 June to Margaret, widow of Thomas *1 July 1385*

[1] Probably means that Autresward was master of the ship bringing the above-mentioned Hanse merchants to London.

de Graunson, knight, and Roger Beauchamp, esquire, of co. Beds, but unclaimed by them.

Membr. 22 *b*
9 Feb. 1385

Richard Glemesford, merchant and fellmonger of London, demanded an account from William Upton his apprentice by a bill directed, according to custom, to the Mayor and Aldermen, in which he complained that on 26 Oct. 1384 at Middelburgh, a merchant town in Zeeland, the said William received by the hands of Thomas Stokton the sum of £40 in gold to trade therewith on behalf of the plaintiff and had refused to render account thereof, to the plaintiff's damage 100s. [*French*]

The defendant, who had been committed to Ludgate prison for lack of mainprise, was brought into court and admitted receipt of the money. Thereupon the court assigned John Reche, Thomas Brawhyng and John Swanton as auditors, and Wednesday 22 March was appointed for hearing the account. On that day the defendant said that he bought from Rubryȝt van Coloyne 3100 *calabers*[1] at a price of £20 7s 8d g̊, one *tymbre*[2] and a half of *bevres* for 51s g̊, 21 *oteres* from Hugh van Bruge for 21s g̊, 3 *furrours*[3] of lamb for 21s g̊, one *pilche*[4] *bevere* for 33s 4d g̊ and a barrel for the *calabers* for 18 g̊. He also paid 4 g̊ for carriage to the ship, 16 g̊ for toll, 12 g̊ for *skutage*[5] and 40 g̊ for a sword, and he had in gold and silver the sum of £3 17s 10d. The above goods and money amounted to £30[6], which he had delivered to his master. He asked that the sum of 26s 8d should be allowed for his board during the four weeks he was at Middelburgh.

[1] The Calabrian squirrel.
[2] 40 half-skins, i.e. 20 pairs.
[3] *Sc. furrura*, a made-up fur.
[4] Med. Lat. *pellicea*, an outer garment of fur.
[5] This is unlikely to be scutage in the feudal sense. Probably derived from *schout* and variants, a municipal or port officer in the Low Countries. Thus the word might denote the due known as "water-bailage" in London.
[6] Counting the Flemish groat at 12 to the Flemish shilling, the apprentice had spent £27 1s 6d Flemish and had in hand £3 17s 10d sterling, which amounted altogether to £30 sterling. This would make £27 1s 6d equal to £26 2s 2d sterling and the Flemish £ amount to a fraction less than 19s 3½d.

The plaintiff prayed judgment on the ground that the defendant had only answered for £31 6s 8d, and asked that the balance of £8 13s 4d should be charged against the defendant. The auditors agreed and on 12 July brought their record of the account into court. It was considered that the defendant pay the balance, and as he was unable to do so, he was committed to Ludgate until *etc.*

Marriage settlement, in the form of a bond and defeasance, between Walter Doget, vintner, Nicholas Brembre, knight, and Henry Vannere, vintner, in order to purchase lands and tenements to the value of £300 for the benefit of John Doget, son of the above Walter, and Idonea his wife, daughter of John Birlyngham and Margaret his wife, which Margaret had married John Philipot as her second husband. Of the £300, the sum of £100 had been left to Idonea by her father, £100 had been contributed as a free gift by her stepfather John Philipot and the remaining £100 was to be supplied by Walter Doget, the father of the bridegroom. In case the latter died, Idonea was to maintain any children of the marriage till they came of age, were married or were otherwise provided for. [*Latin and French*] *15 July 1385*

Nicholas Brembre having died, Henry Vannere came into court and asked that the bond be cancelled, since Walter Doget and the above-mentioned Idonea had gone the way of all flesh (*viam universe carnis sunt ingressi*). *4 Sept. 1394*

Memorandum that Thomas Cheyne, esquire, before setting out on a pilgrimage to Rome, delivered to Nicholas Luke of Florence, Lombard, a small sealed box, called a "*trussyng-coffre*," containing divers goods and jewels, and afterwards died on the journey. The box was claimed by John Cheyne, knight, his executor, and was delivered to him by the said Nicholas Luke, under surety of William Wadesworth, grocer, to save him harmless against any future claim. Membr. 23 *12 Dec. 1385*

Letters patent, dated 16 March 1383, reciting that on 3 Aug. 1382[1] the king had granted to John Clanvou, knight, Nicholas Sharnesfeld, knight, William More, citizen and

[1] *Cal. Pat. Rolls*, 1381–5, pp. 164, 237.

vintner, Paul Gysors, William Fettyngdon, chaplain, and John Boudiche, chaplain, a messuage with a wharf and other appurtenances in Wyndegoslane[1] in Dowgate, of an annual value of 8 marks and formerly held from the king by Richard Lyons, which messuage had escheated to the king because Richard Lyons was a bastard and died without an heir, as appeared by inquisitions made before William Walleworth, late mayor and the king's escheator in the city, whereof the tenor was returned to Chancery. The king now, with the assent of William More, who had lately paid the king 203 marks for the messuage, and with the assent of the said John, Nicholas, Paul and William, John Boudiche having died, and also because they had returned the letters patent to Chancery for cancellation, grants the messuage and wharf to his beloved servant, John Sliegh[2], and his heirs, the said John Sliegh having repaid the said 203 marks to William More.

The above letters patent were enrolled at the request of John Sliegh.

Membr. 23 *b*
18 Jan. 1386

Writ of protection, dated 28 Nov. 1385, in favour of Elias Thorpe, citizen and merchant of London, who was then about to cross the sea on the king's service in the company of John de Drayton, knight, captain of the castle of Guynes[3], for the defence of the same.

By virtue of the above the said Elias was on 18 Jan. 1386 dismissed without a day in suits of debt and account brought against him by John atte Hulle of Sabrichesworth[4].

Membr. 24
1 Feb. 1386

Nicholas Pays, joiner, being deprived of his natural senses, so that he knew not either how to govern himself or to guard and manage his goods according to reason, was entrusted by the Mayor and Aldermen to Peter Feriby, who had

[1] This lane is called Wendegaynelane in 1477, see Husting Roll, 207 (31), perhaps by confusion with the Wendegaynslane or Turnagain Lane in Farringdon Without, which appears to have been a cul-de-sac. The original forms of the name Wendegos, Wadegose, Wyndegos, Wendegoos suggest a different derivation. See *Cal. Pat. Rolls*, 1381–5, pp. 164, 463; *ibid.* 1452–61, p. 286; *Cal. of Husting Wills*, I, p. 149. Harbin's *Dictionary of London*, pp. 594, 619.

[2] Sliegh was king's butler and coroner of London. *Cal. of Letter Book H*, p. 398.

[3] Guines.

[4] Sawbridgeworth co. Herts.

married the daughter of the said Nicholas, in order that he might be supported from the possessions which God had given him, in a manner agreeable to his rank and in accordance with good faith and reason. Accordingly his goods were delivered to the said Peter for so long as his sickness should continue, on condition that the said Peter provide him with food, clothing, bed, shoes and all other necessaries, and render a yearly account before auditors appointed by the Mayor and Aldermen. It was further agreed that if the said Nicholas should die without regaining his senses, and if a will now produced in court, which was said to have been made while he was still *compos mentis*, were proved by law to be valid, then the remainder of his goods should be distributed by the terms of the will, but otherwise they should be expended by the Mayor and Aldermen for the good of his soul and other works of charity, provided always that if by the mercy of God he recovered from his languor, his goods and chattels should be restored to his own disposition. For the fulfilment of the above conditions the said Peter entered into a bond of all his possessions, and for greater security Henry Grenecobbe, dyer, Thomas Haukere, ironmonger, and Gilbert Asshurst, woodmonger, entered into like bonds. John Pays, brother of the said Nicholas, Thomas Fraunkeleyn, chandler, and John Waryner, neighbours of the said Peter, were appointed to see that the said Nicholas was well provided for and to warn the mayor of any default.

Afterwards on 8 Feb. 1386 the sum of £92 4s was delivered to the said Peter by Richard Odyham, chamberlain, and on 11 Aug. a further sum of £11. On 18 Aug. the sum of £10 lent by Nicholas to the late king was paid out, and on 24 Dec. the chamberlain delivered two pieces of silver and a broken piece of silver valued at 40s and two mazers valued at 13s 4d.

Letter of attorney from William Wetenale, taverner, to Peter Bragadyn, merchant of Venice, to recover and sue for debts due to him. Dated 1 Feb. 1386. Membr. 24 *b* *21 Feb. 1386*

Memorandum that on 2 Nov. 1385 William Bonhostel,

Gascon, borrowed from Mark Ernele, grocer, in his house in the parish of St Antholin, the sum of £12 in silver, for which he gave as pledge 5 silver buckles plated with gold (*firmacula argentea foris platata cum platis de auro*) weighing 14 oz., which he asserted to be of pure gold—a statement which was believed by the said Mark and several others, including goldsmiths. Afterwards, however, John Botisham, goldsmith, and other masters of the Goldsmiths, perceiving that the buckles were merely plated with gold in deception of the people, arrested them in the hands of the said Mark, supposing them to be forfeitable. The sheriffs likewise claimed them as forfeit by reason of their office. Accordingly the buckles were handed over by the mayor under his seal to John Fressh, alderman, to be kept until the Mayor and Aldermen had decided to whom they ought to be delivered. Afterwards on 25 Feb. 1386 the buckles were broken and found to be as alleged. And because the said Mark did not offer the buckles for sale or suspect that there was any deceit, but as soon as he learnt of it, caused the said William to be arrested and confined in Newgate, he was held to be innocent of any deception, and it was considered by the court and the sheriffs that the buckles should be returned to him in part satisfaction of his debt. On 13 April they were valued by John Forster, Robert Wadevyll and Michael Brusshele, goldsmiths, as follows: the gold, weighing 4 oz. 9 dwt. at 15s the oz., £3 6s 9d; and the silver, weighing 9 oz. 1 dwt. at 2s 2d the oz., 19s 7d; total, £4 6s 4d.

Membr. 25
17 March 1386

Memorandum that the mayor and good men of Dancastre[1] sent a letter under their common seal reciting that Richard Lewer of their town had consigned 22 sarplers of wool to his servant John Caldham at Middelburgh to trade therewith, which John sold the wool to John Olneye of London and afterwards died. They were informed that John Olneye had in his hands a certain sum of money arising from the sale of the wool and divers bonds, *viz.* two bonds of John Kymbel of London to John Caldham and John Olneye for £80, of which £20 was still in arrears, a bond of James Fane,

[1] Doncaster co. Yorks.

Lombard, to the same John and John for £60, of which £10 was in arrears, and another bond of John Wodecok and Robert Dane to John Olneye in 200 marks to save him harmless as against the executors of John Caldham by reason of certain sums received for a portion of the wool by the said Richard and his wife Katherine. Now whereas the said Richard was dead, they prayed that the said arrears and the bonds might be delivered to Thomas atte Wode and the aforesaid Katherine, now his wife, executrix of Richard's will. Dated at Doncaster 28 Feb. 1386.

The same day another letter was received from Alexander, archbishop of York, certifying that Katherine, widow of Richard Lewer, was named as executrix in his will and that administration had been granted to her. Dated at his manor by Westminster 7 March 1386.

John Olneye willingly appeared in court and produced the following documents: (1) a bond of John Kimbel of London to John Caldam of Pickering and John Olnay of London in £176, by reason of a loan, payable to them or bearer at Christmas 1383, the bond being defeasible if £28 were paid within 20 days of Christmas and £60 at the Easter following. (2) Another bond from the same to the same for £25 payable on 3 May 1384. (3) A bond from Robert Dane and John Wodecok, mercers of London, in 200 marks to secure the payment of 100 marks to the same at Michaelmas 1384.

The two bonds relating to John Kymbel, together with a letter touching a debt of James Fane, were delivered to Thomas atte Wode and the said Katherine. The bond of Robert Dane and John Wodecok was returned to them. Memorandum that Thomas and Katherine admitted having received £80 from John Olneye, who undertook to pay a further sum of £25.

Writ, dated at Westminster 26 Feb. 1386, to Nicholas Brembre, mayor, reciting that he had been ordered to deliver certain goods of William Matys of Ghent from arrest, and asking whether this had been done, what the goods were, and their value.

Endorsed that the execution of the writ was contained in

a schedule annexed, wherein it was stated that the goods, arrested at the suit of Richard Odyham, Matthew Passelewe and John Sutton, still lay under arrest, since no one had demanded their delivery, that they consisted of divers cloths, and that they had been valued by the oath of Richard Hay, fuller, and eleven others as follows: 29 dozens of *russet*, at 16s the dozen, £23 4s; 5 dozens of black *russet* at 22s the dozen, £5 10s; 10 yards of *semdrin*[1] at 2s the yard, 20s; 4 yards black *russet* at 18d the yard, 6s; 3 yards of white *russet* at 20d the yard, 5s; one dozen of *vyolet*, 22s; 31 dozens of *kersey*, at 3s 6d a dozen[2], £6 19s 6d; total £38 6s 6d.

29 March 1386 Recognisance from John Furneux, draper, executor of the will of Adam Fraunceys, of a debt of £200 due to the chaplains of the chapel within the close of Guildhall and payable at Easter a year hence.

Afterwards on 17 July 1387 the said John paid the amount to Richard Odyham, chamberlain, in the presence of Nicholas Exton, mayor, and the recognisance was cancelled.

Membr. 25 *b* John Merssh was summoned to answer Peter Steneby in a plea of debt and detinue, due on a bond of 14 Dec. 1385, whereby he undertook to accept an award in arbitration between the parties.

The defendant pleaded that he and the plaintiff were summoned to meet William de Burgh, knight, the umpire, at the church of St Martin le Grand on 8 Feb. 1386, on which day the umpire refused to give any award. He prayed judgment whether the plaintiff could have execution of the bond against him.

[1] A word of rare occurrence, except in the city records. It may be intended for *Sandrine*, i.e. Alexandrine, a rich striped silk material, cf. *borde Alisaundre*. *Sendal* also denoted a thin rich silken material. *Sindon* was fine lawn, and *sanguine*, *sangwin etc.*, cloth of the same colour. Sharpe, *Cal. of Wills*, II, p. xxxvii, connects the word with old French, *cendrins*, *cendrons*, *couleur de cendre*, and suggests ash-coloured material. To judge from the price and its position in the text, *semdrin* seems to be a woollen material, and Sharpe's suggestion is reasonable.

[2] Here the sense appears to be a dozen yards. Cf. 5 and 6 Edw. VI, c. 6, § 13: "All Devonshire Kersies called Dozens...shall contain in Length at the Water between twelve and thirteen yards." But already "dozen" was becoming a trade-name for kerseys and other coarse woollen cloths.

The plaintiff answered that the parties met on 3 Feb., when the umpire was not sufficiently informed to make an award, whereupon they asked him to continue the matter and agreed to meet on the Monday following, or at a later date, if he were prevented from coming. The umpire was unable to come owing to the king's business and summoned them for the next Wednesday at the third hour after noon, when he awarded that the defendant should deliver to the plaintiff 15 bales of *cordewan*[1] and 10 oxhides sewn (*decem coria bovina suta*), which John Flete, late bailiff of Southampton, had delivered to the plaintiff to carry to London, and which the defendant had arrested in Holebourne. Nevertheless the defendant had refused to fulfil the award.

The defendant pleaded that the umpire on 8 Feb. had asked leave to consider the matter till the next day, and on that day in the parish of St Alban Wood Street in the presence of Geoffrey Clerk and others he refused to arbitrate. And on this pleading the defendant put himself on the country. And the plaintiff did likewise.

Precept was given to John Botkisham, the mayor's serjeant, to summon twelve men of the venue of St Martin le Grand for 26 March. The defendant was committed to prison meanwhile for lack of mainprise.

Letter from the king of Castille and Leon[2], duke of Lancaster, to Sir Nicholas Brembre, mayor of London. Membr. 26 *7 May [1386]*

The mayor will remember that the duke has spoken to him before now on behalf of John Norhampton, John More and Richard Northbury, against whom the mayor's wishes and purposes were unreasonable and outrageous. His redoubtable lordship the king had granted to the duke, on his departure, his special favour, to wit, that these men should have their charters of pardon on condition that they did not approach nearer to the city of London than 40 leagues, but

[1] Originally leather of Cordova, now applied to fine leathers used in shoemaking.

[2] John of Gaunt. These two letters are important evidences of his sympathy with John Norhampton. Cf. Walsingham, *Hist. Angl.* (R.S.), II, p. 116; Higden (R.S.), IX, pp. 46, 74–5, 238; *Cal. of Letter Book H*, pp. 279–82, 307, 359; *Cal. Pat. Rolls*, 1388–92, pp. 296–7, 311.

the duke now learns that after his departure the mayor used all his power to prevent the king's favour thus granted from being performed and accomplished, at which the duke is greatly astonished, since this grant could not be in anyway to the damage of the mayor, and inasmuch as the mayor had promised his good will, it seems to the duke that he might very well have allowed such a thing to be done at his request, which would not be grievous to him or cost him anything. Accordingly he prays the mayor not to hinder the king's favour from being performed and accomplished in such manner as it was granted, so that the duke may not have any cause or occasion for acting in opposition to the mayor in the future. May God have him in his keeping. Given under the duke's signet at Plumpton the 7th day of May. The mayor is asked to certify his intentions to the duke by letter to be delivered to the bearer. [*French*]

Endorsed: "*A nostre trescher & biename monsieur Nichol Brembrer Mair de la Cite de londres.*"

12 May[*1386*] Further letter from the king of Castille and Leon, duke of Lancaster, to Sir Nicholas Brembre, mayor of London.

He informs the mayor that he has learnt that, whereas the king, when the duke was last in his company, granted to him a charter of pardon for John of Norhampton, late mayor of London, the mayor had petitioned so strongly to the contrary, that the charter cannot be sealed or delivered, whereat the duke is greatly astonished and takes it very ill as done in contempt of himself. The mayor knows well that he had previously promised the duke that he would not make any petition or do any other act which would be displeasing or dishonourable to the duke, but in the present case it seems to the duke greatly against his honour that he should be hindered by the mayor in a favour which the king had plainly and expressly granted to him. He informs the mayor, who had suggested to the king that great danger and damage would come to the city if John of Norhampton were allowed to have his pardon, that this suggestion is quite untrue, because the said John wishes and fully intends to absent himself from the kingdom and to accompany the duke to

Spain as soon as the king's grant has been put into effect, for which reason the mayor has no need to make any such suggestion against him. Moreover the duke has now sent to the king to ask his favour for the wife and children of the said John, that they may receive the wife's inheritance. The duke prays the mayor to cease from his opposition and his hindrance of the pardon, even as the mayor would wish that the duke should act towards him, for in the same manner as the mayor shall prove deserving towards the duke, so the duke will behave to the best of his power towards the mayor. Wherefore he begs the mayor to take the matter to heart and may God keep him. Given under the duke's signet at Plympton the 12th day of May. [*French*]

Endorsed as above.

Reply from the Aldermen and Commonalty[1] of the city *23 May [1386]* of London. They recommend themselves to the best of their knowledge and power to his most redoubtable and puissant lordship the duke. They have understood the contents of the letters sent to Sir Nicholas Brembre, mayor, which they recite. In this matter it seems to them that the duke is not duly informed and that untrue suggestions have been made to him against the mayor. Whereas the duke ascribes the above-mentioned actions to the mayor and no one else, they assure his highness that in truth the steps taken to limit the pardon after the duke's departure were not only the action and motion of the mayor but the action and motion of all of them, undertaken for the benefit and peace of the city, and that they had made strong representations to him as their mayor, because at present it seemed to them that the coming of the above-mentioned persons or any of them, and especially of John Norhampton, so near to the city as the duke wished, as appeared by his letters, would be a great cause of unrest to the city and the occasion of great tribulation and discontent within the city, to the subversion of the same, and Membr. 26 *b* thus would prove very displeasing to his lordship the king and to the duke himself and to the whole kingdom, which thing they hoped their honoured lord would in no wise

[1] The Common Council.

desire; and accordingly the mayor, by reason of his office, and they themselves, for their common good and the ease and quietness of the people and in order to prevent any such danger arising in despite of the king and themselves, had agreed that the mayor should move in the matter, and if the duke had remained longer in the country, they would have approached his lordship concerning the same, and especially because the king had previously granted to the commonalty of the city by his letters patent, for greater assurance of peace and quietness, that none of the aforementioned persons should approach nearer to the city than 100 leagues within the boundaries of England, wherefore they hoped that the duke, after good consideration, would hold the mayor and themselves as excused on this point. Furthermore, at the instance of the mayor and aldermen, and in order to give pleasure to the king and the duke, they had by common assent agreed to remit 20 leagues of the 100 leagues aforesaid. They begged his lordship to give no credence to any suggestions made against their request or against themselves or the city until he had received full information therein and considered their answer to the same. They had entire trust in the duke that he was more anxious for their peace and good than to aid and sustain persons who for so long, both in the time of the late king, the duke's father, whom God assoil, and in the time of the present king, had been regarded as rioters, brawlers, disturbers of the peace, initiators and maintainers of common quarrels and riots in the city, and as such notified and published as well in places of record as in the said city, being men engaged to the utmost of their power in oppressing the people and subverting the city, and as such arrested and imprisoned by just commandment of the king and of his noble council and by the mayor and officers of the city, and for such causes, and others more heinous, duly attainted in the time of the present king both on their own confession and in other ways. They prayed that God of his benign grace would give to his redoubtable and puissant lordship a good and long life and good success to him and all his friends and helpers and victory over all his enemies. Written at London under the common seal of the said city the 23rd day of May. From the duke's servants, the Aldermen and Commonalty of the city of London. [*French*]

Reply from Sir Nicholas Brembre in identical terms. As regards the matter touching the inheritance of John Norhampton's wife and children, he had never urged reasons to the contrary. He concludes his letter "*le vostre si vous plest Nichol Brembre.*" [*French*]

Adam Bamme, late one of the sheriffs of London, was summoned to answer Simon Aylsham, mercer, in a plea of debt, wherein the latter complained that on 24 Nov. 1382 in the Sheriffs' Court he sued Nicholas Rudere of Bruges, attorney of Peter Clerk, merchant of Bruges, to render account of £1000. As the said Nicholas was not a freeman and had no goods in the city, he was taken on a *capias* and brought to Adam's compter in Milk Street, whence he escaped on the Wednesday following. And accordingly, since in such a case the sheriff was bound by the use and custom of the city to satisfy the plaintiff for the sum in virtue of which the imprisonment took place, action accrued to the plaintiff for that amount. Membr. 27 *20 July 1385*

The defendant, while protesting that he did not acknowledge the date or the amount or that the custom was as large as was alleged, pleaded that the said Nicholas was attached previous to 30 Nov., that process was continued till a court held on 3 Dec., when friends informed John Norhampton, then mayor, that the said Nicholas was a foreigner and had been long in prison, and prayed the mayor to order the defendant, as sheriff, to deliver him according to custom. Thereupon the mayor, in Simon's presence, had ordered him to send for Nicholas the same day and told Simon to attend the Sheriffs' Court to prosecute his claim if he so wished. The latter made default, whereupon judgment was given that he and his pledges be in mercy and that Nicholas go quit. Moreover, adjournments in the Sheriffs' Court were not to a fixed day, but from one court to another; without that[1] Nicholas left the prison before Simon failed to prosecute.

[1] *Absque hoc*, the words which begin a traverse. They mean "it is not true that *etc.*" See above, p. 95, n. 1.

Accordingly he prayed judgment whether Simon had any action against him.

The plaintiff said that Adam's plea was double: first that, as courts were adjourned from one court to another, no fixed day could be given him, and secondly, that the mayor had ordered him to hear the plea the very same day, and so no fixed day could be given. He asked to be exonerated from one of these pleas.

The said Adam answered that he had alleged all these matters merely to explain how the plaintiff had not prosecuted his claim according to law, which was sufficient to excuse himself. He prayed judgment.

The action was adjourned for the information of the court until 14 Sept., when the plaintiff, while not admitting the defendant's allegations about the mayor's precept, pleaded that adjournments in the Sheriffs' Court were not as alleged, but that the sheriffs, on taking office, arranged to hold their courts alternately, one taking Wednesday and Friday and the other Thursday and Saturday, such days being called "*juridici*[1]," and the defendant, as sheriff, had the two latter days; further that according to custom neither need hold more courts than twice a week, except by consent of the parties or for the delivery of foreigners, this kind of court being called a "foreign" court, and that in such foreign courts no free man ought to be compelled to prosecute his claim of debt or account, except by consent of the parties[2], or unless a day's notice had been given in a case where a plaintiff, having

[1] The practice of the Sheriffs' Courts gave rise to much misunderstanding. The rules given in the Liber Albus (*Munim. Gild. Lond.* (R.S.), I, p. 199), dating from the early part of the 14th century, show that there was a distinction between courts for actions between citizens and those where foreigners were sued. *Et chescun des ditz Viscountz use de tener apar luy deux courtz generalx eǹ la semaigne; et chescun jour, pur deliveraunce des foreyns et estraungers, si mister soit; sils ne soient destourbez pur jours festivalx ou autres causes resonables.* Daily sittings for the convenience of foreigners date back at least to 1221, *ibid.* I, p. 67, and were enjoined by Edw. I in the "statutes ordained by the king and his council" for London in 1285, *ibid.* p. 295. See *Cal. of Plea and Mem. Rolls*, 1323–64, p. xx, and above, p. 95.

[2] Actions between citizens and foreigners were certainly heard in "foreign courts," *ibid.* p. 213, and as such courts were intended to prevent delay for foreign merchants, there was probably no force in the plea that a citizen plaintiff could not be compelled to sue there.

a *dies juridicus* next after the common adjournments, had no counsel then present. The plaintiff further pleaded that the defendant's juridical days were Thursday and Saturday and that on Saturday 29 Nov. the parties appeared in his court, but as there was no opportunity of discussing the case a day was given for Thursday following, yet nevertheless on the Wednesday at 11 o'clock before noon the said Adam suddenly required the plaintiff, without his counsel and without warning, to prosecute his plea, to which, in the presence of Sir William Walworth and other aldermen, he answered that he need not prosecute because the day had not been assigned to him, and his counsel was not present, and he was not warned to plead in a "foreign" court, and he requested the said Adam to defer any steps as to liberating the said Nicholas until the next day, which had been assigned to him. And accordingly, since the delivering of the said Nicholas was without warrant and unjust, he prayed damages against the said Adam.

The defendant pleaded in answer that the court and the authority of the sheriffs were whole and not divided, that according to the custom of the city they could hold personal actions daily and often did so, especially where a foreign merchant was defendant, and that the mayors of London had always had the power, when an impleaded person complained of any delay or wrong in the Sheriffs' Court, to order the sheriffs in the presence of the parties to hold a court the same day, terminate the plea and deliver the parties notwithstanding any common adjournment in the Sheriffs' Court. Moreover the plaintiff, who was present in Guildhall, did not come before him or any of his officers to say that he had no counsel present or make any excuse at all, but clearly did not prosecute his claim, though he was frequently exacted, all of which the defendant was ready to verify by his record or in such manner as the court should direct. Wherefore he prayed judgment whether the plaintiff could assign any injury to him personally or ought to have his action against him.

The plaintiff said that the defendant did not deny his allegation, and as regards his making no excuse about his counsel, he said that he warned the defendant thereof in the Guildhall in the presence of the Mayor and Aldermen, which the defendant had not denied, wherefore he prayed judgment.

Afterwards process being continued day by day until 29 Jan. 1388, the said Simon did not come to prosecute his plea. Therefore he and his pledges in mercy.

Membr. 28
30 Jan. 1386

Richard Gromet, Roger Sket, John Gyot, Arnaud Wrighte, Simon Edelonde, John Pottere, John Soudere, Adam Pottere, Robert Wyse, Thomas Helond, Roger Goudyng and Roger Gromet, fishermen of the country eastwards of London Bridge, were sworn before the Mayor and Aldermen to inform them how and by whom the fish in the Thames were so destroyed that hardly a seasonable fish could be found in it, what the nets in use were and how wide was the mesh, and whether it would be more profitable for the common people that the mesh of the nets for smelts and *gojons* should be of the assize of one inch, or an inch and a half, and for how long they ought to use such nets for such fish.

The fishermen said on oath that destruction was mainly done by *treinkes*[1] and *weres*, and by *hebbyngnettes*[2] put in *fletes*[3] and *shores*[4] in the water and in the *bruche*[5] towards Berkyng, and of these *treinkes*, one each was owned by John Taillour of Wolwych, John Swyft, John Erhithe, Smalbourne, Robert Tripecok of Plumsted, Richard Wayn, John London of Erhithe, John Colyn, John Baterell, Philip Erhithe, Thomas Geffray of Hamme, John Shipman and William Danyel, and there were several others whose names they did not know. They said also that Salomon Prat of Popeler, John Brewere of Hamme, Thomas Wrighte, Daniel de Brambelegh,

[1] Trink-nets were carried by boats or fixed in the stream. A full description of trink-boats, trink-fishing at anchor and trinks is given in the articles and orders of Sir Robert Ducie, lord mayor and conservator of the Thames, A.D. 1630–1, as set out in *A Description of the River Thames* by Roger Griffiths, 1758, pp. 64–76.

[2] Hebbing-nets or ebb-nets were fixed at the mouths of creeks at half-ebb. "Item, that every Hebberman shall fish by the shore, and pitch their Pole at half-ebb and shall have but forty Fathom Rope allowed from the Pitch of their Pole into the River." *Ibid.* p. 75.

[3] Creeks, inlets.

[4] Middle English, *schore*, shore, a sea-marsh or river-marsh.

[5] *Sc.* breach, breaks in the bank.

Walter Taillour, John Thressher of Popeler, John Shipman of Hamme, John Galyon of Wolwyche and John Godesone had each of them *weres*, and there were several others whose names they did not know. Further, the fish usually entered at the *breche* on the land of the abbot of Stratford and the abbess of Berkyng in order to feed on the land there and to be more at ease and more *swef*[1] than in the current of the Thames, and there they stayed till the tide ebbed and they could not pass back to the river but betook themselves to the ditches which remained full of water, which ditches the abbot and abbess hired out to people who put *weres* and other *engyns* in them, against the assize, whereby all fish, great and small, being unable to pass, were destroyed, and thus the abbot and abbess were the principal maintainers of the destruction of fish. They said further that nets of an inch in the mesh were always, time out of mind, used for smelts and *gojons*, and the fishing began fifteen days before Candlemas (2 Feb.) and lasted till the feast of our Lady in Lent (25 March). During this period they held that it would be best for the people to fish with nets of narrow mesh, since smelts and *gojons* could not be taken with larger mesh. No fisherman ought to draw any net called a "*draghenet*[2]" to land during this season between the Tower and London Bridge, and no one ought to fish at any season of the year, except in the time of smelts, with a mesh less than two inches. The fishermen also said that *samoun* and *sturgon* were utterly destroyed by *weres* and *treinkes*, and that there was another kind of net called "*forstate*[3]" with which a man could fish all the year, of which the mesh should be two inches of assize and no narrower. [*French*]

John Heldere, Thomas Fynch, John Spray, Peter Colman, John Couche, Robert Pulter, John Gybon, John Never, Laurence Sprillyng, William Grene, Richard West and William Neve, fishermen of the west of London Bridge, sworn the same day, said that between the Purification (2 Feb.) and the feast of our Lady in Lent (25 March) it

[1] Lat. *suavis*, Old French, *soef*, *suef*, agreeable, comfortable.
[2] Drag-net.
[3] Possibly a net slung from the forestay.

had always been usual to fish with a smeltnet, having a mesh of an inch, for smelts and gudgeons, without dragging these nets anywhere to land near London, but fishing only in the middle of the stream, and hitherto they had had leave to fish with such nets fourteen days before the Purification, if the season required it, i.e. in *swef* and *mol*[1] times when the *scoue*[2] of smelt and gudgeons drew closer to the land, which it did not do in cold and hard times. Also they said they had been used to fish with nets of a two-inch mesh all through the year except nine days before and nine days after the feast of St Mark (25 April), which was the spawning season for roach, that no nets ought to be drawn to land anywhere near London in any season of the year unless the meshes were two inches wide, and that salmon ought (not?) to be taken between the feast of the Nativity of our Lady (8 Sept.) and the feast of St Martin (11 Nov.) because at this time it was *kiper*[3], out of season and of no value. They had been used to take *lampreies* throughout the year except in May, which was their season of spawning. *Lamprons*[4] could be taken at any time except between Hokkeday (Tuesday after Easter-day) and the Feast of St Lawrence (10 Aug.), which was their season of spawning. Also they said that many people had recently made *weres* called "*routes*[5]" near Braynford[6] and Istelworth, whereby small fish were destroyed, that there were other weirs which stopped the common course of the water, so that no vessel could pass without great trouble, and that at the Westwere at Braynford and at Brainte great destruction of fish was done by *engyns* called "*wilwes*[7]."

[*French*]

Thereupon it was agreed by the Mayor and Aldermen that, whereas divers persons fish with smeltnets of one-inch mesh

[1] Lat. *mollis*, soft, open, of weather.
[2] *Scoue, skoue*, school or shoal. Hodgkin's *Proper Terms*, p. 129.
[3] Etymology uncertain, see *N.E.D. sub* "kipper."
[4] The lampron or lampern is defined as a river-lamprey. Probably by lamprey the fishermen were referring to the lamprey-eel, a sea-fish similar to the lampern but of a larger size and spotted. See Roger Griffiths, *Description of the Thames*, pp. 195–6.
[5] Etymology uncertain, see *N.E.D. sub* "rowte-weir."
[6] Brentford.
[7] Weirs made of willows, basket-work fish-traps.

after the season above-mentioned in open destruction of fish large and small, in future anyone wishing to fish with such nets should find sufficient security among the good men of London that within eight days after the said feast of our Lady they would bring their nets to the Guildhall to remain there for the ensuing year under safe custody, permission being given to their owners to come to the Guildhall to see that their nets were well kept, and at a reasonable time to be limited by the Mayor and Aldermen before the feast of the Purification they should have delivery of their nets to mend and repair them and to fish with them during the said season and no longer. Further, each fisherman should swear to do this loyally and not to fish with any net or engine contrary to the ordinance in destruction of fish, and if any one be found fishing with such net after the feast of our Lady in Lent, the nets should be burnt and the owner put to such penance, at the discretion of the Mayor and Aldermen, as befitted one who destroyed the common food.

William Pyg of Westhamme was mainprised by Elias Braybrok and William Pycot not to put any net called "*treinke*" in the Thames except during the time and season when, by ancient custom, such nets were used. *20 June 1386*

Ralph Tot, John Roger, Gilbert Peny, William Smalbourne, Thomas Frost, Adam Clement and John Normanton of Wolwych came before the Mayor and Aldermen in the Inner Chamber of the Guildhall and were charged with having assaulted John Salisbury, surveyor of the Thames, who had been appointed to take, remove and destroy all nets and engines whereby fry were destroyed, by shooting arrows at him, and further, with having put *weres* and other engines of too narrow mesh in the water, contrary to the ancient ordinances of the king and of the city. The defendants admitted the charge and put themselves on the favour of the Mayor and Aldermen, who granted, on account of their humility, that they should be bound over under mainprise. Thereupon they were mainprised by John Horn and others that none of them would interfere in future with John Salisbury or any other officer of the city in the discharge *21 July 1386* Membr. 28 *b* of his duty, nor place too narrow weirs, *treinkes* or other engines in the water, that they would assist and comfort the officers in their work, and that they would hinder and bring to the notice of the mayor all persons so offending, unless they were able to castigate and punish them themselves. They were also sworn not to do any harm to the men of Stebbenhithe[1] or their goods except by due process of law, under penalty of £100.

The said John Horn agreed and promised in good faith to produce, on their return, John Erhithe and John Godessone, who had been charged with the same offences, and were then at sea with the Admiral on the king's service.

The same day John Gyot, Roger Sket, John Pottere and John Soudere of Stebbenhithe were mainprised by John Trigge, fishmonger, not to harm any man of Wolwych under penalty of £40.

Membr. 29
4 May 1386

Reciprocal quitclaims between Margery, widow of John Ittelcote, draper, on the one part, and Thomas de Baketon, archdeacon of London, and Denis de Lopham, clerk, attorneys of Master Richard de Drayton, on the other.

10 May 1386

Adam Botoner of Coventry, by John Kesteven and John Trumpton his attorneys, brought a bill before the Mayor and Aldermen in the Chamber, complaining that John Dilcok, son of the complainant's wife Margaret and her former husband Henry Dilcok, had been bound apprentice to John More and had served five years of his term, during which time his master had not enrolled him, nor given him any instruction during the last year and a half, nor handed him over to any one else of the same trade to learn the trade, nor provided him with food and clothing, as he was bound to do. He prayed that the said John might be released from his apprenticeship.

The court, while agreeing that John More[2] neither could

[1] Stepney.

[2] An adherent of John Norhampton. He was tried in the Tower on 12 Sept. 1384 and sentenced to death, the sentence being commuted to ten years' imprisonment. For accounts of his trial, see *Cal. of Letter Book H*, pp. 264–6, 279; Higden, *Polychronicon* (R.S.), IX, p. 48; Walsingham, *Hist. Angl.* (R.S.), I, p. 116.

nor ought to come to the city, nevertheless desired, on the ground of equity[1], to know whether he had anything to say to the contrary, and accordingly they warned his wife Alice to report the matter to her husband and to appear on 8 June to inform them whether her husband had any objections to offer. The said Alice did not appear nor did any one else come on behalf of John More. Accordingly, since he was reported to be fully informed of the matter and gave no reasons to the contrary, and because he had not enrolled his apprentice within the first year of his term according to custom, as appeared by a scrutiny of the books of the Chamber of Guildhall, nor had he instructed him *etc.*, and further because he had himself been ousted from the freedom of the city by the king's justices sitting at the Tower for certain felonies and treasons confessed by him, and thus was unable to exercise his trade, it was considered, according to custom in the like case, that the said John Dilcok should be exonerated from his apprenticeship and should serve whom he would notwithstanding his indentures, and that his mainpernors in the indentures, namely, the said Adam and Richard Dodenhale, should be released from their mainprise.

Memorandum that Hugh Richardesson of Southampton, *10 June 1386* who was warden and governor (*custos et gubernator*) of a *balinger*[2] called "*le Marie de Excestre,*" was attached in the Sheriffs' Court to answer Philip Travers of Calais, attorney of John Bedon, *scutifer*[3] of Calais, for the profits of the *balinger*, which belonged to John Bedon. The action having been removed to the Mayor's Court, the parties put themselves on the arbitration of Richard de Preston and Richard Toky, good men of the city. On 4 July 1386 the latter reported that John Bedon owed Hugh the sum of £6 for the expenses of the *balinger* and was claiming from him an account of the sum of 40 *frankes*, which Hugh had received for a prisoner of Calais, and of a further sum of 10 marks which had been

[1] *De equitate.*
[2] From Old French, *baleinier*, a whale-ship. A small light ship or sloop.
[3] Possibly a municipal officer of Calais. *Scutifer* is not used in the city records in the sense of "esquire."

entrusted to him, and also of moneys received for freights from Middelburgh to London. This account Hugh could not give in the absence of John Bedon. They awarded that Hugh should enter into security to go to Calais as soon as possible to render an account to John Bedon, and that the £6 should be paid to him.

Membr. 29 *b*
13 July 1386

Baltazar Oubryak, Lombard, was mainprised by Gautron de Bardes, Peter Mark, Nicholas Luk and Bernard Anton, Lombards, for his appearance before the Mayor and Aldermen whenever summoned, under penalty of £1000.

9 April 1386

Precept was issued to summon John Bradele, leatherseller, as executor of Thomas Willyngham, who had married Alice, widow of Richard Gerveys, woolmonger, to bring into court the sum of 10 marks and a moiety of the goods and chattels of the said Richard Gerveys, these being the inheritance of Richard Gerveys' son George. John Bradele appeared on 12 April and asked for an adjournment to take advice, and a day was given him for 28 June. Appearing on that date he pleaded that none of the goods of the late Thomas Willyngham had come into his hands at the time the precept was issued or afterwards. A jury from the venue of Dowgate brought in a verdict for him on this issue. It was considered that the said John go quit and that the said George be not amerced for a false claim because he was an orphan.

Cedula
1385–6

Names[1] of the Common Council of the ninth year of Richard II.

Chepe: Geffrei Crymelford, grocer; Thomas Austyn, mercer; Thomas Vynent, mercer; John Fraunkeleyn, tailor; Geffrey Grigge, vintner; Thomas MakWilliam, grocer.

Bradstret: William Wodehous, skinner; Adam Karlill, grocer; John Clenaunt, woolman; Beneit Cornewaille, draper.

Bisshopesgat: Henry Herbury, vintner; John Sibyle, woolman; Peter Torold, skinner; Adam Ratteseye, hostiller.

Portsokne: William Burford, bellmaker; William Wodeward, founder.

[1] The persons here named served also in the tenth year, with the exception of those marked with an asterisk. See p. 132.

Algate: William Cressewyk; Richard Morell, woolman.

Tower: William Tonge, vintner; Thomas Evesham, woolman; Hugh Boys, ironmonger; Hugh Sprot*, cheesemonger.

Bridge: John Burwell*, fishmonger; Richard Grace, fishmonger; John Mokkyng*, vintner; John Sandhurst*, chandler; Thomas Palmer, fishmonger; John Pountfreyt, saddler.

Lymstret: Richard Gregory, ironmonger; John Clapshethe, poulterer.

Cordewanerstret: John Hoo*, grocer; Richard Hatfeld*, grocer; Geffrei Walderne, draper; Robert Lyndesey, tailor; William Pountfreyt, skinner; Robert Dane*, mercer.

Vinetrie: William Sharpyng, vintner; John Colshull, vintner; Thomas Medelane, vintner; John Tilneye, vintner.

Douegate: William Wotton, woolman; William Wight, woolman; John Wiltshyre, grocer; Nichol Snypston, cordwainer.

Candelwykstret: William Spaldyng*, tailor; William Horston*, draper; William Ivory, butcher; William Gilet*, butcher.

Walbrok: John Sely, skinner; Robert Reson, grocer; John Basse, draper; William Sudbury, tailor.

Langebourne: William FitzHugh, goldsmith; John Studele*, tailor; Thomas Bonaunter, tapicer; John Dyk, tapicer.

Cornhill: John Pynchon, jeweller; Walter Pykenham, skinner; William Wangford, draper; Richard Manhale, chandler.

Billyngesgat: William Ancroft, mercer; John Wade, fishmonger; Thomas Girdlere, corder; John Beaufrount, woolman.

Colmanstret: Richard Whityngton, mercer; Robert Havelok, ironmonger.

Bassyeshawe: Peter Wotton, draper; Peter Morys*, mercer.

Crepulgate: John Furneux, draper; Henry Bamme, goldsmith; John Loveye*, mercer; Robert Asshcoumbe, broderer; Gilbert Prynce*, painter, John Higyn, *fynour*.

Aldrychesgat: Sir Nicholas Twyford*, goldsmith; Thomas Reynham, goldsmith; John Bathe, weaver; John Bockyng, weaver.

Farndon: William Louthe*, goldsmith; John Sechford*,

hatter; William Thorp*, draper; Elis Weston, butcher; William Pershore, chaloner; Simon atte Nax*, cutler.

Castelbaynard: John Vautort, fishmonger; John Asshurst, woodmonger; John Asshele, woodmonger; Thomas Freke, woodmonger.

Queenhithe: William Baret*, grocer; Robert Parys, ironmonger; John Trigge, fishmonger; Richard Sprot, taverner.

Bredstret: Thomas Rolf, skinner; William Shiryngham*, mercer; John Ragonell, fishmonger; John Scorfeyn*, armourer.

Dorso

Oath of the Common Council[1]; and penalty for absence without good cause, 40d. [*French*]

Membr. 30
30 July 1386

Joan Thurkull was summoned to answer Robert Fraunkeleyn, dyer, in a plea that whereas he let to her a tenement in the parish of St James Garlickhithe for a year from Easter 1385 at a rent of 40s, payable quarterly, to be held afterwards at will and given up on reasonable notice, and at the end of the year he gave her a quarter's notice, nevertheless she refused to quit, to his damage 40s.

The defendant pleaded that the plaintiff agreed, in the presence of a certain Robert Kent, who was acting for him, to let the tenement to her for thirty years at 40s a year, and that she gave him a God's penny[2] as earnest of the covenant, and that on Shrove Tuesday (14 Feb.) 1385, as the tenement was empty, he allowed her to occupy it for a year without rent, after which he again recognised the covenant. She prayed that, in accordance with the custom of the city, the said Robert Kent, who acted as broker, should be examined on oath. The plaintiff agreed.

Robert Kent, being summoned, appeared the same day and said on oath that it had been agreed that the defendant should have the tenement for thirty years, if she wished, and that the plaintiff would not expel her or raise the rent.

[1] See *Munim. Gild. Lond.* (R.S.), I, p. 41, for the Latin version; *Cal. of Letter Book D*, p. 192, for the English.

[2] *Denarius ad deum.* It was regarded as giving a divine sanction to a bargain and was sometimes devoted to pious purposes. By the Carta Mercatoria of A.D. 1303 it was made an effectual sanction of a bargain. *Munim. Gild. Lond.* (R.S.), II, p. 206. See Pollock and Maitland, *Hist. Eng. Law*, II, p. 209; *Select Pleas in Manorial Courts* (Seld. Soc.), p. 133; Mary Bateson, *Borough Customs*, I, pp. 217–19.

Accordingly it was considered by the court that the defendant hold the tenement for thirty years, if she wished, and if she died, it should return to the plaintiff, and that the latter be not amerced because he came the first day. But as the plaintiff had slandered her, calling her a prostitute, he was committed to prison. Next day the plaintiff, together with Richard Bruer, John Grenefeld, goldsmith, and William Sherman, who had also slandered and threatened her, were mainprised for their good behaviour, and the plaintiff's servant, John Wakefeld, was likewise bound over under surety of his master.

Memorandum that at Middelburgh in Zeeland, James Neurent, attorney of John Hoo of London, borrowed £60 from William Wodehill, servant of Robert Sutton, merchant of London, and bound himself for repayment by an obligation, dated 17 Dec. 1385, to the said William and a certain Thomas Maperley. The said William having died, Walter Dautrey, claiming to represent Robert Sutton, came to John Hoo and gave him the first letter of payment according to the law merchant and showed him the second letter of payment and the obligation and asked for payment. John Hoo was willing to pay, but the above-mentioned Thomas Maperley put in a claim. The court summoned both parties, and on Thomas Maperley's making default, it was considered that John Hoo should pay the money direct to Robert Sutton on condition that he warranted him against any other claimant.

Membr. 30 *b*
8 Aug. 1386

Deed witnessing that John Shepeye, barber, who had taken Thomas, son of Hugh le Peyntour of Durham, as his apprentice for seven years by indentures dated 2 April, had now sold to Thomas Canoun, marberer, all his rights to the apprentice and the remainder of the term of apprenticeship[1], with the consent of the said apprentice, who appended his seal to the document. Dated 27 July 1386.

[1] See the discussion on the apprentice as a chattel in *Cal. of Plea and Mem. Rolls*, 1364–81, pp. xlii–xliii. It is stated in the early 14th-century London rules preserved in Ricart's *Kalendar* (Camd. Soc.), pp. 102–3, that an apprentice could be sold and devised as a chattel; and the same claim was sometimes made by masters. In an action in 1375, judgment was given that no apprentice was bound to serve any other than his original master against his will. *Cal. of Plea and Mem. Rolls*, 1364–81, p. 202.

ROLL A 28

Mainprises of the time of Nicholas Exton, mayor

Membr. 1
15 July 1387

Giles Combmaker was mainprised by John Ridale and John Marchal, tailors, Ralph Clopham, weaver, and Henry Charles to keep the peace with John Combere, who was likewise mainprised by Simon Gardiner, John Hayne, John Kempe and Laurence Folk.

31 July 1387

Brother Thomas Peverell of the order of the Carmelites was mainprised by James Bilyngford and John Baldok, upholder, for his appearance before the Mayor and Aldermen on reasonable summons, under penalty of £100.

11 Sept. 1388

Richard Burnham, rector of the church of Holy Trinity the Less, was mainprised by Roger Wilford and Roger Torgold to keep the peace with Robert Lyndeseye, draper, who was likewise mainprised by William Ketill, spurrier, and William Shelbourne, haberdasher.

Membr. 1 *b*
5 Nov. 1386

John Keteryng, apprentice of Richard Virly, was committed to prison for non-payment of 8 marks, which he was fined for divers trespasses against his master, as appears by the bill and inquisition thereon, and also on account of fornication in his master's house[1], wherein judgment is still to be given.

6 Nov. 1386

John Bradeley, leatherseller, was committed to prison for 20 marks, due on a bond to John Wells, in which he was condemned. He was released on Good Friday[2] 1387 by consent of the creditor.

Membr. 2
7 Nov. 1386

Bond of Henry Yevele[3], mason and citizen of London, to Maud Holbech and Stephen Speleman in 20 marks, that neither he nor his brother, Richard Foun, would cause her

[1] Which was a breach of the usual covenants in the apprentice's indentures.

[2] *In die paraschues.*

[3] See *D.N.B.*; Henry Yevele, a master-mason and architect, was director of the king's works at Westminster. In the city he served as warden of London Bridge.

or her heirs or executors or the feoffees of her lands and tenements in the parishes of St Aldburgh in Bisshopesgatestrete, St Martin Pomeres in Ismongerlane and St Peter in Bradstrete, any loss by suing on a recognisance which had been made in Chancery to them by Henry atte Mersshe, former tenant of the above-named properties.

Reciprocal quitclaims between Robert de Draycote, prior of the hospital of St Mary within Cripplegate, and the convent of the same on the one part, and John Cyfrewast, knight, and Katerine his wife, formerly wife of the late Adam Stable, mercer, on the other. *14 Nov. 1386*

Richard Haydok, John Andrew, Richard Pattesle, Thomas Jevek, John Lucas, William Wittenhale, vintners of the west (of Walbrook), and Thomas Hayward, Thomas Neel, John Wakelee, Richard Cokham, Thomas Bette and John Wilyngham, vintners of the east, were sworn to make scrutiny of wines and to pour out all such as they found corrupt and unhealthy. Membr. 2 *b* *25 Nov. 1386*

Acquittance from William Rasyn and Isabella Norable, his wife[1], daughter of Richard de Chaddeslee, to Richard Horn, clerk, and Robert West, executors of Richard de Chaddeslee, for the handing over of 100 marks, a small mazer with a covercle of mazer, bound with silvergilt, four plain pieces of silver of one set with a covercle to the same[2] and one second best bed, which goods the said Richard left to Isabella Norable for her marriage. Dated 22 Dec. 1386. *27 Jan. 1387*

Bond, reciting that Stephen Sewale, grocer, had been merchant, factor and attorney of Geoffrey Crymelford, grocer, during the time that he was the latter's apprentice, and had entered into bonds on behalf of his master and himself at home and abroad, whereof he had rendered account before Richard Hatfeld, Thomas Otteley, Richard Toky and William Waddesworth, arbitrators appointed by the mayor, Membr. 3 *21 Feb. 1387*

[1] In his will (Husting Roll 103 (244)) Chaddeslee mentions Margaret Norable his servant, probably mother of Isabella Norable.

[2] *Quatuor pecias argenti planas unius secte cum uno cooperculo ad easdem.* See *Cal. of Wills*, II, p. 670, mentioning a "neste of bowelles" and a "neste of Goblettes" with a cover to each nest.

when it was found that Geoffrey Crymelford had already paid all that Stephen Sewale could claim against him. In order that the master might have security against any further claims arising from the apprentice's trading on his behalf, the said Stephen, together with Sewale Hoddesdon and Robert Sewale, fishmongers, and John Killom bind themselves in £100 that Stephen will acquit his late master of all such claims and will bring letters under the authentic seals of Bruges and Middelburgh, witnessing by proclamation at Middelburgh that he had given satisfaction to all those to whom his master had been indebted by reason of his business dealings, which could be verified by the law merchant, during the time of the war between England and Flanders and for the year ensuing, and further that he would indemnify his master against any loss in the meantime. Dated 12 Feb. 1387.

Memorandum that Bernard Blessyng, merchant of Bohemia, had in the house of Walter Pouke the following goods: 600 white plates (*albas platas*)[1], 50 long plates, 33 plates for the breast, 4 barrels of wine called "*galantwyn*[2]," 5 barrels of beer, one *basenet*[3], one long table with a pair of three-legged stools (*cum pari tripedum*), one stool, one corndish, one axe and a pewter pot, and that on 16 March he proved these goods to be his own by (oath of) John Huwet and John Mundam[4], and that no one had any part therein to the value of 4d, according to the custom of the city of London. And accordingly the goods were delivered to him.

2 March 1387 Francis Vyncheguerre, merchant of Lucca, by John Hende, his attorney, obtained judgment against Bartholomew de Bosano, merchant of Lucca, for £47, arrears of £70 due on a bond of 17 July 1374 and payable at Michaelmas the same year, together with 13s 4d damages. The defendant was committed to prison. Afterwards on the same day John Hende

[1] Plate, one of the thin pieces of steel or iron composing plate-armour. White plate appears to be steel plate, though *N.E.D.* gives "burnished."

[2] Possibly spiced wine, from Old French, *galange, galand, gallente, sorte d'epicérie*. Godefroy, *Dictionnaire de l'ancienne langue Française*.

[3] *Bassinet*, head-piece.

[4] The threefold oath of the garnishee. See above, p. 15, n. 1.

granted that he should have a day of payment and be delivered from prison. Thereupon the said Bartholomew, together with Richard Forster, entered into a recognisance for payment of £27 13s 4d at Easter and £20 at Midsummer.

Salomon Salomon, mercer, acknowledged receipt of a bale of mercery, value £40, from John Chircheman and John Organ, collectors of the king's custom of 12d the £ of merchandise in the port of London, and undertook to save them harmless for the space of a year against all claims concerning the same. *4 March 1387*

Stephen Aphowell of Kaermerdyn[1] with other good men of the same town came here and claimed to be quit of paying custom in London. The payment of 2d the fardel[2] of cloth as custom was put in suspense until Easter, in order that the court might be advised in the meantime as to whether, according to the charters of the king produced by them in court, they were subject to the payment of such custom or not. Membr. 3 *b* *27 March 1387*

Robert Draycote, prior of the hospital of the Blessed Mary of Elsyngspitel within Crepulgate, brought a bill of complaint that he had let a tenement with sollars and other appurtenances in the parish of our Lady atte Bowe for a year from Christmas to Christmas to John Bradlee and Janyn his servant, and that on Wednesday before Michaelmas they had cut down and carried away, by force and arms, i.e. with axes, a counter in a shop for drapery[3], value 13s 4d; a pavement of *Flaundres-till*[4] in a large chamber, 50s; a *parclos*[5] of *Estrichbord*[6] 13 feet long in another chamber, 40s; 3 locks and 4 iron bolts, 3s 4d; another *parclos* in an entrance (*en un huys*) 24 feet long standing in the said great chamber, 40s; a *cuppebord* of *Estrichbord* for the parlour, 40d; a *creste*[7] of *Estrichbord* Membr. 4 *21 Jan. 1387*

[1] Carmarthen. [2] Bundle.

[3] *Une couche en une shope pour draperie ordeigne.* This does not appear to mean a bed but a fixed bench or counter constructed for unrolling and displaying cloth.

[4] Flanders tiles. [5] Partition, screen.

[6] Eastern board, applied to timber coming from Norway and the Baltic.

[7] Cresting or moulding on top of an article of furniture.

over the *speer*[1] in the same parlour, 8d; and a *rierdos*[2] of *Estrichbord* 18 feet long, 13s 4d; all being fixtures[3] of the free tenement of the said prior; and also a great quantity of Maydeston stone to the value of 40s, which trespass they continued until last Christmas, against the peace and the ordinance made thereon, and to the damage of the prior £100. [*French*]

The Mayor and Aldermen visited the tenement on 20 March and in the presence of the prior and the said Janyn, who made no defence, found the bill to be true. It was considered that the prior recover against the said Janyn the sum of 10 marks. The same day, out of reverence for the Mayor and Aldermen, the prior granted that if Janyn would replace the Flemish tiles and clear away all the stinking dung, rubbish and filth out of the tenement before Whitsuntide, he would condone the 10 marks. For greater security John Selton, tailor, and William Coventre, pinner, undertook to perform these conditions if the said Janyn failed to do so. Memorandum that judgment was not given against John Bradlee, who did not appear, because he was in prison.

1 May 1387 Recognisance by Thomas Girdeler, citizen of London, to pay John Hauley of Dartmouth, master of the "*Seynt Marie*" of Dartmouth, for the freight of 86 tuns of red Bordeaux wine at the rate of 27s a tun, the last payment to be made before Michaelmas. [*French*]

22 Oct. John Hauley acknowledged satisfaction and the recognisance was cancelled.

Membr. 4 *b*
24 April 1387 Memorandum that whereas Francis Wincheguerre of Lucca bought from Lord de Neville certain tallies, with which tallies he bought wool at Hull, and whereas Lord de Neville suggested that this wool belonged to Matthew Cheynyn of Florence, the Mayor and Aldermen, on the petition of the said Matthew, summoned Bernard Antonii of Florence, broker, to the Guildhall and asked him to tell all he knew about the buying of the wool. The broker answered

[1] Screen, sometimes the partition of an ingle-nook.
[2] Panelling over a fire-place.
[3] See *Munim. Gild. Lond.* (R.S.), I, p. 432.

on oath as follows: Lord de Neville sold these tallies of the king, amounting to more than £400, to Francis Wincheguerre, who asked the witness to take them to Hull and buy wool with them to that value or beyond. Matthew Cheynyn, hearing that he was going to Hull, also asked him to take a king's tally of £100 and buy wool for him. When he arrived in Hull, the king's customs-officer showed him some wool, but would not strike a bargain because he was himself coming to London in a fortnight and wanted to talk with the principals about the bargain, so that the witness had his journey for nothing. However, when the customs-officer came to London, Francis Wincheguerre, by the witness' agency, bought from him 30 sarplers of wool, 20 of one sort and 10 of another, which amounted to far more than the value of the tallies, whereupon he paid him the balance and everything was settled. It was not true that the petitioner, Matthew Cheynyn, had any part or share in this purchase of wool from Walter Frost.

In an action for debt of £80 due on a bond of Robert de Caunbrugge and William Palmere, executors of Henry Bever, late rector of St Peter of Bradstret, against John Leveryngton, in which the defendant made four defaults, his tenement in the parish of St Stephen Colmanstret was delivered to the plaintiffs as a foreign attachment to hold till the debt was satisfied. A jury of twelve good men of the venue said that the tenement was a brewhouse with three shops annexed of a net annual value of £5 6s 8d, but that the premises were ruinous and that the repairs would cost the first year's annual value. The court allowed the first year's rent for repairs. *10 Dec. 1386*

William Grevell of Campeden paid into court the sum of 20 marks which he owed to William Vale, fishmonger, for two *lasts*[1] of herrings. Membr. 5 *9 May 1387*

Writ demanding the tenor of the will[2] of John Byker, late artilleryman in the Tower, as enrolled in the Husting on 19 July 1361. *14 Dec. 1387*

[1] A reference of 1469 gives 12 barrels to the last. See *N.E.D.*
[2] See *Cal. of Wills*, II, p. 30.

Membr. 5 *b*
9 July 1387

Memorandum that Richard Hatfeld, pepperer, demanded against John Slegh, the king's butler[1], the sum of 17 marks for two tuns of wine, bought by the latter's servant Richard Wellesbourne on 9 Feb. 1385. After four defaults the defendant sent the money on 9 July 1386 and asked that it might be reserved in court till he could appear. Nevertheless on 10 July it was delivered by order of the mayor and William Cheyne, recorder, to the plaintiff, under mainprise of Geoffrey Adam and John Clopton, pepperer, to answer therefor *etc.*

10 July 1387

Memorandum that Andrew Michel, Lombard, in the ninth year of the present reign contributed £8 to a loan of £4000 to the king, which £8 William Grevel of Caumpeden arrested in the hands of Richard Odyham, the chamberlain, in part payment of a larger sum owed to him by the said Andrew. The money was delivered to William Grevel, in virtue of this arrest, and the chamberlain went quit as regards the said Andrew.

27 Sept. 1387

Letter of attorney from John Proude, master and governor of the ship "*Katerine*" of Dartmouth, to Thomas Girdeler of London to receive from Ramon Monedcys, burgess of Bordeaux, certain sums for freightage, which he had recovered by proceedings in the Sheriffs' Court.

Cedula

The Common Council by wards in the time of Nicholas Exton, mayor, in the tenth year of King Richard II.

[As in the preceding year, see p. 122, with the following changes.]

Broad Street: John Clenaunt appears as "Clenhond."

Tower: John Norwych, woolman, *vice* Sprot.

Bridge: William Radewell, fishmonger, Richard Spenser, tailor, and John Millyng, fishmonger, *vice* Burwell, Mokkyng and Sandhurst.

Cordwainer Street: Fulk Horewod, grocer, William Culham, grocer, and Thomas Hayward, vintner, *vice* Hoo, Hatfeld and Dane.

Candlewick Street: John Walcote, draper, John Olneye, woolman, and John Brownesbury, butcher, *vice* Spaldyng, Horston and Gilet.

[1] See above, p. 46, n. 1.

Langbourn: Thomas Noket, draper, *vice* Studele.

Bread Street: William Prest, mercer, and William Stapulte *vice* Shiryngham and Scorfeyn.

Queenhithe: Thomas Frankeleyn *vice* Baret.

Farringdon: John Hille, mercer, John Cantoys, Thomas Davy, goldsmith, John Walworth, vintner, and William Savage, hostiller (excused), *vice* Louthe, Sechford, Thorp, Pershore and atte Nax.

Aldersgate: Thomas Dancastre *vice* Twyford.

Cripplegate: John Forster, goldsmith, and William Larke, painter, *vice* Loveye and Prince.

Bassishaw: Richard Burton *vice* Morys.

Acquittance from Thomas Noket, citizen of London, John Reche and Richard Palmer of Langedon to Aubrey de Veer, knight, and William Tasburgh, chaplain, for the receipt of £100 in part payment of a debt of 800 marks. Membr. 6 *7 Oct. 1387*

Quitclaim from Thomas Bonde, vicar of South Mymmes[1] co. Middlesex, to John Symond, chandler, and Alice his wife, widow of Robert Rotheley, chandler. *23 Oct. 1387*

This day William Prophet, mariner, of Westlenne, plaintiff, offered himself against William Jay of Swyneshеved[2], merchant, who had this day by foreign attachment, according to the custom of the city, in a plea of debt on demand of £7 12s 6d. By his bill of complaint, the plaintiff alleged that on 8 Oct. last at Wasshecrosse near Fossedyke[3] the defendant freighted his ship "*Seintemariebote*" with 30 weys of salt to be carried to London at 5s the wey, which salt the plaintiff carried to London, where the defendant unloaded the greater part of it without paying the plaintiff anything for the freight. Accordingly he prayed that £7 12s 6d arising from the sale of the salt might be arrested as a foreign attachment and delivered to him according to the custom of the city, and he produced the covenant between them dated 8 Oct. Membr. 6 *b–7* *13 Dec. 1387*

The defendant having made four defaults, the plaintiff

[1] South Mimms. [2] Swineshead co. Lincs.

[3] Washcross near Fossdyke co. Lincs, villages at the head of Fossdyke Wash.

prayed that John Wykes, the serjeant of the Chamber, who had made and received the aforesaid sum out of the sale of part of the salt, should pay it to him. Thereupon, according to the custom, the plaintiff was put on oath as to how much was really owed to him. He said the amount was as abovesaid, but he had borrowed 40s from the defendant. Accordingly it was considered that this sum should be deducted and that the plaintiff receive £5 12s 6d. But as it was clear from the indenture that the defendant had agreed to pay the plaintiff for his freightage within seven days after he had tied up in London, and if he failed to do so or to land the salt he should after the seven days pay the plaintiff 3s 4d a day for his expenses, and since the plaintiff had tarried with his ship for ten further days, with his freight unpaid and with the salt still not discharged, owing to the defendant's default, as was testified by many witnesses, it was considered that he receive 33s 4d more. The serjeant of the Chamber then paid him the two amounts and he was mainprised by Edmund Bys and Nicholas Brandon to restore it, if the defendant within a year and a day submitted to justice and was able to prove reasonably that he was not liable for the debt and damages.

Nicholas Brembre, knight, came before the mayor and recorder and acknowledged the following writing to be his deed: Grant from Nicholas Brembre to William Venour, Henry Vanner, Edmund Halsted, Thomas Broun and John Soles, citizens and merchants of London, of all his goods and chattels, live and dead, of whatsoever kind and wherever they might be, as well within the city as elsewhere this side of or beyond the seas, to have and to hold to them, to do and dispose thereof as their own goods without any reclamation or condition whatsoever. Sealed with the donor's seal and given in London on 15 Oct. 1387[1].

[1] Nicholas Brembre with others was appealed of high treason on 14 Nov. 1387. On the following Sunday, 17 Nov., the appeal was again made in Westminster Hall. The king accepted the appeal and a day was given at the next Parliament. Soon after, probably on 19 Nov., proclamation was made of a special protection for the appellors and appealed. Brembre was apprehended and brought to trial on 20 Feb. 1388 by the "Merciless Parliament," which met on 3 Feb. He was found guilty, and drawn and hanged the same day. See *Rot. Parl.* III, pp. 229–38; Higden's *Poly-*

Adam Fraunceys, knight, appeared before the Mayor and Aldermen on 30th July 1386 and prayed that it might be recorded that on 17 June, at Barton-on-Humber co. Yorks, thieves broke into his room in John Davy's inn and stole two coffers belonging to him, in which were his seal, bearing his arms and the words "*sigillum Ade Fraunceys*," divers sums of money in gold and silver and certain jewels, and that he repudiated all bonds and other documents which might be sealed with his seal after that date. *30 July 1386*

William, son of John Algate of St Albans, who had been apprenticed on 24 June 1380 for ten years to Roger Streyt, ironmonger, complained by bill that his master in Dec. 1386 went to Middelburgh in Zeeland and immediately afterwards his goods in England were arrested and sold for the benefit of his creditors, so that the complainant received no instruction, food or clothing and had become a vagabond, contrary to the good customs of the city, wherefore he prayed to be released from his apprenticeship. Membr. 7 *b* *29 Jan. 1388*

The Mayor and Aldermen sent for Robert Parys and Robert Havelok, masters of the mistery of Ironmongers, who said on oath that the master had no shop in London after Dec. 1386 and did not provide for his apprentice. Afterwards the Mayor and Aldermen, hearing that John Grove, armourer, was attorney of the said master in England, sent for him in order to have fuller information. He admitted the truth of the complaint but opposed the exoneration on the ground that the apprentice had not rendered account. To this the apprentice replied that he had given security by a bond in £600 from himself, John Marchal and John Algate to render account, which bond John Grove had accepted. Evidence was given that he had gone to his master in Middelburgh to make the account, but his master refused to receive it. On the above facts, it was considered by the court that the complainant be exonerated from his apprenticeship and be allowed to serve whom he would.

chronicon (R.S.), IX, pp. 107–8; Walsingham, *Hist. Angl.* (R.S.), II, pp. 173–4; Knighton, *Chron.* (R.S.), II, p. 249; *Cal. of Letter Book H*, pp. 320–1; Cobbett's *State Trials*, I, pp. 90–123. Brembre took the precaution of conveying away his goods and chattels so as to prevent their forfeiture as "felons' chattels." For a similar conveyance of his lands and tenements, dated 13 Nov. 1387, see Guildhall Library original deeds, Add. MS. 36.

14 Feb. 1388 Adam de St Ives reported to the mayor and recorder that he had put a seal engraved with his arms in a room of his house near the Stokkes[1] and about a fortnight before Christmas, when he went to get it, he found that it had been removed and he could not find it. He prayed that the matter be recorded so that he should not be responsible for any deeds sealed with the seal after that date.

Whereas a bill was brought before the Mayor and Aldermen by John Burwell, claiming from Nicholas Horne 86 tuns and one pipe of Rochelle wine, the mayor appointed Thomas Gurdeler, Thomas Newton, John Vatote and Richard Toky as arbitrators. They awarded that as regards 78 tuns of the wine, which Nicholas Horne had sold at Middelburgh, he ought to pay John Burwell the sum of £42 12s 6d *gros*, which amounted in sterling, counting the noble at 7s 10d *gros*, to £36 5s 2d[2]. As regards the remaining 8 tuns and one pipe, which were then in Middelburgh in the custody of John Laward and Thomas Dove, they ought to be sold and the proceeds divided, John Burwell receiving five-eighths and Nicholas Horne three-eighths. But as regards a further amount of £17 18s ¾d, which John Burwell claimed from Nicholas Horne as his contribution towards the expenses of *takelyng*, victuals and wages of the masters and mariners of a ship called "*la Cristofre*" of London, in which they were partners, the arbitrators would not make any award without the aid of merchants cognisant of the facts. [*French*]

Membr. 8
31 Jan. 1388 Precept was issued to William Venour and Hugh Fastolf, sheriffs, to bring before the Mayor and Aldermen at the Guildhall on 31 Jan. 1388 the bodies of Roger Wygemor, John Donyngton, draper, Robert Lyndeseye, tailor, and William Sheryngham to answer concerning divers evildoings and misprisions whereof they were indicted, and also twelve good and lawful men of their bailiwick, not of the affinity of the said Roger *etc.*, to make delivery of the same and

[1] The Stocks Market, at the junction of Cornhill, Lombard Street and the Poultry.

[2] Thus the Flemish £ was now worth no more than 17s and a fraction of a penny sterling.

further to fulfil those things which should be required of them by the court according to the law and custom of the city. On which day the said Roger came by William Sheryngham his attorney and the said John, Robert and William in their proper persons. And the said indictment was seen by the court, whereof the tenor follows in these words: Inquest taken at Guildhall on Monday (16 Sept. 1387)[1] after the feast of the Exaltation of the Holy Cross A° 11 Ric. II before Nicholas Exton, mayor, William More and William Standon, sheriffs, and William Cheyne, recorder, to inquire who were maintainers, advisers or in any way guilty of the evil misprisions lately committed against the king and the condition and governance of the city by John Northampton, John More, Richard Norbury and William Essex and also to inquire concerning the goods and chattels of the same John, John, Richard and William and of Peter Mildenhale, which jurors said upon their oath that Roger Wygemor, John Maudeleyne, Robert Riseby, John Donyngton, draper, William Norton, Robert Lyndeseye, tailor, John Chedder, mercer, William Sheryngham and John Vyne, mercer, were maintainers, advisers and helpers, for the more part, in all the evils and misprisions done against Nicholas Brembre, knight, late mayor of London, the sheriffs, aldermen and governance of the city, and as regards any goods and chattels of John Norhampton *etc.* they say they know nothing thereof, nor do they make any presentment. In witness whereof the jurors to this inquest have set their seals.

And because the said indictment made no mention of a certain time or place and thus was of no force at law, the said John Donyngton *etc.* were told by the court that they were not bound to answer the indictment, and if it were of any force, they could exonerate themselves by the king's letters patent whereby he pardoned to his liege men of London and

[1] This indictment against John Norhampton's supporters was presented when Brembre was still in the king's favour, and it was due for trial before the Mayor and Aldermen as justices of the peace. But meanwhile Brembre himself had been appealed of treason and there was little doubt as to his coming fate. It is open to question whether the court would have been so solicitous on behalf of the defendants, if the proceedings had taken place six months earlier.

each of them and the whole commonalty of London—except those who were adjudged to be convicted of the discord and dissension in the city, and others who had withdrawn themselves outside the city for the said causes and hitherto had not returned to their obedience and to surrender to the peace, whose names were exhibited in the king's chancery to be entered of record—the suit of his peace which pertains to him for all treasons, felonies, insurrections, trespasses, conspiracies, confederacies, leagues and all other misprisions against his royal majesty within the city before the date of his letters patent, whereof any, being indicted or accused, had not been convicted or might in future be indicted or accused, and granted his sure peace to them in the premises, which letters patent were dated 22 June A° 9 (1385).

The said John Donyngton *etc.* said they did not wish to seek any benefit from the above letters and craved leave to answer the indictment, whereupon they were severally charged and pleaded not guilty and put themselves for good or ill upon the country. A jury of John Colshull and his fellows, being sworn and charged, found them not guilty. Accordingly it was considered that they go quit thereof; and because it seemed to the court that the indictment was of no force nor was anyone bound to answer to it by law, it was considered that no process be made on it against John Maudeleyne, Robert Riseby, William Norton, John Chedder, mercer, and John Vyne, mercer, who were likewise named in it. And it was agreed that the indictment be so endorsed.

Membr. 8 *b*
2 May 1388

Quitclaim from Peter Porter, goldsmith, of Malyns[1] in Brabant, to Sir John de Sproxston, parson of the church of Groundesburgh[2] co. Suffolk, of all actions, real and personal, suits, plaints and demands from the beginning of the world to the present day.

Membr. 9
22 Jan. 1388

Alice, widow of John Coterell and executrix of his will, was summoned, on a bill of John Body and Joan his wife, to bring into court the sum of £100 and the third part of the residue of the goods of the said John Coterell. In the bill

[1] Malines, Mechlin. [2] Grundisburgh.

the plaintiffs alleged that the said John by his will of 23 July 1349 left £40 to his son Thomas, £20 to his son John and £40 to his daughter Joan, now plaintiff, with a proviso that if any died under age their share was to be divided among the others, and that he also left a third part of the residue of his goods to the said children and the wardship of the children to their stepmother Alice, the defendant. Afterwards Thomas died aged two years and John aged three years, and accordingly their shares fell in to Joan.

The defendant pleaded that Geoffrey Colewelle and others were also appointed executors, that the goods came into the hands of the said Geoffrey, and that she herself neither received nor administered them.

The plaintiffs answered that Geoffrey was the testator's apprentice and continued as Alice's apprentice for seven years and that together they administered the goods in the parish of St Pancras.

On this issue a jury of the venue, which was summoned for 2 May 1388, brought in a verdict that the defendant, as executrix, administered the goods. Therefore it was considered that she be committed to prison because she had not the money at hand to pay, there to remain until she brought in the sum of £100 and found security to answer for the third part of the residue. No damages were given as the plaintiffs demanded none in their bill.

Protection and safe conduct for a year under letters patent, dated at Westminster 2 June 1388 and addressed to all and singular admirals, captains, castellans and their lieutenants, wardens of the ports and other maritime places, sheriffs, mayors, constables, bailiffs, ministers and all other faithful lieges and subjects constituted as well by land as by sea, in favour of Matthew Cenyng[1] of Florence, merchant, giving him permission to enter, travel in and leave the country, together with his merchandise, and exempting him from all prosecutions for any past offences. Membr. 9 *b* *2 June 1388*

Acquittance from Guydo de Bryene to Bartholomew de *20 June 1388*

[1] *Alias* Matthew Chenyn. *Cal. Close Rolls,* 1385–9, p. 188.

Bosano for the receipt of £2000 sterling due on a statute merchant.

Membr. 10
28 Jan. 1387

Thomas Haukere, ironmonger, brought a bill of complaint before the Mayor and Aldermen against Edmund Olyver, stockfishmonger, reciting that John Northampton, son of John Northampton of Lincoln, became his apprentice for a term of 12 years at midsummer 1382, and that the said Edmund as surety undertook to make good any damage done by him, and that on 20 Oct. 1386 he sent the apprentice to Middelburgh in Zeeland to receive from Thomas atte Hoke, the plaintiff's attorney, the sum of £90 and to bring the money or its value in merchandise to London by a ship sailing from the town of Ver, called Caunfer[1], but the apprentice, having received the money on 9 Dec. 1386, left his service the next day and departed to some place unknown, though he might have had passage in many ships sailing from Caunfer to London; and accordingly the plaintiff claimed damages of £200 from the said Edmund in accordance with the law merchant. [*French*]

The defendant appeared on 13 Feb. and a day was given him on 30 July, that he might in the meantime make inquiries among merchants trading at Middelburgh. On that day the parties chose arbitrators, John Walcote and Richard Wyllesdon, on behalf of the plaintiff, and Thomas Girdlere and Richard Toky, on behalf of the defendant, to give an award on 19 Dec.

Before that date, however, a certain William Brampton came into court with a bill, in which he stated that he had been chosen umpire, because the arbitrators could not agree, and that he had come into the Chamber of the Guildhall on 17 Dec. to give an award as regards one part of the dispute, his award being that a certain letter under the great seal of the Staple of Middelburgh, which had been delivered to Thomas Hoke, the plaintiff's attorney, by William Brampton, governor of the Staple, should be annulled and cancelled, because it had been issued only to establish a right over the apprentice and not to prejudice any proceedings in England,

[1] *Sc. Campoveria*, Veere, in Walcheren, Holland.

and thereupon the letter had been handed over to Henry Perot, clerk of the Guildhall[1], to be destroyed, and that further he had adjudged that no plea should be begun till Easter, the matter remaining in his hands meanwhile, since he intended either to appear personally then or to send a final award under his seal. [*French*]

As the said William Brampton did not send his award at Easter, the plaintiff craved leave to proceed to a plea. But the court, wishing to know whether he had made a definite award or not, and considering that a letter from Middelburgh might easily have been delayed by contrary winds or other causes, wrote to him a letter under the mayoralty seal [*French*] Membr. 10 *b*
on 11 April 1388, urging him to send the award. To this he replied by a letter dated at Middelburgh on 20 May, excusing himself for not attending in London, because he was unable to come, and stating that the apprentice, John Northampton, had arrived in Middelburgh without any merchandise, gold or silver, except his bare expenses, and while there he had neither bought nor sold anything nor made any exchanges, as was clear from the evidence of merchants and from a search which he had made in the books where such exchanges were registered, but that all such exchanges had been made by the plaintiff's attorney, Thomas Hoke—the days, months, years and terms of payment all being duly entered in the registers. Accordingly he found the boy not guilty of what was surmised against him by his master, namely, that he had received so great a sum of money, for it was well known that Thomas Haukere had no merchandise on that voyage to Middelburgh except a fardel of cloth which was not worth £20, and Thomas Hoke told the writer that he could not sell it for any sum of money so large as was alleged. Further, as to whether the boy made his journey by command of his master or of the attorney, or whether he was dead or alive or what had become of him, the writer could not gain any certainty or information from the inquiries he had made, but he knew that many English merchants, whom God assoil, had within the last two years been drowned and had lost their lives on the journey between England and Zeeland

[1] Common clerk, or town-clerk, from 1375 to *c.* 1402.

and in the straits of Holland. Accordingly, taking all these matters into consideration, he gave as his final award that the defendant, Edmund Olyver, be quit of all claims from the plaintiff, saving to the latter the right of proceeding against the boy, if, which God grant, he were still alive. The writer begged the Mayor and Aldermen not to be displeased by his delay in answering, which had been caused by a long wait at Orewell on his passage out and much business on his arrival at Middelburgh. [*French*]

On receipt of this letter, the Mayor and Aldermen ordered the parties to be summoned for 2 July, on which day the plaintiff did not come and the defendant prayed that the award be enrolled.

Membr. 11
12 June 1388

Simon Broun, son of the late Robert Broun of London, was attached to answer John Bishop, mercer, and Katerine his wife, in a plea of contempt and trespass, in that he took service with the said Katerine, when she was sole, on 29 Dec. 1374 for seven years, receiving food and clothing as his wages, and left on 18 April 1375 without permission or reasonable cause, contrary to the ordinance[1] of the king and his council that any servant so leaving his service before the end of the contract should incur the penalty of imprisonment, whereby the plaintiff had damage £10.

The defendant pleaded that long before 29 Dec. 1374 he became apprentice of a certain John Aunger, bottlemaker, for eight years, and that on that date his master sold the unexpired portion of his apprenticeship to the said Katerine without his consent[2] and gave her the counterpart of his indentures, which was against the custom of the city, since the plaintiff was not a freewoman either then or at any time during his apprenticeship and had no trade in the city, whereby he might be made a freeman, and the plaintiff, thus being seised of him as an apprentice by colour of the said sale, set him to minding horses outside the liberty of the city and gave him no instruction in his trade; and it was for this reason that he left her service, as he was entitled to do, for

[1] The Ordinance of 18 June 1349, c. 2. *Statutes of the Realm*, I, pp. 307–8.

[2] See above, p. 125, n. 1.

at no time did he make any covenant to serve her. He offered to verify his pleading and demanded judgment.

The plaintiffs answered that the defendant of his own free will agreed to serve the said Katerine, which the defendant again denied, whereupon both parties put themselves on the country. On 26 June a jury of the venue of the parish of St Bride said on oath that the defendant made no agreement with the plaintiff Katerine and entered her service in no other way than by colour of the sale of the apprenticeship. Therefore it was considered that the plaintiffs take nothing by their bill, but be in mercy and that the defendant go quit thereof.

Membr. 11 *b*
18 July 1388

Writ, dated at Westminster 14 July 1388. Whereas the merchants of the cities of London and Norwich and the boroughs of Lenne, Great Yernemuth, St Botolph[1] and Kyngeston-on-Hull had complained that the men of Lubik, Rustok, Wissemere, Sounde[2] and Hamburgh in Almaine had arrested their servants and goods in the town of La Sounde, threatening to keep them in prison and their goods under arrest until they received redress for certain alleged wrongs done to them on the sea and elsewhere by Englishmen, whereof the said merchants were innocent, the king commands the mayor and sheriffs of London to arrest all the men, goods and merchandise of the towns of Lubik, Rustok, Wissemere, Sounde and Hamburgh and other parts of Almaine, being in the port of London or elsewhere within their bailiwick or district, and to detain them until they find sufficient security not to depart from the country without leave and to answer such charges as may be made against them on behalf of the king or the said merchants.

By virtue of this writ the following merchants of Almaine[3], Hermann Vynthorp, Frawyn Stupyn, Conerad de Ulpey, Bernard van Lune, Henry Smytman, Andrew Kilmere, Broun Dycof, William van Borne, Herri Meyresbek, John Knyghtkyn, Hilbrond Isplyngrote, Nicholas Lure, Frawyn Balke, Albert Clippyng, John Wystrete, John Espenkethe,

[1] Boston co. Lincs.

[2] Lübeck, Rostock, Wismar, Stralsund.

[3] See above, pp. 90, 100, for variants of these names.

Bernard Mekelynghous and Nicholas Paternostermaker, appeared in Guildhall and were mainprised by John Shadeworth and other citizens to appear before the chancellor on his next arrival in London or before others of the king's council, and further to save the mayor and sheriffs harmless by reason of their delivery.

Afterwards came a writ exonerating the merchants and their sureties, which was enrolled in the roll of Nicholas Twyford's mayoralty.

20 Sept. 1388 Writ, dated at Cantebrigg[1] 20 Sept. 1388. Whereas it had been granted by the king's predecessors to the merchants of the Hanse of Almaine that they should not be arrested for debts in which they were not sureties or principals or for trespasses committed by others, and recently the king had ordered that the merchants and goods of Lubik *etc.* in London should be arrested, nevertheless the king, in consideration of the above liberties and because Hermann Vynthorpe, John Pape, William de Borne, Hermann Husman and Mathias Walkemole had entered into a pledge before the king and his council that English merchants at Lubik, Rustok, Wissemere and Hamburgh should come and go freely without molestation, commands that the Hanse merchants be allowed to go at large with their goods. By the council.

And because this writ did not seem sufficient to the Mayor and Aldermen, the merchants were told to obtain another writ. Afterwards in the mayoralty of Nicholas Twyford, knight, they brought another writ[2], and they and their mainpernors were then exonerated.

Membr. 12, 13 and *cedula* A list of 490 aldermen and citizens under their respective wards, and 93 rectors, vicars and curates, who took the oath before Nicholas Exton, mayor, and the sheriffs, according to a writ and *cedula* entered in Letter Book H, fo. 228. A note that the names of lay citizens followed one after another, with no mention of their wards, in the return which accompanied the writ and *cedula* to Chancery.

[1] Cambridge.
[2] See below, p. 149.

[The oath, given in Letter Book H, had been taken by those attending parliament on 3 June 1388 and pledged them not to suffer the acts recently passed to be repealed. The writ requiring the aldermen and chief men of the city to take the oath was issued next day, 4 June.]

Henry Derby, ironmonger, was summoned to answer William Avenell, son of Giles Avenell of London, in a plea of covenant, wherein the latter complained that he became apprentice in Feb. 1382 to the defendant, who turned him away last Christmas, saying he wanted no more of his service, and this was without reasonable cause and not owing to any demerit of the plaintiff, in consequence of which he received no food, clothing or teaching and had heavy charges in keeping himself, since he could not take service with any one else, wherefore he prayed to be exonerated from his apprenticeship and to be reimbursed for his expenses, according to the custom of the city. Membr. 14 *1 July 1388*

On the master's denying these allegations, a jury of the parish of St Botolph by Billingsgate found for the plaintiff and assessed damages at 6s 8d. Therefore it was considered that the said William be exonerated from his apprenticeship and recover the damages taxed by the jury.

Letters patent of Sir Guy de Bryene, knight, testifying that, whereas a certain John Grede sued a writ of *scire facias* against him returnable on the octave of St John the Baptist concerning his manor of Haselbere[1] co. Dorset, in order to defend his estate he had searched in his treasury in his manor of Rammesham[2] and in several other places for the muniments relating to the said manor and could not find them, and that, having a great suspicion that they had been taken away in a box by his son William to his (Guy's) house in London, he had, on his coming to London, of his own accord and without any suggestion from others, broken into the box on 30 June 1388 and there found fines, charters and other documents relating to the manor aforesaid and several others of his manors, which muniments he took away with *6 July 1388*

[1] Haselbury Bryan. Cf. *Cal. Close Rolls*, 1385–9, p. 593.
[2] Rampisham co. Dorset.

him, leaving in the box such muniments as concerned his son's own lands and tenements. He issues these letters patent to explain his action, for which no one was responsible but himself. Sealed with his seal on 6 July 1388. [*French*]

Membr. 14 *b*
18 Sept. 1388

Bargain and sale by Roger Brymmor, grocer, to John Weneton, fishmonger, and William Romesseie, tailor, of three quarters of a *craier* called "*le Andrew*" of Dertemouth with the proportion of rigging belonging thereto. Dated at London 23 June 1388. [*French*]

5 Sept. 1388

Letter of attorney from John Cook, chaplain, to Richard Odyham, chamberlain of the Guildhall, and Sir John Leicestre, chaplain, to demand moneys due on letters of exchange from Angel Cristopher and Peter Mark and their partners, Lombards.

2 Oct. 1388

In a dispute between Ralph Node, spurrier, and his late apprentice, Simon Hobbe, who complained that his master had not instructed him sufficiently in his trade, the arbitrators, Simon Winter, goldsmith, Simon Abraham, girdler, John Stafford, pinner, and Edward Law, junior, glover, awarded that the apprentice remain with his master for a further period and receive pay at the rate of 60s the year and his food and drink, and that the master make him free of the city as soon as he had learnt his trade and had paid 20s. [*French*]

Membr. 15
6 May 1387

Memorandum that on 6 May 1387 John Banham, late apprentice and servant of Thomas Austyn, mercer, came before the Mayor and Aldermen and complained that his master had sued him in the Sheriffs' Court for £500, and though he did not owe that sum he agreed to judgment on the promise of his master that all previous accounts between them should be satisfactorily settled, but when he was committed to prison for the debt his master allowed him to remain there, wherefore he prayed that the Mayor and Aldermen would appoint auditors and permit him to render account.

The Mayor and Aldermen, wishing to do justice between the parties, summoned the master before them. He said that he had made no such promise, but for his good name he would agree to the appointment of certain mercers as auditors to hear an account out of court, so long as the sheriffs' judgment was allowed to stand, and he promised to recover from the complainant only what the auditors should award. Afterwards by consent of the parties William Sheryngham, John Loveye, John Ottele and Robert Guphay, mercers, were elected and having heard the complainant's account produced their award in court on 8 Oct. 1387 as follows:

The said Thomas Austyn having discharged John Banham of rendering account for the period between Christmas 1382 and Christmas 1384 and having agreed to accept the oath and hand of John Hore, another of his servants, for the ensuing year, and the latter having given evidence, the auditors awarded that John Banham be quit for all receipts from his master during these three years, but that he ought to remain liable for any debts arising out of loans made by him. [*French*]

The parties again appeared on 29 Nov. 1387, Thomas Austyn, who had been committed to prison on divers accusations of the complainant and John Hore, having been liberated and being now on mainprise. All papers and memoranda were read relating to the three years for which the account had been taken and for the half year during which the complainant had served Thomas Austyn in his shop. It was found that £110 was owed to the latter by divers persons for goods sold to them by John Banham. Thereupon Thomas Austyn said he would give the said John a sufficient warrant to recover these debts, but he would not himself assume any responsibility. If, however, any acquittances were given or moneys received by him or his agents, he would make allowance for them. He was also willing, if the said John would find security for paying the sum of £110 by instalments, that the sheriffs should discharge him from prison, and he would give him an acquittance for all debts except the sum of £110.

Afterwards, when the said Thomas himself was delivered from prison, he received from the chamberlain the sum of £6 6s 8d which John Cartere of St Albans had paid.

ROLL A 29

Divers men adjudicated to prison in the time of Nicholas Twyford, knight, mayor

Membr. 1
1 June 1389

Thomas Derby, *brodurer*, was committed to prison at the suit of Lionel Vyvarde, merchant of Genoa, for a debt of £20 due to the said Lionel for an embroidered silk curtain.

28 Aug. 1389

John Whyte, *lymenour*, was committed to prison for a debt of 16s which Henry Gaysle, *scriveyn*, recovered against him on the award of the masters of the *Lymenours*[1], and for 40d which the court adjudged that he should pay to the chamberlain for disobeying the ordinances of his mistery.

30 Aug. 1389

John Kempe, boatman, unmarried (*solutus*), who was taken in adultery with Isabella Smyth, wife of Richard Smyth, in Billingsgate ward by John Kempe, smith, constable of the ward, was mainprised the same day by the said John Kempe and John Chiltre to appear before the Mayor and Aldermen where and when *etc.*, under penalty of £40[2].

Membr. 1 *b*
23 Jan. 1389

Whereas divers charters of divers misteries, granted to them by the king and his progenitors, had in the time of Nicholas Brembre, knight, been taken into the Chamber of the Guildhall into the custody of Richard Odyham, chamberlain[3],

[1] Illuminators, Limners. Mentioned as an organised craft in the list of 1422 preserved in the records of the Brewers' Company.

[2] This offence, which was usually a matter for the ecclesiastical courts, had been made punishable in the Mayor's Court by a recent ordinance promulgated during Norhampton's mayoralty. Walsingham, *Hist. Angl.* (R.S.), II, pp. 65–6, tells us that there was a campaign against immorality while Norhampton was mayor, and that he and his followers were animated by the teaching of Wiclif. The Bishop of London resented the infringing of episcopal rights but was afraid to protest. See *Cal. of Letter Book H*, pp. 176, 189; *Munim. Gild. Lond.*, I, pp. 457–60. This was not entirely new, since offences against morals had been punished in accordance with previous ordinances, probably as conduct likely to lead to a breach of the peace. *Ibid.*, I, pp. 591–2 for civic ordinances on the subject.

[3] During the first mayoralty of Nicholas Brembre, 21 March 1377 to 13 Oct. 1378, the Common Council ordered that all masters of misteries should bring in their charters for the governance of their misteries to the mayor and chamberlain. *Cal. of Letter Book H*, p. 193. Unwin, *Gilds of London*, p. 156, regards this as aimed against the manufacturing guilds, but it appears to have applied to all the misteries, and was probably a move

there to remain *etc.*, and afterwards, when it should be necessary to the men of the misteries, to be handed back to them for production before the king and his council, the charter of the Drapers was on 23 Jan. 1389 delivered by the chamberlain to John Basse, Thomas Noket, Thomas Weylond and John Eston, drapers, who were mainprised to produce it before the Mayor and Aldermen and their successors where and when *etc.*

The same day the chamberlain delivered to Roger Excestre, Thomas Depham, Thomas Kirwode and Thomas Cole, saddlers, the charter of their mistery, under the same conditions[1].

24 Jan. 1389

The charter of the Goldsmiths was similarly handed over on mainprise of Thomas Polle, Thomas Panton, Andrew Stamelden and Reymund Standulf, goldsmiths; the charter of the Skinners by mainprise of William Olyver and William Horscroft, skinners; the charter of the Girdlers by mainprise of John Nasyng, William Sewall, William Picot and William Potenham, girdlers; and the charter of the Tailors by mainprise of John Dymmok, John Wilby, William Horston, Richard Rose, John Garnet and John Ballard, tailors.

15 July 1389

Martin Falimonica was mainprised by Ciprian de Mare and Isuellus Spinula to appear before the Mayor and Aldermen where and when *etc.* and to answer if any wished to sue against him.

Membr. 2
20 Sept. 1388

Further writ relating to the arrest of Hanse merchants in London in reprisal for the arrest of English merchants at La Sounde by men of Lubyk *etc.*[2] The king commands that the merchants, *viz.* Hermann Vynthorpe, Frowyn Stepyng, William de Bourne, Conrad de Ulpe, Bernard van Lunen,

to strengthen the authority of the city government over the misteries. A writ of 1 Nov. 1388 ordered the misteries to produce their charters in Chancery before 2 Feb. 1389, *Cal. of Letter Book H*, p. 336, for which reason they were returned by the chamberlain. See Unwin, *Gilds of London*, pp. 157–8; Toulmin Smith, *English Gilds*, pp. 127–31.

[1] The Saddlers had refused to surrender their charter, and only obeyed when Brembre threatened to drive them out of the city by the sword. See Sherwell, *Saddlers*, p. 41.

[2] See above, p. 144.

Henry Smythman, John Epenschede, Henry Mayresbek, John Knyght and Bernard Mekilkus, all of Cologne, Andrew Kilmere, Brunus Dycof, Hilbrand Ispelyngrode, Nicholas Leure, Frowin Balke, Albert Cleppyng and John Wystrote, all of Dortmund (*Tremonia*), and Nicholas Paternostermaker of *Ungaria*, should be disarrested and allowed to go at large, because the said Hermann Vynthorp, William de Bourne, John Pape, Hermann Huseman and Matthew Walkemolle had appeared before the king and his council and had entered into mainprise that English merchants should go and come with their goods, without injury or arrest, in the towns of Lubyk, Rustok, Wyssemere and Hamburgh and the districts of the same, excepting the town of La Sounde. Dated at Cantebrigg 20 Sept. 1388.

By virtue of this writ the mainprise of the merchants of Almaine was cancelled and they and their mainpernors were exonerated.

Membr. 2 *b*
16 Jan. 1389

Quitclaim from John Wantynge, son of Sibil, sister of Robert Hamull, citizen, whose heir he is, to William de Briene, knight, his heirs and assigns and other persons holding[1] the manor of Esthall co. Kent, of all his right and claim to the same manor and to a messuage, mill, 4 carucates of land, 13 acres of meadow, 60 acres of wood, £10 annual rent and a rent in kind of 120 hens and 400 eggs, in Esthall, Crei St Mary, Orpinton, Doune, Codham, Okeholte, Hese, Farneburgh, Pintham and Frenigham co. Kent[2], which the said Robert his uncle acquired of Richard de Esthall and Margaret his wife. Dated 15 Jan. 1389.

3 Oct. 1388

Writ of protection, dated at Cambridge 3 Oct. 1388, in favour of John Holbech of London, who was prosecuting divers pleas touching himself and the king in divers courts in England and was afraid of personal violence and damage to his goods by his enemies.

[1] *Et ceteris tenentibus manerium.*

[2] East Hall, St Mary Cray, Orpington, Down, Cudham, Okeholte *alias* Shottys, a small manor held by the family of Shelley in Knockholt, Hayes, Farnborough, either Petham, Pedham Place west of Farningham, or Petham, Pedham Court in Eynesford, Farningham. See Hasted's *Kent*, I, pp. 304, 308.

Further writ to the mayor and sheriffs ordering them to proclaim the above protection in the city and not to molest or trouble the said John.

Writ to the mayor that whereas letters patent of pardon[1] had been issued to Margery, widow of Hugh Bromhull, pinner, for all offences entailing penalty of life, limb or forfeiture, between 1 Oct. 1382 and 31 May 1388, whereof she might have been indicted, accused or appealed, the king wished to be certified as to whether the said Margery was one of the citizens of the city. *23 Jan. 1389*

Return of Nicholas Twyford, mayor, that the said Margery was one of the citizens according to the custom of the city.

Memorandum that Robert de Whiteby, clerk and servant of John, duke of Lancaster, lately entrusted to Peter Mildenhale, skinner, a counterpane of ermine for a bed belonging to the duke, which the said Peter pledged as security to Thomas de Kent and Walter Pykenham, skinners, executors of Stephen Daubeneye, skinner, for a debt of £101 1s 8d, which he owed to Stephen, and afterwards the said Peter was arrested and imprisoned in the king's castle of Nottingham[2] on charges of felony and treason. Subsequently, when Robert asked for the counterpane, the executors refused to deliver it to him. Thereupon the king on 16 Jan. 1389 sent letters under his privy seal to the mayor and sheriffs demanding that they return the counterpane to Robert, as appears more fully in the file of letters received from the king and other lords and magnates. The mayor and sheriffs caused the executors to deliver the counterpane, and the latter were exonerated thereof. *16 Jan. 1389*

Pleas held in the Chamber of the Guildhall according to the custom of the city before the Mayor and Aldermen 2 Dec. 1388

Membr. 3
2 Dec. 1388

Gilbert Bonet, executor of the will of Richard Lyons, was summoned, together with his co-executors John Warde and

[1] *Cal. Pat. Rolls*, 1385–9, p. 519. [2] *Cal. of Letter Book H*, p. 312.

Thomas Medelane, to answer Isabella, widow of the said Richard, for detinue of 1500 marks, being her portion of the goods and chattels of her late husband according to the custom of the city, whereby a widow took a third part if there were children, and one half if there were no children. She alleged that when her husband died without issue on Corpus Christi day (13 June) 1381 he possessed goods and chattels in the parish of St James Garlikhithe to the value of 3000 marks, *viz.* gold and silver in money, silver vessels, linen, woollen and silk cloth, wine in tuns, pepper, ginger and other merchandise.

John Warde and Thomas Medelane making default, the defendant Gilbert appeared, after the great distress had been put upon him, and protested that he did not acknowledge the custom to be as alleged, or that the plaintiff was ever *de jure* the wife of Richard Lyons, or that the said Richard had any goods and chattels on the day of his death. He alleged that in 1363 before John Harald, commissary-official of the bishop of London, in St Paul's church the said Richard and Isabella, by the name of Isabella Pledour, were divorced at the suit of the said Richard on account of certain impediments, and such marriage as there was between them, so far as it went in fact, was declared annulled by definitive sentence. He demanded judgment whether the plaintiff could have any action against him.

The plaintiff answered that she was married (*desponsata*) to the said Richard long before the time of the alleged divorce and that the marriage (*sponsalia*) continued till the death of her husband, and that at the Husting of Common Pleas on 13 Nov. 1385 she sued John Wakelee and Maud his wife on a writ of dower for the third part of two messuages and sixteen shops in London, which John and Maud afterwards alleged that her union with Richard Lyons was not lawful wedlock. To this she had replied that she was married at the door of St Mary de Stanynge church in Aldrichesgate. As the court then considered that the case belonged to ecclesiastical jurisdiction and they had no power to demand information from the bishop of London, and they wished to consult further, the action had been adjourned from Husting to Husting until 12 Nov. 1386, when the king sent a writ of *certiorari*, returnable to Chancery, demanding the record and process, and afterwards sent the return with another writ to the justices of the Bench[1] to deal with it. She had appeared before the justices and, on the default of the said John and Maud, prayed that a writ of *certiorari* be sent to the bishop. After several writs had been sent to him, the bishop at last sent to the justices his letters patent and close saying that he had summoned the parties before himself and his commissaries and, the matter having been thoroughly discussed, it had been found that Richard Lyons and Isabella Pledour had lawfully contracted matrimony, which was solemnised according to the accustomed form of the church. Afterwards the king sent his writs to Robert Bealknappe, justice of the Bench, and to Thomas Haxeye, keeper of the writs of the Bench, ordering them to send to Chancery their certificate with all matters connected, which certificate they duly sent. Thereupon the king sent the record and process with the certificate to the Husting on 27 April 1388 in order that they might proceed. She said further that there had been no divorce, which she was prepared to verify, wherefore she prayed judgment.

As the court considered that the cognisance of the case belonged to the ecclesiastical court and that they had no power to demand information from the bishop, and because they wished to consult further, a day was given to the parties and process was continued until 15 Feb. 1389. Meanwhile the king by a writ of 8 Feb. demanded that the writ and process be returned to Chancery. Finally on 10 May 1390 the king sent a writ, *sub pede sigilli sui*, reciting the proceedings and informing them that the record and process had been forwarded by Chancery to Robert Cherlton and other justices of the Bench, who had obtained from the bishop of London a certificate, dated 15 Nov. 1389, to the effect that the marriage contracted between Richard Lyons and Isabella Pledour had been quashed and annulled[2].

Membr. 3 *b*

Membr. 4

William Shrympelmerssh was attached to answer John

Membr. 5
10 Feb. 1389

[1] *De Banco*, the Court of Common Pleas at Westminster.
[2] For further proceedings see below, p. 185.

Pygeon, piebaker, in a plea of deceit[1], wherein the latter complained that on 24 Sept. 1386 the defendant offered to sell him a house in the parish of St Andrew Baynardescastell in fee simple, free of all encumbrances, and guaranteed that it would let at 20 marks per annum and that he would rent it himself for 20 years at that amount, whereupon the plaintiff bought it for 100 marks, but found that it was burdened by two statute-staples, one to William Venour in £100 and another to Edmund Gyssyng in £40, and that it was worth only 12 marks per annum; and moreover the defendant, instead of finding security as promised and renting the house, fled to sanctuary at Westminster.

The defendant in bar of action pleaded an agreement of 2 Nov. 1386 in the parish of St Gregory as regards all claims of the plaintiff against him, except a claim for the enrolment of a deed in Guildhall, which claim he did not acknowledge, and that in accordance with the agreement he paid the plaintiff 21 marks.

The plaintiff answered that the agreement was made not in the parish of St Gregory but in that of St Mary Wolcherchehawe and that it was conditional on the defendant enrolling the deed of feoffment of the house, sealing indentures of a twenty years lease of the same and paying an old debt of 21 marks, which conditions, as regards the enrolment and the indentures, were not fulfilled.

On these issues a jury of the two parishes of St Gregory and St Mary brought in a verdict that the agreement was made in the latter parish and was conditional, and they assessed damages at 5s. Accordingly it was considered that the plaintiff recover damages as taxed by the jury and that the defendant be in mercy.

20 March 1389 Letter of attorney from Hugelin Gerard of Bolonia Crassa to Philip de Matuan of the same.

Membr. 5 *b*
15 March 1389 Robert Somersete, draper, who had been named in the will of Thomas Carleton, grocer, as an executor, together with the widow, Joan, and John Arnold, chaplain, came into court and

[1] An offence at common law and by statute 3 Edw. I, c. 29.

renounced his executorship and prayed that his renunciation might be entered of record.

Membr. 6
16 Feb. 1389

Indentures between Thomas Sampson of co. Suffolk and John Otteleye, citizen of London, for a settlement on the marriage of Simon Sampson, son of the said Thomas, with Margaret, daughter of the late William Knightcote of London, and ward of the said John. The said John agreed to pay over to the said Thomas the said Margaret's inheritance, *viz.* £333 6s 8d, namely £100 in money and the remainder for the purchase of real property, when an opportunity should occur, for the benefit of Simon and Margaret and their children, or, failing children, the legitimate children of the survivor, with remainder to Thomas Sampson. It was further agreed that half of any goods and chattels which might accrue under the will of William Knightcote be used for the same purpose and half be paid to the said Thomas. Dated 9 Feb. 1389. [*French*]

18 Feb. 1389

Recognisance by Egbert Ludykesone of Campe[1] to Richard, earl of Arundel and Surrey, of a debt of £500 payable at Christmas at the earl's town-house (*hostiel*) of Pulteneys[2] in London. [*French*]

Membr. 6 *b*
8 April 1389

Letter of attorney from William Bacoun, son and heir of the late Richard Bacoun, stockfishmonger, to Sir John Gardyner, parson of the church of St Martin Oteswich, and John Douve to receive from Richard Bedewynd and Margaret his wife a quitrent of half-a-mark issuing from their tenement in the occupation of John Chircheman and situate in the parish of St Michael Crokedlane in Tamestret. Dated 1 Feb. 1389.

[1] Kampen, Holland.

[2] See Kingsford's *Stow*, II, p. 322; *Archaeologia*, LVII, pp. 268–9.

Membr. 7
27 Nov. 1388

Pleas held in the Chamber of the Guildhall before Nicholas Twyford, knight, Mayor, the Sheriffs and Aldermen[1] *according to the custom of the city on Friday 27 Nov. A° 12 Ric. II*

Whereas John Walpoll, tailor, and others had brought divers bills of trespass before the mayor against John Bodesham of Bury, late serjeant of the city, the said John was arrested and taken to the compter of Thomas Austyn, one of the sheriffs, on 5 Nov. 1388. Afterwards on 12 Nov. he was mainprised by Robert Litle, fishmonger, and seven others to keep the peace with the complainants and for his appearance in court where and when *etc.*

Among the bills above-mentioned was one affirmed at the suit of John Reymes, cordwainer, who complained that the said John Botelesham (*sic*)[2] on 19 Dec. 1384 in the parish of St Peter Westcheap, with several others in his company, sought for the plaintiff in his house and from house to house, with force and arms, in order to kill him, so that the plaintiff did not dare to approach his house to carry on his trade and make his profit for a quarter of a year, to his damage £100, and moreover the said John was the chief abettor of all the indictments made against the plaintiff. [*French*]

Thereupon the sheriff was ordered to bring the body of the defendant into court on 27 Nov. and to warn the mainpernors to have him there. But though the sheriff testified that the mainpernors had been warned, the defendant did not come. Accordingly, since the Mayor and Aldermen wished to be more fully informed as to the truth of the matter contained in the bill and as to the damages to be awarded, precept was given to summon a jury of the venue for 2 Dec. On that day came a jury of William Maryner and others, who said on oath that all the matter contained in the bill was true and that the said John Botelesham was guilty of the trespass alleged, to the plaintiff's damage £50. Judgment was reserved until 5 April, when, the sheriff's serjeant having

[1] Sitting for the conservation of the peace, in accordance with the city's jurisdiction therein.

[2] *Alias* Botkysham, Botlesham *etc.*

testified that the mainpernors had been warned, judgment was given that the plaintiff recover his damages as taxed by the jury. The plaintiff then prayed that the defendant and the mainpernors be committed to prison until the damages be paid. Order having been given for their arrest, the sheriffs' serjeants, Nicholas Covele and Richard Clare, testified that the mainpernors Robert Litle, Thomas Neel, Thomas Prentys, William Poull, John Blake and Simon Rous had been arrested and committed to prison, but that the defendant and the other mainpernors Stephen Sedere and Walter Lynot could not be found within the liberty of the city.

Similar proceedings on a bill [*French*] of John Payn, goldsmith, and Joan his wife, who complained that when the said Joan on 1 Aug. 1386 was in Ludgate prison at the suit of Sir Nicholas Brembre, whom God assoil, the said John Botesham, then being keeper of the prisoners of Ludgate, out of envy, strong rancour and ill-will, conspired to ruin her and, desiring to please the said Sir Nicholas, procured and abetted the prisoners there to beat her in her bed and elsewhere so continually and so horribly that her life scarce endured, and then, venomously despoiling her of all her goods, he drove her, naked except for a single gown, to Newgate, where he confined her in a cell so hard and piteous that she came near to death, all of which horrible and outrageous hardship she would not willingly have suffered for £100.

Since the Mayor and Aldermen wished to be fully and completely informed, and since the more important men of the venue of Ludgate were either mainpernors of the defendant or belonged to his covin, they gave orders that 12 good men who were confined in Ludgate[1] at the time of the alleged trespass and were now at large should be summoned for 4 Dec. On that day the jury of William Strange and others said on oath that the whole matter contained in the bill was true, to the plaintiff's damage 20s. On 5 April 1389 judgment was given accordingly.

[1] See *Cal. of Early Mayor's Court Rolls*, pp. xlii–xliii, on the jury as a body of witnesses whose duty it was to inform the court. Cf. Pollock and Maitland, *Hist. Eng. Law*, II, p. 622; Maitland, *Social England*, I, p. 291.

Membr. 7 *b*
27 Nov. 1388

Similar proceedings on a bill [*French*] of William Waleys, tailor, who complained that John Bodesham, when he was keeper of Ludgate prison, deprived him of his right to alms, during his imprisonment, to his great undoing, and also of his rights of Holy Church at Easter and at all other times, to his discomfort and unhappiness, and further, when the plaintiff received a grant of 26s 8d for his deliverance from prison, the keeper heard of it and out of enmity to him prevented his being set free. The plaintiff prayed a remedy, so that no other poor persons might in the future suffer such injustice.

The same jury as above said on oath that the defendant did not receive or retain the sum of 26s 8d as was charged against him, but all the rest of the material in the bill was true, and they taxed damages at 40s.

Membr. 8
27 Nov. 1388

Similar proceedings on a bill [*French*] of John Horlee of the parish of All Hallows Stanyng, who complained that when he was a prisoner for debt in Ludgate a year or more ago for 14 weeks, during which time he lay in his own clothes, borrowing no garments from any one else, some of his acquaintances gave the keeper the sum of 3s 4d for him, as the keeper himself admitted, and a certain Shalyngford also gave another 3s 4d, but the keeper not only retained these moneys but also charged him 3s for sleeping on the bare ground in the plaintiff's own bed and bed clothes, and demanded 8d more, taking a lined cloak (*cloche double*) from him as security, and then later, when the plaintiff, being delivered, went with his wife to ask humbly for the cloak and the alms due to him, the keeper suddenly leapt out on them and would have killed them with his drawn baselard, if they had not fallen on their knees and piteously begged for mercy.

The same jury found the defendant not guilty of retaining the cloak, but said that the rest of the bill was true and assessed damages at 13s 4d. Judgment was given on 10 April 1389 that the plaintiff recover the above amount, but be in mercy for his false claim as regards the cloak.

Membr. 8 *b*
27 Nov. 1388

Similar proceedings on a bill [*French*] of John Walpoll, tailor, formerly a prisoner in Ludgate, who complained that the keeper, John Bodesham, and his clerk, William Rounde, had ruled the prison extortionately and evilly, *viz.* when alms of 100s or 10 marks were received for the deliverance of poor and feeble prisoners, they put down in the calendar of deliveries the names of their own servants and the officers of the prison, who were at large, so that they might receive the alms, thus depriving the poor prisoners of their deliverance; and further, the common alms-box was shared out in the keeper's own chamber against the wishes of the prisoners, and he chose three or four prisoners, as he pleased, to share out the alms and do with them as they wished, whereas the box ought to be shared out in the presence of all the prisoners in their common room; and lately, when the prisoners had raised a great clamour against this unjust division of the alms, he had allowed them to divide the alms themselves, as was right and reasonable, but being angry because he could not have control of the box, he had forbidden the usual begging by two prisoners outside the prison of alms for the sustenance of the prisoners; and when the plaintiff prepared a bill of complaint to the mayor, containing all these matters, the officers of the prison delayed it for three weeks, so that when it reached the mayor, it found him too busy to deal with it; and then the keeper, to punish the plaintiff for his share of the bill, put him in the stocks and in irons for five weeks to the great damage of his legs and limbs, during which time, when a grant of 40s was made for his deliverance, the keeper heard of it and detained the money and by evil suggestion to the mayor had him transferred from Ludgate to Newgate, thus depriving him of his deliverance, and moreover he told charitable people that the plaintiff had been indicted, and he also detained his clothes and other things, of all of which matters and many others the plaintiff would inform the Mayor and Aldermen by word of mouth, if they would graciously listen to him.

The same jury appeared on 4 Dec., when the plaintiff prayed leave to amend his bill, which the court refused. The jury then said on oath that the defendant was guilty of the bodily trespass against the plaintiff to his damage £30.

Afterwards on 2 Feb. 1389 the plaintiff brought another bill [*French*], reciting the above proceedings and mentioning that his action had been abundantly affirmed by the verdict of the jury given in answer to questions by the court. On this occasion the plaintiff had submitted to the court that he was not learned in the law, and that his bill had been drawn up by lay persons and did not contain the day or year of the alleged trespass or the value of the goods detained or the amount of the damages, and he had prayed that his bill might be amended and that matters omitted might be inserted, in accordance with the advice of his counsel, as follows: the date of his imprisonment in Ludgate, 19 June 1388; the value of the goods, £10; and the damages, £60. The plaintiff again prayed that the bill might be amended, or alternately that the present bill might be put in the file and annexed to the former bill and record, and that judgment might be given.

The sheriff's counsel and the counsel of the mainpernors prayed that the above bill might remain in court among other bills to which objection could be made. The court agreed.

Process being continued, the plaintiff appeared on 10 April 1389 and prayed judgment. Whereupon, the record and process being heard, it appeared to the court that the original bill was defective for the reasons alleged by the plaintiff and for other reasons, that the bill was false in matter, since John Bodesham was not keeper of Ludgate during the mayoralty mentioned but had previously been relieved of his office, that the verdict of the jury had been taken inadvisedly, and that therefore judgment could not be rendered on that verdict, and further that by the custom of the city a bill in such a case could not be amended. Wherefore it was considered by the court that the bill be quashed and that the said John Walpole and his pledges be in mercy[1].

[1] For the sequel to this action see *Cal. of Letter Book H*, pp. 368, 374, 392–3, 395–6. The mayor and aldermen, not being expert in the law, had left the matter to the recorder on condition that he consulted with John Tremayn, the common serjeant, and William Cressewyk, an alderman. Though the common serjeant advised that the bill could not well be abated, as a verdict had already been taken, the recorder had abated the

Writ of *certiorari* demanding the record and process of the actions brought by John Reymes and John Payn against John Botelesham and of the judgments against the mainpernors. Dated at Westminster 14 April 1389. Membr. 9 *14 April 1389*

Return to the same.

Note that the king sent a writ of *corpus cum causa*, followed by a similar writ *sicut alias*, and a further writ *sicut pluries*, demanding that the mainpernors imprisoned in connection with the above actions be brought to Chancery, together with the cause of their taking and detaining. *28 April 1389*

Return to the *sicut alias* of 28 April 1389.

Afterwards the record and process of the pleas between John Reymes, John Payn and John Horlee, on the one part, and John Bottlesham on the other, were sent before the justices at St Martin le Grand.

Writ of protection in favour of John Swan, son of Henry Swan of Mertok[1] co. Somerset, then about to proceed to Scotland on the king's service with Thomas, earl of Nottingham, marshal of England and warden of Rokesburgh Castle[2], to join the garrison of the castle under Thomas Swynburne, knight, the earl's lieutenant. Dated at Westminster 10 May 1389. Membr. 10 *10 May 1389*

Writ of *certiorari*, to Nicholas Twyford, mayor, and Richard Odyham, chamberlain, inquiring whether John Nichol, son of Geoffrey Nichol of Bordeaux, was a freeman of London, and if so in what manner. Dated at Westminster 20 June 1389. Membr. 10 *b* *20 June 1389*

bill and given judgment against Walpole. The matter was taken on appeal to the justices at St Martin le Grand, but in 1393 Walpole was still unsatisfied and petitioned the duke of Lancaster. In 1395 Walpole attempted to bully the then mayor into taking up his case and was committed to prison. Two years later he was bound over in £100 for his good behaviour and released. See below, pp. 229, 242. Meanwhile Botelesham, the unjust gaoler, remained an officer of the city. William Cheyne, the recorder, was succeeded by John Tremayne, who is mentioned as recorder on 18 June 1390. *Cal. of Letter Book F*, p. 273.

[1] Martock.

[2] Thomas Mowbray, warden of the Scottish Marches, and afterwards first duke of Norfolk (1397).

Return, that the said John had served his apprenticeship with John Clopton, late citizen and vintner, and was accepted as a freeman in the Husting of Common Pleas on Monday before the feast of St Dunstan (19 May) A° 8 Ric. II (1385).

Membr. 11
12 June 1389

Letter of attorney from Robert de Grafton, burgess of Shrewsbury, to John Levere, fishmonger, to receive from the prior and convent of the house of the Salutation of the Mother of God of the order of the Carthusians near London, an annual pension of £10, and another annual pension of £10 owed to him by the prior and convent of the hospital of the Blessed Mary without Bishopsgate.

6 July 1389

John Costace, merchant of Gascony, demanded against John Forteneye, apprentice and attorney of John Mokkyng, merchant of London, the sum of £57 18s 4d due for 10 casks of Gascon wine at 110s 7d the cask, bought by the defendant at Sandwich on 9 Nov. 1388, which sum ought to have been paid on the quay late of Henry Picard in the parish of St Martin Vintry immediately the casks were put on shore, but though the casks were landed, gauged and filled, according to the agreement, the defendant refused to accept delivery or to pay the money. He demanded a remedy according to the custom of the city and the law merchant.

The defendant admitted the agreement, but declared that the plaintiff was not prepared to deliver the casks as agreed, and on this issue he put himself on the country. Précept was given to summon a jury of whom one half should be Gascons, according to the custom. After making default, the jury appeared by distress on 16 July, when the parties agreed to put themselves on the arbitration of four men of the mistery of Vintners chosen by Robert Herry, *viz.* William Sharpyng, Richard Patesle, Richard Lyttlyngton and Thomas Say, who were sworn. The jury were exonerated. As the said William Sharpyng had to leave town (*devillare*) on business, the arbitrators went next day to the mayor's house next to the church of St John Zakary, and announced their award in favour of the plaintiff, which award the mayor recited and recorded before the aldermen in court on the following Monday. The defendant was committed to prison until he should pay the sum due, after which the wine was to be delivered to him.

Afterwards the said John Forteneye brought a bill against his master, John Mokkyng, complaining that the latter had sent him to Sandwich with 13s 4d to buy the wine, which he did, sending word by a certain Robert Grey to his master, who approved of the bargain and assigned a portion of the wine to John Doget, and afterwards when the plaintiff returned to London, the master again said that he was content, but when the wine arrived in London, delivery was delayed for awhile owing to its being arrested by the sheriffs, after which the master refused to accept it. Since the bargain was not for his own but for his master's profit, he prayed a remedy. Membr. 11 *b*

The matter having been thoroughly examined in accordance with the law merchant, it appeared to the court that the apprentice had bought the wine for the use and profit of his master, in which case the latter was bound to save him harmless. Accordingly it was considered that John Mokkyng pay £57 18s 4d to John Costace and that the apprentice be delivered from prison. As the master had not that sum ready he was committed to prison. An account being held, 51s 8d was deducted for gauging and other expenses, and on 20 March 1390 the defendant paid the residue.

Information having been given to the mayor and chamberlain by Ralph de Cromwell, knight, lord of Tateshale[1], that a certain John Slory occupied a plot of waste ground annexed to his tenement in the parish of St Sepulchre without Newgate, claiming it as an appurtenance of his free tenement, whereas it was the soil and free tenement of the commonalty of the city[2]—the mayor and chamberlain ordered John Wykes,

[1] Lord Cromwell of Tattershall co. Lincs.

[2] The city authorities exercised oversight on common and waste lands from an early time. In 1376 an Act of Common Council mentions a complaint that the Mayor and Aldermen had been granting *pleusours terres et tenementz de comune soyl* under the common seal without consulting the commonalty. *Cal. of Letter Book H*, p. 38. In 1435 it is stated as a law and custom of the city that tenements situated near the walls and gates should be distant sixteen feet or more, the space between being the common soil of the city. In 1444 the charter of Henry VI granted to the citizens all common soils, purprestures and approvements, in all wastes, commons,

the serjeant of the Chamber, to summon an inquest of office from the neighbourhood to give a verdict. On 17 May 1389 a jury of Thomas Ermelyn and others were separately sworn to tell the truth. They said that at present they were not fully informed, but that certain good men of the neighbourhood, *viz.* Richard Storm, John Squyer, Henry Godchep, Richard Asshewell and Roger Totyng, were fully cognisant of the matter, and they prayed that they might be sworn to give them information. The above-named persons were summoned for the following Monday to be sworn and the jurors were ordered to attend on the plot of land on Thursday, when the informers would be there with them, so that they might give their verdict on 31 May. In addition Thomas Mallyng and Richard atte Chirche, masons, and Stephen Warde and William Endcote, carpenters, who were sworn to the city, were ordered to attend on Thursday to advise them, so that the law of the city might be observed in all things. The jurors with two of the informers duly appeared in the Chamber and declared that John Slory had met them on Thursday and had shown them deeds, which had been enrolled in the Husting, manifestly proving that he had certain messuages, houses and shops there, held from the king by service of 4d per annum, of which the plot in dispute was a parcel, and that the commonalty of the city had no title to the same. At the same time the masons and carpenters certified to the same effect.

Membr. 12
14 Jan. 1389

Stephen Brunne, grocer, came before the Mayor and Aldermen and, in accordance with the custom of the city and the law merchant, brought a bill of complaint, as administrator of William Barkham, grocer, who died intestate, against John Beaufrount. The bill alleged that the plaintiff and William Barkham had entered into a bond dated 28 Oct. 1374 to pay the said John Beaufrount and a certain William de Lubenham

streets and ways...together with the profits thereof. Though in the time of Car. I (Birch, *Historical Charters*, p. 166) this grant was claimed to have been abrogated by the proceedings in the parliament of 28 Henry VI (*Rot. Parl.* v, pp. 183 *seq.*), it was not so understood at the time. Meanwhile, under licenses in mortmain and the charter of Edw. IV, A.D. 1478, lands were acquired by devise or purchase, which, with the common soils above-mentioned, were the foundation of the present City Lands.

the sum of £200. Afterwards on 4 Oct. 1375 in the parish of St Thomas the Apostle John Beaufrount agreed that if William Barkham would deliver to him cloth to the value of £200, taking in return a payment of £40, he would restore the bond and give him an acquittance. But though the cloth was delivered at Winchester, as witnessed by certificates under the mayoralty seal of Winchester, John Beaufrount had not returned the bond or fulfilled the conditions. [*French*]

The defendant was summoned by John Harewell, the mayor's serjeant, and made default. Thereupon order was given to sequestrate him, by way of distress, by locking and sealing one door of his house, according to the custom of the city. On a second default another door was locked and sealed. On a third all the doors were locked and sealed. The defendant having failed to appear on a fourth summons, the plaintiff demanded judgment and damages, and in further proof of his action produced the following documents.

(1) Bond of William Berkham and Stephen Brune to pay £200 to John Beaufrount, woolman of London, and William de Lubbenham of co. Northampton. Dated 28 Oct. 1374. [*French*]

(2) Covenant of 4 Oct. 1375. [*French*]

(3) Testimonial letter of John Bette, mayor of Winchester, that in the presence of himself, John Moryne and John Broun, bailiffs of the same city, Thomas Warner, Richard le Frye, John atte ȝerd and Water Hogyn, clerk, and other neighbours, William Berkham of London had delivered 51½ cloths of divers colours to John Beaufrount, partner of William Lobbenham, of which cloths 27 were of Bristol, 2 of Winchester, one was blanket and the remainder were in dozens (*en doseynes*)[1], with which John Beaufrount acknowledged himself satisfied, the delivery taking place outside Stephen Haym's house. Dated at Winchester 30 April 1376. [*French*]

(4) Testimonial letter of John Chamberlayn, mayor of Winchester, Thomas Smyth and John Peverell, bailiffs, and John Craan, clerk, confirming the above. Dated at Winchester 18 May 1388. [*French*]

[1] Here used in the sense of kersies and other coarse woollen cloths. See above, p. 108, n. 2.

(5) A letter of administration under the seal of the President[1] of London to Stephen Brunne of the goods of William Berkham. Dated at London 10 Nov. 1382.

Before judgment could be given a writ of *supersedeatis* was received reciting that John Beaufrount and William de Lubbenham were suing Stephen Brunne, pepperer, before the justices of the Bench at Westminster for £400 due on a bond, and that the said John Beaufrount had complained that the proceedings before the Mayor and Aldermen were merely intended to hinder the plaintiffs in their action and defraud them of their debt. The king, thinking it not consonant with reason that, where an action was pending for judgment before the justices of the Bench, the matter of that action or anything touching it should be dealt with in an inferior court, ordered the Mayor and Aldermen to supersede proceedings on the bill of Stephen Brunne. Dated at Westminster 20 Jan. 1389.

Membr. 12 *b*

Afterwards on 8 July 1389 Stephen Brunne brought a writ of *procedendo* to the effect that John Beaufrount and William de Lubbenham had made default before the justices of the Bench, wherefore the Mayor and Aldermen were ordered to proceed. Dated 7 July 1389.

Accordingly John Beaufrount was summoned to show cause why judgment should not be given, but did not come. It was considered that the plaintiff recover the bond. A jury of the venue of St Thomas the Apostle, where the abovementioned covenant was made, taxed the plaintiff's damages at £10. Thereupon the plaintiff alleged in full court that too small a sum for damages had been allowed, since he had spent more than £40 in the action, and he prayed that the sum for damages might be increased in accordance with custom and the law merchant. The Mayor and Aldermen raised the damages to a further 5 marks, and gave judgment for the return of the bond and the damages. The plaintiff prayed that the defendant be taken and committed to prison until he paid, which was granted under condition that if the

[1] Another name for the "official," the presiding officer or judge of an archbishop's, bishop's or archdeacon's court. The letter is sealed *sigillo officialitatis*.

defendant appeared within a year and a day to submit to justice, he should be admitted to answer.

Letter of attorney from John de Mauernec, merchant of Bayon, to Arnald Brokas, Richard Wedon, stockfishmonger of London, John Newark and Arnald Gillyam of Cesze, to sue for and receive from Domyngo...de Valence the sum of £60 and damages. Dated at London 16 Aug. 1389. *16 Aug. 1389*

Alice[1], widow of William de Wyndesore, knight, brings a plaint of intrusion against John Wyndesore, *squyer*, John Elmeshall and William Preston, touching her free tenement in the parish of All Hallows the Less. Membr. 13 *12 July 1389*

Quitclaim from John Southereye, tapicer, and Cecilia his wife to Neapolinus de Spinula, merchant of Venice. *7 Sept. 1389*

Simon Rede was exonerated from his apprenticeship to John Wenborn, ironmonger, on the ground that the latter had not enrolled him and had fled the city for debt. Evidence was given by John Faukoner and Roger Parys, masters of the mistery of Ironmongers, that the said John Wenborn had no shop in the city and had not transferred the apprentice to any one else. *1 Oct. 1389*

In an action for debt at the suit of John Frankeleyn, draper, against Edmund Peyton, mercer, for the sum of £90 due on a bond, the defendant made four defaults and fled to the liberty of St Martin le Grand, whereupon the goods whereby he had been distrained were valued as a foreign attachment by oath of Thomas Prudaunce and Simon Casteleyn, mercers, Thomas Bacheler and John Hunte, drapers, John Wilyngham and Thomas Kirton, vintners, and John Lorymer and John Osby, as follows: *2 Oct. 1389* Membr. 13 *b*

One *dosser*, one *coster*[2], 3 *bankers* and 2 *quisshyns*, 8s; 2 pieces of *kanevas*, 12d; one stuffed *jakke*[3], 3s 4d; one

[1] Commonly known as Alice Perrers. William Wyndesore, summoned to Parliament 1381 to 1384, was king's deputy and lieutenant in Ireland *temp*. Edw. III. He died in 1384.

[2] A side-hanging for a chair, bed *etc*.

[3] Jacket; when made of leather, stuffed and quilted or covered with iron plates, it was known as a *jakke of defense*.

stauntys[1], 2d; *ridelrynges*[2] and *countours*, 2d; 5½ yards of black fustian, 3s 4d; 14 yards of *syndon*[3], 9s 8d; 4 lbs of wax, 16d; one curtain of *kanevas*, 6d; 2 *launternes*, 4d; six stools, 3s; one yard of white worsted, 2d; one box, 3s 4d; one grate, 6d; one candlestick and one *brandyre*[4], 4d; 2 bows, 6d; one *polhax*, 8d; one sword, 4d; one pound of yarn and one *reell*, 2d; one piece of *wardemol*[5], 2d; one *kanevas*, 12d; one *sarse*[6], 8d; one *mosefalle*[7], 1d; one remnant of *kanevas*, 12d; earthenware pots, 4d; vessels (*vesselementa*) of wood, 4d; one *risshbolt*[8], 2d; one wooden bowl, 2d; *talwode*[9], 20d; one chair, 4d; one table with *trestells*, 16d; one large watertankard, 2s; one mortar with two pestles, 20d; one tub, 2d; one little form (*formula*) and one table with *trestills*, 6d; coal, 12d; one hogshead, 4d; one *kemelyn*[10], 2d; 7 empty tuns and one pipe, 10s; two *kanevas* in the cellar, 8d; three little forms, 12d; one quartpot of pewter, 8d; 6 tuns and one pipe of red wine, £13; 10 dozens of woollen cloth, £4; 2¾ yards of *fustyan* of Naples, 3s 8d; 9 ells of linen cloth, 6s 4½d; 5 yards of *karde*[11], 20d; 10 ells of linen cloth of Brabant, 5s 10d; 2 ells of *bulters*[12], 16d; one piece of *bukerham*, 8s 4d; one *quylte*, 3s 4d; one *materas*, 5s 6d; 2 lbs of *lyure*[13], 12d; 92½ yards of *sengle worsted*, 23s 1½d; one *volaunt*[14] of red worsted, 2s; 60 ostrich feathers, 20s; one breastplate, 2s; grapes (*uvas*), 3s 4d; total, £24 10s 1d.

Out of this sum was deducted £4 due to Peter Wotton for house-rent, 40s due to William Sele for the same, and 18s 4d due to William Hawe for the rent of a cellar, leaving £17 11s 9d.

As the court was informed that a certain Richard Langele,

[1] *Sc. standysh*, a pen-tray.
[2] Curtain-rings.
[3] A fine linen fabric.
[4] Brandiron, in various senses, gridiron, trivet and andiron, see *N.E.D.*
[5] Wadmal, a coarse woollen material.
[6] *Sc. searce*, a cloth-sieve or strainer.
[7] Mousetrap.
[8] Rushbolt, possibly a rush-sieve for boulting meal.
[9] Firewood.
[10] *Sc. kimnel*, a tub.
[11] *Sc. carde*, a material used for canopies, curtains and linings.
[12] Boulting-cloths.
[13] There was a cloth of Lyre, i.e. of Lire or Liere in Brabant, but not usually sold by the lb., unless yarn or fringe is intended.
[14] Something floating or flying, a sleeve, cape or flounce.

tymbermongere, owed the defendant £14 6s 8d, he was summoned. He proved by a deed that the money was not yet due. Accordingly judgment was given that the plaintiff receive the above-mentioned goods to the value of £17 11s 9d and the sum of £14 6s 8d when it fell due, under security of Richard Cornewaill, tailor, and Terry Trepston, *broudurer*, to answer therefor *etc.*

ROLL A 30

Divers men committed to prison in the time of Adam Bamme, mayor

Membr. 1
22 Sept. 1390 Richard Langele, *tymbermonger*, for a debt of £13 which he acknowledged as due to John Frankeleyn, draper.

4 Nov. 1390 Robert Tethyngman, apprentice of Richard Ledyerd, tailor, for refusing to serve his master.

20 Jan. 1391 John Sewale for a debt of £42 10s due to Bartholomew Bosano, Lombard.

15 Dec. 1390 John Heysterre and John Norwych at the suit of the said Bartholomew for £55, and 20s damages taxed by a jury.

Membr. 1 *b*
17 Nov. 1390 John Walpole, tailor, was mainprised by William Kirkeby and nine others to keep the peace with the officers of the city under penalty of £100.

20 April 1391 Peter Brake and John Kent, Flemings, were mainprised by John Bryan, junior, and Thomas Rose for their appearance in court.

Membr. 2
5 July 1390 Margaret, widow and executrix of Roger de Beauchamp, knight, and Thomas Olyver, chaplain, her co-executor, brought an action against Thomas Newenton and Robert Upgate, executors of John Philippot, knight, for detinue of the sum of £80, which they alleged had been entrusted on 4 Nov. 1374 to John Philippot by Robert Wytherley, master of the college of St Lawrence Pulteney, on behalf of Roger de Beauchamp. In proof, they cited a deed of John Philippot, acknowledging receipt of the above amount.

The defendants, while protesting that they did not admit any of the facts alleged, pleaded that John Philippot had subsequently acted as executor of Roger de Beauchamp and had duly administered his goods and chattels to a value exceeding £80, and offered to verify their pleading.

The plaintiffs in turn did not admit the truth of the defendants' plea and prayed judgment on the ground that the defendants had put in no defence to their action. They were not bound, they said, by the law of the land, to answer the plea made by the defendants.

The defendants pleaded that the plaintiffs had not denied the truth of the matters advanced by them, which were a sufficient defence in law, and accordingly they prayed judgment that the plaintiffs be excluded from their action.

The court, after consultation, gave judgment on 14 Nov. for the defendants.

Appointment by Adam de Foxleye, rector of St Andrew in Holbourne, of John Bygonet and Roger Hillom to let to lease and receive the rents from houses and tenements left by Avice, widow of William Edyman[1], for the support of a priest to say masses for the souls of those mentioned in her will, in accordance with the wishes of the testator, who directed that after the death of her executors, two of the better men of the parish should be chosen by the rector to receive the houses and rents for the said purpose. Dated in the said parish 3 June 1390. Membr. 2 *b* *29 Nov. 1390*

Writ directed to the Mayor and Aldermen reciting a complaint of Francis de Conago of Milan, merchant, that Philip de Matuleano of Boloigne de Grace had impleaded him by bill in the Chamber of the Guildhall, in order to make him contributory to divers expenses incurred by Hugelin Gerard of Bologna, and although the complainant offered to answer the said Philip by competent counsel, the Mayor and Aldermen would not admit him to make this kind of answer. The king commands the Mayor and Aldermen to admit the said Francis to make his answer with competent counsel, or in person if he preferred, and to do justice in the matter. Dated at Westminster 25 Nov. 1390. *25 Nov. 1390*

Return to the above that the Mayor and Aldermen for the time being had been accustomed, time out of mind, to hold and terminate plaints and pleas merchant brought before them in the Chamber of the Guildhall, as well by bill exhibited as without, where both parties were merchants, and on such bills and plaints to summon and do justice to such

[1] Cf. *Cal. of Wills*, I, p. 181; II, p. 540.

merchants, foreign and native, whether dwelling in the city or resorting to it, who made complaint to the Mayor and Aldermen concerning mercantile matters and their merchandise, by the law merchant used within the city from of old, and further to examine such merchants of either party when they were present upon the matters and grievances specified in such bills and plaints. Moreover the Mayor and Aldermen and their predecessors had been accustomed, from a time whereof the memory of man runneth not to the contrary, to take the oaths of such merchants and to examine them and put questions to them and to use other means of eliciting the truth, and then to terminate and bring to a final decision such bills and plaints pending before them according to their discretion and the truth discovered by examination, without any counsel or any other form of plea. This was the reason why the Mayor and Aldermen did not admit Francis de Conago to make his answer with his counsel on the matter specified in the writ, but caused him to answer by the law merchant by way of examination and other methods according to the ancient custom of the city, because he and his adversary were both merchants resident in the city and the matter of the bill exhibited entirely concerned merchandise.

16 Feb. 1391 Letter of attorney from Lodewicus Burnel, merchant of Lucca, to Naufreus Johannis, merchant of Lucca. Dated 13 Feb. 1391.

Membr. 3
5 Dec. 1390 Richard Moris, *hostiler*, and John his servant were summoned, by virtue of a bill exhibited before the Mayor and Aldermen in the Chamber of the Guildhall, to answer John Prene, clerk, who complained that, whereas throughout England it was the custom for innkeepers, keeping common hostelries, and their servants to guard the goods and chattels which guests had in their chambers within the inns, he came and lodged with the said Richard in his inn in the parish of St Benet in Castle Baynard Ward with his horse and other things, *viz.* a trunk (*mala*) and two small boxes, and the innkeeper assigned him a room in the inn, in which he placed his things, and afterwards on 24 Nov. the plaintiff went on

business of the University of Oxford to Westminster, and while he was away, evil men broke through the wall of his room and carried away the boxes, in which were 100s in silver coin and a bond of 100s made by a certain John Hore, and this came about by lack of good custody on the part of the innkeeper and his servants, to the plaintiff's damage £10, whereof he prayed a remedy.

The defendant, while protesting that he did not acknowledge that the plaintiff brought any boxes or that the goods were in the boxes or of the value alleged or that they were carried away, pleaded that long before the plaintiff entered the room or placed anything in it, he hired, by his servant John Shilyngton, a certain apartment (*mansionem*) from the defendant, *viz.* a hall, chamber, buttery and kitchen, at 6s 8d a week, on condition that neither the defendant nor his servants were to have anything to do with the said dwelling, or with the plaintiff or his servants, or with any goods brought in by them, and that the plaintiff was to buy his own victuals and other necessaries wherever he wished without interference by the defendant or his servants during his tenure of the apartment. By virtue of these conditions the plaintiff occupied the apartment until the day when the goods were alleged to have been carried away and long afterwards, during which time he bought his own necessaries outside the defendant's inn and the defendant and his servants did not interfere, nor did the defendant have any horse in his inn or buy any food for the plaintiff, nor did the plaintiff in any manner lodge with him, nor did any goods of the plaintiff come in any way into his custody, as he was prepared to verify, without that *etc.* He demanded judgment whether the plaintiff could impute any default of custody to him, and whether the plaintiff ought to have any ground of action against him for the loss of his goods.

The plaintiff did not admit the truth of these allegations and pleaded that the defendant was a common innkeeper, that the house which he, the plaintiff, occupied was a common hostelry and a part of the common inn kept by the defendant, and that the room in which the goods were placed was parcel of the hostelry and within it, and since the defendant did not deny that the goods were actually stolen, and since further every common innkeeper was bound by the law and custom of the realm to guard his inn, he claimed that he was under no necessity to answer the allegations put forward by the defendant [breaks off].

2 Sept. 1391 Letter of attorney from John Donat, citizen and apothecary, to Guynus Bartholomei, merchant of Siena.

Membr. 3 *b*
7 Sept. 1390 Geoffrey Grigge, taverner, was summoned to answer Nicholas Benyngton, mercer, for arrears of rent due on two houses, the one called "*le Bole on the Hope*" and the other "*le Caban*," both being in the parish of All Hallows in Honeylane. The defendant pleaded that a certain John Oxenford had leased the former house to a certain John Blaunche for 60 years, who assigned the lease to the plaintiff who again assigned it to the defendant, whose wife Agnes had paid the arrears. As regards *le Caban*, he said it was part and parcel of the other house and was included in the lease. The plaintiff answered that not John Oxenford but Robert Turk, knight, had made the original lease. He denied that the two houses were conveyed by the same lease or that the arrears had been paid. A jury of Richard Brendewode and others found for him with separate damages on his two bills, of 20s and 6s 8d. Judgment accordingly.

Membr. 4
8 Feb. 1391 Since in these days the scarcity of wheat and especially of corn has been greatly increased and since the Most High of His abundant grace has permitted a great part of the wheat, coming from distant foreign parts for the sustenance and aid of His common people, to be brought to the city of London, so that scarcity has in great part been diminished there and wheat is more plentiful and sold at a less price than in other cities and districts of England, Adam Bamme, the Mayor, and the Aldermen[1], noting that under God's providence there was a plenitude of wheat in the city, and being desirous, in their careful foresight for the common weal, to provide against any scarcity which might arise in the city in the coming summer, caused the good men of the city to be summoned

[1] The Court of Aldermen.

for common counsel in the Chamber of the Guildhall on 8 Feb. 1391, when it was agreed and ordained that £400 of the goods of orphans in the custody of Richard Odyham, chamberlain, should be delivered to Adam Bamme for buying wheat therewith in case the commonalty of the city should have need of it, and since this money belonged to the orphans and had been entrusted to the chamberlain, the said Adam, under the style of "Adam Bamme, citizen and goldsmith," entered into a recognisance to repay the above sum to the chamberlain at Michaelmas following, as appears in Letter Book H, fo. 258, under the condition that if meanwhile any orphan claimed delivery of his goods, and the Mayor and Aldermen ordered payment, the said Adam should satisfy the orphan for the sum due to him and acquit the chamberlain and his successors and the commonalty thereof; and if no orphans so claimed, the said Adam should repay the whole amount as abovesaid, it being always understood that if any loss or damage occurred in the buying of the wheat, it should fall upon the commonalty of the city, and be charged upon the profits of the Chamber.

William Bretford brought a bill complaining that William Goryngg, citizen and weigher of lead of London, on 12 Nov. 1390 under colour of his office had arrested a wooden balance and certain leaden weights weighing 8 cwt. 1 qr., of the value of 100s, claiming them as forfeit, against right and reason, and to the plaintiff's damage 40s. He prayed the Mayor and Aldermen to have the balance and weights brought into court, so that they might discuss whether they were forfeitable or not. [*French*] *16 Feb. 1391*

The defendant appeared on summons on 18 Feb. and pleaded that the plaintiff had no ground of action against him, because from time immemorial all balances, used by persons weighing lead between merchant and merchant, which were not sealed with the seal of the city, were forfeitable to the use of the sheriffs and went towards the payment of the king's farm. Further the present sheriffs had committed the weighing of lead to the defendant in virtue of their office. The plaintiff having weighed lead with balance and weights which were not sealed, the sheriffs had arrested them as forfeitable and sold them to the defendant, who was in possession of them for that reason; without that[1] he was an official of the sheriffs or by colour of his office had arrested them, as the plaintiff supposed by his bill.

The plaintiff repeated that the defendant had arrested the balance and weights of his own ill-will, and on this he put himself on the country, and the defendant did likewise.

A jury of the venue of St Dunstan in the East, *viz.* Walter Coupere and his fellows, said on oath that the defendant arrested the balance of his own ill-will, to the plaintiff's damage 10 marks. Therefore it was considered that the plaintiff recover *etc.*

23 Aug. 1391 Grant from Hugh Fastolf, citizen of London, to John Hadley, William Cressewyk, citizens of London, Robert Houtoft, Geoffrey Somerton, James Billingford and Sir Nicholas, perpetual chaplain of *la Charnell* in Great Jernemuthe (Yarmouth), of all his goods and chattels. Dated at London 21 Aug. 1391.

Membr. 4 *b*
19 Nov. 1390 Action of account by the abbot of Rewley near Oxford against Hugh Talbot, tailor, with regard to moneys received by the latter to trade therewith by the hands of William Wynferthyng, William Isbrond, Thomasina Hukstere, Hans Clokkemaker and other tenants of the abbot in London [breaks off].

Membr. 5
20 Nov. 1390 John Holmton of Sleaford, merchant, brought a petition claiming from John Walworth, vintner, the sum of £120, which the complainant's attorney overseas, John Feryour, had lent to John Walworth's apprentice and attorney, Richard Edmund, at Middelburgh two years before for the purchase of wines, under condition that the money should be repaid in England. He prayed that John Walworth and his apprentice be examined in court according to the law merchant, in order that a reasonable end might be made to the matter. [*French*]

[1] The defendant pleaded that he was only concerned with the weighing and that it was not true that as an official he had arrested the balance and weights. The plaintiff pleaded that the defendant had exceeded his duties and had made the arrest.

John Walworth having denied on 1 Dec. that the loan had been made for his use, the parties agreed to put themselves on an examination of the apprentice, Richard Edmund, and to accept his testimony. The said Richard on 7 Jan., having sworn to tell the truth without concealment, favour or fear, said that his master had in his keeping certain charters and muniments relating to his (Richard's) lands and tenements, and being afraid that his master might treat him unjustly in the future, he had borrowed the money in dispute for his own use and profit, and that none of it ever accrued to the use and profit of his master, as by the petition of John Holmton was supposed.

Acquittance from Alice, widow of William Ancroft, mercer, to William Hyde, grocer, John Pountefreit, saddler, Robert Sewale, fishmonger, and John Drew, executors of her late husband's will, for the sum of 500 marks, being her third part of her husband's goods and chattels coming to her as dower and purparty, and for the clothes belonging to her chamber[1], to wit, linen and wool for the beds and all the clothing for her body, as appeared more fully in her husband's will. Given under her seal 1 May 1391. [*French*] *9 May 1391*

Acquittance [*Latin*] to the same effect, to which, as her seal was unknown to many, Mary, abbess of the Minoresses of St Clare without Aldgate, had added the common seal of the convent.

[1] According to Calthrop, *Divers ancient customs and usages of the City of London*, A.D. 1655, p. 165, the "widow's chamber" consisted of the tenement wherein she and her husband were dwelling at the time of his death, of which she was to enjoy to her own use the hall, principal chamber, the cellar underneath, and have the use of the oven, stable, privy and yard, so long as she remained unmarried. Cf. *Cal. of Wills*, I, p. 448, where Knopwed in 1341 says his wife is to have her entire chamber with all vessels and utensils belonging to his hall, larder, chamber and kitchen. In a case before Lord Parker on 18 March 1728, Biddle *v.* Biddle, it was decided that a widow was entitled to the furniture of her chamber, or in case the estate exceeded £2000, then to £50 thereof. *Viner's Abr.*, VII, 200.

Note, that whereas "free bench" outside London was dower according to the custom of the manor, in London it is distinguished from dower and is a convertible term with "widow's chamber." See *Munim. Gild. Lond.*, I, p. 393; *Cal. of Letter Book H*, p. 253; *Cases in Equity temp. Lord Chanc. Talbot*, 1741, case 257.

A further acquittance by the abbess on behalf of the convent and their *consoror*, Alice, widow of William Ancroft. Dated 2 May 1391.

6 Sept. 1391 Report of Simon Hoke and Henry Godard, the sworn masons, and Richard Bornham and Walter Wiltshire, the sworn carpenters of the city, with regard to a stone building called the "*Fermory*[1]" at Austin Friars. They found that one gable-crest[2] had fallen and another was in danger of falling, owing to bad work on the part of Richard Salyng, mason, whom they charged with the renewal thereof at his own cost and expense. [*French*]

Membr. 5 *b*
19 June 1391 Robert Bardolf, knight, and Amicia his wife demand an Assize of Nuisance against William Bealhome, leatherseller, touching their free tenement in the parish of All Hallows on the Wall.

Report of the four sworn masters of the Masons and Carpenters as to a stone wall of Robert Lyndeseye's tenement at the Tabard in Wood Street in the parish of St Alban. [*French*]

Membr. 6
8 May 1391 Writ of *certiorari* demanding the tenor of a letter under the signet from the king to John Norhampton, late mayor, ordering him to arrest Hugelin Gerard, Lombard, with all the goods and chattels, papers and letters found in his lodging, and to deliver him to Sir Thomas Murreux, late constable of the Tower. Dated at Westminster 8 May 1391.

Return giving a letter under the signet dated at the king's manor of Shene on 29 Jan.[3], ordering that Ogolyne Gerard be delivered to Thomas Morrieux, constable of the Tower, and his papers be sent to the *continuel conseil* in London. [*French*]

2 Aug. 1391 Appointment of Thomas Davy, John Hunte, Thomas Lamport and William Harper, wardens of the mistery of Goldsmiths, William Louthe, John Lyncoln, Stephen de

[1] Infirmary. [2] The cresting or finial of a gable.
[3] Probably 1383. On 13 Feb. 1383 a writ was issued for his delivery, as he had been mainprised in Chancery. *Cal. Close Rolls*, 1381–5, pp. 288, 419.

Thorpe and John de Luton, goldsmiths, as arbitrators in an action between Henry Bamme, plaintiff, and Hervy Rokhawe, defendant, with regard to lands in Fulham, Braynford and Illyng[1].

Membr. 6 *b*
6 Aug. 1391

John Fraunceys, one of the sheriffs, brought a bill of complaint setting forth that a certain John Gentyll had been condemned in the court of his predecessor, John Loveye, and in his own court in several actions for debt brought against him by John Hayne, tailor, John French, prior of the Carmelite Friars, and John Denys, jeweller. On 20 June he was allowed to escape to the sanctuary of St Martin le Grand through the negligence of Thomas Clerc, who was servant of the sheriffs' serjeant, John Starlyng, without having paid the debts recovered against him, in consequence of which the plaintiff became chargeable for those amounts. Although every sheriffs' serjeant was responsible for the misdeeds of his servants, the said John Starlyng had refused to find security to save the plaintiff harmless against the abovementioned claims. [*French*]

John Starlyng was brought before the Mayor and Aldermen and was asked if he could give any reason why he should not exonerate the sheriff against the plaintiffs in the said actions. He pleaded that John Gentyll had been handed over by the court to his servant, Thomas Clerc, without his knowing anything about it, and therefore he was not responsible for his escape.

As it seemed to the court that, according to the custom of the city, sheriffs' serjeants were bound to answer to their masters not only for their own offences but also for such misdeeds of their servants as concerned the sheriffs, and since the serjeant's servant, who had been ordered by the court to take the prisoner to Newgate, had allowed him to escape, it was considered that John Starlyng find sufficient security to indemnify his master against any claims of the plaintiffs in the aforesaid actions, and since John Starlyng could not find such security, he was committed to Ludgate until he could do so.

[1] Brentford and Ealing.

6 Sept. 1391

Writ of protection in favour of Henry Tamworth, esquire, who was then on the king's service in the company of Thomas, earl of Nottingham and earl marshal, captain of the town of Calais. Dated at Westminster 6 Sept. 1391.

By virtue of this protection a plea of trespass brought against the said Henry by Walter atte Welle was adjourned without a day.

Membr. 7
10 Oct. 1391

John, son of William Shynguler of Bermyngham co. Warwick, brought a bill showing that his master, Roger Grymston, draper, to whom he had been apprenticed at Easter for eight years, had absconded for debt on Tuesday after Michaelmas, leaving him destitute and homeless and without food and drink except what was given to him by good people for the love of God. He prayed to be exonerated from his apprenticeship. [*French*]

The master, on being several times summoned, failed to appear, and since evidence was given by the neighbours that he had left no goods and chattels in the city to carry on his trade and had not put his apprentice to any one else to learn the trade, the latter was exonerated, on condition that if the master returned within a year and a day and had any action against his apprentice, he should be allowed to sue it.

Membr. 7 *b*
1 April 1391

Letter under the mayoralty seal to the duke of Gyene and Lancastre[1] and to all royal and other lords. Whereas a certain Robert Ospreng, claiming to be executor of Thomas William, had complained to the duke that William Venour, during his mayoralty, had given him a letter under the mayoralty seal confirming the impression of the seal used by the testator during his lifetime, but had afterwards sent for him to bring to Guildhall a bond of £200 made by William Page to the testator, and had imprisoned him and taken away from him the letter under the mayoralty seal, in consequence of which he could not have execution of the bond—the real truth was as follows: The said Robert had come to the mayor saying that he had been appointed administrator of the goods and chattels of Thomas William by the abbot of Westminster, whereupon the mayor had given him a letter witnessing that

[1] John of Gaunt, duke of Guyenne and Lancaster.

a lease of a shop in Bokelersbury[1] from Thomas Medelane, vintner, to the testator, bore the seal used by the testator in his lifetime, but afterwards the Mayor and Aldermen were advised that this testimonial letter might turn to the prejudice of other persons, since they had no full information or knowledge of the seal of the testator and did not truly know whether it had been used by him in his lifetime or not, except on the word of the said Robert and other insufficient persons, and accordingly, with the assent of the aldermen and the city's counsel, the mayor had taken back the letter. It was not true that the said Robert had been in any way imprisoned or grieved or molested in his person, as he alleged. They begged the duke to give credence to this explanation and to hold the said William Venour excused. [*French*]

[1] Bucklersbury.

ROLL A31

Roll of Memoranda of the time of Edward Dalyngregge, knight, warden of the city of London[1]*, in the sixteenth year of the reign of King Richard the Second* (1392)

Membr. 1
6 July 1392

Whereas John Harmesthorpe, master of St Katherine by the Tower[2], placed a certain William Gynne, a boy of about ten years of age who was in his wardship, to school with Richard Exton near the Friars of the Holy Cross[3], certain of the friars came to the boy and told him to translate into Latin the words—" *Y oblisshe me to be a frere of the croys,*" and when the boy had done so, one of the friars kissed him and said that all the bishops in England could not absolve him from becoming a friar of their order, and so they took the boy away on 4 July 1392 and dressed him in the habit of their order and withdrew him from the custody of the said Richard Exton. And when the latter complained to Edward Dalyngregge, warden of the city, praying for a just remedy, the warden on 5 July ordered the friars to send the boy to him, and next day, on the ground that the boy was of tender age and not of marriageable years and was a servant of the master of St Katherine, without whose consent he could not legally bind himself, and further because the friars had gained possession of the boy by deception, the warden sent him back to the master of St Katherine.

9 July 1392

Bond by John Loveye, William Shiryngham and Thomas Vynent, citizens and mercers, before William Venour, deputy of Edward Dalyngregge, in £3000, to Bernard Brocas,

[1] He appeared at Guildhall on 1 July 1392 and there read his commission appointing him warden and king's escheator. The mayor and sheriffs had been dismissed, apparently because the citizens had refused a loan to the king, but had privately lent the money to a Lombard who accommodated him. The reason given in our records was "certain defects in a commission under the common seal and other causes." See *Cal. of Letter Book H*, pp. 378–9; Higden, *Polychronicon* (R.S.), IX, pp. 270–3; Walsingham, *Hist. Angl.* (R.S.), II, pp. 208–9; Sharpe, *London and the Kingdom*, I, pp. 240–2.

[2] The hospital of St Katherine by the Tower.

[3] The house of the crouched or crossed Friars in Hart Street in Aldgate Ward, now called Crutchedfriars.

knight, to save the latter harmless within one month, in case John Shadworth[1], who was in his custody, should escape or absent himself.

Afterwards on 18 Oct. the said Bernard came before the Warden and Aldermen and acknowledged that the above covenants had been fully observed, and agreed that they should be cancelled.

Acquittance by Lefardus Blumendale, merchant of Prussia, before the Warden and Aldermen, to Sir John Montagu, knight[2], lord of Werk, for the receipt of 1000 nobles, owed by the said Sir John, as principal, and John, Lord Bemund[3], William, Lord de Botreaux, knights, Peter Byxton, John Bever and Edmund Faukes, citizens in Danczik, and Robert Ko, English merchant, as his sureties, on a recognisance to Sir Wynand Ostinchusen, consul in Danczik, and the said Lefardus. Dated in London under his seal, 12 July 1392, and sealed, for further evidence of the true identity of the said Lefardus, with the seals of Frowin Stepyng, John Swarte and Henry Smytman, merchants of Almaine, dwelling in London. *13 July 1392*

Bond by the said Lefardus, Frowin, John and Henry to John Mountagu, knight, in 1000 nobles to indemnify him and his sureties against any further claims for the money paid as above.

[1] John Shadworth, alderman, was one of the two sheriffs dismissed. Higden says he was sent to Odiham Castle (IX, p. 272), of which Bernard Brocas was constable. He was released under surety on 23 July and pardoned on 19 Sept. *Cal. of Letter Book H*, p. 383.

[2] The honour or barony of Wark by Tweed in Northumberland, granted for life to William Montagu in 1329 and subsequently entailed, descended to his son John in 1344, and to his grandson John in 1370, who exchanged it in 1397 for other lands with Ralph Neville, later earl of Northumberland. See *History of Northumberland*, XI (Kenneth Vickers), pp. 38–41; *Inquis. post mortem*, 13 Ric. II, no. 34; Husting Rolls, 118 (124), 119 (101), *etc.* for the possessions of this family in London, where they appear to have dwelt.

[3] Beaumont.

Of the time of Baldewyn Radyngton[1], *knight, warden of the city of London*

Membr. 1 *b* Letter of attorney from Francis Johan, merchant of Sene[2], to Guy de Port of Lucca and William Palmere of London.

23 Aug. 1392 Bond of James Clabaud, son of James Clabaud, merchant of Amiens, in £200 to William Wende, hosier, that he would not take away Joan, wife of the said William, or communicate with her, or do the said William any harm either in his person or his goods.

21 Oct. 1392 Letter of attorney from Bernard Dalem, *alias* Bernard Doat, esquire, of Gascony to Sir Bertrand de la Traw, clerk, John Frankeleyn, draper, and Arnald Guilliam of Sedzes[3], dwelling in London, to receive from the king or the treasurer of England an annual pension of 40 marks, granted to him for life by the king, and to give acquittances for the same. Sealed by Sir Baudewyn Radyngton, warden of the city, with the seal of his office, for greater credence, since the seal of the said Bernard was unknown to many. Dated at London 17 Sept. 1392. [*French*]

Membr. 2
5 June 1391

Pleas held in the Chamber of the Guildhall before Adam Bamme, Mayor, and the Aldermen, according to the custom of the city, on Monday 5 June 1391

Gilbert Bonet, executor of the will of Richard Lyons, was summoned to answer Isabella, widow of the said Richard, for detinue of 5000 marks, her widow's portion of her late husband's goods.

The defendant pleaded that Isabella had already sued a bill against him on 2 Dec. 1388, proceedings on which were still pending, and he prayed judgment as regards a bill sued, when

[1] Dalyngregge held office as warden for three weeks, his successor's commission being dated 22 July 1392. *Cal. of Letter Book H*, p. 382. According to Stow, *Annales*, p. 482, he was removed because he favoured the citizens. Cf. Higden, *Polychronicon*, IX, p. 274.

[2] Siena.

[3] Séez, Orne, Normandy?

a previous one was still pending. On being told to answer further, he pleaded the record of the previous proceedings to the effect that the plaintiff was divorced in 1363 owing to certain impediments and that such marriage as there was between her and Richard Lyons was annulled[1].

The plaintiff now pleaded that after the bishop of London had given a certificate that she had been divorced, she appealed against the divorce to Robert, bishop of London, who instructed his commissary, William Laas, to hear the appeal, and the latter annulled the divorce and confirmed the marriage. She offered to verify this in such manner as the court required.

Thereupon the defendant, saying that he did not acknowledge these allegations, prayed judgment on the ground that the plaintiff had not disputed the certificate or his pleading.

Nicholas Benyngton, mercer, brought a bill against Geoffrey Grigge, taverner, for refusing to quit certain tenements, the "*bol othe hope*" and a house late in the tenure of John Hamerton which he held as a tenant at will[2]. [*French*] Membr. 2 *b* *15 Nov. 1391*

On the defendant's pleading that he held the unexpired portion of a lease of 60 years originally granted by a certain John Oxenford, the plaintiff cited the record of a previous suit for rent due, wherein the bill alleged that the defendant was a tenant at will, in which suit judgment was given for the plaintiff. He prayed judgment whether the defendant could be admitted to verify his plea against the said record. The defendant then pleaded that the record was not sufficient in law to bar his proof, and prayed judgment.

Pleas in the Chamber of the Guildhall according to law merchant and the custom of the city before John Hende, Mayor, and the Aldermen, A° 15 Ric. II Membr. 3

Francekyn Johan, merchant of Siena, brought a bill against Nicholas Donat, son of John Donat, and John Tervyn, clerk, administrators of the goods of John Donat, late citizen and merchant of London, setting forth that John Donat had had *14 May 1392*

[1] See above, pp. 151–3.
[2] See above, p. 174.

charge of certain jewels of the value of 1000 francs belonging to the plaintiff, *viz.* two *nouches* and two gold rings, on condition that if the Duke de Berry, who owed John's brother Nicholas the sum of 1430 francs on a bond, should pay that amount to the plaintiff before Easter, then John Donat should keep the jewels, but otherwise he should return them, receiving back the bond, as appeared in examination before the court[1]. On John Donat's death, the administrators received the jewels in the presence of the court. But though the plaintiff had often asked that they should be returned to him, according to the conditions, the administrators refused. The plaintiff prayed that they should be forced to return them—and speedily, in deference to the king's letters sent to the court, and in accordance with the law merchant. [*French*]

Order having been given to summon the defendants, John Covelee, the mayor's serjeant, reported that John Tervyn could not be found and had no goods in the city or suburbs whereby he might be summoned. He was arrested and taken to the compter of John Shadworth, sheriff. Thereupon Amy, widow of John Donat, brought the jewels into court and asked for his release, which was granted. He then found sureties for his appearance, John Shalyngford and John Creek, draper, and asked that the jewels might be returned to Amy, which the court refused on the ground that his sureties were not substantial enough. The other defendant Francis Donat was also arrested.

The parties appeared on 5 Aug., when Nicholas acknowledged the truth of the bill. The other defendant, John Tervyn, pleaded that the bill was insufficient in law, because it did not mention or allege that the Duke de Berry had failed to pay the money due before Easter. The plaintiff answered that there was sufficient matter in the bill to maintain his action and that the other defendant, Nicholas, had acknowledged the truth of it. He prayed judgment.

The action was adjourned until 10 Dec. in order that the court might be advised according to the law merchant and the custom of the city. On that day it was considered that

[1] I.e. the plaintiff had sold his jewels for a bond, but he was to have them back if the bond was not met.

the plaintiff take nothing by his bill and be in mercy, and the jewels were returned to the said Amy.

Marginal note: *The record sent to the king's Chancery.*

Writ of *certiorari*, demanding the true and full tenor of the record and process of the above action. Dated at Westminster 28 Oct. 1393. *28 Oct. 1393*

Return that the complete tenor of the record was being returned with the writ.

Roll of memoranda of the time of John Hende, mayor of London, A° 15 Ric. II Membr. 4

Writ of *certiorari*, reciting that John Botelesham and his mainpernors had appeared before Walter Clopton and his fellow-justices, who were sitting at St Martin le Grand to hear pleas of error in the actions John Reymes *v.* John Botelesham[1], and John Payn and wife *v.* John Botelesham[2], and had alleged error in the record and process of these actions, which had been heard before the Mayor, Sheriffs and Aldermen on 27 Nov. 1388, to wit, that the Mayor, Sheriffs and Aldermen on the first day of the process had ordered the arrest of the said John Botelesham, whereas he was a freeman and as such had the right to make three defaults in a case where process was made against him by summons or attachment, to which John Reymes, John Payn and his wife had severally answered that as soon as such a plaint was affirmed and it had been reported to the Mayor, Sheriffs and Aldermen by two freemen of the city, not necessarily officers, that the defendant was a fugitive and insufficient in goods and chattels to be attached, such a defendant ought to be arrested, and further that, immediately after they had affirmed their plaints, they had brought John Rede and John Cole, sufficient men of the city, on 4 Nov. 1388, who witnessed that the said John Botelesham was a fugitive and did not possess goods whereby he might be summoned or attached, whereupon by precept of the mayor the said John Botelesham had been arrested by his body; and to this John *10 Nov. 1391*

[1] See above, p. 156. [2] See above, p. 157.

Botelesham and his mainpernors had pleaded before the justices that such witnesses must by the custom of the city be officers, and further that John Rede and John Cole had not given their evidence after the plaints had been affirmed. As the justices desired information on these points the mayor was directed to inform them as to the custom of the city. Witness W. Clopton at St Martin le Grand, 10 Nov. 1391.

Return to the above by the Mayor and Aldermen that John Rede and John Cole gave their evidence after the plaints had been affirmed, and that it was not necessary that the two witnesses should be officers, but only that they should be freemen.

7 Dec. 1391 Letter of attorney from Bernard Dalem *alias* Bernard Doat to Bernard du Siguer. Sealed at the request of the said Bernard Dalem by Sir Richard Craddoc, knight. Dated at London 1 Dec. 1391. [*French*]

Revocation of the above, 12 Sept. 1392.

Membr. 4 *b*
13 Feb. 1392 Robert Excestre, prior of Christ Church, London, appeared in court and acknowledged that the following indenture between William Rysyng, late prior, and the convent, on the one part, and John Caumpe and William, Thomas and Robert, his brothers, on the other part, was the deed of the prior and convent and sealed with their common seal.

Indenture of covenant, dated at London, 15 March 1386, in the presence of John, bishop of Durham and treasurer of England, and Walter, Lord Fitzwauter, between Sir William de Risyng, prior of Crischirche, and the convent, on the one part, and John, William, Thomas and Robert Caumpe, on the other, recites that by common agreement of Sir Aubrey de Veer, knight[1], and the said John Caumpe and his brothers, a quitclaim by the said Sir Aubrey to them had been entrusted to the prior and convent on the following conditions:

If it were proved by Sir Aubrey or his heirs by due process of law within eight years that John and his brothers or any

[1] Earl of Oxford, 1392 to 1400, when he died.

of them were villeins of Sir Aubrey, as *regardant*[1] to his manor of Dullyngham co. Cambridge, and this proof were shown to the prior and convent, the quitclaim should be returned to Sir Aubrey.

If it were not so proved, or if the said Sir Aubrey or his heirs delayed the delivery of the said John and his brothers, in case they were taken by Sir Aubrey or his heirs, after they had claimed their delivery by law, or if Sir Aubrey or his heirs put them in prison with the punishment of the stocks, irons, manacles or other engines in grievous pain of their bodies, or if the said John Caumpe or any of his brothers were proved by matter of record to be free and of free condition as regards Sir Aubrey and his heirs, then the quitclaim should be delivered to John Caumpe and his brothers and their heirs without hindrance.

Provided always that any suit sued within the said eight years by John Caumpe or his brothers should be sued to the end without nonsuit[2], after villeinage in their persons had been alleged against them by Sir Aubrey or his heirs, with the exception of the suit which the said John had pending at present against Sir Aubrey, which in consideration of this covenant should be discontinued.

And the said Sir Aubrey granted, in the presence of the above-mentioned lords, that he would not arrest the bodies of the said John and his brothers during the term of eight years unless he had more sufficient proof of their villeinage than at present, and that if he or his heirs arrested them for the said cause, he would guard them, without hardship of the villein's prison, until they were replevied.

In witness of the above, the common seal of the prior and convent and the seals of the said John, William, Thomas and Robert Caumpe were interchangeably set to these indentures.

[*French*]

Letter of attorney from Walter Cachemayd, merchant of Bristol, to Thomas Witton of London, dwelling in Podyng-lane, to receive from John Solak the sum of £76 17s 6d recovered against him by bill in the court of Guildhall, which *7 March 1392*

1 *Come regardantz a son manoir etc.*
2 The discontinuance of an action by demandant or plaintiff.

money was due on a bond to the said Walter and Robert Walrond, apprentice of William Whyt of Bristol. Dated at London in Brigestret 28 Sept. 1391.

15 Dec. 1391 Hervy Rokhawe, goldsmith, and Richard Darell, esquire, brought a bill of complaint against Maude Holbeche for detaining two deeds, relating to properties in Fulham and Braynford belonging to Margaret the widow of John de Norwich, goldsmith, which deeds they had placed in her hands for safe custody and return when required. [*French*]

When the action came on for hearing Richard Darell did not appear and after two defaults the co-plaintiff Hervy Rokhawe received permission to sue alone. The defendant pleaded that in the bill the plaintiff alleged that he and Richard delivered the deeds to her, and she said it was agreed that she should return the deeds to both of them, and as Richard had not appeared, she prayed judgment whether Hervy Rokhawe could have his action against her.

The plaintiff denied that there was any such agreement and pleaded the court's permission to sue alone. It was considered that he recover the deeds and damages of 40d.

Membr. 5
19 Jan. 1392 John Baldeswell, citizen and cook, brought a bill against Robert Carter for having obtained from him by falsehood and deceit the sum of 9 marks 12s 4d under the following circumstances. A certain Bartholomew Berford, who owed the plaintiff £120 and had fled to sanctuary at Westminster, owned 4 tuns of woad, which lay in a cellar hired from John Pycard on his behalf by a certain Mark Hunt. The said Robert came to him in the parish of St Mary at Hill and said that he knew where the tuns of woad were and that on these tuns 8 marks were due to a certain John Pycard and 23s 8d to himself, but the woad was worth more than this, and if the plaintiff would pay him the amounts mentioned, he might have the tuns. Accordingly he paid the said Robert; whereas the truth was that Robert had nothing to do with the woad, and the only amount due on it was 8s to John Pycard for cellarage. [*French*]

The defendant pleaded that the plaintiff came to his wharf next to the Wolkeye in the parish of St Dunstan in the East, and walked up and down, sighing and wailing (*suspirando et ululando*); so he asked him why he had come and what he was looking for. The plaintiff answered that he was given to understand that Bartholomew Berford had 4 tuns of woad in a house on the wharf, but he did not know which house. He told the plaintiff that there were 4 tuns in John Pycard's house, but to whom they belonged he did not know. Thereupon the plaintiff asked him to go to Pycard to make inquiries, which he did, learning that they belonged to Bartholomew Berford and had been pledged to Pycard by a certain Mark Hunt for 10 marks 7 shillings, in connection with some debt or other. The plaintiff then gave him this amount and asked him to pay Pycard, which he did the same day, whereupon the plaintiff received delivery of the tuns. He prayed judgment whether the plaintiff ought to have any action against him.

The plaintiff repeated that the defendant was guilty of deceit and put himself on the country.

A jury of the venue, consisting of William Bastard, Hugh Roos, John Dromayn and others, related the facts[1] in the same manner as the defendant had done, and said he was not guilty of any deception. Judgment that he be acquitted of the bill and that the plaintiff take nothing and be in mercy.

Recognisance by Cataneus de Spinola, Leonellus Vyvald, Matheus Grymald and George Granell, merchants of Genoa, of a debt of £545 6s 9d payable on 1 June to John Nichol, Thomas Bere and Ralph Glovere, merchants of Cornwall, and John Job. Membr. 5 *b* *8 May 1392*

Lease for three years, in consideration of a sum of money and an annual rent of one grain of wheat, from Thomas and Robert Broun, sons of Matthew Broun, late woolmonger of London, to John Skut, citizen and merchant, of *25 May 1392*

1. A tenement in Themestrete in the parish of St Dunstan by the Tower, bounded on the west by the tenement of Peter Ferye, tailor, and on the east by the shop of John Bere, cordwainer.

2. A shop bounded on the west by the shop of John

[1] After telling their story in eighty words, the jury adds (*ulterius*) that the defendant is not guilty. See above, p. 157, n. 1, on the jury as witnesses.

Parson, chandler, and on the east by the shop of Isabella Phippe, *shepster.*

3. A tenement with a small wharf[1] in Petywalys lane in the parish of All Hallows Berkyngchirche, lying between the street and the Thames, bounded on the east by the tenement belonging to a chantry in the said church, and on the west by the tenement of William Talworth, shipwright.

4. Three shops in Poortes lane by St Dunstan's Church.

Membr. 6
26 April 1392

Action of John Broun against Walter Ludneye, draper, for a debt of 80 marks awarded to him on the arbitration of John Stapulton, William Berdevile, William Beset and Edmund Cappemaker. The defendant pleaded that the action was a prolongation of disputes which had already been settled by a concord made between the parties at Westminster before Richard Ravenser, clerk, when mutual quitclaims were enrolled in Chancery [breaks off].

Membr. 6 *b*
7 Feb. 1392

John Prentys, draper, was summoned to answer a bill of John Mawsyn, parson of the church of St Peter Cornhill, executor of the will of John Strowsburgh, late citizen and *browderer*, claiming from him a debt of £56 13s 4d. The plaintiff alleged that a certain John Bradfeld, grocer, owed the said John Strowsburgh the sum of £60, and that on 12 March 1388 the defendant took the debt upon himself, of which a portion was paid in John Strowsburgh's lifetime, leaving the above sum in arrears.

By request of both parties a day, 14 Feb., was given for them to come to an agreement. On that day the defendant denied that he owed any debt to John Mawsyn and waged his law[2] as a freeman of the city according to the custom. The plaintiff granted that he should have his law. Thereupon the defendant made his law with six other men that he owed nothing. It was considered that the plaintiff take nothing by his bill *etc.*

[1] The easternmost of the four small quays which were later known as "Marowe's New Quay." See *Dugdale Society*, IV, pp. xxv–xli. It is now represented by part of the Wool Quay.

[2] The "law," or sevenfold oath, was permissible in actions of debt where there was no writing or tally to prove the debt. *Munim. Gild. Lond.* (R.S.), I, pp. 203, 294–5. The law could be forbarred if the plaintiff produced witnesses. See *Cal. of Early Mayor's Court Rolls*, pp. xxxvi–xxxvii.

ROLL A 32

Rolls of Memoranda of the time of William Staundon, mayor, A° 16 Ric. II

Thomas Wade brought a bill against his master John Crosseby, tapicer, to whom he had been apprenticed about three years before, and whom he had served faithfully until God, of his grace, visited the petitioner with diverse infirmities, so that he was unable to help himself, complaining that when he asked his master for money for medicines and to give him sufficient food and clothing, the said master refused and ordered him to go to his friends; whereupon he went to those who had stood surety for him, and he was supported by them at their costs, and afterwards, when he regained his health, he had several times, by the masters of his mistery, required the said John to provide him with food and clothing and teach him his trade, as he was bound to do by the custom of the city, or else to make a reasonable agreement with him, but the master refused and would neither accept the award of the said masters nor of any one else. Membr. 1 *11 Nov. 1392*

The master, on being summoned by the mayor's serjeant, twice made default and told the serjeant that he would not come. Thereupon the masters of the mistery of Tapicers, Walter Shank, Richard atte Welle, Edmund atte Wode and John Ricolf, testified that by the mayor's orders and on the plaintiff's request, they had on several occasions gone to see the defendant at White Chapelle outside the liberties of the city and that he had refused to come to a reasonable agreement with his apprentice. Accordingly it was considered, for the above reasons and because the master was living outside the liberties and was rebellious towards the mayor's serjeant, that the apprentice be exonerated from his indentures.

Writ to the mayor and sheriffs, that whereas Leonellus de Vivaldis[1], merchant of Genoa, was reported to have caused jewellery of great value and other goods and chattels to be brought into the city and secretly sold to divers persons of *7 Nov. 1392*

[1] Cf. *Cal. Close Rolls*, 1392–6, pp. 23, 36–7.

the realm, without any payment of custom or subsidy, the king commanded that the said Leonellus be arrested and kept in custody till he found security to appear before the king and his council on the octave of St Hilary next, and that meanwhile his papers be kept safely till further command be received. Dated at York 7 Nov. 1392.

Return that the said Leonellus was arrested on 16 Nov. and his papers were placed in a sealed bag in the Chamber of the Guildhall, and that afterwards George de Vivaldis, Teramus Catanius, Dominicus de Mari and Thobias Lomelyn, merchants of Genoa, mainprised him for his appearance *etc.*

30 Sept. 1392 Thomas Lynne, master of the barge "*Seintmarie*" of Dartmouth, owned by John Hawley, brought a bill against Octobone Grelo and Messer Pelegrin Cataigne and their partners, Tyrame Catane and George Vivalde, all merchants of Genoa, complaining that the said Octobone and Pelegrin on 1 March 1392 at Cyvyle[1] chartered the barge to be laden with 150 tons of merchandise within four weeks at 4½ francs the ton, amounting to 675 francs, with a further 25 francs for shoe-money[2], after which the ship was to sail to Hampton[3], remaining there four days while part of the cargo was discharged, and then proceed to London to discharge the remainder of the merchandise, and if the barge were not loaded at Cyvyle within four weeks by default of the merchants, they should pay the master the sum of 300 *doubles*[4] and the expenses of his stay there. The plaintiff remained at Cyvyle in the river with the barge and 40 sailors for ten weeks beyond the four weeks mentioned, because the merchants did not load their cargo, and he arrived at Hampton on 30 June 1392, where part of the cargo was delivered to the said Tyrame and George, and finally came to London on 12 Aug. where he delivered the rest of the cargo to them. By the law merchant he was entitled to 675 francs for freight, 25 francs for shoe-money, and 300 *doubles* penalty for delay, but though he had demanded these sums from the merchants, they refused to pay, to his damage £1000. [*French*]

[1] Seville.
[2] *Chaux*, *chauces*, a phrase equivalent to modern *pourboire*, a gratuity.
[3] Southampton.
[4] See below, p. 197, n. 1.

The plaintiff found pledges for prosecution, *viz.* John Hawley and Nicholas Macclesfeld, and produced a copy of the charter, the tenor of which appears in a schedule sown to this roll [see below].

The defendants, Tyrame Catane and George Vivalde, who were mainprised by Leonellus Vivalde, Angel Seba, Jerome le Conell and George Segale, appeared on 5 Oct. and pleaded that the present plaintiff had been sued for divers debts by Amfreon Bekevile, merchant of Genoa, John Birche of Bristol, John Hawley of Dartmouth, Richard Grove of Bristol and John Garcio, burgess of St Andrew's, and that in connection with those actions, the above-mentioned sum of 700 francs due for freight and shoes had been arrested in their, the defendants', hands by precept of Baldewyn Radyngton, knight, warden of the city, and delivered to Gilbert Maughfeld, sheriff, until it was decided to whom it should be paid. As regards 500 francs of that amount they prayed judgment as to whether they were liable to the plaintiff twice over, and as regards 200 francs they pleaded that the said Octobone and Pelegrin had lent that sum to the plaintiff at Civile on 1 March 1392 for the provisioning of the barge and crew, on condition that he should repay it at the port where the cargo was discharged, as soon as he received satisfaction for the freight, under penalty of one franc each day for delay. In proof of this plea they submitted a deed [*French*] of the plaintiff, admitting receipt of 200 francs from Octobone Grelo and Pelegryn Caitaneo, which he promised to repay without taking advantage of any exception of the law or any royal protection, and giving the justices, judges and bailiffs of all ports in any country power to levy the money, if unpaid, on the barge and its gear. Membr. 1 *b* *5 Oct. 1392*

The defendants pleaded that since the money due for the freight was then in the hands of the sheriffs, they had complied with the conditions of their charter and they prayed for the return of 200 francs in accordance with the above deed. As regards the claim for 300 *doubles* they pleaded that the plaintiff could not maintain his action against them, since they agreed to load the barge within four weeks at Civile and the plaintiff agreed to cross to St Luke de Barameda to receive cargo, and the said Octobone and Pelegrin had fulfilled all the conditions in their charter[1], which they produced:

Charter, dated 1 March 1392 at Siville, in the name of Thomas de Lynne, burgess of Dartmouth, master of the barge "*Seinte Marie*," witnessing that he had affreighted the barge to Pelegryn Catane and Octobon Grille to be laden with 150 tons of merchandise at the port of Civile within four weeks and then to go by river to St Luke de Barameda without delay and thence to Hampton, to remain four days discharging cargo, and afterwards to London to discharge the remainder, on condition that the master receive $4\frac{1}{2}$ gold francs of the coinage of the king of France for each ton and 25 francs for shoes, to be paid on arrival in London, where the cargo should be unloaded within 25 days. It was agreed that the merchants provide a pilot from Civile and that they caulk the cabin of the barge[2], and that the master was bound to provide the barge well equipped and found with sailors and all its gear, and that he should have a boat
Membr. 2 and cocket fitted for taking and discharging cargo in any port in which they tarried, paying the boat-crews their right, and that he should provide the merchants with fresh water, salt, firewood and cressets burning fore and aft, while towage[3] and little pilotages were to be a charge upon the goods

[1] Though the parties refused to admit each other's charters, the gist of the two documents is the same, the considerable differences of phraseology not affecting the general sense.

[2] Plaintiff's charter: *Et vous les ditz merchantz me devez doner pillotte dicy de Civyle tanqz a mon descharge et vous calefaiteez le tilat de la dicte barge.* Defendants' charter: ...*et qe vous ferrez calofater la couverture de la Barge.* Travers Twiss, *Black Book of the Admiralty* (R.S.), I, p. 30; IV, p. 194, translates *tylat* as deck, upper deck, "*pons tiliaceus* (linden-wood), made of harder wood than pine. *Il tillado* in old Spanish." *Calefaiter, calofater*, apparently not derived from Lat. *calefacere*, mean "to caulk." If *tilat* means "deck," the reason for this somewhat onerous charge on the merchants may be the rule that merchants had no claim for goods spoilt by wet if the deck was well pitched or, in case of an open boat, if the tarpaulin was watertight and if these coverings were higher than the bulwark, *Ibid.* III, pp. 94, 431, and accordingly merchants undertook the responsibility themselves. On the other hand there is a possibility that *tilat* is derived from French, *tille*, Engl. *tilette, tilt*, a deck-house or cabin. The waterproofing of a cabin or deck-house seems a more reasonable charge.

[3] Plaintiff's charter: *Et qe vous doie doner en ceste viage aque douce seel & bussh et crescetz ardauntz devant & derere—towages & petites lodman-*

of the merchants, and whatsoever should be found of the gift of God in fresh or salt water should be divided, one part for the merchants, one for the barge and the third for the master, and further the master and sailors should defend the merchants and their goods against all men except those of the master's own country. Either party not keeping the terms of the charters must pay the other the sum of 300 *doubles Moreskes dor*[1], chargeable on the barge or the merchants' goods as the case might be. [*French*]

The plaintiff pleaded that as regards 500 francs of the 700 francs, the defendants had said nothing to acquit themselves, and as regards the 200 francs which they alleged had been lent to him he was not bound by law to answer them, and as regards the 300 *doubles* penalty mentioned in his charter he was prepared to verify his plea. And the defendants pleaded as before, refusing to accept the plaintiff's charter.

The court asked for information from the sheriffs as to the actions for debt against the plaintiff and learnt that all except that of Amfrion Bekevile for £21 2s 6d were pending unsettled without a day owing to the king's letters of protection to the plaintiff. Accordingly it was considered that the plaintiff recover 675 francs for freight, 25 francs shoemoney and 20s damages, less the amount claimed by the said Amfrion, together with 300 *doubles* penalty, and that the sheriff deliver to him 700 francs, less the amount claimed by Amfrion.

Schedule annexed containing a copy of the charter put in by the plaintiff. *Cedula*

Recognisance by William Bartelot, citizen and mercer, to Membr. 2 *b* *4 Dec. 1392*

nages seront sur les biens de vous ditz merchantz. Defendants' charter: *Et qe jeo vous doigne ceste viage ewe douce & siel & busche & cressets ardantz devant & derere towailles & lez petitz lemanes qe soit sur lavor de vous lez merchantz. Lemanes, sc. lomanes, lodmannages* are pilotages. *Petitz lemanes* are harbour or coastal pilotages. See *Black Book of the Admiralty* (R.S.), II, p. 385. *Ibid.* Law of Oleron, III, p. 19. A coastal pilot was *petit lomant. Towailles* ought to mean napery, but is probably a variant of towage, which was a charge on merchants. *Ibid.*

[1] Godefroy, *Dictionnaire: monnaie d'Espagne qui venait des Maures...* "*une grant piece de monnoye d'or, nommee double morisque d'Espaigne.*" *Invent. des D. de Bourg*, 4182, *Laborde*.

Robert Guppey and Simon Bartelot, mercers, of a debt of £1000 payable at Michaelmas. Dated 10 Sept.

Grant from the same to the same of all his goods and chattels. Dated 9 Oct.

Marginal note: Robert Guppey and Simon Bartelot on 16 July 1395 acknowledged satisfaction concerning the above obligations, which were cancelled.

7 Oct. 1392 Writ of protection in favour of Thomas Lynne, master of the barge "*Seinte Marie*" of Dartmouth, who was then on the king's service with John Golafre, knight, captain of the town and castle of Chirburgh[1], for the provisioning of the same. Dated at Woodstock 7 Oct. 1392.

18 Dec. 1392 Quitclaim from Idonea, widow of John Clenhond, merchant of London, to William Walpole, otherwise called William, son of William Wynkfeld of Walpole in Mersshelond[2], late servant of her husband. Dated 16 Dec. 1392.

18 Jan. 1393 Bond from Leonellus Vyvald, George Vyvald and Leonellus Gautier, merchants of Genoa, to Sir John, Lord de Beaumont, knight, in £1000 to submit to the arbitration of Sir Thomas Percy, knight, Sir Henry Grene, knight, John Hadlee and William Brampton before the end of the next parliament, in disputes between the said Leonellus Vyvald and Lord Beaumont.

19 Jan. 1393 Acquittance by Drew Barentyn, goldsmith, William Cressewyk, John Luton, goldsmith, and Laurence Kelshill, chaplain, executors of the will of Nicholas Twyford, knight, to John Fraunceys, goldsmith, for the receipt of a sum of money owed by him for the reversion of a tenement called "*le Grifon*[3]" in Cheap, which remained to him after the death of Margerie, wife of the said Drew and formerly wife of Sir Nicholas Twyford. Dated at London 7 Dec. 1392.

[1] Cherbourg.

[2] Marshland Fen now lies some miles south of Walpole St Andrew and Walpole St Peter. The whole district could be described as marshland in 1392.

[3] The "*Griffon on the hope*," on the east side of Friday Street, directly south of a corner-tenement of St Paul's, which abutted on Friday Street and Cheapside. Husting Roll, 128 (73).

Marion Stok having complained that John Ruddok, *text-scriveyn*[1], to whom her son John had been apprenticed for eight years, had withdrawn himself from the liberty of the city and did not support or instruct the apprentice, and John Newent, cordwainer, William Broun, chandler, Thomas Burton, fuller, and other neighbours having given evidence to the same effect, the boy was exonerated from his apprenticeship. Membr. 3 *12 March 1393*

Pleas held in the Chamber of the Guildhall according to the custom of the city before William Staundon, Mayor, and the Aldermen on 21 Feb. A° 16 Ric. II [1393]

John Lotolli, merchant and burgess of Bordeaux, son of Master Ramond Bernard Lotolli, jurisconsult (*sage endroit*), was summoned to answer Robert Normant, master of the ship "*Christofre*" of Yarmouth, in a plea of debt of £32 1s 8d, due on a recognisance of 15 April 1388, made at Leybourne[2], a merchant town in Gascony. By this recognisance the defendant, who had promised to freight the plaintiff's ship with 60 casks of wine at 15s the cask to London, Hampton or Sandwich, and 20s the cask to Midelburu[3] and had failed to do so, bound himself to pay to the plaintiff the sum of £30, being half the freight, and also to repay £2 1s 8d borrowed from the plaintiff in London, the recognisance being attested by the seals of the mayor of Leibourne and Arnaud de Favols, burgess of the same, and witnessed by Bernard de la Barca, Aymeric de Jal Rostit, Amand Leucer, Berthon Dalbiera and Guassias Chivaler, public notary of the duchy of Aquitaine. [*French*] *21 Feb. 1393* Membr. 3 *b*

The defendant denied that the deed was his own, and a jury was summoned of merchants, of whom half were merchants of Gascony. On 19 March a jury of Robert Henry, John Gyllyng, Geoffrey Haket, Thomas Jeveek, Geoffrey Chauflour and John Andrew, English merchants, Arnald

[1] A writer of the ordinary book-hand, as distinguished from the writers of the court-hands. They were separate crafts in 1422. Unwin, *Gilds of London*, pp. 167, 370–1.

[2] Libourne.

[3] Middelburg, Holland.

Guyllyam, Peter Favere, John Narrant, Naudinus Bouv, John Nicholl and Perynot Robert, merchants of Gascony, said on oath that the deed was the deed of John Lotolly and assessed the damages at 4d. Judgment for the same.

Membr. 4 Memorandum that Jorwerth ap Reys of North Wales on 18 Feb. 1393 obtained from Nicholas Luke, Lombard, an exchange of London[1] for 30s, payable to the said Jorwerth in Venice, but that he went no further than Rome, owing to sickness, and returned to Sandwich, where he died, having appointed Jorwerth ap Evan his executor, to whom the said Luke repaid the 30s.

2 Aug. 1393 Melianus de Mare, merchant of Genoa, offered himself in a plea of debt of £15 against William Averey, citizen and clerk, who was summoned by foreign attachment. On the defendant making four defaults, the said Melianus prayed that the attachment be valued and delivered to him under security according to the custom of the city. The goods were valued by oath of John Clopton, shearman, John Devenyssh, shearman, and John Iryssh, tailor, and delivered to the plaintiff under security *etc.*, as follows:

One dozen of *plunket*[2] cloth, 20s; one dozen and 2 yds. of red cloth, 16s; one dozen and one yd. of green, 21s 8d; one dozen and one yd. of blanket, 13s; one dozen and 2 yds. of red, 18s 8d; one dozen and 2 yds. of *morey*[3], 28s; 1½ dozen and 1½ yds. of *melley*[4], 27s; one dozen and one yd. of blanket, 15s 2d; one dozen of *russet*, 14s; 1½ dozen of green, 14s; one dozen of *blew*, 24s; one dozen of blanket, 12s; one bed of *tapicerie* worked with a lion lying under a tree, of middle size, 40s; total, £14 3s 6d.

Membr. 4 *b*
6 Oct. 1393 William Wakeryng, master of the hospital of St Bartholomew in Smithfield, brings a plaint of intrusion against William Badby, citizen and grocer, touching his free tenement in the parish of St Peter upon Cornhill.

[1] I.e. a traveller's cheque.

[2] *N.E.D.* a woollen fabric of varying texture, apparently of a grey or light blue colour.

[3] Murrey, murrey-coloured cloth.

[4] Medley.

Thomas Pynchon, an orphan of the city, son of John Pynchon, late citizen and jeweller, brought a bill before the Mayor and Aldermen in the Chamber against Robert Excestre, prior of the church of Crichirche, London, William Cressewyk, William Baret, Hugh Sprot, Walter Pynchon and John Edmond, executors of the will of his father, for detaining his third part of the goods and chattels and debts owed to his father on the day of his death, contrary to the custom of the city, by which an only child, who had not been advanced, was entitled to a third part. The said orphan alleged that he was the only child of his father and Margaret his wife, and that his father died on 24 Sept. 1392, leaving goods and chattels of the value of £2200 and debts owed to him of the value of £1000 and 100 marks. [*French*] Membr. 5 *5 Nov. 1392*

Robert Peek, common pleader of the city[1], prosecuted on behalf of the orphan. The defendants, by Philip Rykhalle their attorney, while not admitting that the testator left goods of the value named, pleaded that they had paid over £300 debts owed by him, that he made certain bequests in his will, that the funeral cost over 200 marks, in addition to other expenses, that the testator on the death of his first wife married Idonea, leaving no issue by her, and that where a man died leaving a wife without issue by her, there was no custom in the city that the issue of a previous wife, even though he had not been advanced, should have the third part of the goods and chattels of his father[2].

[1] *Communis narrator*, common pleader or counter, sometimes called "common serjeant."

[2] This contention was doubtless founded on an extraordinary judgment of 1369, when the Mayor and Aldermen recorded that it was the custom for a second wife, left a widow, to have a moiety of her late husband's goods, even though he had issue surviving by the first wife and none by the second. Letter Book G, fo. 234 *b*. A marginal note in a later hand appears: "no such custome." The action was copied into Liber Albus (*Munim. Gild. Lond.* (R.S.), p. 393), and in the Elizabethan copy is a marginal note in a 17th-century hand: "This must bee intended that the two sonnes which the husband had by his first wife were fully advanced by there father in his life time, and then the second wife (havinge no children by him) may by the custome have a moity, as if he had dyed without children; but if the two sonnes were not advanced as aforesaid, then is this judgment against the custome and constant practize in all times, for by the custome she ought and by constant practiz never had but a third part, where there are child or children unadvanced." The Mayor and Aldermen here disregarded the precedent of 1369 and made the orphan an offer, roughly equal to the third due to an unadvanced child.

The plaintiff answered that it was immemorial custom that such a son should have a third part on the death of his father, even though the latter left a widow without issue.

As the court was not fully advised as to this custom, or how such a custom ought to be tried (*triari*), the action was adjourned from day to day until 3 July 1393, when the parties appeared. But since there was great doubt and difference of opinion among the Mayor and Aldermen as to the custom of the city, the action was again adjourned, and these differences continued, retarding the execution of the will, until the executors produced the will, in which a clause stated that the testator wished the orphan to be remunerated (*remuneraretur*) from the goods and chattels after the legacies had been paid. In order to fulfil the will and for the sake of peace, the executors offered the plaintiff the sum of £600 as his "remuneration," if approved by the court, in full satisfaction of his claims, under the condition that if he died under the age of sixteen years, the money should be returned to the executors, to be treated by them as the money of the testator and expended for the good of the testator's soul. They stated that this sum was a third of the testator's goods and chattels, omitting certain debts owed to him by magnates, which might be regarded as desperate debts.

Thereupon the will was read in court, and since the testator willed that all feoffees of his lands and tenements should enfeoff the plaintiff therewith, such lands being of great value, and thus the orphan had in a manner been advanced at his father's death, the court asked whether the orphan and his friends would be satisfied with this offer by way of "remuneration," according to the form of the will. The plaintiff, with the consent of the court and by the advice of the Mayor and Aldermen as guardians of the orphans of the city, and also with the consent of Richard Felde, the king's clerk, and Walter Pynchon his uncle, in the presence of John Markham, Hugh Holes, William Gascoigne and John Woderove, serjeants-at-law, and Thomas Skelton and William Skrene, his counsel, accepted the offer. Accordingly it was considered that the orphan be content with the above sum and take nothing by his bill and be precluded from his action, and that the executors be quit thereof, and that, as the plaintiff was an orphan, his amercement be condoned.

Letter of attorney from John Coventre, formerly apprentice of the late William Sharpyng, vintner, to John Cloos and John Kyrkeby to demand and recover against John Hadle, Richard Odyham, John Shelford, draper, Henry Frowyk and Richard Norbery, his hereditary right to a tenement, or shops and rents, called "*le Brodeseld*[1]" in the parish of St Pancras in Westchepe. Dated 1 May 1393. Membr. 6 *6 May 1393*

Similar letter, containing the name of John Thorp in place of John Cloos. Dated 5 May 1393.

Thomas Bowyer, saddler, was summoned to answer William Burdevyll, *fuystour*[2], in a plea of debt, in which the latter alleged that in the court of Thomas Vynent, sheriff, he had sued the defendant for £40 and the defendant had admitted a debt of £7, for which judgment was given. This sum the defendant refused to pay. *19 March 1393*

The defendant, by William Sydyngbourne his attorney, pleaded that by the custom of the city from time out of mind the sheriffs had been accustomed in their compters to receive and enter plaints of debt, account, trespass and other contracts and that when a defendant was committed to prison for debt and the plaintiff afterwards acknowledged satisfaction and demanded the defendant's release, the sheriffs were used to release such a debtor, and whereas the plaintiff came to the sheriffs' compter in the parish of St Mildred by the Stocks[3] and acknowledged satisfaction, the debtor was released, and accordingly he prayed judgment whether the plaintiff could maintain his action against him.

The plaintiff pleaded that there was no such record to

[1] A substantial stone building, consisting of shops and warehouses. It stood on the west side of Soper Lane, now Queen Street, next to a corner warehouse belonging to St Martin le Grand, which abutted on Cheapside and Soper Lane. See Husting Rolls, 70 (77–8) (80), 161 (24). Harbin, *Dictionary of London*, gives much useful information but places the building on the wrong side of the street.

[2] Maker of saddletrees, the woodwork of saddles. For details of this craft, see *Cal. of Plea and Mem. Rolls*, 1323–64, pp. 238–40.

[3] St Mildred in the Poultry.

exclude him from his action. A day was given to the defendant to produce the record, and the latter produced a record under the shrievalty seal[1], wherein it was stated that the plaintiff came into the sheriffs' compter and granted the release of the body of the said Thomas Bowyer, whereupon the latter had been released [breaks off].

Membr. 6 *b*
25 June 1393

Acquittance from Idonea, relict of John Pyncheon, to William Cressewyk, Robert Excestre, prior of Crichurch, Walter Pyncheon, William Barette, Hugh Sprot and John Edmund, executors of the will of the said John, for certain jewels and a competent sum of money, being her widow's portion. Witnessed by the mayor, aldermen and sheriffs, and dated in the Chamber of Guildhall 5 June 1393.

Memorandum that whereas John Carbonell, chaplain, proctor of Sir John de Wendlyngburgh, prebendary of Wodeland in the cathedral church of Crydyton[2], delivered to Peter Plentee the sum of £7 14s 6d to be paid to the said Sir John in London in return for a general acquittance, and the said Peter, having refused to pay without this general acquittance, was forced to do so in the Sheriffs' Court, receiving an acquittance there, the said Sir John appeared before the Mayor and Aldermen and promised to save the said Peter harmless as against the said John Carbonell.

[*French*]

[1] *Sigillum officii vicecomitatus.*
[2] Crediton.

ROLL A 33

[*Of the time of John Hadle, mayor*]

Robert Durham brought a bill of complaint against Thomas Adam for detinue of certain goods to the value of £54 3s 2d contained in a schedule, which he had committed to his charge by the hands of John Mapulton in the parish of St Lawrence Jewry, and which the defendant refused to return to him, to his damage £10. Membr. 1 *14 Nov. 1393*

Schedule: 4 beds, each with coverlet and tester, 5 marks; another coverlet, 13s 4d; 4 blankets, 6s 8d; 2 pairs of sheets, 10s; another pair of sheets, 4s; one new *celour de carde*[1] with 3 curtains, 15s; 4 pairs of jet beads with the *gaudees*[2] silvergilt and one *furmaille*[3] silvergilt, 26s 8d; 2 gold rings, one with a sapphire and the other with a diamond, 30s; 2 silvergilt rings, 3s 4d; 2 *forcerez*[4] and 2 *bursez*[5] of cloth of gold, 6s 8d; one hauberk, 40s; one *baselard*[6] harnessed with silver, 13s 4d; four bows with one *trusse* of *setes*[7], 20s; one dozen pewter vessels *garnish*[8], 16s; 3 pewter pots, i.e., one pottle, one quart and one pint, 2s 6d; 2 pewter salt-cellars, 8d; 3 candlesticks of *laton*, 2s; one large *cofre*, 10s; divers colours: azure, *cynopre*[9] *etc.*, 100s; divers books belonging to the trade of a painter, 40s; 40 *quaiers* of paper *real*[10] and other paper, 16s 8d; another coffer, 2s; 4 *piers*

[1] *Sc. celure*, a canopy of *carde*, a material used for hangings, probably linen.

[2] *Sc. gaud.* A rosary of 165 beads was composed of 150 *Aves* and 15 *Paternosters*. The latter were ornamental beads and so arranged as to make one *Paternoster* come after every 10 *Aves*. See *Cal. of Wills*, II, p. 25, n. 1; *N.E.D.* "gaud"; Riley, *Memorials*, p. 455.

[3] *Sc. fermail*, from mediaeval Latin, *firmaculum*, a buckle or clasp.

[4] *Sc.* forcers, boxes.

[5] Purses.

[6] A kind of dagger or hanger.

[7] A bundle of arrows.

[8] A set of vessels for table use. In 1587 (see *N.E.D.*) it consisted of 12 platters, 12 dishes and 12 saucers. Here the word seems to mean "of a set."

[9] *Sc.* cinnabar, an ore of quicksilver yielding a red pigment, more brick-red than vermilion.

[10] *Sc.* royal, now 24 by 19 inches for writing and 25 by 20 inches for printing.

of *marble*[1] with 8 *molours*[2], 13s 4d; one pair of *matyns*[3], 6s 8d; one *sautere*[4], 13s 4d; 2 *bordclothes*[5], 13s 4d; 2 *tuaills*, 6s 8d; 2 *savenapes*[6], 2s; one *basenet* with *aventaille*[7], 40s; one long gown of *baudekyn*[8], 40s; one *materas*, 6s 8d; one long sword and buckler, 10s; one silver girdle, 20s; 2 *mazeres*[9], 18s; one half-dozen silver spoons, 12s; 2 *chaperouns*[10] of scarlet, 8s; 2 of green cloth, 3s 4d; one of blue, 2s 6d; 2 of *ray*, 6s 8d; one pair of silk *poynettez*[11], 3s; 2 pairs of poignets of red cloth, 2s; 2 pairs of scarlet shoes (*chaux*), 13s 4d; 2 pairs of hose (*chauz*)[12] of red cloth, 6s; 5 yds. of black cloth, 13s 4d; 6 yds. of cloth *linee*[13], 6s; 4½ yds. of the same, 4s 6d; 7 yds. of russet, 23s 4d; 11 yds. of blanket, 22s; 2 *warde-corsez*[14], 5s; one doublet of fustian, 5s; one gown of green, the *lynyng* of blanket, 13s 4d; one gown of blue, 10s; one long (gown) of *ray plonket*[15] and one *chaperoun* of the same, 11s 6d; one *sloppe*[16] of fustian, 6s 8d; 4 banners of the arms of the Prince *batuz*[17], 26s 8d; *sandel*, *taffata* and satin to the value of 10s; *sanguin*[18] with *brimyngstone* to the value of £10; 2 *hachettz*, 2s; 2 planes, 2s; 6 *cheselz* and 4 *fournours*[19],

[1] Stones of marble.
[2] *Sc. muller*, a grindstone for painters' colours.
[3] Matin or matins were one of the hours of the breviary. It seems to correspond with the *primere* which the defendant acknowledged receiving.
[4] Psalter. [5] Board-cloths, table-cloths.
[6] *Sc. sanap*, a strip placed on a table-cloth to keep it clean.
[7] A basinet or light headpiece with visor.
[8] A rich embroidered stuff, rich brocade.
[9] Mazer-cups. [10] A hood or cap.
[11] *Sc. poignet*, a wristlet or armlet of stuff worn over a sleeve as an ornament.
[12] It is difficult to distinguish between shoes and hose in city documents. Whereas in classical Latin, *calceus*, *calceamentum* and *caliga* denote a shoe, *par caligarum* in the city appears to mean a pair of hose, and *caligarius* is a hosier; a shoe-maker being *allutarius* or cordwainer.
[13] Probably linen-cloth, being cheaper than the woollen cloths mentioned.
[14] An overgarment for outdoor use, *N.E.D.*
[15] Striped plunket.
[16] A loose outer garment.
[17] Beaten, i.e. inlaid, overlaid, embroidered. See *N.E.D.*: "*c.* 1400, *Roland*, 287, Baners beten with gold."
[18] Blood-coloured pigment.
[19] Some implement for a furnace or oven, a malkin or mop for cleaning out an oven. See *N.E.D. sub* "furner" (2). Possibly it is mistakenly written for *fourmours*, which the defendant acknowledged receiving, i.e. chisels or gouges, see *N.E.D. sub* "former."

3s 4d; one half-dozen *hokes*, 2s; pots, platters (*esquelez*) and lead belonging to the trade of a painter, 5s; 5 yards of russet, 16s 8d. [*French*]

Afterwards the parties put themselves on the award of John London, Richard Knettere, cutler, Robert Guppeye and John Lane, as regards the above goods, and also concerning a recognisance of John Mapilton, mason, to John Goodman, tailor, John Pecham, chandler, and Thomas Adam, for the payment of £52 to the plaintiff.

The award stated that the defendant admitted receiving only a portion of the above-mentioned goods, including a *bastard mazer*[1], with a covercle, and certain kirtles and *abbitz* delivered to the Friars Minors, together with other goods including *one primere*[2], *fourmours*[3], 2 hammers, 2 *pynssouns*[4], 2 files, one *hanefeld*[5], 2 saws, one *shepebelle*, one pair of *tables blank*[6], one pair of tables without *meyne*[7], one quart bottle, one pint bottle and 2 *fenestralles*[8]. They awarded that the defendant return the above goods to the plaintiff and recover for him those delivered to the Friars Minors. As regards the recognisance the defendant should be quit except for 100s, and the plaintiff should have the recognisance in order to recover what was due to him. [*French*]

Bonds of John Mokkyng, vintner, and Richard Spencer, spicer, in £100 to abide by the award of Adam Carlell, John Walcot, William Brampton and Henry Yevele, arbitrators chosen by the mayor, or, if they failed to agree, of Adam Bamme, chosen by the mayor as an independent umpire. Membr. 1 *b* *3 Dec. 1393*

Whereas Richard Spenser, spicer, had sued a bill of deceit against Henry Yevele before John Hadle, Mayor, and the Aldermen, the parties submitted themselves to the award of the said Adam, John and William, and of Adam Bamme, in order to settle their differences before the octave of the

[1] A mazer made of other wood than maple.
[2] A prayer-book. See *N.E.D.* "1530 Palsg. 183 *Unes heures*, a primer or a mattyns boke."
[3] Chisels or gouges.
[4] Pincers.
[5] *Sc. anefeld*, anvil.
[6] A playing-board without squares.
[7] A playing-board without *meinie*, i.e. pieces or men.
[8] A window-frame, sometimes a window-pane.

Purification, on condition that if no award were given, they should be in the same position as before.

Membr. 2
4 Dec. 1393

Philip Vale, merchant of Bristol, who had married an orphan of the city, Eleanour, daughter of Richard Toky, grocer, deceased, brought a bill before the Mayor and Aldermen praying that William Bys, John Olney and William Pountfreit, executors of the will of the said Richard, give account of certain tenements and rents of the value of 1000 marks, devised to them by the testator to be sold and the proceeds divided equally between Richard, William, John, Maude and Eleanour, children of the said Richard, and also of the goods and chattels of the testator, which were of the value of £100. According to the will, if any child died under age, his or her share should be divided between the survivors. Since then, the children William and John had died. [*French*]

Robert Pek, the common pleader, affirmed the matter contained in the bill on behalf of the orphans, Eleanour, Richard and Maude. The defendant William Bys, by Philip Rykhall his attorney, did not acknowledge that the goods and chattels were of the value alleged and, as regards the lands and tenements, pleaded that the custom from time out of mind was as follows: that every freeman and freewoman of the city could devise his tenements within the city to his executors to be sold as movable chattels, and if his movable chattels did not suffice to pay his debts, the executors from the money received from the sale of the tenements were charged to pay his debts, in the same manner as they would from his goods and chattels. They pleaded further that the tenements were sold to a certain John Sandhurst for £322 8s 4d, that the children Richard and Maude were under age, and that Eleanour on 6 June 1393, being of full age, married the plaintiff Philip Vale against the executors' wishes. They had paid to him the share due to his wife and had received from him an acquittance, produced in court, as follows:

Acquittance from Philip Vale for his wife's portion of her father's goods and chattels, as set forth in an inventory, and also for her portion of £322 6s 8d coming from the sale of tenements, saving the right to claim a further share, if any of the children died or took the religious habit under age, a share of any debts still unpaid to the executors, and a share of any portion of £19 2s 9d, reserved for paying the testator's debts, which might be unexpended. Dated at London 6 Aug. 1393.

The defendant further pleaded that the goods and chattels at no time amounted to more than £57 9s 1d, and that the testator was indebted to divers persons in the sum of £137 6s 11d, as appeared by the following inventory:

INVENTORY of the goods and chattels of Richard Toky, deceased, made on 26 Oct. 1391 by Geoffrey Baldok, upholder, Richard Lygthfelow, brasier, John Borham, stockfishmonger, Thomas Panton and Philip Wynter, goldsmiths, Stephen Verderne, skinner, John Page and Roger Couton, armourers, and Richard Mymmes, joiner.

HALL. One *dorser*, 2 *costiers*, 4 *quysshyns* of red and *blod*[1] worsted, 8 *bankers*[2] lined with canvas, 10s; one painted table for cups, 5s; a wash-bowl and stand (*lavatorium cum stipite*) of lead, 2s 6d; 3 basins with 3 washbowls of *denaunt*[3] work, Membr. 2 *b*
11s 4d; one large bowl, 5s; one table with trestles, 2s 6d; another painted table, 8d; 6 *quisshyns* of tapestry work, 20d; one pair of tables of *sprews*, 2s; 3 *quisshyns* of red tapestry work, 12d; one *braunch*[4] of iron, 4d; one *pees* of a wash-bowl, 2d; 3 forms, 12d; one pair of *aundirens*, 14d; an iron candlestick, 6d; one lance with a shield, 2s; *polaxes*, 3s; one *arblast*[5] with the *takell*, 2s; 2 *dorsers*, 2 *bankers*, 6 *quisshyns*, 3s 4d; 2 chairs, 20d; 2 *dorsers* and 2 *bankers* of *blod* and black, 20d; one pair of *aundirens*, 20d. Total, £3 0s 2d.

CHAMBER. 3 *redells*[6], one *selour* of *blod carde* with 3 posts (*stipis*) for a bed, 6s 8d; one other *selour* of *blod carde*, 20d; one large feather-pillow[7] with bolster, 6s 8d; 3 mattrasses covered with *blod carde*, 6s 8d; one small *presse* for caps

[1] From *blodius*, said to mean blood-cloured, but more probably blue.
[2] Covering for a bench or chair.
[3] Of Dinant in Belgium, a town which exported large quantities of *dinanderie*, i.e. vessels of copper and brass.
[4] Candelabrum.
[5] Cross-bow.
[6] Curtains.
[7] *Plumale*, possibly feather-bed.

(*capuciis*), 4d; 3 painted cloths, 6d; 2 *tapets*[1] of *taune*, 16d; one green *banquer*, 4d; one silk quilt *paled*[2] with red and green and lined with *bokeram*, 10s; one bed with *tester* of worsted, 20s; one bed with *tester* of *say*[3] with roses, 5s; one bed with *tester* of green, 4s; one bed with a stained (*steynat'*)[4] *tester*, 5s; 2 coverlets, 2s; one coverlet (*cooportorium*) made at Wynchestre, 3s 4d; a bed of red and *blod* with roses, 3s 4d; one *tester* of red and *blod*, 18d; one *chaloun*[5], 2s 6d; 4 pairs of sheets, 13s 2d; 3 sheets, 12d; 5 ells of linen at 7d the ell, 35d; 3 ells of cloth of Cologne[6], 20d; 3 feather-pillows (*plumalia*) of *sendal*[7], 20d; one small piece of *sendal*, 2d; 4 old feather-pillows, 12d; 2 ells of stained cloth, 12d; 3 pairs of linen cloths, 20d; one long shirt (*camisia*), one night-gown (*flame-olum*) and one night-cap, 12d; one *vernicle*[8], 4d; 2 *fossers*, one pair of gloves, 8d; 3 handbags (*mantice*), 3s; one chest, 16d; one large chest, 3s 4d; 2 pairs of top-boots (*ocrearum*), 16d; one pair of spurs, 4d; 2 lances, 3s; 2 *quisshyns* of *sendale*, 2s; one gown (*gonella*) slashed (*bipartita*) with russet, furred with lambswool, 6s 8d; one short gown, 3s 4d; two pieces of woollen cloth of shot colours (*stragulatus*)[9], 6s 8d; one slashed gown of the Grocers' livery (*secta*), 3s 4d; one gown of russet with caps, 2s 6d; one gown of black *fresed*[10], 4s; one fur of *otir*, 5s; one white fur, 2s; one *pilche*[11] of black, 2s 6d; 3 *kirtelles*, 18d; one doublet, 2s; 6 caps, 3s; 5 pairs of hose (*caligarum*), 2s 6d; 2 pairs of *meteyns*, 10d; one beaver hat, 12d; one gown of blood-colour (*sanguinei*) furred with *crestigray*[12], 33s 4d; one gown of *blod* colour furred with *cristigray*, 20s; one russet gown furred with *bys*[13], 8s; one

[1] Hangings of tawny-colour. [2] Striped.

[3] With a back-curtain of say, which was a kind of serge.

[4] Stencilled or dyed in patterns.

[5] *Sc.* shalloon, a blanket or rug.

[6] Cologne exported linen and linen-thread.

[7] A fine silky material.

[8] The picture of the face of Christ impressed on the handkerchief of St Veronica. Small ornaments representing this miracle were worn as tokens by pilgrims. See Prologue, *Canterbury Tales*, ll. 685–7.

[9] *Stragulatus* is defined as *diverso colore variatus*.

[10] Friesed, i.e. combed out into a woolly nap.

[11] A fur coat, from medieval Latin, *pellicea*. Cf. later "pelisse."

[12] See above, p. 91, n. 3.

[13] *Ibid.*

gown of scarlet, 4s; one gown of *vyolett*, 2s; one tunic of scarlet, 20d; one kirtle of violet, 8d; one kirtle of russet, 18d; 2 other old kirtles, 16d; one kirtle of blanket, 20d; 2 pieces of *cristigray*, 4s; 3 caps, 2s 4d; one cloak of *blod* lined with blanket, 5s; one other old cloak, 16d; one worn-out cloak, 8d; one stool, 8d; one *cradell*, 12d; 2 *paunchers*[1], 6d; *bed-bords*, 2s 3d; one *pilche*, 8d. Total, £13 0s 10d.

Jewels in the Chamber. One gold signet, 9s; one silver seal with a chain weighing 3½ oz. 4 dwt., 9s 9d; a pair of tables of ivory, 12d; 3 plain (*plane*) pieces of silver with a covercle, weighing 2½ lbs. 1½ oz., at 26s the lb., £3 8s 3d; one nut[2] with a covercle, 20s; one mazer bound with silver with silver covercle and foot, 13s 4d; one cup bound with silver, 10s; one small cup bound with silver, 6s 8d; 2 cups of mazer, 2s; 13 silver spoons, 19s 10d; one *baselard* harnessed with silver, 6s 8d; another small one, 3s; a belt partly garnished with silver, 3s 4d; one horn with a *braser*[3] harnessed with silver, 6s 8d; one dagger harnessed, 2s; one *bokell* and one *pendaunt* of silver, 26d; broken silver, 4s 11d; one small box of *sprews*, 5s; one lace of green silk, 12d; one *knoppe*[4] of *perles*, 6d; one pair of coral beads with an *agnus dei*[5], 23s 4d; another pair of red coral, 6s 8d; one pair of amber, 5s; one pair of beads, 2s; 3 *gett* buttons and 3 silver conies (*coniculi*), 6d. Total, £11 12s 7d.

Pantry and Buttery. One ambry[6], 40d; one hanging ambry, 10d; one candlestick of *laton*, 26d; one *pouderbox*, 2d; two *painted* (depicti) plates, 2d; one pair of table-knives, 20d; one pair of bellows (*par utrium*), 2s; two iron funnels (*fonella*), 2d; 8 *tolett*[7], 2d; one table cloth (*mappa mensalis*), 4s; 2 large towels, 10s; another table cloth and a small towel, 5s 6d; 4 old tablecloths, 20d; one small towel, 4d; 2 *chargeours*, 12 *plateres*, 10 dishes, 11 saucers (*salsaria*),

[1] Either a piece of armour to cover the stomach or a belt or girdle.
[2] A cup made of a coco-nut.
[3] Bracer, a piece of armour for the arm, but here probably a brace, in the sense of a strap.
[4] A knob, ornamental boss or even a tassel.
[5] A representation of the Lamb of God.
[6] A cupboard, locker or press.
[7] Possibly a diminutive of French *toile*, a small piece of cloth, or from French *telle*, a coarse cooking-pot.

9 *trenchours*, 2 half-gallon pots, 3 quart pots, one pint pot, salt-cellars (*salers*), one *halywattirstoppe*[1] and one candle-stick weighing 86 lbs., at 2d the lb., 14s 4d; 2 *flaskett*[2] of pewter, 18d; one *gorde*[3], 2d; one hamper, 4d; one box, 12d; 8 lbs. of *lynenyerne*, 2s 4d; 14 lbs. of *wollenyerne*, 4s; 3 round basins, 20d; one jar (*cadus*) for ale, 4d; one earthenware pot, 2d. Total, 58s 6d.

KITCHEN. 3 brass pots (*olle enee*), 2 *pocenetts*[4], one *chauf-four*[5], one broken copper pot (*olla erea*), 2 *keteles* and 2 pieces of broken brass, 20s; 4 copper pans, 5s 6d; 3 iron *spetys*[6], 20d; one mortar of stone with 2 pestles, 12d; one *grespanne*, one *flesshok* and one pair of tongs, 14d; 2 axes, 2 hatchets, 12d; one pipe for corn, 4d; 4 tables, 2s; one grate, 6d; 2 tripods, 6d; one *dressyngknyf*, 10d; one *rakke*, 8d; 2 *wassyngtubbes* and one barrel, 12d; one pair of tongs and one *scomour*[7], 8d; one frying-pan (*frixorium*) and 2 ladles, 6d; one *bely*[8] and one mortar, 2d; one water-tankard, 12d; 2 gridirons (*craticule*), 6d; one *knedyngtubbe*, 14d; *wode* and *cole*, 4s 4d; one pair of *gromes*[9], 6d.

COUNTING-HOUSE. One large box bound with iron, 12s; one small *forcer*, 8d; one book of the statutes, 3s 4d; one quire of paper, 8d; 3 hooks (*hami*) of *laton*, 4d; one lock of *laton* with one *fane*[10], and one balance of *laton*, 12d; 3 pieces of *blod carde*, 8d; 4 bows, 2s 6d; 18 arrows and 2 bolts, 16d; 3 *stantifs*[11], 36 *countours* and one pair of pincers (*fortisipium*), 18d; one pair of *balaunces*, 4d; one *pennar*[12] and ink-horn (*hincornu*), 4d; one pair of tables of box, 8d; one pyx, bound with iron, for silver, 12d; one ell of old canvas, 4d; 2 pieces of deer hide, 14d; one *bascinet* with *aventaill*, 13s 4d; one breastplate, 13s 4d; one *palett*[13] with *aventaill*, 4s; one *pauncher* of mail, 2s; one *legharnes*, 10s; one pair of *vaumbras*

[1] Holywater-stoop.

[2] A shallow receptacle, made of wood, osier or metal; not used at this period in the sense of a small flask or bottle.

[3] A bottle or cup, derived from "gourd," but used generally of any material.

[4] A little pot.

[5] Chafer, chafing-pan.

[6] Spits.

[7] Skimmer.

[8] Bellows.

[9] *Sc. crome*, a hook at the end of a stick, a flesh-hook.

[10] Possibly meaning a ward or bolt of a lock.

[11] *Sc. standish*, a pen-tray.

[12] Pen-case.

[13] A head-piece with visor.

and *rerebras*[1], 4s; one pair of gauntlets of plate, 3s; one image of the Blessed Mary in *aleblastre*, 2s; one image of St John the Baptist in *aleblastre*, 16d; one yard of *blod frised*, 10d; 9 heads for arrows, 4d; bags (*sacule*) for silver, 4d; one breastplate, 10s. Total, £4 12s 4d.

STOREHOUSE. One beam with the scales, 6s 8d; *wyghtes* weighing 3½ cwt. 6 lbs. at 6s the cwt., 21s 4d; 4 pairs of balances, 16d; another pair, 16d; one jar full of *bromston*, 10s 5d; one *malesadell*[2], 2s 8d; another saddle, 4s; a saddle for a woman, 4s; one *sadelclothe*, 5d; one counting-board (*computorium*), 5s; broken iron, 3s 11d; iron bolts and staples, 13d; one shovel (*vanga*), 3d; one *auncer*[3] of *bras*, 12d; one ladder, 4d; one *latys*, 6d; one *rowel*[4], 6d; 2 windows, 7d; one saw, 6d; one small saw, one axe, two hammers, one pair of *pynsons*, one old plane[5] and 2 trowels, 12d; 5 *boules*[6], 1d; one door with a *wykett*, 3s 4d; 40 pieces of timber and broken tables, 5s; one deer skin (purse?) with the maidenhead[7] and one cage, 10d; 8 locks and 120 keys, 20d; cords and *bastis*[8], 2d; one small broken box, 4d; 2 painted papers (2 *papir' depict'*), 2d; 6 *pors nettis*[9], 6d. Total, £3 19s 5d. Membr. 3

FROM THE SALE OF TENEMENTS. From John Sandhurst, chandler, £317 1s 8d; from Thomas Austyn for a house called "*Colhous*" lying within the testator's house, £5 6s 8d. Total, £322 8s 4d.

MONEYS PAID. By Henry Barbour, £3 6s 8d; John Pountfreyt, 15s; Agnes Frowe, 9s 10d; Herman Goldesmyth, 46s 8d; John Corbet, capper, 11s 3d; John Corsour, scrivener, £4; John Kent, tailor, 22s 6d. Total, £12 11s 11d.

MONEY FOUND, £3 6s 8d.

SUM TOTAL OF ALL THE AFORESAID GOODS: £379 15s 9d.

[1] Vambrace and rerebrace, pieces of armour for the forearm and upper-arm.

[2] A saddle for carrying *males*, i.e. leather bags or trunks.

[3] A small balance for weighing.

[4] A wheel-shaped candle-stand.

[5] Probably a plasterer's trowel; not a plane in the later sense.

[6] Bowls.

[7] *Unum corium de cervo cum capite domicelle.* A frequent ornament—the representation of the Virgin's head. See *N.E.D. sub* "maidenhead."

[8] Cords or ropes made of bast. Cf. *bastil cordes, Cal. of Plea and Mem. Rolls*, 1364–81, p. 158.

[9] Pursenets, bag-shaped nets.

Debts owed by the testator. To Thomas Wilford, fishmonger, £92 3s 4d; William Bys, £30 6s 8d; Roger Snell of Winchester, £12; Robert Crosse of Hull, £5 5s; Walter Toky, £4 13s 4d; Robert Cherteseye, 43s 10d; John Pope, waxchandler, 10s 9d; John Campyon, waxchandler, 13s 6d; Maud Goldman, 21s; John Cawode of Waterford, 3s; Reginald atte More, draper, 6s 8d; Henry Colbrook, skinner, 4s 4d; William Skynner, 2s 2d; John Newent, cordwainer, 2s 6d; William Plomer, 4s; John Beauchaumpe, 7s; John Goryng, tiler, 7s; Thomas Maghfeld of Waddon, 20d; Richard Spencer, draper, 2s 5d; Edmund Bys, 7s 11d; William Waddesworthe, 4s 8d; Robert Hardekyn, 2s 10d; John Sandhurst, chaundeler, 9d; Nicholas Neuenham, chaplain, 53s 4d; Henry Whitwell, £3 6s 8d; Nicholas Bokeby, broker, 6s 8d; Henry Draper, *scholemaister*, 3s; Robert Taverner, 2s 6d; Martin Seman, 20d; John Shritwyth, 40s; Eva, widow of Ralph Person, 10s; to the *kercheflauendre*[1], 2s 6d; to the joiner in Lumbard Strete, 12d; William Canterbury, 8s 6d; William Man, 6d; Walter Tyler, 6s 8d; Maud atte Vyne, £13 6s 8d; the church of St Mary at Hill, £4 3s 4d; the church of St Edmund in Lumbardstrete, £6 3s 4d; the church of Holy Trinity, 17s 4d; John Wakefeld, 33s 4d; Master John Cook, £4 4s; Andrew de Bardes, Lumbard, £3 6s 8d. Total, £194 16s.

Legacies. To the High Altar of St Edmund in Lombard Street, 6s 8d; to 3 chaplains celebrating in the same church, 5s; to the master-clerk of the same, 20d; to the sub-clerk, 12d; to the fabric of the same, 20s; to 2 chaplains in the same celebrating for the soul of the testator for one year, £12. Total, £13 14s 4d.

Funeral expenses of the testator, his wife and son. On the day of death and the month's mind[2], £14 9s 1d; anniversary days of the testator, his wife and son, £10; repairs to the tenements of the testator for three quarters of a year after his death, 29s 10½d; advice of counsel for levying

[1] Kerchief-laundress.

[2] A commemorative service held 30 days after death. Testators sometimes left moneys for candles and tapers for this occasion. See *Cal. of Wills*, II, pp. 15, n. 2, 17, 42, *etc.*

debts and selling the tenements to the best advantage, £7; expenses in valuation and sale of the above-mentioned goods, and in breakfasts (*jantaculis*) and drinks at divers times, £3; paid to William Bys, executor, for his labour, 40s; for the making of an inventory, probate of the will and acquittance of the same, 40s; for expenses of the orphan John, 2s. Total, £40 0s 11½d.

DESPERATE DEBTS. John Bramyot of Hertford, £10; John Presford of the Isle of Wight, £3 13s 4d; John Monketon, £30; William atte Wode, £13 10s; William Pokynbye, £20; Jacob Horyng, Fleming, £30; Thomas Depyng, mason, 16s 8d; William Cookford of Lynne, 24s; Reginald Coopperton and Isabel his wife, 53s 4d; Robert Cherteseye, £5; Alice Wetherisfeld, 3s 4d; Elmyn Legat, 7s; Henry Frowyk, 16s 7d; Henry Neweporte, 20s; Sir John Dymmok, 2s 6d; John Kew, 23d; John Pygelton, 4s 4d; John Lyoun, 3s 7d; John Couelee, 10s; John Looke, 33s 4d; Sir John West, 6s 2d; Nicholas Saddeler, 10s; Roger Bokyngham, 3s 4d; Reginald Skreveyn, 5s; Ralph Steynour, 3s 7d; Richard Preston, 20s; Thomas Paryssh of Shrouesbury, 6s; William Baille of Bekynton, 29s 10d; William Wirhale, cardemakker, 2s 9d. Total, £126 6s 8d.

Exhibited before the official of the archdeacon of London, 17 Kalends of February (16 Jan.) 1392, and pronounced a true inventory and sealed with the seal of the office.

The defendant pleaded that he had satisfied the creditors and that altogether he had spent on the funeral expenses the sum of £40 9s 1½d (*sic*) and had paid the legacies amounting to £13 14s 4d, for which he desired to be acquitted. After paying the share of the said Eleanour there remained in his hands only the sum of £91 13s ¾d for the use of the children Richard and Maude, which he was prepared to pay into the Chamber.

Thereupon the Mayor and Aldermen assigned Gilbert Maghfeld and William Brampton, aldermen, to hear the account. The latter confirmed the amounts received for the goods and chattels and the sale of tenements, i.e. £379 15s 9d, and the amounts expended or to be expended on paying the

Membr. 3 *b* testator's debts and legacies, i.e. £208 10s 4d, but as regards the other expenses they allowed 100s for the funerals, 60s for anniversaries, 100s for counsel, 40s for food and drink, 40s for the executor's labour, 40s for proving the will and inventory and 2s expenses for the child John, who survived his father for 14 days, making a total of £19 2s, as compared with £40 0s 11½d estimated in the inventory, and making a grand total of payments £227 12s 4d, thus leaving a balance of £152 3s 5d to be divided between the orphans Richard, William, Eleanour and Maude, i.e. £38 0s 10¼d each.

And whereas the orphan William was in the charge of the executor for three years from his father's death on 22 Oct. 1390 to 13 Oct. 1393 when he died, the sum of £7 15s, at 12d a week, was deducted from his portion, leaving £30 6s 3¼[1] to be divided among his three surviving brothers and sisters, i.e. £10 2s 1d each, thus increasing each child's share to £48 3s 4¼d.

And whereas the orphan Eleanour was in charge of the executor for 50 weeks after the death of her father, 50s was deducted from her share, leaving £45 13s 4¼d, of which 50 marks (£33 6s 8d) had been delivered to Philippot Vale her husband, leaving a balance due to her of £12 6s 8¼d.

And whereas the other two orphans Richard and Maude remained in charge of the executor for 3 years 42 weeks, from 22 Oct. 1390 to 15 Aug. 1394, at 12d a week, the sum of £9 18s was deducted from the share of each, leaving to each £38 5s 4¼d.

Accordingly it was considered that the executor bring into the Chamber the sum of £88 17s 4¾d, which he did.

Afterwards, 1 Sept. 1394, Philippot Vale acknowledged receipt of £45 13s 4¼d. By consent of John Hadlee the mayor, the chamberlain paid to the prioress of the house of Kylbourne, where the orphan Maude became a nun, the sum of £38 5s 4¼d, as appears in Letter Book H, fo. 288, and the same amount to the orphan Richard when he came of age, as appears in Letter Book H, fo. 324.

Membr. 4
13 Feb. 1394
Grant from Alan Walsyngham, cordwainer, to John Corbet,

[1] There is an error of 5d here which is carried on through the rest of the account.

squire of the duke of Gloucester, William Vaggescombe, grocer, and Richard Mildenhale, cordwainer, of all his goods and chattels. Witnesses John Pountfreyt, Godfrey Cost and John Dyk. Dated at London 24 Jan. 1394.

Bond of Salamon Oxeneye to Bartholomew de Bosano and Lodewyc de Port, Lombards, to pay the sum of 40s on condition that James de Boo, Lombard, sent certain proof before Christmas that "Sire Hans Chivaler" owed him that amount. *9 March 1394*

Quitclaim from Richard Ryner, coppersmith, to Richard[1], lord of Talbot, Irchenfeld[2] and Blakemere. Dated 16 March 1394. *26 March 1394*

Membr. 4 *b*

The merchants of the Hanse of Almaine dwelling in London demand an Assize of Nuisance against John Slegh touching their free tenement in the parish of All Hallows in the Hay[3]. *13 July 1394*

Membr. 5

John Billyng, esquire, and Elizabeth Beauchamp brought a bill of complaint against Amye Donat for detaining a bond dated 31 July 1394 whereby they were bound in £80 to a certain Philip Vannoche of Siena, which bond they had entrusted to her in the parish of St Dunstan in the west on the same day. [*French*] *20 March 1394*

A day having been given to the parties on 20 May, the said Philip Vannoche also appeared and brought a bill of complaint against the same defendant for detinue of the same bond, which he alleged had been entrusted to her on 5 Aug. 1394 in the parish of St Peter Cornhull. [*Latin*]

The defendant pleaded that the bond had been entrusted to her by consent of the parties on condition that she should return it to the plaintiff Philip if he should deliver to the said Elizabeth within three days a set (*sectam sive sortam*) of pearls of the value of £10, other sets of the value of £20, £15 and £30, and one of large pearls valued at £70, a tally for £100 and a fictitious (*fictam*) bond for £100, wherein

[1] Richard Talbot, who married Ankaret, sister and sole heir of John, baron Strange of Blackmere. He succeeded his father in the barony of Talbot in 1387.

[2] Archenfield co. Hereford.

[3] The Guildhall of the Teutonic merchants, later known as the Steelyard.

three bags of dust, made of rape[1], radish roots and old, rotten *cetuall*[2], unhealthy for human use, found in the house of Walter Kyng, grocer, in the parish of All Hallows in the Hay in Dowgate Ward, and exposed for sale by the said Walter's apprentice as being good powdered ginger, in deceit of the people and to the scandal of the whole mistery of Grocers. The said Walter admitted this and other offences committed by his servants and put himself on the mercy of the Mayor and Aldermen. Thereupon it was considered that he pay a fine of £200 to the Chamber, unless he received the favour of the court. Upon this the defendant offered to pay...to the Chamberlain before Michaelmas and found mainprise, namely, John Walcote and others, for payment, and he was then sworn not to commit any such deception in future.

Apparet per compotum quod soluit l *li.*

21 Aug. 1394 John Hunte, supervisor of strangers bringing Thames fish to the city and having their stand in Chepe, presented William Talworth, servant of Geoffrey Hardeby, fishmonger at the Stokkes, for coming to Chepe and buying eels to regrate them for the profit of his master, against the ordinance of the city[3] and as tending to produce a scarcity of victuals for sale to the people. The Mayor and Aldermen considered that the said Geoffrey pay a fine of £40 unless meanwhile he obtained the favour of the court, and upon this he begged to be allowed to compound for 10 marks.

1 Sept. 1394 William Crowmere, John Olyver, ...Haddon[4] and ...., masters of the mistery of Drapers, came before the Mayor and Aldermen and presented a yard-measure found in the house of John Derlyng, draper, on Cornhill, which measure was used by him and his servants for buying and selling woollen cloth and was half-an-inch too long, to the deceit of the people and the scandal of the mistery.

[1] Possibly wild rape, charlock or field-mustard is meant.

[2] *Sc. setwall*, the root of the zedoary, a plant having qualities resembling those of ginger.

[3] See *Cal. of Letter Book H*, pp. 243, 274–5. Citizen-fishmongers were allowed to buy from the foreigners for resale, but only after an interval of some hours. This was an attempt to corner eels.

[4] Probably the John Haddone, draper, who was excused in 1420 from serving on juries owing to increasing old age. *Cal. of Letter Book I*, p. 244.

On being charged, John Derlyng denied that he had bought or sold cloth with the measure or that he had ever seen it before. He was asked whether any of his servants or apprentices had used it and answered no. He prayed to be allowed to have a talk with them, which was granted, and meanwhile he was committed to prison. Next day he said that one of his servants had used it, but without his knowledge, and he put himself on the mercy of the court. Thereupon the Mayor and Aldermen, considering that this deception was harmful to the people and a scandal to the mistery, ordered that he pay a fine of £40 to the Chamber, unless *etc.* Upon this, the said John Derlyng agreed to pay 10 marks at Michaelmas by way of recognisance.

Thomas Spencer, *galochemaker*[1], informed the Mayor and Aldermen that he had recovered against John Toky, late his apprentice, the sum of £11 10s debt and damages in the court of Richard Whityngton, one of the sheriffs, for which the said John was now a prisoner in Ludgate, and that the said John was suing him and others by bills before the Mayor and Aldermen in the Chamber of the Guildhall. *20 May 1394*

The Mayor and Aldermen, considering the imprisonment and poverty of John Toky and desiring that a good agreement should be made between the parties, ordained that the said John should give a bond for the sum of £11 10s due, and serve the said Thomas at his trade for 3s 4d a week, retaining 20d for himself while the rest should go to the payment of the debt, and that all proceedings between them should be quashed.

The master agreed; but the said John was unwilling to enter into bond for the debt or to sue on his bills. Accordingly he was ordered back to Ludgate to remain there by virtue of the judgment in the Sheriffs' Court[2].

[1] Galoshes were shoes either made entirely of leather or with a wooden sole. The Pouchmakers in 1400 were given oversight of wooden galoshes (*galoches de feust*), *Cal. of Letter Book I*, p. 9, and in 1415 the two crafts had combined, *ibid.* p. 150. By 1488 the Pattenmakers had come into the combination, *Cal. of Letter Book L*, p. 251, though they were afterwards incorporated as a separate company in 1670. All these were trades using fine, soft leathers. At different times the Whitetawyers, Purser-Glovers and Pouchmakers all combined with the Leathersellers. Journal 8, fo. 206; Letter Books M, fos. 13, 59–60; N, fos. 59–61.

[2] See below, p. 223.

6 July 1394 Writ of *certiorari*, directed to the mayor and chamberlain, demanding the tenor of a quitclaim from John Rumbold of Kelcil[1] to John Davy, citizen of London, of all claims to tenements formerly belonging to Nicholas Rumbold. Dated at Westminster 6 July 1394.

Note that the tenor of the above quitclaim, which was enrolled in the Husting of Pleas of Land on 21 July 1371, was returned to Chancery.

18 Oct. 1394 Writ requiring the tenor of a recognisance by the prior of *Seintmariespitell* not to harm Roger Assent or his servants. Witness Edmund, duke of York, *custos* of England, at Westminster 18 Oct. 1394.

Return by the mayor and sheriffs that on 10 July 1394 John Mildenhale, prior of the hospital of S[t] Mary without Bishopsgate, was mainprised by William Horston and William Palmere to keep the peace with Thomas Fyncham and Roger Assent.

Membr. 6 *b*
20 Aug. 1394 Letter of attorney from Conrad Uterolp, merchant of Almaine, to Vrowyn Epensheth, merchant of Almaine, and Philip Rykhall. Dated at London 15 Aug. 1394.

11 Sept. 1394 Memorandum that William Bys, stockfishmonger, one of the executors of Richard Toky, delivered to Stephen Speleman, chamberlain of Guildhall, the sum of £19 12s 9d owed to divers creditors, of whom Robert Hardekyn, William Caunterbury and Andrew de Bardes appeared and received payment on swearing upon the Gospels that the money was due to them. One third of the unpaid balance, *viz.* £5 4s 9d, was paid to Philip Vale, husband of Eleanour, one of the orphans, under mainprise of Nicholas Walsyngham, mercer, and John Knesworth, goldsmith, to pay a proportionate share, if any of the creditors still unpaid proved their claims against William Bys, the executor.

[1] Kelsale. Husting Roll 99 (86). These tenements, extending eastwards from the Coleman Street Ward boundary on London Wall, were left by will by Nicholas Rumbold, whitetawyer, for life to his wife Agatha, who afterwards married John Davy, with remainder to the Whitetawyers. They were escheated to the Crown and finally purchased by the Leathersellers' Company. See Black's *Leathersellers*.

Afterwards John Wydecombe, draper, and Agnes his wife, widow of Walter Toky, son of Walter Toky of Corse[1], senior, burgess of Gloucester, together with John Wyghale, co-executor of Walter Toky, recovered against William Bys the sum of 7 marks. Thereupon the chamberlain of Guildhall paid his portion, *viz.* 62s 2½d, and the mainpernors of Philip Vale paid their portion, *viz.* 31s 1½d. *11 March 1401*

John Barton, clerk, administrator of the goods of Nicholas Newenham, recovered the sum of 53s 4d, due to the said Nicholas, of which the chamberlain paid two parts and the above mainpernors paid the third part. *27 Sept. 1403*

Membr. 7 *b*

Stephen Speleman, chamberlain, paid to Richard Toky, son of Richard Toky, deceased, the sum of 56s 6¾d under mainprise of Thomas Duffhouse, fishmonger, and John Moore, brewer, that he would pay his third part of the debts owed by his late father if they were claimed by the creditors Robert Crosse and Master John Cook. *7 April 1406*

Stephen Speleman, chamberlain, paid the like sum to Richard Toky under mainprise of Thomas Loche and John Borham to pay the above debts if claimed. *27 Feb. 1409*

Membr. 6 *b*

Bond of John Seint Germyn, grocer, to pay James de Monald and his partners of the society of the Albertini the sum of £4 10s in case they were forced to pay the like sum to the heirs or executors of Philip Ley, chaplain, for an exchange made for him. *11 Sept. 1394*

Thomas Spencer brought a bill before the Mayor, John Fressh, and the Aldermen against Richard Qwytyngton, late sheriff, complaining that whereas he recovered against John Toky in the Sheriffs' Court a debt of £11 10s and 3s 4d damages, for which the said John was committed to Ludgate, the sheriff allowed the prisoner to go at large on Whit Sunday last, whereby action accrued to the plaintiff to demand the debt and damages from the sheriff. [*French*] *14 Oct. 1394*

The defendant, Richard Whytyngton, appeared by John Bottesham his attorney and pleaded that on 21 May the

[1] co. Gloucester.

plaintiff granted that John Toky should be delivered from prison and that neither the sheriff nor John Bottesham, who was then keeper of Ludgate, should be called into question for his liberation.

The plaintiff in answer pleaded an ordinance of the city that where a defendant in a personal action pleaded a peremptory plea, he could, on the demand of the plaintiff, be called upon to take a peremptory oath to tell the truth about his plea, and if he did not take such oath, he should be condemned, wherefore he demanded that the said Richard Whytyngton and John Bottesham, as the keeper of his prison, should be sworn and examined peremptorily. The court allowed the demand and gave a day on 8 Feb. 1395. On that day the defendants failed to appear. On the next court day it was considered, after deliberation and advice, that the plaintiff recover against Richard Whytyngton the sum of £11 13s 4d and damages taxed at 6s 8d, and that the said Richard be in mercy.

Membr. 7
21 Oct. 1394

Proceedings by John Devenissh, assignee of Nicholas Benyngton, against Geoffrey Grigge for refusing to quit the "*Bolle othe Hoppe*" and other premises. He alleged the record of a plea by Nicholas Benyngton, who recovered 13s 4d for rent due, in which it was stated that the defendant held the premises for three years and afterwards year by year. A day was given that the court might be advised, but afterwards the plaintiff made default.

Membr. 8
23 Oct. 1394

Salamon Salmon, mercer, brought a bill of complaint against Robert Dane, mercer, as executor of the will of John Bussheye, mercer, for non-payment of £47 10s 2d due on a recognisance of 31 March 1394 from the testator to the plaintiff. [*French*]

After three defaults the defendant appeared and pleaded that he was neither executor nor administrator of the testator's goods and chattels, but that the testator, being indebted to him in the sum of £246 due on a statute staple, had granted to him all his goods and chattels by a deed of 1 Dec. 1391 in part payment of his debt, and on 24 March 1394 had given and delivered to him all the goods which he had in his shop, together with his apprentice, and had given orders to his servants, Robert Fyncheden and John Grace, to levy his debts and pay them to the defendant and to hand over to him the bonds in part payment of the aforesaid £246, in virtue of which grants he obtained possession of divers goods of the deceased to the value of £80, as follows:

86½ ells of *West' estr'*[1] at 2d the ell; 8 ells of canvas at 3d the ell; one coverlet, 3s; another coverlet of *reys*[2], 8d; 4 pieces of *worsteyde* at 13s 4d the piece; 13 dozen 2 pieces of *paris*[3] at 17s the dozen; 23 *chesiblez*[4] at 8s each; 6 dozen 11 lbs. of *fil de coll'*[5] at 8s the dozen; 3 *hattis* of *bever*, 2s; 4 lbs. 3 oz. of *bedys* of *aumbre* at 5s the lb.; 12 dozen bone beads at 18d the dozen; 12 whips, 6s; 3 lbs. 2 oz. *yvori combes* at 6s the lb.; 7 pieces of *bokeram* at 4s the piece; 18 silk banners at 18d each; 9 pieces *kerchers* of *Cortrik*[6] at 12d the piece; 2 pieces 2 yds. of *sarsenet* at 16s the piece; 75 silk garters, 6s 3d; 10 *pli3t Crymyll'*[7] of silk at 10s each; one piece *Cambr' kerchers*[8], 3s 4d; 6 *volettez*[9] of *Cambr'*, 3s 6d; one piece of red *relisaunce* of 3 *purl*[10], 2s; 7 pieces *relisaunce* of *purl* at 2s the piece; 18 pieces *crymyll* of thread at 3s the piece; 2 pieces towel of Henaude[11] containing 380 ells at 6d the ell; 2 pieces towel of Custaunce[12] containing 60 ells at 4d the ell; 2 dozens 11 pieces *twaill* at 8d the piece; 30½ pieces of

[1] *Sc. Westvale,* Westphalian, coarse wool or canvas, of strait or narrow width. See *N.E.D. sub* "Westvale" and "strait," 4 *b*.

[2] *Sc. rays*, a kind of striped cloth. Cf. cloth of ray.

[3] Paris thread or cloth, probably linen.

[4] Chasubles.

[5] Thread of Cologne.

[6] Kerchiefs of Courtrai.

[7] *Sc.* plite, pleat, plait. It appears to mean a definite quantity of silk folded or pleated. *Crymyl, sc. cremil,* is a border of openwork or lace or a fringe. *N.E.D.* quotes W. H. Stevenson, *Nottingham Borough Records*, II, p. 52: *Pro ii plyces de coton cremyll iis vid.*

[8] Kerchiefs of cambric, i.e. of Cambrai, where fine white linen was woven.

[9] *Sc. volet,* a kerchief or veil worn at the back of the head by ladies.

[10] *Relisaunce* or *relusauncz* was some kind of lustrous, sheeny material, not very heavy, since it was used for coverchiefs or light head-dresses. See *Cal. of Plea and Mem. Rolls*, 1323–64, pp. 244, 262. The word *purl*, of which this is a very early example, means bordering, edging, frilling. The whole phrase probably means silk lawn with a threefold frilled border.

[11] Hainault.

[12] Constance.

borde[1] of *iiii k*, at 16d the piece; 2 *orfrez*, 16d; 5 dozen 10 ells of silver at 2s 6d the dozen; 4 pieces of fustian at 12s the piece; 11 *laton* rings, 11d; 5 dozen 10 rings of *her*[2], 6d; 1 roll of *bultel* of *reynez*[3] at 2s 4d the piece; 2 pieces of *bokeram ynde*[4] at 3s the piece; $3\frac{1}{4}$ yds. of the same at 8d the yd.; 3 pieces of *borde* and 3 pieces of *twaill* of *denaunt*[5] containing 54 yds. at 8d the yd.; 4 pieces of *spynall*[6] containing 210 ells at 2d the ell; 2 remnants of *borde alisaundre*[7], 8s; 3 ells of *west lib*[8] at 4d the ell; $8\frac{1}{2}$ pieces of *bokeram esteyned*[9] at 2s the piece; 3 pieces of *bokeram esteyned* for an altar at 10d the piece; one coverlet and one *testre*[10], 14s; 84 yds. of *bultel* of *Melane*[11] at 2d the yd.; one piece of *bultel large*[12], 10s; 3 ells of silver, 12d; 5 gross of gold and silver[13] at 8d the gross; 7 gross of *laton* rings at 3d the gross; 14 silk *lacez*, 12d; one half piece of green *sendel*[14], 3s; 4 pieces of *dornek*[15] at 15s 4d the piece; $3\frac{1}{2}$ lbs. of *frengez*[16] at 12d the lb.; $5\frac{1}{4}$ lbs. of *fill*[17] at 8d the lb.; 4 beds of *worsteyd* at 8s each; 4 pairs of *curteyns*, 8s 6d; one *bultell* of *worsteyd*, 4s 10d; half a *sele*[18] of *worsteyd*, 2s; one red *tester*, 3s; 55 yds. of red *worsteyd* at 2d the yd.; 24 *reys*[19] at 2d the *reye*; 3 *beris*[20], 3s; one net, 12d; 2 dozens of red cloth, 40s.

[1] *Borde*, see n. 7 on *borde alisaundre*, appears to be some kind of striped material. Beck, *Draper's Dictionary*, p. 3, says "*bord*" in Arabic means a striped cloth and that St Augustine speaks of a stuff called "*burda*." *iiii k* seems to have some analogy with "iii purl" above. One may suggest "material of 4 stripes," but this is mere conjecture.

[2] This should mean "hair," but *er*, *sc. erei*, of copper, is not impossible.

[3] Sieve, sievecloth of Rennes, Brittany.

[4] Buckram dyed with indigo.

[5] Towel of Dinant, not necessarily a drying-towel, but linen-cloth generally, sometimes used of an altar-cloth.

[6] A textile fabric, probably coarse linen.

[7] *Sc.* Alexander, Alexandrine, a kind of striped silk material, see Beck, *Draper's Dictionary*.

[8] Meaning of *lib* uncertain. The cloth is *Westvale*.

[9] *Sc.* stained, stencilled in designs. The Stainers applied colour which penetrated the material. They were decorators rather than colour-dyers and amalgamated with the Painters in 1501.

[10] *Sc.* tester.

[11] Milan.

[12] Wide, as opposed to strait, see above, p. 225, n. 1.

[13] Gold and silver braid or ornaments, tinsel.

[14] A thin rich silken material.

[15] A fabric of Tournai used for hangings.

[16] *Sc.* fringes.

[17] Thread, usually linen.

[18] *Sc.* ceil, a canopy.

[19] Probably spangles.

[20] A covering for a pillow, pillow-slip, usually "pillow-beres."

In addition to the above goods, the testator's servants had levied divers debts owed to him by William Wychelse and others and had delivered these amounts to the defendant in part payment of the debt owed to him. The defendant prayed judgment as to whether the plaintiff had any action against him. Membr. 8 *b*

The plaintiff answered that long after 1 Dec. 1391 he delivered to the testator divers goods for which the testator entered into a bond for £47 10s 2d, and that these and other goods belonged to the testator at the time of his death, and that two days before his death he asked the defendant to administer all his goods and chattels, to pay the plaintiff and other creditors, and from the residue to recoup himself for his own claims, and then to pay the balance to the testator's wife. He offered to verify his plea that the defendant administered the goods as executor of the will.

The defendant repeated that the only administration carried out by him was in virtue of the deed of 1391 and the assignation of effects of 31 March 1394, and that he did not administer any other goods or debts which might have belonged to the testator at his death.

On this issue a jury of the parish of St Lawrence Jewry said on oath that the defendant did not administer any goods belonging to the testator at the time of his death as executor, but that he received the above goods in the testator's lifetime in part satisfaction of the debt owed to him, and that he received the debts above-mentioned after the testator's death on the ground of the agreement to assign them to him. As regards £20 owed by a certain John Reynold to the testator, the defendant had exchanged this for a new bond payable to himself. They assessed the damages at 40s, if the court gave judgment for the plaintiff for £47 10s 2d, and at 20s, if the court gave judgment for £20 only. The court reserved judgment [breaks off].

ROLL A 34

Rolls of Memoranda of the time of John Fressh, mayor of the city of London, A° 18 Ric. II

Membr. 1
4 Nov. 1394

Memorandum that Christopher Tyldeslegh complained that though he had served a ten years' apprenticeship, his master John Grenefeld, goldsmith, refused to have him admitted to the freedom of the city. On the master failing to appear, the said Christopher was received into the freedom on the testimony of John Forster, John Bolstrode, John Standelf and William Donn, wardens of the mistery of Goldsmiths, and others.

4 Jan. 1395

Quitclaim from Matthew Cheyne, merchant of Florence, to Zanobius Ser Benozii, merchant of Florence. Dated at London 2 Jan. 1395.

Membr. 1 *b*
26 Jan. 1395

William, Lord la Sowche, knight, brings a plaint of intrusion against Margaret, widow of Nicholas Sharnesfeld, knight, Lewis Clyfford, knight, Richard Stury, knight, Baldewyn Radyngton, knight, and John Cheyne, knight, touching his free tenement in the parish of St Andrew in Lyme Street Ward.

26 Feb. 1395

Letter of attorney from William Waterman of Southwark to Alice Mockyng of Southwark to receive the sum of £13 18s due on a bond from Thomas Ponyngges, knight, lord of St John[1].

1 Feb. 1395

Letter of attorney from William atte Bourne, merchant of Almaine, to Hildebrand van Brekefeld, merchant of Almaine, and Philip Rykhall, clerk.

Membr. 2

Examination of two men charged with immorality, of whom one implicated several persons, male and female, in religious orders.

6 Feb. 1395

Inquest taken before John Fressh, Mayor, and the Aldermen in the Chamber of the Guildhall, by oath of Thomas

[1] Cf. Husting Roll, 125 (72). He was son of Luke Poynings, who was summoned to parliament from 42 to 49 Edw. III, and Isabel de St John. He was never himself summoned to parliament.

Coton, John Jeweler, Thomas Prentys, John Hay, John Hendelee and William Colyn of the parish of St Martin Ludgate, Walter Wynter, Nicholas Spe... and Henry Broun of the parish of St Faith, Richard Frenches and William Asshe of the parish of St Audoen. The jurors said on oath that on 29 Jan., when the mayor was outside Ludgate on the business of the city, John Walpole, tailor[1], followed him from the gate to St Paul's Church and took him by the sleeve, shouting and saying derisively, "Oh mayor, do justice to me," to whom the mayor said: "show it by bill and justice will be done to you," and thereupon John Walpole said noisily: "What use is it to make you a bill when all the magnates of England have made my plea and acknowledge my action?" and he said further to those passing by: "it is a fine thing to make a bill for him"; and when the mayor arrived in the churchyard and there met Sir John Busheye and Sir William Bagot, knights, the said John Walpole wrangled with the mayor and called John Botesham, serjeant and official of the city, "a false ribald and harlot[2]," and said that if he was not a false harlot, he would make him one, and then the said John Walpole said to the mayor: "it is a great honour for you, the mayor and judge of London, to play at tables with Richard Clare your serjeant, such a harlot as he is," and after this he followed the mayor from the churchyard through the church, every now and then taking him by the sleeve and shouting and arguing with him, until they reached Paternosterrowe, where the said John shouted angrily: "mayor, do me justice, or I will bring such a mob about you that you will be glad to do justice"; for which dangerous words the mayor committed him to Newgate prison, and then the said John Walpole, while going from the mayor's presence towards the prison, raised the hue and cry with a loud voice, saying: "the mayor of London wants to have me falsely imprisoned because I sue for justice"; and when he arrived at Newgate the said John publicly told the men there that Adam Bamme, John Hende, William Staundon and John Hadlee, late mayors of

[1] See above, pp. 158–160.

[2] *Sc.* vagabond, low fellow, rogue, but sometimes used, not as a term of abuse, to denote a menial, hireling.

London, were false in exercising their mayoralties, and that of all the mayors John Hadlee was outwardly the finest talker but inwardly the falsest. The jury said further that a great part of the uproar and rancour in the city from the time of Nicholas Twyford to the present day was made and spread by the ill-will of John Walpole, who was a great disseminator of discord.

30 March 1397 The aforesaid John Walpole was mainprised by Robert Croukern, Richard Plymmouth, William Whyteby and Geoffrey Asshwell, tailors, Simon Ede, baker, and Robert de Eye, weaver, for his good behaviour towards the king and people and especially towards the officers and citizens of the city under several penalties of £100.

Membr. 2 *b*
18 Oct. 1395 Thomas Duk, citizen and skinner, demands an Assize of Nuisance against William Sleford, clerk, dean, and the college of the king's free chapel of St Stephen within the king's palace of Westminster, touching his free tenement in the parish of St Dunstan in the West.

19 Oct. 1395 Henry Parmystede, draper, brought a bill of complaint against John Pountfreyt, saddler, for a debt of 7 marks owed by him as surety for John Mountacu, who had purchased cloth from the plaintiff to the value of £9. [*French*]

The defendant denied the debt and offered to make his law incontinently as a freeman of the city according to the custom. Thereupon the plaintiff granted that if the said John would swear alone that his defence was true he should be precluded from his action. The defendant swore on the Gospels that he owed the plaintiff nothing. Therefore it was considered that the plaintiff take nothing by his bill and be in mercy and that the defendant be quit thereof.

Membr. 3
17 April 1395 Robert Guppey, mercer, was summoned as administrator of the goods and chattels of John Chiveley, intestate, to answer John Cholsey, merchant, in a plea of debt of £200, which sum the said John Cholsey had bound himself to pay as surety for the intestate in a bond to Thomas Neuton and Henry Burton, merchants of London. On the death of the intestate by shipwreck, the plaintiff has been forced to pay

this sum at Middelburgh by the law of the Staple of Middelburgh, and he now claimed it from the administrator.

The defendant denied that he was general administrator of the intestate's goods and chattels, and pleaded that the intestate owed him £100 and that he had sued the real administrator, Thomas atte More of co. Cambridge, for payment in the Sheriffs' Court. He produced the record of the action, which showed that on Thomas atte More's making default, he had been awarded the right of collecting a number of debts owed to the intestate and also, as a foreign attachment, a quantity of goods belonging to the intestate, which were then in his (the present defendant's) custody. These goods were valued in the Sheriffs' Court by John Cosham and Thomas Merton, mercer, as follows:

82 lbs. of *brasile*[1] at 3s the lb.; 9 pieces of red *bukeram* at 3s the piece; 20 *groos* of gold of Lucca[2], 10s; 33,000 chestnuts (*castons*) at 16d the thousand; 7000 small white plates[3] at 8s the thousand; 211 lbs. of *coperwire* at 4d the lb.; one long sword, 6s 8d; one *cappe* of *bevere*, 2s 6d; one box of *cipres*, 8d; an old *basynett* with *visere*, 4s; 4 pieces of *bokasyns* of *barbarie*[4] at 18s the piece.

The plaintiff then pleaded that the goods and chattels and debts received by the defendant were greater in value than the £100 due to him.

The parties submitted to the arbitration of William Brampton, Thomas Aleyn, John Shaddeworth, Hugh Clerk, William Parker, John More, William Marchesforth and William Sonnyngwell, who awarded that, as the goods and debts exceeded the debt of £100 by 100 marks, the defendant should pay the plaintiff the latter sum and also supply him with a list of the names of certain persons who owed money to the intestate, and that both parties should quitclaim to each other all actions; which was done. The names of the debtors were William Mordon, £22; Katherine Swyft, £4 4d; John Brook,

[1] A red dye from the East Indian tree *Caesalpinia Sappan*. See *N.E.D.*

[2] 20 gross of gold of Lucca, either gold thread used for weaving into fabric or small ornaments, spangles, tinsel, *etc.*

[3] Steel plates for armour.

[4] An early use of the word "*bocasin.*" It means some kind of fine material, generally used for linings, in this case woven in Barbary.

16s 8d; Adam Chapman, £22; William Geffrey of Colchestre, 13s 4d; John Balsham of Calais, £3; John Ware, 46s 8d; William Greyston, 40s; Thomas Philipp, £7 13s; John Westby, 6s 6d; John Canynges of Bristol, 40s.

Membr. 3 *b*
4 May 1395

John Hotot of Newmarket co. Cambridge, who had served a seven years' apprenticeship to Andrew de Preston, vintner, complained that his master refused to make him free of the city. The said Andrew declared that the apprentice had caused him losses and had behaved badly, which he would complain of by bill at the next court. As he failed to do so, the apprentice was admitted to the freedom on the testimony of John Walworth, Simon Bodham and Robert Aston, masters of the Vintners.

4 July 1395

An inquest of office was taken at the Guildhall before the Mayor and Aldermen by oath of William Bacon and others, who said that a certain bond by which John Thorpe, clerk, was alleged to be bound to Richard Norhampton in £500 and 10 marks, was a forgery made by Robert Morton, chaplain, and Robert Bulby on 6 May 1388 in the parish of St Andrew Holborn, as they understood, and that it was not the deed of John Thorpe.

ROLL A 35

[*William More, mayor*]

William Hoo of London brought a bill of complaint against William Shiryngham and Roger Elys, sheriffs, for a debt of £182 18s 8d, wherein they had become liable by allowing a certain Manuel Zakarie, merchant of Genoa, to escape from Newgate, to which the said Manuel had been committed after the plaintiff had obtained judgment against him in the Sheriffs' Court for the above-mentioned sum due on a bond. [*French*] Membr. 1 *26 Nov. 1395*

The defendants appeared after three defaults and pleaded that all sheriffs had the power of choosing deputies to guard the gaol and the prisoners, that they had appointed a certain William Popelton and others, who were dwelling in the city and had sufficient goods and chattels to satisfy the plaintiff's claim, and that action lay against the latter and not against the sheriffs themselves. They prayed judgment whether they ought to be charged with the debt.

The plaintiff pleaded that he had no need to answer the defendants' plea, since they had admitted that they were and at the time of the escape had been keepers of the gaol.

After an adjournment that the court might be advised, it was considered that the plaintiff recover the above-mentioned debt against the sheriffs and damages taxed at 13s 4d, and upon this the sheriffs were committed to prison on 6 Feb. 1396 until they paid.

Memorandum that on 14 Dec. 1395 William Venour, John Hamerton, clerk, John Stapulford and Roger Wikwane, executors of William Venour, senior, deceased, brought a bill against the said William Hoo for a debt of £200 due on a bond dated 22 Aug. 1394, by virtue of which Hugh Battisford, common serjeant-at-arms of the city, on 15 Dec. 1394 arrested the sum of £182 18s 8d in the hands of the sheriffs. William Hoo having made four defaults, the sheriffs on 23 Feb. 1395 brought the money into court and prayed that they might be liberated from prison, informing the court that of the aforesaid money the sum of £50 had been attached at the suit of Nicholas Bacon, mercer, in the Sheriffs' Court Membr. 1 *b* *14 Dec. 1395* on 15 Dec. 1394. The sheriffs were liberated and the record of Bacon's action was produced, which showed that William Hoo owed £50 to a certain Thomas Appelby, mercer, deceased, whose administrator, John Michellesonne, was sued by Bacon.

After deliberation, the court gave judgment that the executors of William Venour should receive the sum of £182 2s in part payment of their claim to £200 and that Nicholas Bacon and William Hoo receive nothing.

Membr. 2
4 Dec. 1395

John Cosham, who had been admitted to the freedom of the city in the mistery of Haberdashers on 1 Oct. 1379 during the mayoralty of John Philipott and the chamberlainship of John Ussher, and who now exercised the trade both of a haberdasher and a mercer, but was clothed yearly in the livery[1] of the Mercers and had no connection with the Haberdashers, petitioned the Mayor and Aldermen that he might be admitted to the freedom as a mercer. At the instance of the good men of the mistery of Mercers who appeared in court, the Mayor and Aldermen granted the request and remitted the usual fine.

31 Jan. 1396

Writ to the mayor and sheriffs that whereas Thomas Polle, Robert Fraunceys, Richard Barton and John Emond, goldsmiths, had been charged with causing the death of Robert Baroun, horner, outside the Bar of the New Temple and had been committed to prison, which homicide they declared had been committed by evildoers unknown to them, and whereas they were ready to answer the charge and stand to justice, the king commanded that if they were mainprised by John Hadlee, Adam Bamme, Drew Barentyn and William Brampton under sufficient penalty, they should be released from prison. Dated at Worcester 23 Jan. 1396.

By virtue of the above the said Thomas and his fellows were released under the above mainprise under penalty of 400 marks. The same day Henry Bamme, John Forster, Thomas Panton, Thomas Hay, Thomas Exton, William de Lowthe, John Frenssh, John Bulstrode, John Luton, Stephen

[1] *Secta*. The Mercers already had a livery in 1347, worn by all the members. The restriction of the livery to the wealthier members was a development of the next century. Unwin's *Guilds*, pp. 103, 166.

Mapelesden, John Standelf, John Carbonel and William Stamelden, goldsmiths, entered into a bond to save the said mainpernors harmless.

Deed of sale from Henry Sanday of Lucca, burgess of Venice, owner and master of the ship "*Seinte Mariknyght*," to Gilbert Maghfeld, merchant of London, of the above-named ship with all her gear and appurtenances, which the vendor warranted for a year and a day according to the Law of Olyron[1] and the custom of the sea, the adventure of the sea and the act of enemies alone being excepted from the warranty. Sealed at the special request of the vendor with the mayoralty seal for better evidence and security and marked with the accustomed mark of Martin Seman, papal and imperial notary. Dated at London 26 Sept. 1395. Witnesses, Angel Christofre, Lodewic de Port, merchants of Lucca, John Joan, merchant of Venice, Bernard George, merchant of Florence, Reginald Grille, merchant of Genoa, and many others. Membr. 2 *b* *30 Nov. 1395*

Bond of William Brampton and William Askham, citizens of London, John Pasford and Richard Shelle, clerk, in £200 that Thomas Shelle, esquire, and Dame Juliane his wife would acquit and discharge John Fabyan and Thomas Paynel and the lands, tenants, executors and heirs of Sir Bernard Brocas, knight, senior, of any claim to 200 marks, that being the sum in which Sir Bernard and Dame Juliane and the said John Fabyan and Thomas Paynel as their sureties had been bound in the Exchequer for the wardship of the manor of Ferle[2] co. Southampton, and the marriage of Bernard, son and heir of Sir Edmund de Mussenden, knight. Membr. 3 *4 Feb. 1396*

Writ of protection in favour of Emanuel Zakarie, who was then engaged in certain urgent business affecting the king and the realm, such protection to continue till Michaelmas following. Dated at Notyngham 17 Feb. 1396. *17 Feb. 1396*

[1] Neither version of the Law of Oleron preserved in the city's Liber Horn and Liber Memorandorum contains any rule as to warranty of ships sold, nor does there appear to be any such rule in the customs of the sea as collected in the *Black Book of the Admiralty*. Warranty of title was not unusual. See Holdsworth, *Hist. Eng. Law*, VIII, p. 246. *Select Pleas of the Admiralty* (Seld. Soc.), I, pp. 141–3; II, pp. 16, 82, 91, 99.

[2] Farley Chamberlayne. *Cal. Pat. Rolls*, 1391–6, p. 575.

Note that a close writ *de proteccione allocanda* was received on 23 Feb.

9 March 1396 Assignment by John Balsham, apothecary, to William Thorgerton, apothecary, of all his rights to the unexpired portion of the apprenticeship of William Brokeman. Witnesses, Edmund Fraunceys and Mark Everlee, masters of the art of Grocers of London, William Chichely, Robert Chichely, John Lew, John Feyrrer, John Spark, clerk, and others. Dated 8 Feb. 1396.

Membr. 3 *b*
14 April 1396 Writ of *certiorari* demanding the cause of the taking and detaining in Newgate of John Walpull of London, tailor. Dated at Westminster 14 April 1396.

Note that a return was made on 4 May of the cause as enrolled in the Memoranda Roll of John Fressh, mayor.

12 May 1396 Writ of protection in favour of John Basse, draper, who was then in the king's service in the company of Sir William de Hoo, knight, captain of the castle of Oye in Picardy. Dated at York 28 March 1396.

Close writ *de proteccione allocanda* of the same date.

Membr. 4
12 March 1396 Acquittance from John Mannyng, warden of the Guildhall Chapel, John Depham, Walter Adekyn, William Holme and John Draycote, chaplains of the same, to William Parker and William Cressewyk for the receipt of £160, paid by them in the presence of Stephen Speleman, chamberlain, which money they owed to Edmund Noreys, late warden, Peter Wysbech and John Dangy, chaplains, deceased, and to the above-mentioned John Depham and Walter Adekyn. Given under their seals and the seal of the chamberlainship in the Chamber of the Guildhall, 9 March 1396.

Membr. 4 *b*
18 May 1396 Bond of John Sely, skinner, to Tydemann Wauschede and Henry Smytman, merchants of Almaine, for the payment of £132 13s 4d by quarterly payments of 50s. Dated 17 May 1396.

Membr. 5
19 June 1396 Acquittance from Gerard, (son of) Sir Benedict de Albertis[1],

[1] *Gerardus domini Benedicti de Albertis*. Cf. p. 240. *Gerardus filius Benedicti per nomen Gerardi domini Benedicti de Albertis*.

and James Monald of the society of the Albertines, administrators of the goods and chattels of James Dyne, intestate, for the receipt of £173 12s 11d due, on two letters of exchange, from Alamann Mannyn and Antony Mannyn his brother.

Bond of the said Gerard and James to save the said Alamann and Antony harmless against all claims arising from the letters of exchange.

Writ from the king to the mayor and sheriffs informing them that he had lately confirmed the charters of the town of Northampton, given by his predecessors, which granted to them, among other liberties, freedom from toll and lastage throughout all England and the seaports, and which empowered the *prepositus* of Northampton to take a pledge there in case anyone infringed these liberties, and commanding the said mayor and sheriffs to allow the said burgesses to be free thereof. Dated at Westminster 2 May 1396. *2 May 1396*

Return to the above from Thomas More, mayor, Roger Elys and William Shiryngham, sheriffs, that they and their fellow-citizens and their predecessors held London and Middlesex to farm together with divers liberties, free customs, tolls and lastages of merchandise coming to London, by payment of a certain sum of money yearly to the Exchequer, and that they had been accustomed to take from the burgesses of Northampton and others toll and lastage[1] on all merchandise coming to London in aid of the farm aforesaid, and moreover these liberties, tolls, privileges and customs had been confirmed and ratified by divers statutes and by the charters of the king himself and his progenitors, against which liberties and customs the burgesses of Northampton had shown no cause why they should be exonerated from payment, and whereas the mayor and sheriffs were bound by oath to observe what was a royal as well as a civic right, they were unable and ought not to exonerate the burgesses of Northampton from the payment of such toll and lastage.

Bond of Robert Denny, knight, to pay William More, vintner, the sum of £20 in case the said Robert survived his *9 May 1396*

[1] A toll payable by traders on the last or burden of merchandise.

wife Amy and recovered her dowry, to wit, a tenement with appurtenances in the parish of St James Garlickhithe, with which he had enfeoffed William More, Thomas Brounflete and Simon Barber.

Membr. 5 *b*
1 July 1396

Lease from William Lyghtegrave, goldsmith, to Thomas de Tildeslegh, of a tenement with a large garden and two shops on the north side of the entrance thereof, for a term of 50 years at an annual rent of a rose for the first three years and afterwards of 26s 8d, the property being on the east side of Whitecrouchestrete[1], whereof the tenements were bounded on the north by the tenement of John Bokelsmyth and on the south by that of Walter Abraham, and the garden on the north by that of John Bokelsmyth and on the south by that of Thomas Charlton, and the whole property on the east by the garden of Thomas Marys. The lessee covenanted to keep the buildings in repair against wind and rain, to amend the pavement when necessary, to surrender the property on completion of the term in good condition, except for damage from fires caused by others, sudden ruin and horrible tempest, and to give the lessor a yearly right of entry. Dated at London 23 June 1396.

16 Oct. 1396

Quitclaim from Fermyn de Haunchies, brother and attorney of John de Haunchies, Danish merchant, to Thomas Newenton, late sheriff, of all claims arising from the delivery from prison of John Hater, merchant of Coventry, during his shrievalty.

Membr. 6
6 July 1396

Assignment by John Isylham and Maud his wife, widow of Peter Widyton, pepperer, to Thomas Peroun, grocer, of the remaining period of a lease of a tenement in Bridge Street next to the Bars of the Bridge in the parish of St Magnus at a yearly rent of £22 10s for the first four years and one clove[2] afterwards, which premises the assignors had on a lease of 30 years, dating from 8 Dec. 1373, from Henry Hale, fishmonger, and John Patyn, *fleccher*, masters of the fraternity of the Blessed Mary of Salve [Regina] in the church of St Magnus at London Bridge, Sir Walter Broun, rector

[1] Whitecross Street. [2] *Unum clavum gariofoli.*

of the same church, William de Kyngeston, Henry Yivele and William Bys, citizens and brethren of the same fraternity. Dated 9 May 1396.

Bond of Thomas Peroun and Hamo Elyot, grocers, to pay the sum of £200 to John Isylham and Matilda his wife by half-yearly payments of £25.

Brother John Lyes, warden of the house of the Friars Minor of London, demands an Assize of Nuisance against John Norhampton, draper, touching his free tenement in the parish of St Nicholas *ad Macellas*[1], London. Membr. 6 *b* *7 Aug. 1396*

Campyne Pinell brought a bill of complaint against William Halton, draper, William Horwich, tailor, William Roter, draper, and John Clopton, shearman, for detinue of two bonds, in which the said Campyne and Richard Underwode were severally bound to each other for the payment of £10. [*French*] Membr. 7 *16 May 1396*

The defendants, being summoned by Robert Harry, the mayor's serjeant, appeared on 18 May and pleaded that the said Campyne and Richard had submitted themselves to their arbitration on terms specified in the bonds and under the agreement that, if one party disobeyed their award, the other party should have the bonds, and since they did not know whether the parties had obeyed the award or not, they prayed that the said Richard might be summoned to the next court.

On being summoned by Richard Walden, the sheriffs' serjeant, the said Richard made default. Therefore it was considered that the bonds be delivered to the plaintiff with damages against the said Richard taxed by the court at 40d.

Bond of John Colwell, *alias* Croydon, son and heir of Thomas Colwell, in £100 to William Fitzhugh, goldsmith, and Richard Rede, that he would leave the latter in undisturbed possession of lands and tenements in Mynchenlane[2] and elsewhere in the parish of St Dunstan by the Tower, acquired by them by demise of William de Forde, clerk, William Scryn, Robert Hethe and Walter Roo, the latter having obtained the property by feoffment of Thomas Mortemer, knight. *12 Feb. 1396*

[1] St Nicholas Fleshshambles. [2] Mincing Lane.

ROLL A 36

[*Adam Bamme, mayor*]

Membr. 1
25 Nov. 1396

Letter of attorney, dated at Burton-on-Trent, from William Prudhomme of the same to John Snypston, citizen of London, and John Bullok to receive from the society of the Ancient Albertines of Florence the sum of 312½ nobles 2s 8d of English money, due on a bond from the society to Thomas Wyght and John Dalston, for the collection of which William Prudhomme had a letter of attorney from the said Thomas and John.

24 Jan. 1397

Writ *corpus cum causa*, dated at Westminster 24 Jan. 1397, demanding that Margery Borham, *brouderer*, then a prisoner in Newgate, be brought before the king in Chancery on Thursday following with the cause of her taking.

Return by Adam Bamme, mayor, that information having been given that the said Margery, before she was made a citizen of the city, had retained a certain woman to dwell with her for a term of years in the manner of an apprentice by indentures, contrary to the liberties and laudable customs of the city hitherto used and approved, he had caused her to appear before him to show her part of the indentures, in order that he might do justice in the matter, but that she had refused with contumely to do so or to obey him, for which reason he had ordered her to be confined in prison; nevertheless she would be brought before the king promptly in obedience to the writ.

Membr. 1 *b*
23 Jan. 1397

Writ of protection in favour of Peter Cornelha, *alias* Cornolha, *alias* Cornewaill, of London, merchant, who was then on the king's service in the company of Sir John Stanley, captain of the castle of Rokesburgh in Scotland.

3 Feb. 1397

Writ of *certiorari*, demanding the cause of the committal to prison of Gerard, son of Benedict de Albertis, knight, Philip Thomas de Albertis and John Andrewe, to be certified in Chancery on the Tuesday following.

Return by Adam Bamme, mayor, that Gerard, son of Benedict, under the name of "Gerard of Sir Benedict de Albertis, knight," Philip Thomas and John Andrewe, foreigners, were committed to prison by virtue of a bill of detinue of goods and chattels which had been brought against them by Stephen Speleman, chamberlain of the city, and Walter Marwe, as executors of the will of Margaret, widow of James Dyne, late citizen, to compel them to render to the said executors one half of the goods and chattels of the said James, to the value of £1600, which belonged to the said Margaret by the law and custom of the city.

Action by Robert Curson and Sara his wife against Stephen Speleman, chamberlain, for detinue of a box of deeds. The chamberlain pleaded that the box was entrusted to him by William More, mayor, in obedience to certain letters under the king's signet, until it should be decided whether the box belonged to the above Robert and Sara or to William Bedyngton, who claimed them by right of his wife, Alice, sister of the said Sara and daughter of William Willesdon. After interpleader, judgment was given for William Bedyngton. Membr. 2 *4 Dec. 1396*

[*French and Latin*]

John Edmond of London, as factor of William Wykenden, executor of William Leche of Lynn, merchant, acknowledged receipt from Gerard, [son] of Sir Benedict de Albertis of Florence, factor of the society of the Albertines in England, of the true value of 100 ducats due on an exchange between William Leche and the society, to wit, 38d for every ducat, amounting to £15 16s 8d in all. As the said John had lost the letter of exchange and had no hope of finding it in the future, he acknowledged himself bound to exonerate the said Gerard and the society against any claims of William Wykenden or others arising from the exchange. Membr. 3 *16 Feb. 1397*

Bond of William, Burdeux herald of arms[1], John Coveham, draper, John Boteer, saddler, Robert Larden, carpenter, and John Serle, brewer, to William Byker, the king's artilleryman[2] at the Tower, to pay the latter £60 at the feast of the Purifica- *27 Feb. 1397*

[1] *Heraud darmes.* See Guillim's *Heraldry*, 1724, Suppl. p. 39.
[2] *Artillar' domini Regis.*

tion next following in the church of Holy Trinity within Aldgate. Dated at London 10 Feb. 1397.

Membr. 3 *b*
12 Feb. 1397

Writ of *corpus cum causa* to the Mayor and Aldermen to bring John Walpole[1], tailor, then detained in prison, before the king in his council in Chancery, together with the cause of his taking and detaining, in order that the king might give order for his delivery according to right and the law and custom of the realm. Dated at Westminster 12 Feb. 1397.

Membr. 4
7 April 1397

Bond of John Grene, cordwainer, to Stephen Speleman, chamberlain, in £20, to keep the peace, to be of good behaviour towards the mayor, aldermen and officers of the city, and to obey the lawful and reasonable ordinances of the mistery of Cordwainers. The same day the masters of the mistery released the said John of all previous offences against the mistery.

18 Feb. 1397

Writ of *certiorari* demanding the record and process of an action of trespass brought by John Neel, gardener, against John Sewale, carter. Dated at Westminster 18 Feb. 1397.

Record and process of the above action:

The Mayor and Aldermen being given to understand that a plea of trespass pending in the court of Thomas Wilford, sheriff, between John Neel, gardener, and John Sewale, carter, was being unduly disturbed both in court and outside by immoderate maintenance as well by citizens as by foreigners, and desiring to do full and speedy justice to both parties in accordance with the custom of the city, ordered the sheriff to bring the aforesaid plea with all matters concerning it before the Mayor and Aldermen in the Chamber of the Guildhall on 1 Feb. 1397 and to warn the parties to be there to do and receive what justice should require according to the custom of the city, which sheriff the same day brought the aforesaid plea with all matters concerning it in these words:

Wednesday 10 Jan. 1397 John Neel, gardener, levied a certain plaint of trespass in the compter of Thomas Wilford, one of the sheriffs, in these words: John Sewale, carter, is

[1] See above, pp. 160, 229.

attached *versus* John Neel, gardener, in a plea of trespass. Pledges of prosecution, John Stokesle, skinner, and Roger Ward.

Court of the lord king held before Thomas Wilford, one of the sheriffs of London, on Wednesday after the feast of St Hilary [13 Jan.] A° 20 Ric. II [1397]. *17 Jan. 1397*

John Sewale, carter, was attached to answer John Neel, gardener, in a plea of trespass that on Monday before Christmas in the parish of St Botolph without Aldersgate in the suburb of London he assaulted the plaintiff with force and arms and beat, wounded and ill-treated him against the peace and to his damage £100, and therein he produced suit. The defendant pleaded not guilty within the liberty of the city and put himself on the country. And the said John Neel likewise.

And upon this the Mayor and Aldermen gave precept to summon a jury for 16 Feb. when the parties appeared and the jury said on oath that the defendant was guilty within the liberty of the city to the plaintiff's damage 40 marks. Accordingly it was considered that the plaintiff recover the said 40 marks and that the defendant be committed to prison until he pay a fine to the king and the said damages.

Membr. 4 *b*
20 Feb. 1397

Bond of Gerard, son of Sir Benedict de Albertis, one of the executors of James Dyne, citizen of London, and Bartholomew de Bosano to Stephen Speleman, mercer, and Walter Merwe, executors of Margery, daughter of the said James Dyne, to pay to Lodewic, son of the late Nicholas Dyne, when he came of age, the sum of £12 devised to him by the said Margery, which sum the said Stephen and Walter had paid out to the said Gerard and Bartholomew for the use of the said Lodewic.

Membr. 5
22 May 1397

Writ of error to the mayor and sheriffs of London with regard to a plea of trespass brought by Thomas atte Hay, brewer, against William Rothewell, chaplain, before John Fressh, late Mayor, and the Aldermen, whereof the said William had complained that there was manifest error in the record and process. The king, having assigned William

Thirnyng, John Cassy, Hugh Huls, John Markham and John Woderove, his justices, to examine the record and process and correct the errors therein, if any, by the law and custom of the realm and of the city, in the presence of the mayor and aldermen, if they wished to be present, at the church of St Martin le Grand—commands the sheriffs to warn the said Thomas atte Hay to be present, and further to deliver the said William Rothewell from prison, since he had been mainprised in Chancery by John Rothewell of Cirencester, Nicholas Halle of Cirencester, Reginald Grace, tailor, of the parish of St Andrew without the Bar of the Old Temple, and Thomas Alcestre of the parish of St Clement Danes without the Bar of the New Temple for the payment of the fine, or for his return to prison, if the judgment were affirmed. Dated at Westminster 22 May 1397.

Precept of the above justices to the Mayor and Aldermen to produce the record and process of the above-mentioned plea and to warn the said Thomas atte Hay to appear before them on 5 June 1397.

Return of the Mayor and Aldermen that it was the custom of the city time out of mind that no mayor or aldermen ought to send or return the record and process of such plea, wherefore they could not do so at present, but there was a custom that the mayor and aldermen, after an interval of forty days at least for consultation, allowed to them by the justices after their first coming, ought to render the record and process by the recorder of the city by word of mouth, which they were prepared to do.

Membr. 5 *b*
6 April 1397

Writ of error to the Mayor and Aldermen demanding that the record and process of a plea of debt between Salamon Salman, mercer, and Robert Dane, mercer, be produced before John Cassy, Hugh Huls, John Markham and John Woderove, the king's justices, at the church of St Martin le Grand, and further ordering the Mayor and Aldermen, if the said Robert Dane found sufficient security to pay the debt if it were affirmed, to deliver him or his mainpernors from prison. Dated at Westminster 6 April 1397.

Precept of the above-named justices to the mayor, aldermen and sheriffs to produce the record and process on 28 June 1397. Dated at Westminster 1 June 1397.

Return of Richard Whityngton, Mayor, and the Aldermen, claiming the custom of forty days respite and the communication of the record and process *oretenus* by the recorder.

Record and process of the action above-mentioned: Salamon Salman, mercer, sued Robert Dane, mercer, by bill, for £40, that sum having been awarded to the plaintiff on the arbitration of Richard Norbury, Thomas Aleyn, William Sonyngwell and Thomas Prudance, who laid down that it should be paid by half-yearly instalments of 5 marks, but that the whole amount should become due if a half-yearly payment were in arrears. The defendant denied that there was any such condition as to payment or that they submitted themselves unconditionally to the arbitration, and said that the parties agreed that if either of them refused to accept the award, he should be bound to the masters and mistery of Mercers in £20, and since he had refused the award, he was liable only for that amount. A jury was summoned which found that the parties had submitted themselves to the arbitration in high and low. Judgment for the plaintiff with 40s damages. Membr. 6 *8 Feb. 1397*

Richard Northbury and John More, mercers, in whose hands had been entrusted reciprocal bonds for £100 by Edmund Fraunceys, grocer, and Thomas Lydyard, were sued by the former for detaining the bonds. They pleaded that the bonds were handed to them to be given up under certain conditions, and since they did not know whether the conditions had been fulfilled, they asked that Thomas Lydyard be summoned. Membr. 6 *b* *24 Feb. 1397*

The said Thomas appeared and pleaded that a dispute between himself and the plaintiff about a house in Oxford had been submitted to the arbitration of John More, John Sutton, grocer, Richard Northbury and Thomas Prudance, mercers, who awarded that Edmund Fraunceys should enfeoff him with the house within six days and levy a fine in the king's court in order to debar any claim of Edmund's wife Agnes on the ground of dower, for which he was to pay

Edmund a rent of £10 for life, and thereupon they had deposited bonds for £100 to be delivered to one party if the other failed to fulfil the award. The said Edmund, he pleaded, had not made the feoffment.

The plaintiff denied that there was any condition of making a feoffment, and as regards the fine, he said that he and his wife had fulfilled the award, but that the said Thomas had not given him security for paying the rent.

The court adjourned the case till 13 July to consult as to their judgment, on which day the said Thomas made default. Accordingly judgment was given for delivery of the bonds to the plaintiff with damages 20s.

Membr. 7
22 May 1397

Margery, widow of Richard Godard, and Thomas Sybseye, tailor, brought a bill wherein they complained that John Godard, goldsmith, had expelled them from two messuages with a quay adjacent in the parish of St Bennet of Baynardescastell next to Paul's Wharf. These premises had been leased to Richard Godard on 29 March 1378 by John de Lyndeseye, prior, and the convent of the hospital of St Mary without Bishopsgate for 60 years, which lease was assigned by him on 12 May 1387 to John Neuport and Andrew Neuport his brother, then serjeant-at-arms of the king, and John Yonge, mariner, the two last-named re-assigning it on 20 Oct. 1396 to the plaintiffs, who enjoyed possession until 6 Jan. 1397, when, as they alleged, the defendant expelled them.

The defendant pleaded that Richard Godard had sublet one portion of the premises in the fifth year of the present king (1381–2) to Reginald Thorneye, woodmonger, and Margaret his wife, for fifty years at an annual rent of 33s 4d, and the remaining portion in the eighth year (1384–5) to John Seman for 50 years at an annual rent of 8 marks 6s 4d, and that neither of them attorned to John Neuport, Andrew Neuport and John Yonge, and that finally on 6 Oct. 1397 the said Richard granted these annual rents to him, the defendant, to whom the tenants attorned, and that on the day of the supposed expulsion he entered the tenements to take a distress for his rents as he was entitled to do, but that he did not expel the plaintiffs.

The parties went to a jury on the issue of the expulsion, and the jury brought in a verdict that the defendant expelled the plaintiffs, and taxed damages at 10 marks. Judgment was given that the plaintiffs recover their damages.

Note of payments made by William Oxford, who had married Alice, widow of William Potenham, girdler, and by Peter atte Hethe, co-executor with the said Alice, on behalf of the orphans of the said William Potenham[1]. Membr. 8 *2 April 1395*

Further proceedings relating to Alice, orphan daughter of the said William Potenham. *24 Jan. 1397*

[1] See Letter Book H, fo. 303.

ROLL A 37

Further rolls of Memoranda of R. Whityngton

Membr. 1
28 April 1398 Writ of *certiorari* to the mayor and sheriffs, demanding the cause of the taking and detaining of John Sewale of Isildon, carter, in Newgate gaol.

Return of Richard Whityngton, mayor, and John Wodecok and William Askham, sheriffs, that John Sewale was committed to prison on the appeal of Richard Hawtyn, glover, as follows:

On Thursday 27 Dec. 1397 Richard Hawtyn, glover, came to Newgate before the mayor and sheriffs, John Cokayn, recorder, and John Michel, coroner, and appealed John Sewale, carter, because that the said John on 15 Sept. 1397 in the church of St Martin le Grand said to him that there was no peace or love in England since the present king became king, and that he was not a right king[1].

Further the said John Sewale was detained in prison for a debt of 40 marks recovered against him in a plea of trespass before Adam Bamme, late mayor.

1 Aug. 1397 Writ, directed to the mayor and sheriffs, reciting that among the liberties of Oxford[2] which the king had confirmed, it had been granted that the burgesses should be quit of toll, passage and every other custom throughout England and Normandy, *bilande & bistrande*, and that they and their heirs should have their liberties, laws, customs and tenures, with *soch* and *sach*, *thol* and *theam* and *infangfthef*, even as the citizens of London had them, and that if any one took toll or other custom, of which the burgesses were quit, the mayor and bailiffs at Oxford should take a pledge (*namium*) at Oxford until restitution was made. The citizens of London are commanded to permit the enjoyment of these liberties and to release any distress made for this reason, or show cause to the contrary. Dated at Westminster 1 Aug. 1397.

[1] *Quod ipse non fuit rectus Rex.* Probably the sense is proper or fitting, rather than upright or rightful.

[2] The reference is to the original charter of Oxford of 16 Feb. 1229. See *Munim. Gild. Lond.* (R.S.), II, pp. 671–3.

Return of the mayor and sheriffs that from time immemorial they and their fellow-citizens had held London and Middlesex to farm with divers liberties, customs, tolls, passages and lastages on merchandise coming to London, for a certain sum of money payable annually to the Exchequer, and that the sheriffs had been accustomed to take toll and passage as well from the burgesses of Oxford as others in aid of the farm aforesaid, which liberties, free customs, privileges, passages and lastages had been confirmed both by statutes and by charters with the clause *licet*, contrary to which the burgesses of Oxford had showed no cause why they should be exonerated. Since the mayor and sheriffs were bound by oath to observe the liberties of the city, they were unable to exonerate the burgesses of Oxford from payment of toll and passage, which were parcel of the aforesaid farm.

Bond of Robert Broun, skinner, to pay Albright Brant, merchant of Almaine, the sum of £19 4s 8d, by half-yearly payments of 40s. In case of default it was agreed that the said Albright be at liberty to enter upon a tenement of the said Robert in Petywalys[1] in the parish of All Hallows Berkyng, of 2 marks annual value, 4s quitrent formerly belonging to William Talworth in the same parish, three shops in Porteslane in the parish of St Dunstan by the Tower of 28s annual value, and 16s 8d quitrent from tenements in the parish of St Margaret Patyns in the occupation of Lady la Mortimer and Sir John Wilteshire, knight. Membr. 1 *b* *25 May 1398*

Writ of error to the Mayor and Aldermen with regard to the plea of trespass brought by Thomas atte Hay, brewer, against William Rothewell, chaplain, which plea was then being examined by Hugh Huls and his fellows, the king's justices, at St Martin le Grand. As the defendant William Rothewell had alleged error in the record and process of the plea, in that the plaintiff had not affirmed his bill of complaint by pledges, it is ordered that the bill be produced to Membr. 2 *8 Nov. 1397*

[1] The portion of Lower Thames Street from the Custom House to the Tower precincts. Robert Broun's quay and the two quays formerly belonging to William Capelyn de Taleworth afterwards formed the greater portion of Marowe's New Quay.

the justices at S[t] Martin le Grand. Moreover, immediately after the affirmation of the bill without pledges, the mayor's serjeant had been ordered to attach the said William, as a stranger, by his body. The justices required to know whether it was an ancient custom of the city thus to attach a stranger on the first day. Witnesses, William Thurnyng and Hugh Huls at S[t] Martin le Grand 8 Nov. 1397.

Return of Richard Whityngton, Mayor, and the Aldermen, that they were sending the bill as duly affirmed by pledges, and that it was immemorial custom in the city that when any one affirmed a bill of trespass or debt with pledges against a stranger, the latter ought to be attached on the first day.

8 Nov. 1397 Writ of error to the Mayor and Aldermen with regard to the plea of debt of £40 brought by Salamon Salmon against Robert Dane, mercer, then under examination as above. As the defendant alleged error in the record and process, in that the plaintiff affirmed his bill without pledges, it is ordered that the bill be produced before the justices. Moreover, after the jury had been sworn on 21 March 1397 they had demanded a day till the morrow to give their verdict and this was granted to them by consent of the parties. As this was alleged to be contrary to custom, the justices required to be certified as to the custom on 13 Nov. Witness John Cassy at S[t] Martin le Grand, 8 Nov. 1397.

Return that the Mayor and Aldermen were sending the bill as duly affirmed and that they were prepared to testify as to the custom by the mouth of the recorder, as was customary in the city, at the date and place mentioned.

Further return that it was immemorial custom for a jury in personal actions in the Mayor's and Sheriffs' Courts to demand and receive, by consent of the parties, a reasonable day to give their verdict, in order that meanwhile they might have more mature deliberation.

Membr. 2 *b*
4 Oct. 1397 Writ of error to the Mayor and Aldermen with regard to the plea of trespass brought by John Neel, gardener, against John Sewale, carter, in the court of Thomas Wilford, sheriff,

which was removed into the Chamber before the Mayor and Aldermen and was then under review by the king's justices at St Martin le Grand, the said John Sewale having complained that there was manifest error in the record and process and the rendering of judgment, namely, that whereas Adam Bamme, late Mayor, and the Aldermen ordered the sheriff to bring the plea before them in the Chamber on 1 Feb. 1397 and to warn the parties to be present, there was no mention in the record and process of the sheriff's having warned the parties and the complainant was not so warned, to which John Neel had replied that the sheriff did in fact warn the parties and that the said John Sewale, being warned, appeared, although both the warning and appearance were omitted from the record as sent to the justices—the Mayor and Aldermen are required to send the full record and process before the justices on 17 Nov. 1397. Witness William Thirnyng, 4 Oct. 1397.

Return of Richard Whityngton, Mayor, and the Aldermen that the sheriff did not certify them that he had summoned the parties, but that it was immemorial custom, when they caused an action pending in the Sheriffs' Court to come before them, for the sheriffs or the mayor's serjeants to warn the parties to appear on a certain day, and on this occasion Richard Jargeville, the mayor's serjeant, warned the parties to appear, and in obedience to this warning they appeared and pleaded as appears in the record already sent.

Plaint levied in the compter of William Askham, one of the sheriffs of London, on 11 March 1398: Membr. 3 *11 March 1398*

John Barker, haberdasher, and Margaret his wife, widow and executrix of Roger Crane, were summoned to answer William Crane, haberdasher, in a plea of debt of £32; pledges of prosecution, John Deux and Robert Northflete.

The sheriffs' serjeant was ordered, according to custom, to summon the said John and Margaret for the next court of the king, to wit, Wednesday 13 March, on which day the said John came. The sheriffs' serjeant testified that he had summoned the said John and Margaret. Thereupon the court ordered the said John to bring his wife to answer with him according to the custom of the city. Both defendants appearing on 15 March, the plaintiff made his declaration, in which he complained that the late Roger Crane was found to be in arrears to him in the sum of £32 by an account made before John Broun, auditor, on 28 Aug. 1394, which sum the said Margaret his executrix refused to pay, to his damage £20.

Upon this, in accordance with the custom whereby the Mayor and Aldermen at their pleasure could cause a plea pending in the Sheriffs' Court to come before them at the request of either party and could terminate it after examination of the parties, or in any other due manner according to the law merchant and the custom of the city, Richard Whityngton, mayor, instructed his serjeant to order the sheriff to bring the plea before him and to warn the parties to appear the same day, which was done. The said William Crane and John Barker appeared in person and the said Margaret by John Barker as her attorney. A day was given to them, by their consent, on Friday 22 March, when the parties appeared. The mayor then asked the defendants whether, if the plaintiff together with John Broun and John Deux would swear that the said John Broun heard the account and that the sum of £32 was due, they would be willing to be condemned in £32 according to the law merchant and the custom of the city and to be committed to prison.
Membr. 3 *b* The defendants peremptorily agreed, and the plaintiff for his part agreed to be excluded from his action if he and the said John Broun and John Dreux were unwilling to swear.

Thereupon the plaintiff, John Broun and John Dreux being examined, swore as abovesaid. And because it is and has been the custom of the city of London from a time whereof the memory of man runneth not to the contrary, that when the defendant in any bills or plaints before the Mayor and Aldermen in the Chamber of the Guildhall or before either of the Sheriffs is willing to put himself peremptorily on the oath of the plaintiff that the matter contained in the bill or count is true, if the plaintiff is unwilling so to swear, he ought by the law merchant and the custom of the city to be excluded from his action and demand, but if he so swears, the defendant ought to be condemned in the plaintiff's action and demand, and because it is also the custom that when the defendant offers to put himself peremptorily on the oath of the plaintiff and other good men with him[1], as upon the oath of the plaintiff alone upon any point, matter or thing contained in such bill or count, the same consequences ensue—therefore it was considered that the plaintiff recover against the defendants the said sum of £32. The plaintiff remitted the damages. The defendant John Barker, being present in court, was committed to Ludgate until he paid.

Writ of *certiorari*, dated at Westminster 2 Aug. 1398, demanding the record and process of the plea between William Crane, haberdasher, and John Barker and Margaret his wife, executrix of Roger Crane.

Membr. 4
10 June 1398

John Godolf, son of William Godolf, late citizen and currier, brought a bill praying to be exonerated from his apprenticeship to Richard Essex, draper, who had left his trade and was residing outside the liberties of the city. [*French*]

The said Richard was summoned four times at his house in the city and also by favour at Southwark, where he was living, to show cause, but did not appear. Accordingly on 26 June the apprentice was ordered to find security to serve the remainder of his term if Richard Essex within a year and a day came and proved that before his departure he had transferred his apprentice to an honest man of the same trade, or had assigned any one to provide for him and teach him his trade.

31 Aug. 1398

Letter of attorney from Naveryna, widow and executrix of John Thornbury, knight, reciting that on 30 March 1398, she had, together with Philip, son of John Thornbury, and

[1] The only peremptory oath was a single oath, and if either plaintiff or defendant refused to swear, he thereby lost his action. The present instance, as explained above, pp. 15, n. 1, 44, was merely a challenge, and there was no custom that two other good men could be associated in the oath. See *Munim. Gild. Lond.* (R.S.), 1, pp. 217–18.

Thomas Eston, recovered against Matheu de Magnane of Bologna, moneychanger, and Gerard de Ferrar, executors of the will of William Gold, Englishman, the third part of 6000 marks sterling and of other goods and chattels to the value of 2000 marks, belonging to William Gold at the time of his death, and that in part execution of the recovery, they had received three chests containing silk cloth of gold, silk kerchiefs and other silk, a coffer containing jewels of gold and precious stones, to wit, rubies, sapphires, *balaces*[1], diamonds and pearls, and a paper with divers letters and accounts, which had been arrested by the mayor's serjeant in the house of Thomas Fortebras, merchant of Lucca and factor and attorney of the "*companye*" of Guynyse, and in the hands of Jacob Manyan, son of the said Matheu, as being the goods and chattels of William Gold, which goods had been appraised at the value of £1200. She grants the above goods to Balduche, son of John Parghia de Intermenell of Lucca, with power to sell and dispose of them as his own, and at the same time she appoints him her special attorney to execute the remainder of the recovery. Dated at London 1 May 1398. [*French*]

Membr. 4*b*
3 May 1398

Similar letters from Philip, son of Sir John Thornbury, and Thomas Eston.

Membr. 5
6 Nov. 1397

Naveryna, widow of John Thornbury, knight, Philip, son of the above John Thornbury, and Thomas Eston, executors of the will of the said John, brought a bill of complaint by Balduchius Parghia of Lucca, their attorney, in their own names and that of William Grevell, their co-executor, against Matheu de Magnane of Bologna, moneychanger, and Gerard de Ferrar, executors of the will of William Gold, Englishman, for the detinue of the third part of 6000 marks and of other goods and chattels to the value of 2000 marks, *viz.* horses, harness, jewels, pearls, rings *etc.*, which was due to the executors in accordance with an indenture of 24 Nov. 1379, whereby the late Sir John Thornbury and William Golde had agreed that the survivor of them should have a third

[1] Balas-rubies.

part of the goods of the other, and they claimed further 2000 marks damages. [*French*]

At the same court William Grevell appeared and disclaimed being an executor or taking any part in this action. Accordingly he was separated from the action.

The remaining plaintiffs alleged that Matheu and Gerard were foreign merchants dwelling outside the realm, but had certain goods in the house of Thomas Fortebrace, factor of the society of Guynes, merchants of Lucca, and in the custody of Jacob Magnane, merchant of Bologna, which belonged to William Golde, and they prayed that these goods might be arrested as a foreign attachment. Order was given to attach the goods and summon the said Matheu and Gerard to appear on 12 Nov. The latter having made four defaults, judgment was given for the plaintiffs on 30 March 1398 and the goods were valued at £1200. The plaintiffs then agreed that the goods should remain in the custody of the said Jacob Magnane in case the defendants should appear within a year and a day to defend the action, and the said Jacob and Thomas, being at that time in London, entered into a bond to deliver the goods and chattels if the defendants Matheu and Gerard made no claim to them.

Membr. 5 *b*
1 April 1398

Writ of *certiorari* demanding that the record and process of the above action be sent to Chancery. Dated at Westminster 1 April 1398.

Return to the same.

21 Nov. 1397

Inquisition *post mortem* taken before Richard Whityngton, Mayor, and the Aldermen by oath of Richard Mustell and others as to the lands and tenements whereof Richard Cok died seised. The jurors said that he died seised in fee tail of certain lands and tenements within the city by virtue of the will of Robert Cok, glover, his father, enrolled in the Husting[1] A° 11, Ric. II, *viz.* certain tenements with an adjacent wharf called "*Dryngwatereswharf*" in the parish of St Magnus by the Bridge of £16 13s 4d annual value, a bakehouse with dwellings above in the parish of Holy Trinity the Less in Knyghtriderstrete in the ward of Cordwanerstrete of 6 marks annual

[1] *Cal. of Wills*, II, p. 268.

value, and also of a tenement called "*Litellondon*[1]," with houses built above and gardens adjacent, in the parish of All Hallows atte Wall in Bradstrete Ward of 5 marks annual value, but charged with an annual rent of 12s to the new hospital of St Mary without Bishopsgate. As the last-named rent had been in arrears for four years, John Mildenhall, prior of the hospital, had entered into the property and had occupied it until 23 Nov. 1393, when he and his convent by a deed enrolled in the Husting demised it to the said Richard Cok and Ellen his wife and his heirs, which Richard died jointly seised, with his wife, of the said property in fee tail. The date of his death was 19 June 1397, when all the rents issuing from the properties were arrested in the hands of the tenants by one of the serjeants of the Chamber. A certain Agnes, his daughter, was Richard's next heir, being over the age of two years, and a certain Thomas Peroun, since his death, had been in occupation of *Litellondon.*

Membr. 7
1 July 1397

Thomas Somersete, brother and heir of John Lylleston, brought a bill of complaint against John Skete that whereas John Lylleston devised to Joan his wife, her heirs and assigns a shop with solar and yard in Shytbournelane[2] in the parish of St Mary Abbechirche, which he bought of William Tapyser, and the said Joan afterwards married John Skete and died, and the complainant thereupon entered as heir, on the ground that a man by the custom of the city could not devise to his wife more than a life interest in his tenement, the said John Skete on 9 Jan. 1397 entered forcibly into the tenement, breaking two doors to the value of 20s and carrying away four locks to the value of 4s. [*French*]

The defendant, after three defaults, appeared on 9 July and pleaded not guilty of force and arms, but admitted entering the tenement, for which he alleged that the plaintiff had no action

[1] On the south side of London Wall. First mentioned by this name in 1371. It was bounded on the east by land belonging to London Bridge and on the west by a tenement of William Kyng, which later belonged to the Leathersellers and afterwards became the Ward School. It had a frontage of 60 feet 4 inches. In 1540 it passed into the possession of the Saddlers, with whom a portion still remains. Husting Rolls, 99 (126), 116 (123), 122 (26), 130 (33), 162 (78), 240 (6), 243 (24).

[2] Sherborne Lane. Derivation uncertain.

against him, because men of the city could by the custom of the city devise their tenements to their wives in fee simple, and the said Joan became seised of the tenement after her husband's death, and she, together with the defendant, granted the tenement to John Cappe and Walter Hoper and others, whose status he, the defendant, now possessed.

Both parties offered to verify their pleadings as to the custom of the city. On 8 July a jury of the venue was summoned and brought in a verdict that the defendant entered into the tenement in the manner and form alleged by the plaintiff[1], and taxed the damages at 3s 4d.

Therefore it was considered that the plaintiff possess his tenement and receive the damages taxed by the jury, and that the defendant pay a fine of 2s to the king for his contempt.

Writ to the mayor, sheriffs and recorder, appointing them, with the assent of the king's council, to inquire by a jury into the matter of a complaint made to the king by Donyna[2], widow of John Haucwod, knight, who asserted that certain persons enfeoffed with lands to the use of her husband, for the purchase of which he had from time to time sent sums of money, were detaining these lands and other goods and chattels, and had rendered no account of the profits thereof either to her husband or herself, and further that they had removed from St Paul's church a box of muniments belonging to her husband and relating to these transactions. A return was required to the council before the quindene of Easter. Dated at Westminster 24 Feb. 1398. Membr. 7 *b* *24 Feb. 1398*

[1] Though the parties pleaded as to right, the court considered only the question of forcible entry in accordance with 5 Ric. II, c. 7, 15 Ric. II, c. 2.

[2] Donnina, natural daughter of Bernabo Visconti, who married Sir John Hawkwood, the leader of the White Company and a notable figure in Florentine history. Hawkwood had purchased the Leadenhall through feoffees for the purposes of his will. In 1409 the surviving feoffee executed several deeds, the effect of which was to sell the property to the Mayor and Commonalty of London, who still possess it. The proceeds appear to have been used for the foundation of chantries, for the souls of Hawkwood and his companions, at Sible Hedingham and Castle Hedingham. Husting Roll 108 (87); Temple Leader and Marcotti, *Sir John Hawkwood*; Letter Book I, fo. 103 *b*; *Cal. Pat. Rolls*, 1408–13, p. 482; *London Topographical Record*, XIII, pp. 10–15, "Notes on the History of the Leadenhall."

Inquisition taken before Richard Whityngton, mayor, William Askham and John Wodecok, sheriffs, on 11 April 1398 by oath of John Byle, John Mogoun, John Bret, Peter Mason and Nicholas Cros of the parish of St Peter on Cornhill; Laurence Bakoun, Thomas Somerton, Walter Pope and Peter Briklesworth of the parish of St Christopher; Robert Cauntbrigg, Morice Archer, Thomas Drake, turner, and Henry Anketil, shearman, of the parish of St Benet Fynk; John Deux, Richard Lambard, Roger Horsley and John Bussh of the parish of St Michael at Corn, who said on oath that John Haucwod, knight, sent certain sums of money to John Serjeant, Robert Rikedon, Thomas Coggeshale, Robert Lyndeseye and John Sampson, who bought a tenement called "*Ledenhalle*" in the parish of St Peter with a part of the money, *viz.* the sum of 1200 marks, to the use of John Haucwod, which tenement was of an annual value of £28 3s 8d, and that since John Haucwod's death these persons had received the issues of the property, but to whose use the jurors did not know. They said further that the said John and the others had taken a chest to St Paul's church for safe custody and had afterwards removed it, but the jurors knew nothing of its contents. Sealed with the seals of the jurors and dated as above.

Membr. 8
20 July 1397

Writ of error to the mayor and sheriffs, demanding that the record and process of the action of trespass brought by Margery, widow of Richard Godard of London, and Thomas Sybseye, tailor, against John Godard, goldsmith, before the mayor, be brought into the next Court of Husting, and that the execution of the judgment against the defendant be suspended if he could find sufficient security to answer for the damages adjudged against him, in case the judgment were affirmed. Dated at Westminster 20 July 1397.

Similar writ, *sicut alias*, dated 6 Oct. 1397.

16 Nov. 1397

Writ ordering the mayor and sheriffs to return the former writs to Chancery, since they had been issued thoughtlessly (*improvide*[1]) from the king's court, in order that

[1] There was no appeal from the Mayor's Court to the Husting, but only to a special commission of justices sitting at St Martin le Grand.

other procedure might be taken. Dated at Westminster 16 Nov. 1397.

Grant from Adam Profete of Canterbury to William Parker, stockfishmonger, of all his goods and chattels, for better evidence of which he puts the said William in possession thereof by delivering to him a baselard plated with silver (*stipatum argento*). Witnesses, John Osbern, Robert Frankleyn, John Combe, William Rouchestre, John Walsingham and others. Dated at London 22 Nov. 1397. Membr. 8 *b* *27 Nov. 1397*

ROLL A 38

Rolls of Memoranda and Pleas of the time of Drew Barentyn, mayor, A° 22 Ric. II

Membr. 1
17 Feb. 1398

Writ of attorney recording that Perynanton de Blay, master of the ship "*Sabater*" of Bayonne, had appointed, *coram nobis*, Arnald William of Sedze and Henry Tylnay of London, vintner, his attornies in all pleas and actions in all courts of England during his absence abroad. Dated at Westminster 17 Feb. 1398.

5 Nov. 1398

Writ of *habeas corpus*, directed to the Mayor and Aldermen, declaring that it was a royal prerogative that debts owed to the king should be paid before satisfaction was made to other creditors, and requiring them to bring before the barons of the Exchequer the body of Ralph Gonyly, *scrutator*[1] in the port of Plymouth and all ports and places of Cornwall, who was engaged in accounting before the barons of the Exchequer concerning the issues of his office and was indebted to the king in divers amounts, which Ralph had been committed to prison by the Mayor and Aldermen at the suit of Perynanton de Blay. Witness, L. de Allerthorpe at Westminster, 5 Nov. 1398. By the Red Book of the Exchequer and by the barons.

Return of Drew Barentyn, Mayor, and the Aldermen that the said Ralph Gonyly, having nothing within the liberty of the city whereby he might be attached, had been arrested to answer Perynanton de Blay on a bill of complaint, of which a copy accompanied the return. Nevertheless the said Ralph would be brought before the barons as required.

Membr. 2
20 Nov. 1398

Precept directed to Drew Barentyn, mayor, the king's escheator in the city of London, to inquire by the oath of

[1] The king's "searcher." According to the plaintiff's story, he had been driven by stress of weather into Plymouth, where he customed his merchandise and took a cocket thereon, and Gonyly unjustly seized and retained both the cocket and the merchandise. *Cal. Close Rolls*, 1396–9, pp. 442–3.

good and lawful men of his bailiwick as to the lands and tenements held by Henry Caliser of London on the day of his death, and to return the finding to Chancery. Dated at Westminster 20 Nov. 1398.

Inquisition taken on 8 Jan. 1399 by oath of Thomas Coton and others, who said on oath that Henry Caliser on the day of his death held of the king in free burgage, as all the rest of the city is held, a tenement of the annual value of 4 marks in Bowyerowe within Ludgate in the parish of St Martin, situate between a tenement of the Friars Preachers in the occupation of Thomas Coton, bowyer, on the west, a tenement of Nicholas Spencer on the east, Ludgatestrete on the north, and a tenement of the Friars Preachers on the south; further that Henry Caliser died on 15 April 1312, that William Leek, tailor, is his next heir and of the age of 50 years and more, that Henry Caliser's widow Agnes occupied the house, by virtue of a legacy from her husband, until she died, that afterwards Nicholas Myle and his wife Ellen occupied it by virtue of a legacy from Henry Caliser to Ellen for her lifetime, that Nicholas then held it for life without any title, and on his death a certain Nicholas Henxtworth occupied the house by intrusion until his death, when Joan his widow entered by intrusion and took as her husband a certain Clement Lavendere, and on her death a certain John Henxtworth entered the house as her heir and held it until last Michaelmas, when by his consent William Leek, the true heir of Henry Caliser, entered into occupation.

Writ of protection in favour of Andrew Preston, vintner, who was then in the company of John, duke of Exeter, captain of the town of Calais. Dated at Westminster 10 April 1399. *10 April 1399*

Writ of *certiorari* to the Mayor, Aldermen and Sheriffs requiring information as to the probate of wills in the city. Dated at Westminster 18 April 1399. *18 April 1399*

Return that no testament of lands and tenements in the city ought to be admitted to probate or enrolment unless the seal of the testator were affixed or appended to it, and unless sufficient witnesses, two at least, were able to testify expressly concerning the seal of the testator, having sufficient knowledge of that seal.

Membr. 2 *b*
29 April 1399

Writ of protection in favour of Saer Parkesgate then about to cross in the king's company to Ireland. Dated at Westminster 29 April 1399.

18 June 1399

Quitclaim from Wynandus[1] van de Brule, executor of John Palyng, late citizen and goldsmith, to John Frensshe, Raymond Standelf, goldsmith, and William Sauvage, citizens of London.

Writ of *certiorari* demanding the cause of the taking and detaining of Beatrice, widow of Ralph Seintleger, otherwise known as Beatrice, wife of John Curson, knight. Witness Edmund, duke of York, *custos* of England, 10 June 1399.

Return of Drew Barentyn, mayor, that the said Beatrice had been taken and detained in prison at the suit of Alexander Shessh by virtue of a bill pending before the Mayor and Aldermen in the Chamber of the Guildhall, the tenor of which bill accompanied the return.

Membr. 3
11 Dec. 1398

Plaint levied before John Warner, sheriff, 11 Dec. 1398.

John Boudyer and John Molyn, merchants, summoned against Peter de Craon, knight, merchant, in a plea of account of goods and chattels received to the value of 250 marks. Pledges of prosecution: William Permestede and William Cosso.

By virtue of which plaint, the said John and John were taken and detained in the prison of Newgate until 26 June 1399, when John Clopidas brought into the Chamber a writ of attorney, dated at Haverford, 24 May 1399, whereby he or any one appointed by him was authorised to act on behalf of the plaintiff, who was then about to cross to Ireland in the king's service. Thereupon he appointed Matthew Trefours, chaplain, as his attorney, and together with the said Matthew agreed to the delivery of the two defendants from Newgate.

[1] Said to be Lat. of Wynkyn. Martin, *Record Interpreter*.

At the same court the defendant, John Boudyer, appeared and acknowledged a recognisance of debt. This document, dated 10 Nov. 1388, was issued by John Buridam, esquire, keeper of the seal of the bailiwick of Vermendois established at Peronne, and witnessed that John Boudyer, *surgien de muraus*[1] at Paris, had personally appeared before his lieutenant, Raymond Douiler, and had acknowledged a debt of 200 gold florins called "francs" as due to Sir Peter de Craon, knight, *seigneur de la frete Barnart*[2], and payable in even portions at Pentecost and Christmas following. [*French*]

Membr. 4
10 May 1399

Alice, daughter of Robert Osprenge, late citizen of London, brought a bill before the Mayor and Aldermen against John Olneye, junior, of Weston, Richard Blomville and John Middelton, mercer, executors of the will of John Olneye, senior, woolman, complaining that whereas the late John Olneye by his will made on 10 Aug. 1396 had devised to her the sum of £40, the said executors on 16 Sept., when the testator was dead, had embezzled the will and forged[3] another will, in which there was no mention of the legacy. [*French*]

As the plaintiff was under age, the court appointed John Dalton to prosecute her bill. The defendants having made three defaults, John Middelton appeared alone on 4 June, when he appointed Lambert Frampton his attorney and was mainprised for his appearance on 9 June.

Membr. 4 *b*

On that day the said John Middelton prayed judgment as to whether the court had any cognisance of the matter in the bill, which dealt with testamentary dispositions, the cognisance of which belonged to the Court Christian. Notwithstanding this exception to its jurisdiction, the court ordered him to plead further.

He then pleaded that on 16 Sept. 1396, when he was alleged to have forged a will, the testator having died, the testator was in fact alive at Lavendene[4] co. Bucks and for two days after. He prayed that the bill be quashed. He was

[1] "Of the walls?"
[2] Lord of la Ferté Bernart. *Cal. Pat. Rolls*, 1396–9, p. 423.
[3] *Forgerent fauxement.* [4] Lavendon.

ordered to plead further, notwithstanding this exception to the bill.

Thereupon the defendant, while not admitting any embezzlement of the first will or forging of the second, declared that he would make his plea as follows—it was true that John Olneye had devised the sum of £40 to the plaintiff on 10 Aug. but afterwards on 1 Sept., believing that he could not fulfil the legacies, the testator changed his will and made another one at Lavendene, revoking the former will, which second will the defendant now produced in court, and that afterwards the testator died, when his will was proved according to ecclesiastical law before the ordinary in that county, and was duly administered, and this was the will which the plaintiff alleged to be a forgery, which he was prepared to verify *etc.*

The plaintiff, while protesting that she did not admit anything pleaded by the defendant, chose as her plea the statements made in her declaration, which she was prepared to verify. She demanded judgment whether she was bound by law to answer the defendant's allegations.

As the court wished to consult more fully as to rendering of judgment, a day was given on the quindene of St Michael, before which day the action remained without a day because the lord Richard, late king of England, dismissed himself from the rule of his kingdom[1]. The plaintiff appeared on the quindene and prayed that the parties should be summoned to hear judgment on the 22 Oct. After several adjournments, and Richard Blomville having died, the parties appeared on 21 Jan., when the court, wishing for information as to the
Membr. 5 amount of damages to be adjudged in case judgment were given against the defendant, ordered a jury of the parish of St Michael Crokydlane to be summoned for 18 Feb. The jury said on oath that the plaintiff sustained damages, by reason of the deception alleged in her bill, if judgment were given for her, to the value of £55.

And since it seemed to the court that the matter alleged by the defendant was not sufficient in law, according to the custom of the city, to exclude the plaintiff from her action,

[1] *De regimine regni sui se dimisit.*

it was considered that she recover against the said John Middelton and his mainpernors the sum of £55 taxed by the jury. And upon this, the plaintiff, by her guardian, acknowledged that she did not wish to prosecute her bill further against John Olneye, junior. Accordingly it was ordered that she have execution against John Middelton and his mainpernors, and on her request, precept was issued to take and detain them in prison until the money be paid.

Whereas, according to the custom used and approved in the city from a time whereof the memory of man runneth not to the contrary, every mayor or warden of the city for the time being is able, whensoever it shall please him, to take and cause to come before himself and the Aldermen in the Chamber of the Guildhall all kinds of plaints or pleas, begun or pending undetermined before any of the Sheriffs of the city, as well at the petition and request of the defendants as of the plaintiffs, and to determine them by examination of the parties or in any other lawful manner—on 10 July 1399 the mayor, at the request of a certain Amy Donat, ordered his serjeant to warn John Wade, sheriff, to bring before him in the Chamber a plaint levied before the said sheriff between John Tervyn, clerk, administrator of the goods and chattels of John Donat, intestate, and the said Amy in an action of trespass, and to give the plaintiff John Tervyn a day, namely 12 July, to prosecute his plaint before the Mayor and Aldermen in the Chamber. Membr. 5 *b* *10 July 1399*

The plaint, beginning with the words: "Plaint levied in the house of John Wade, one of the sheriffs of London, on Thursday 10 July 1399," was produced, and the plaintiff John Tervyn then made his count, in which he alleged that on 13 Feb. 1392 the defendant Amy Donat took and carried away by force and arms the sum of £20, belonging to John Donat and then in the custody of the plaintiff, against the peace and to his damage £40. The defendant found mainprise for her appearance to answer the count on 22 Oct., the plea remaining without a day during the interval, because the lord Richard, late king of England, had dismissed himself from the rule of his kingdom.

On 22 Oct., at the request of the plaintiff, precept was issued to re-attach the defendant for her appearance on 27 Oct. The plaintiff having declared as before, she pleaded not guilty. A jury of the parish of St Helen Bishopsgate on 3 Dec. prayed for a week's interval before giving their verdict, and on 10 Dec. found her guilty and taxed damages at £21. Judgment was given for that amount, and the defendant and her mainpernors were committed to prison.

ROLL A 39

Rolls of Memoranda and Pleas of the time of William Askham, mayor, A° 5 Henry IV [1403–4]

Writ of *certiorari* demanding that the tenor of the ordinances made between the Cordwainers and Cobblers of the city be sent before the king in his council. Dated at Westminster 2 May 1404. Membr. 1 *2 May 1404*

Return giving the ordinances of 2 Dec. 1375 [set out in H. T. Riley's *Memorials*, pp. 391–2], 23 Jan. 1376 [R. R. Sharpe, *Cal. of Letter Book H*, p. 20] and 14 Aug. 1395 [set out in *Memorials*, pp. 539–41].

Quitclaim by Agnes Benyngton to John Devenyssh of all her interest in the "*Bole*" tavern in West Cheap in the parish of All Hallows, Honeylane, a shop with two solars above next to the tavern and two tenements next to the church. Dated 8 June 1404. Membr. 1 *b* *10 June 1404*

Bond of John Devenyssh, whereby he conveyed his title to the above properties and the rents issuing from the same, to John Bullok and Roger Hunte, on condition that if he came to an agreement with William Sacom as to certain debts before 15 Aug., he should re-enter into possession. The bond mentions that he had acquired his title from Nicholas Benyngton, and that he had subsequently let the one tenement to Alexander Davy, grocer, and the other to Thomas Bacheler, draper, and Joan his wife, and the shop to Alexander Goodyng. Dated 9 June 1404.

Grant by Arnald Guilliam of Sedse, citizen and vintner, to Philip Bangor, draper, and John Brid, vintner, of four pieces of silver with silver covercles and all other his goods, jewels and chattels. Dated 27 Sept. 1404. *7 Oct. 1404*

Writ of error, dated at Westminster 9 Nov. 1403, ordering that the record and process of an action begun in the Sheriffs' Court before Richard Merlowe, sheriff, between Thomas Aleyn, mercer, plaintiff, and Joan, widow and executrix of Bartholomew de Bosano, mercer, Peter Burton, clerk, and Membr. 2 *9 Nov. 1403*

William Sowthows, her co-executors, defendants, and subsequently removed into the Chamber of the Guildhall before John Walcote, late Mayor, and the Aldermen, which action was for the recovery of £200 from the executors, be rendered at the church of St Martin le Grand before William Gascoigne, John Markham, William Haukeford and William Brenchesley, the king's justices assigned to examine the same and to correct the errors therein, if any, and to do justice in the matter.

12 Nov. 1403 Precept of the above-named justices to the same effect, but describing the defendant Joan as widow of Bartholomew de "Basano," and fixing a day, 28 Nov., for the production of the record and process.

Membr. 2 *b* Return of William Askham, Mayor, and the Aldermen to the above writ, claiming the city's privilege of rendering the record and process *oretenus* by the recorder after a respite of forty days.

Membr. 4
11 Feb. 1404 Precept of the justices at St Martin le Grand reciting that when the Mayor and Aldermen on 25 Jan. had produced, *oretenus* by the recorder, the record and process of the action between Thomas Aleyn, mercer, and Joan, widow of Bartholomew de Basano, and Peter Burton and William Sowthows, her co-executors, the executors had complained of several omissions in the recorder's statement, as follows:

They had claimed judgment because the name mentioned in the bond, on which the money was claimed, was written as "Basano," whereas it was "Bosano" in the plaint, and the court had not allowed their exception.

Item, William Vaux, attorney of the defendant Joan, had stated that Bartholomew de Bosano, coming from Scotland in the king's company, had fallen sick at Newark and made his will, appointing as his executors Joan his wife, John Duffeld, John Corne and John Bilte, who administered his goods and chattels after his death, and as these persons were not named in the plaint, he demanded judgment, whereupon the plaintiff had denied that John Duffeld and the others were executors and had challenged the defendant, in accordance with the custom of the city, to an oath that her pleading was true, to which William Vaux had replied that the defendant Joan was not bound to answer as regards the alleged custom, but that he, as her attorney, would take the oath, and the court, not allowing his exceptions, had ordered him to continue pleading.

Item, the plaint was levied against the said Joan and her co-executors in common, and as the co-executors did not appear, she prayed judgment whether she need answer without them, and the court had not allowed her exception and had ordered her to answer further.

Item, though the plaintiff made his declaration against the defendant Joan only, in the absence of her co-executors, on the supposition that this action was sufficient, nevertheless he prosecuted process of *capias* against the co-executors to answer together with her, thus waiving and renouncing the advantage conferred on him by statute[1], whereupon she prayed judgment whether the court wished to call on her to answer before the appearance of her co-executors, and notwithstanding this exception, the court ordered her to answer further.

Item, when her co-executor William Sowthows appeared by his attorneys Richard Legge and William Rokesburgh, and pleaded that the testator, falling sick at Newark, appointed him, together with John Duffeld, John Corne, John Bilte and John Taillour as executors, and the names of these executors were not named in the plaint, whereof he prayed judgment, notwithstanding this exception the court ordered him to answer further.

Item, during the process divers precepts were issued and there were continuations of the action by putting the jury in respite, and judgment was deferred that the court might consult.

Item, judgment having been rendered for Thomas Aleyn, the plaintiff, execution of the judgment was made against the defendant Joan.

[1] 9 Edw. III, c. 3, which says that "all the executors do represent the person of the testator as one person," and that, where there is action against them, "he or they that do first appear in the court shall answer to the plaintiff." The court held that even though the plaintiff had sued a *capias* to force the co-executors to appear, he did not lose the right to sue one executor in the absence of the others.

Since it was complained that none of the above matters appeared in the record as produced *oretenus* by the recorder, the Mayor and Aldermen are ordered to produce the omissions, if any, and the original plaint before the justices at St Martin le Grand on 16 Feb. 1404. Dated at St Martin le Grand 11 Feb. 1404.

Membr. 4 *b* Return that the precept arrived too late for answer.

16 Feb. 1404 Further precept to the same effect, demanding the omissions and original plaint on 21 Feb. Dated at St Martin le Grand 16 Feb. 1404.

Membr. 2 *b* Return that the recorder had already explained that there was no such action as "Aleyn *versus* Basano," and so there could be no omissions or original plaint, but that there was an original bill on the sheriffs' roll in "Aleyn *versus* Bosano," as was recorded by the recorder on 25 Jan. 1404.

Membr. 3 *21 Feb. 1404* Further precept of the justices, demanding the omissions and original plaint in "Aleyn *versus* Basano" to be produced on 24 April 1404. Dated at St Martin le Grand 21 Feb. 1404.

Membr. 7–7 *b* *27 Jan. 1405* Further precept of the justices, demanding *etc.* on 3 Feb. 1405. Dated at St Martin le Grand 27 Jan. 1405.

Return that there was no such plea, but that there was one in the name of "Bosano."

Membr. 6–6 *b* *3 Feb. 1405* Further precept of the justices, reciting previous precepts and returns. Although the Mayor and Aldermen had returned that there was no such plea as "Aleyn against Basano," the executors maintained that in the sheriffs' roll the name appeared clearly as "Basano" and that in the plaint there enrolled there was also a spelling "civitaes." Accordingly the justices demand the original plaint to be produced on 10 Feb. 1405.

Return that the precept arrived too late for answer.

Membr. 2 *12 Nov. 1403* Writ to the mayor and sheriffs notifying that by ancient custom the men and tenants of the honour of Walyngford were quit of toll throughout England, and demanding that this exemption be allowed to them in London, or that cause be shown to the contrary. Dated at Westminster 12 Nov. 1403.

Similar writ in stronger terms. *14 Nov. 1403*

Return of William Askham, mayor, Thomas Polle and Thomas Fauconer, sheriffs, that they and their fellow-citizens and their predecessors held London and Middlesex to farm with divers liberties and free customs, tolls, passages and lastages, by an annual payment to the Exchequer, that the sheriffs had always taken custom from the men of Walyngford as from other men, in aid of the aforesaid farm, which liberties had been confirmed by statutes and charters of the king and his progenitors, wherefore they could not and ought not to exonerate the men of Walyngford from payment of the same.

Writ demanding that all sheriffs of London since 24 June 1396 appear before the barons of the Exchequer on 9 May to show by what title they claimed certain dues from boats bringing rushes, which dues a certain John Clerk of London had lately taken to farm from the king, and that the mayor bring the names of the sheriffs. Witness J. Cokayn at Westminster, 12 April 1404, by the roll of memoranda XI of Hilary term, and the writ is returnable in three weeks of Easter (20 April). Membr. 5 *12 April 1404*

Return as follows:

A° 20 Ric. II, Roger Elys and William Shiryngham, both dead.

A° 21 Ric. II, Thomas Welford, attached for his appearance by John Roo and Robert Dryffeld. William Parker, dead.

A° 22 Ric. II, William Askham, att. by William Gay and Nicholas Bridport. John Wodecok, att. by William Neuport and Ralph Bray.

A° 23 Ric. II, John Warner, att. by Edmund Bys and Edmund atte Perye. John Wade, att. by James Symmes and William Kyngeston.

A° 1 Henry IV, William Walderne, att. by John Blosse and Henry Broun. William Hyde, dead.

A° 2 Henry IV, John Wakelee, att. by John Donne and Thomas Hert. William Evote, dead.

A° 3 Henry IV, William Fremelyngham, att. by Henry

Hoddon and Philip Bray. William Venour, att. by Nicholas Godeman and Ralph Bate.

A° 4 Henry IV, Robert Chichelee, att. by Thomas Stable and Richard Kyng. Richard Merlawe, att. by Simon Bale and John Gode.

A° 5 Henry IV, Thomas Polle, att. by William Norton and Henry Horton. Thomas Fauconer, att. by Henry Gedenham and Stephen Bridlepe.

Membr. 5 *b*
8 Oct. 1404

Lease from John Chaumbre, knight, of Lyllyngstonlovell[1] co. Oxon, and Joan his wife, daughter and heiress of William Glendale, late citizen of London, to William Langford, armourer, for seven years of two shops in Friday Street on the south side of the inn called "*le Fesaunt on the hope.*"

Lease to the same of a shop, south of the above, in the occupation of William Porter, saddler.

9 Oct. 1404

Quitclaim of John Marchall, tailor, to John Chambre, knight, and Roger his son, of all claims on a statute staple of Westminster for the sum of £200.

Membr. 7
12 Oct. 1404

Acquittance from John Chambre, knight, to Thomas Stone, hostiller, and Joan his wife, for £40 rent for an inn called "*le lyon on the hoope*" in Friday Street and a small shop by the north door of the inn.

Membr. 8
22 Nov. 1404

Letters patent constituting John Hende, mayor, William Gascoigne, William Thirnyng, John Cokayn, William Rikhill, Hugh Huls and Thomas Thornburgh, any six, five, four, three or two of them, of whom the mayor should be one, justices of Gaol Delivery of Newgate. Dated at Westminster 22 Nov. 1404.

20 Jan. 1405

Writ demanding that John Seint Germayn, Walter Gawtron and Thomas Craft, citizens of London, be arrested and brought before the king and his council on Friday next, there to answer *etc.*

Return that the above-named persons had been arrested.

[1] Lillingstone Lovell.

Elisabeth Golafre, prioress of the house of the Blessed Mary Magdalene at Ankerwyk-on-Thames co. Bucks., brings a plaint of intrusion against Robert Comberton[1], James Northampton and Henry Somer touching her free tenement in the parish of All Hallows at Hay, London. *9 Feb. 1405*

John Chaumberleyn and Thomas Notecroft, perpetual chaplains of the chantry in the church of St Michael Paternosterchirche in the Ryole, bring a plaint of intrusion against Richard Broun, John Hovell and William Arnold, bakers, touching their free tenement in the same parish. Membr. 8 *b* *6 July 1405*

Bond of Roger Batt, skinner, to John Proffyt, chamberlain, for his good behaviour towards the masters and mistery of Skinners, under penalty of £20, to be applied as to one half to the use of the city and the other half to the charitable purposes of the mistery, if he were convicted by testimony of eight good men of the mistery. Membr. 9 *20 Oct. 1405*

The Mayor and Commonalty of the city of London demand an Assize of Nuisance against John Shadeworth and John Wodecok, mercers, William Cressewyk and John Wakefeld, touching their free tenement in the parish of St Michael Bassyngeshawe. *26 Oct. 1405*

Richard Forster, Walter Pope and Guy Lawrence, citizens of London, entered into a bond of £40 that neither the prior nor convent of Merton, nor anyone in their name, would from henceforth place in the Thames any branches or rods called "*ryses*[2]" for the destruction of fish or hindrance of *shouts*[3], barges, boats or other vessels between the prior's weir and the meadow opposite in the county of Surrey. Thereupon a *shout*, a long boat and a net belonging to the prior, which had been taken by Alexander Boner, serjeant of the city and supervisor of the Thames, were handed back. Membr. 9 *b* *4 July 1405*

Afterwards on 20 July 1407, as it was found by the Mayor and Aldermen on their view of the Thames[4] that the prior

[1] Brother of John Northampton. *Cal. of Letter Book H*, p. 229.

[2] *Ramos sive virgas vocat' ryses*. See *rice* in *N.E.D.*, twigs or small branches.

[3] Dutch, *schuit*, a flat-bottomed boat.

[4] See above, p. 71, n. 2.

and his deputies had placed *rises* in the water contrary to the above bond, John Brokford, serjeant of the Chamber, was ordered to summon the above-mentioned Richard, Walter and Guy to hear judgment on 28 July. As they could not deny the record, it was considered that John Profyt, chamberlain, levy the sum of £40 from their lands, tenements, goods and chattels. Afterwards, for divers reasons moving the Mayor and Aldermen, the said £40 was condoned for £10, which was paid, and thereupon the bond was cancelled.

Membr. 10
1 Sept. 1405

John Chapman, son of Hamon Chapman of Ash co. Kent, brought a bill complaining that Thomas Clyfton, vintner, to whom he had been apprenticed for eleven years, had given him no instruction during the first five years of his term, and had then beaten and wounded and driven him from his service, to his damage £40.

The master, being summoned, made four defaults, wherefore on 28 Sept. it was considered that the plaintiff be exonerated from his apprenticeship and be quit thereof.

Membr. 11

Seven rolls and one *scrowell*[1] of memoranda and pleas of the time of John Wodecok, mayor, A° 7 Henry IV.

Memorandum that Robert Domenyk, mercer, and William Norton, draper, having been appointed as arbitrators between Roger Moordon, skinner, and John Tettysbury, skinner, brought in their award as follows:

Whereas John Tettysbury had entered into a bond of £80 to Robert Markele, skinner, that he would pay the sum of £40, which had been left as a legacy by John Leycestre[2] to

[1] The rolls are full-sized membranes, the *scrowell* or scroll is a half-skin.

[2] John Leycestre, a maternal uncle, left £40 to John Tettysbury's daughters Joan and Joan, aged twelve and three years respectively. The money was entrusted on 10 March 1394 by the Chamberlain to John Tettysbury as guardian for his daughters, on condition that he paid 4s in the £ interest per annum, "in accordance with city custom." When the younger daughter Joan died, John Tettysbury rendered account in the Chamber on 10 June 1402 for the £40 legacy and £66 interest, the latter amount having been expended on the girls' upbringing, leaving a debt of £40. Roger Mordon and Robert Markelee acted as sureties to John Tettysbury when the legacy was paid to him. Ultimately the elder daughter Joan married a certain William Fraunceys without permission of the Court of Aldermen, and on 12 May 1408 the latter paid a fine of

John Tettysbury's daughters Joan and Joan, it was awarded that Roger Moordon should pay this amount on his behalf, and that Roger Moordon should also pay him the sum of £20 due for divers debts. As a help towards these payments, Roger Moordon was to receive certain rents from John Tettysbury's tenements in Thames Street. [*French*]

Writ of *certiorari*. Whereas John Rede, weaver, had recently sued Thomas Polle and Thomas Fauconer, late sheriffs of London, on a writ of the Exchequer, for having under colour of their office on 13 May 1405 arrested, imprisoned and detained him until he entered into a bond of 100 marks for his delivery, and for having taken and carried away 3 cloths of blanket, 2 pieces of silver with a silver covercle, 3 mazers harnessed with silver and one dozen silver spoons, value £100, belonging to him, as he alleged, and whereas the present sheriffs of London, at the suit of the late sheriffs, had recently arrested the said John, and a writ of *corpus cum causa* had been sent to the sheriffs, who had returned that the said John Rede had been taken and committed to prison for certain causes pending before the mayor, the mayor is ordered to certify the cause of the taking, arresting and committing to prison of the said John before the barons of the Exchequer at Westminster on 21 May 1406. Witness J. Cokayn at Westminster, 19 May 1406. *19 May 1406*

Further writ, dated 25 May 1406. Membr. 11 *b* *25 May 1406*

Return of the mayor that John Rede had been committed to prison on 8 May 1406 as a punishment for opprobrious, unseemly and rebellious words openly spoken to himself and the aldermen, to the great scandal of the Mayoralty Court of the city (*curie Maioratus Civitatis*), in order that others henceforth might be deterred from speaking the like words.

Writ to the mayor and sheriffs that among other liberties and quittances granted to the citizens of Winchester by the Membr. 12 *17 Nov. 1405*

40s and was allowed to receive the legacy, which was paid by Philip Bangor, who had probably assumed Mordon's responsibility. The case shows how little actual money passed at this period, payments being largely a matter of bonds, bills and assignments. See Letter Book H, fo. 291 *b*; I, fo. 18.

king's predecessors and confirmed by himself, it was granted that they should have all the liberties and customs which they had in the time of King Henry I[1], their purchases (*acata*) and pledges (*vadia*), and that they should be quit of toll, lastage, stallage, pontage[2], passage, chiminage, murage, pavage, cayage and picage[3] and all other customs, wherefore the mayor and sheriffs are commanded not to hinder or oppress the said citizens against the tenor of the said charters. Dated at Westminster 17 Nov. 1405.

27 Sept. 1406 Writ of protection in favour of Thomas Brige, *alias* Thomas Parker, of Eltham, who was then in Ireland in the company of the king's son, Thomas Lancastre[4], steward of England and the king's lieutenant in Ireland. Dated at Westminster 27 Sept. 1406.

Membr. 12 *b*
26 Feb. 1406 Bond of Thomas Meygneld, grocer, to John Sadler, vintner, in £40, that Hankyn van Hannard, whom the said John had brought before the Mayor and Aldermen as a native of Flanders and an adherent of the king's enemies, would produce authentic letters under seal to prove that he was born in Holland and was not an adherent of the king's enemies.

21 June 1406 Thomas de Nevyll, lord of Fournyvall, brings a plaint of intrusion against Thomasine, widow of William de Fournyvall, knight, touching his free tenement in the parish of St Andrew, Holborn[5].

[1] No charter of Henry I to Winchester is extant. The writ quotes part of what is known as the "second charter" of Henry II, which may be dated either 1155 or 1158. See J. S. Furley, *Winchester Records*, pp. 28–9; Stubbs' *Charters*, pp. 165–6.

[2] Bridge-toll.

[3] Dues for passing, the repair of roads and walls, paving, quay-dues, and dues for breaking ground in markets and fairs for the erection of stalls. See Ballard and Tate, *British Borough Charters*.

[4] Second son of Henry IV, created earl of Albemarle and duke of Clarence in 1411.

[5] Described in *Inq. post Mort.* of 6 Ric. II as 2 messuages and 13 shops. It is called "Fournyvalles Inne" in *Inq. post Mort.* of 32 Henry VI. Acquired by William Furnyvall in 1350. See Husting Roll, 104 (76) (77) (149) (150). Thomas Nevill married Joan, d. of the above, and was summoned to Parliament as Thomas Nevyll of Halumshire. His daughter Maud married John Talbot, who was summoned to Parliament in 1409, as John Talbot, lord of Furnyvall, and afterwards became earl of Shrewsbury.

Writ to the sheriffs that, whereas by charters lately confirmed by the king the burgesses of Colchester were free of all toll, lastage, passage, pontage and customs, and had the right of taking as much from the burgesses of any town as in that town had been taken from the burgesses of Colchester, and further were free of murage, picage and pavage, the said sheriffs are ordered to allow the said burgesses to enjoy their liberties. Dated at Westminster 10 Nov. 1405. Membr. 13 *10 Nov. 1405*

Return of the sheriffs that they were unable to exonerate the burgesses of Colchester from payment of toll, lastage and passage, since the money thus obtained was a part of the feefarm, payable at the Exchequer, for London and Middlesex, as granted by statutes and charters and confirmed by the present king.

Writ to the sheriffs that, although parliament had been summoned to Coventry on 15 Feb. for certain arduous and urgent business touching the realm and the church, nevertheless, since the king had assigned his son the prince of Wales to make war against and punish the rebels in Wales and believed that victory would be the more certain if the lords, nobles, magnates and commonalty of the realm were nearer to the prince and his forces, he had, by the advice of his council, ordained that parliament should be held at Gloucester, wherefore the sheriffs were bidden to cause four of the more discreet and sufficient citizens to be chosen to attend at the place and time named, having sufficient power on behalf of themselves and the commonalty of the city to do and consent to those things which should be ordained of the common counsel of the realm[1], but the king did not wish that the sheriffs or any other sheriffs of the realm should be chosen. Dated at Westminster 1 Jan. 1406. Membr. 13 *b* *1 Jan. 1406*

Whereas Roger Batte, skinner, had entered into a recognisance to the chamberlain in £20 on 20 Oct. 1405 for his good behaviour towards the masters and mistery of Skinners, and to observe the laws, customs and liberties of the city, Membr. 14 *10 May 1406*

[1] *Que tunc ibidem de communi consilio dicti regni...ordinari contigerit.*

the masters and wardens on 10 May 1406 came before the Mayor and Aldermen complaining that the said Roger was daily working to their detriment, against the form of his recognisance. The said Roger, who was present, denied having committed any trespass. Thereupon the parties put themselves on the judgment of the Mayor and Aldermen, who on 18 May, having examined both parties, awarded that Roger Batte humbly submit himself to the masters, wardens and good men of the mistery and crave pardon for his offences, and that the said masters, wardens and good men should then pardon him. This having been done, the bond was quashed and the said Roger entered into another recognisance to the chamberlain in £20 to the same effect.

Membr. 14 *b*
11 July 1406

William Louthe, Thomas Polle, Thomas Exton, John Blakeden, William Grantham, George Cressy, Richard Barton, William Fitzhugh, Salamon Oxney, John Palyng, John Frenssh, John Osborne, John Standelf, Peter Thorold, John Lenham, John Lagage, Thomas Lamport, John Emond, William Adye, John Halle, Robert Halle, William Randolf, Richard George and Robert Broun, goldsmiths, and many others of the same mistery keeping inns in the city, whose names are preserved in a register (*papiro*) in the court, came before the Mayor and Aldermen in the Chamber and entered into recognisances in £200 to the chamberlain, for the good behaviour of themselves and their servants towards the king and people and all officers and servants of the city.

Membr. 15
18 Feb. 1406

Memorandum that whereas a writ had been issued from the Exchequer to the sheriffs ordering them to distrain Thomas Polle and Thomas Fauconer, late sheriffs, to appear in the Exchequer to answer John Rede, weaver, for having taken and imprisoned him until he entered into a recognisance of 100 marks for his release and for having taken and carried away his goods to the value of £100, the Mayor and Aldermen summoned the parties on 18 Feb. 1406 and questioned them separately as to whether they would accept their arbitration on all disputes between them, and both parties consented to do so. Thereupon John Rede agreed to withdraw his writ in the Exchequer and not to prosecute it on the Thursday following. The late sheriffs were ordered to bring in the bond, and both parties entered into recognisances to accept the award. On 2 March Cecilia, widow of William Denton, appeared in court and also agreed to accept the award in so far as it concerned herself.

Afterwards on 8 May the Mayor and Aldermen, having fully considered the trespasses committed by both parties, gave as their award that John Rede, for certain trespasses against Thomas Polle and Thomas Fauconer, should pay them the sum of £20, and that the latter, for their trespasses against John Rede, should pay him the sum of £4 or goods and chattels to the same value, and that the obligation for 100 marks should be cancelled, further that John Rede should not prosecute his suit in the Exchequer on 9 May, and that out of the goods which the above-mentioned Cecilia had intrusted to him for her keep he should provide for her in the same manner as he had done before the dispute between himself and the sheriffs, or account to her by due process of law[1].

John Talbot and Maud his wife bring a plaint of intrusion against John Penros touching their free tenement in the parish of St Andrew Holborne[2]. *8 March 1406*

John Osbarne, in the presence of John Wodecok, mayor, John Preston, recorder, Hugh Waterton, knight, and Richard Whityngton and Drew Barantyn, aldermen, in the parish of St Mary Magdalene, Castle Baynard Ward, took an oath that all the statements in a sealed document, which he prayed might be entered of record in the Chamber of the Guildhall, were true, as follows: Membr. 16 *9 July 1406*

"I John Osbarne knowleche here by for yow and fully bere wytnesse as I will answere a fore God and man on all manere perill that may befalle to body or to sowle, that y the same John Osbarne in the age of syxtene wynter beyng w^t my fader John Osbarne that tyme Conestable of the Castell of Dunsterre and Styward of the same lordship and beyng a chyld at scole seyghe and herde and was ther present whan

[1] See above, p. 275. [2] See above, p. 276, n. 5.

Sire John the lord Mohun enfeffed William Fordeham and Maude of Burton of the same castell and lordship of Dunsterre and other maners lygyng thertoo in fee symple and here upon was a livere of seysyn y made to the same William and Maude by Robert Parnecote and William Howthorpe by vertue of a lettre of atturne then opynly i redde att which tyme the same lord Mohun was att Tychefeld[1] and my lady his wyf atte Beneham[2] a towne of the Abbotes of Clyve[3] and att the same tyme of lyveree ther were twey children in the same Castell and weren bore oute and broght to Beneham a forsayd to her moder that was the Contesse of Salesbury that now is and here suster that Meneresse aftir that[4] and within a fourtenyght or thre wekes after that, the forsayd William and Maude comen in propre persone to Dunsterre and made a dede of feffement to the same lord Mohun and Johane his wyf and to the heirs of here twey bodies frely bygetyn, and delivered hem fully seysyn afore all men of the forsaid castell, lordship and maneres att which tyme all men that there were were glad that the children should be enherited. And that all this is sothe I will do to sothe upon what book or relik that ye will do come afor me and also sette herto my sele of myn armes. In witnessyng of verray trowthe and in more opyn prove herto i have sett my sele a forsayd. I wryten att London in the parissh a forsayde the ix day of Juylle the yeer of the regnyng of kyng harry the fourthe after the conquest sevenethe."

10 July 1406 Walter Gregory appeared before the mayor, recorder and aldermen and prayed that the following words, which he swore to be true, might be entered of record in the Chamber.

"I Wautier Gregorye Vicaer of the Chirche of...knowleche and fully bere witnes here a fore yow as I will answere

[1] Titchfield.

[2] Binham. J. Collinson, *Hist. of Somerset*, III, p. 511.

[3] Of the Cistercian abbey of Cleeve co. Somerset, near Old Cleeve.

[4] John de Mohun's daughters were Elisabeth, wife of William de Montacute, earl of Salisbury; Philippa, who married (1) Walter, Lord Fitzwalter, (2) Sir John Golafre, lord of Langley, and (3) Edward, duke of York; and Maud, who married John le Strange, Lord le Strange of Knockyn. The minoress would appear to be an unknown second sister, unless Maud took the veil after her husband's death in 1397.

afor god and man on perill of my soule that Sir John Mohun lord of Dunster went to the kyng for to over see with hym, and at that tyme hym dred of his home comyng a yene and therfor he pursuyed to the kyng to have licence to aliene his londes to certein persones that is to sey to William Fordham, clerk, and to Maude of Burton a woman soule for the grete trist and affeccioun that he hadde to hem byfor eny other by cause that William was his mayster and Maude was maistresse to my lady his wyf by assignement of Sir Bartholomew Borewessh[1] here fader that tyme that they were wedded, and the kyng graunted it, and after that the same lord made a dede of feffement in fee symple to the same William and Maude of the castell and Burghe of Dunsterre, and of the maneres of Carampton[2], Mynehevede[3] and Culvetone[4], and ther upon was a lettre of attourne y made to Robert Parnecote and to William Howthorpe by the same lord to delivere hem seisine in his name of the forsaid castell, Burghe and maners, and by vertue of that lettre they delivered the forsaid William Fordham and Maude seysyne acordyng to the forseyd dede, and att that tyme the same lord was att Tychefeld and long tyme after for the kyng abood ther in Contrey a grete whyle abydyng passage, and my lady Mohun his wyf remuede to Beneham a manere of þe Abbotes of Clyve and soiourned there and here children with here in the mene tyme that the forsayd William Fordham and Maude were in possessioun and duryng here possessioun they helde courtes and token attournementes of all the tenauntz, and with in thre wekes or a monethe after that the forsaid lord Mohun and my lady his wyf comyn to Dunsterre and ther the forsaid William Fordham and Maude of Burton made a dede of feffement to the same lord and to Jone his wyf and to the heirs of her twey bodies frely begetyn of the forsaid castell, burghe and maners and therupon the forseyd William Foordham and Maude delivered hem fully seysyn in propre persone acordyng therto afor all men, and by vertue therof the forsayd lord continued possessioun to hys endyngday, and att the same tyme I was of the age of xviii wynter and beyng ther att

[1] Burghersh.
[2] Carhampton.
[3] Minehead.
[4] Kilton.

scole and fye[1] and was present ther whan the forseid feffementz weren made, and that y wole do to sothe as a preste ought to do in what manere that eny man will ordeigne me to done. In witnesse of which thing I the forseid Watier have sette to my sele the x day of Juylle the yeer of the regnyng of kyng herry the fourth after the conquest sevenethe."

Membr. 16 *b*
28 July 1406

Covenant whereby, in consideration of the cancelling of a bond for £8, Thomas Depham, saddler, and Agnes Vyntener his wife, formerly servant of Sir Robert Turk, knight, conveyed to Thomas Knolles, grocer, the right of collecting for four years a quitrent of 40s from a tenement called "*The Peynted taverne*[2]" in the occupation of John Cosyn, which quitrent the said Agnes had received for the term of her life by grant of John de Scardeburgh, rector of Orewell[3] co. Cambs, Richard Jepe, rector of All Hallows Honeylane, Bartholomew Seman, *goldbetere*, and Thomas Burwell.

Membr. 17
13 Aug. 1406

Precept from John Wodecok, mayor, to the sheriff of Middlesex, dated at London 13 Aug. 1406. He refers to the statute of Westminster II[4], which enacted that salmon should not be taken or destroyed by engines or nets in millponds from mid April till 24 June, to the statute of 13 Ric. II[5], which confirmed the above and enacted that salmon should not be so taken in millponds or elsewhere and that no fisherman or *garthman*[6] or other should place in the Thames, Humber, Ouse, Trent or elsewhere during that period any nets called "*stalkers*[7]" or other engines, by which the *frye* or *brode* of salmon, lampreys or other fish should be taken, and that there should be chosen and sworn good and sufficient conservators of the statute in accordance with the earlier

[1] *Sc.* fay, faith, allegiance.

[2] In the parish of S[t] Martin Vintry in a lane of the same name, which was later called "Three Cranes Lane," Kingsford's *Stow*, I, p. 239. Agnes Vyntener had a grant for life of the quitrent from Bartholomew Seman, executor of Sir Robert Turk. Husting Roll, 136 (14). See also *Cal. of Wills*, II, p. 460.

[3] Orwell.

[4] 13 Edw. I, c. 47.

[5] 13 Ric. II, Stat. I, c. 19.

[6] Garth, according to *Termes de la Ley*, 1721, p. 373, is a dam or weir for taking fish.

[7] *N.E.D.* derives this from stalk, to creep stealthily, and describes it as a net used by poachers.

statute, and to the statute of 17 Ric. II[1], which enacted that the justices of the peace should be conservators in their own counties, to ensure that weirs should not be too strait for the destruction of fry but of a reasonable wideness, to punish offenders, to appoint good and sufficient subconservators and to hold inquiries both *de officio* and on the information of their subconservators, and which also enacted that, whereas the king's predecessors had granted to the citizens of London the right of removing *kydels*[2] in Thames and Medway and of having the punishments pertaining to the king, the mayor or warden of London for the time being should have the conservation of the statutes and the same duties as were given to justices of the peace, from Stanes Bridge to London, and from thence in the same water and in the water of Medway as far as it was granted to the said citizens. Accordingly the sheriff of Middlesex is ordered on the king's behalf to summon twenty-four good and lawful men to come before the mayor at Stanes on 19 Aug. 1406, in order that he might inquire as to the nets and other engines by which the fry of salmon, lampreys and other fish were destroyed, and to appear in person with the names of the jurors.

Similar precept to the sheriff of Surrey. Membr. 17 *b*

Similar precept to the sheriff of Essex for a jury at Stratford Langthorne[3] on 26 Aug. 1406, with return by the sheriff that the precept arrived too late to be obeyed, and note that a further precept was issued for 18 Sept. 1406. Membr. 18 *16 Aug. 1406*

Similar precept to the sheriff of Kent for a jury at Grenewych[4] on 17 Sept. 1406. Membr. 18 *b* *27 Aug. 1406*

Commission for Gaol Delivery of Newgate to Richard Whityngton, mayor, William Gascoigne, William Thirnyng, John Cokayn, William Rykhill, William Haukeford and John Preston, of whom six, five, four, three or two, of whom the mayor should be one, were to serve. Dated at Westminster 8 Nov. 1406. Membr. 19 *8 Nov. 1406*

[1] 17 Ric. II, c. 9. [2] A fish-weir. See above, p. 71, n. 2.
[3] The abbey of Stratford Langthorne in the marshes, west of West Ham. [4] Greenwich.

10 Nov. 1406 Lease from Robert Denny, knight, to Roger Hiller, joiner, and John Aldelond, plumber, of his tenements in the parish of St James Garlekhithe, bounded on the east by Kyronelane[1], on the west by a tenement belonging to the church, on the north by the church and on the south by the highway, for a term of 10 years at an annual rent of a red rose for five years, and of £6 for five years, the lessees to keep the pavement in repair. A bond of £30 to be cancelled if the lessees enjoy undisturbed possession.

Membr. 19 *b*
8 Oct. 1406 Covenant whereby Robert Broun, skinner, in consideration of a debt of £21, conveyed to William Framelyngham, skinner, the rents accruing from a plot of ground in Thames Street by Sprotteskey[2] in the parish of St Dunstan by the Tower, which he had recently let to John Hyde *alias* Scut for two years at an annual rent of £4, occupation to take place after two years and to continue till the debt was paid. Dated 31 July 1406.

7 Feb. 1407 Bond of Robert Lynford and Edmund Hamelyn, skinners, to Robert Gare of York to bring authentic proof that 3½ lasts of herrings arrested in the ship of James Snycope by the bailiff of Billingsgate as the goods of John Persay, merchant of York, John Sparow of Lund on the Wald[3], William Rumlay, merchant of York, and John Persay, son of Robert Persay of Helmsley, at the suit of the said Robert Gare for a debt of £32 13s 4d, were the goods of John Helmesley of York at the time of the arrest.

Membr. 20
7 March 1407 Robert Weller, son of Peter Weller, tailor, exonerated from his apprenticeship to John Godewyn, salter, who had left the city.

[1] Now Maiden Lane in Vintry Ward.

[2] Described in 1504 as "Hatterskey, formerly Sprotteskey," with wharf and crane, bounded on the north by Thames Street, on the south by the Thames, on the east by Water Lane and on the west by the tenement of Richard Knyghtley and Joan his wife, called "Crownekey." Husting Roll, 231 (33). It now forms the eastern end of Custom House Quay.

[3] Lund on the Wolds, near Beverley co. Yorks.

Alexander Bryan came before the Mayor and Aldermen and complained that the previous year he had entrusted a quantity of soap to a certain Alexander Reve to be sold in Bordeaux or exchanged for other goods, and that the said Alexander had traded it for one pipe and two hogsheads (*pro duabus*[1] *capitibus porcorum*) of Gascon wine, and that subsequently a certain Alan Roys, mercer, levied a plaint of account against him in the compter of Nicholas Wotton, sheriff, which plaint was removed before the Mayor and Aldermen in the Chamber of the Guildhall, in which he alleged that this wine had been sent to the complainant by Alexander Reve, in order that he might pay part of a debt of £7 owed by the latter to himself. The Mayor and Aldermen, having inspected a letter sent by Alexander Reve to the complainant and another letter sent by the same to Alan Roys, together with other evidences put in by the parties, adjudged that the wine belonged to Alexander Bryan and that Alan Roys take nothing by his plaint. *13 April 1407*

Philip de Albertis, merchant of Florence, brought a bill before the Mayor and Aldermen demanding from John Megre, merchant[2], 139 cwt. 60 lbs. of tin of the value of £150, unjustly detained by him. This tin he claimed to have bought in the parish of St Nicholas Acon from William Venour for £125 11s 8d, who in turn had bought it from the said John Megre, giving him a bond of £150 for payment, a certain Marcus Marcat acting as broker in both sales. The said John Megre had agreed to deliver the tin to him but had afterwards refused to do so, to the plaintiff's damage £200. Membr. 21 *16 June 1407*

After three defaults the defendant appeared on 27 June and appointed John Hethyngham his attorney to answer the plaintiff. Next day, by his attorney, he protested that he did not acknowledge that the tin was of the value named, and pleaded, as his plea, that the plaintiff ought not to have an action against him, because the purchase by William

[1] *Sic.*

[2] See below, p. 287, for previous proceedings in equity, by the law merchant.

Venour took place in the parish of St Mary Wolnoth and the said William Venour undertook to find other sufficient persons to enter into bonds with him for the payment of £150, after which the tin was to be delivered, but had failed to do so. He prayed that the matter be inquired into by a jury, of whom one half should be of the plaintiff's language, namely Florentines. The plaintiff pleaded that the facts were as set forth in his bill and likewise prayed a jury.

Precept was issued to summon a jury of the parishes of St Nicholas Acon and St Mary Wolnoth, which came and found a verdict for the plaintiff with 100s damages. Being asked by the plaintiff how much was due for his own expenses and how much for damages owing to detinue of the tin, the jury answered 50s for the one and 50s for the other. As it seemed to the court that too little was allowed for expenses, judgment was given that the plaintiff recover the tin, if possible, together with the aforesaid damages and another 100s for his expenses, or otherwise the price of the tin together with damages as aforesaid.

Membr. 22
23 July 1407

Writ that whereas the king by letters patent had lately granted to the abbess and minoresses without London[1] that no justice, mayor, sheriff, bailiff, coroner, escheator, serjeant, constable, beadle or other officer should exercise any jurisdiction, such as summons, distress or arrest, within the close or precinct of the abbey aforesaid, except only in treason and felonies touching the crown, the mayor and sheriffs of London are commanded to permit the abbess and sisters to enjoy this liberty, and if they have exercised such jurisdiction, to make amends or show cause to the contrary. Dated at Westminster 23 July 1407.

[1] The abbey of the minoresses of St Mary of the order of St Clare without Aldgate, which was exempted from the jurisdiction of the city of London. See Tomlinson, *History of the Minories*. Recently the abbey had received an inspeximus charter confirming its privileges and granting that the abbess and sisters and their successors should have this liberty, that no justice, mayor, sheriff *etc.* should exercise or cause to be exercised any jurisdiction whatsoever by summons, distress or arrest or any other jurisdiction within the close or precinct of the said abbey, except for treason and felony touching the crown. *Ibid.* p. 44; *Cal. Pat. Rolls*, 1399–1401, p. 543.

Return of Richard Whityngton, mayor, Geoffrey Brook and Nicholas Wotton, sheriffs, that they have not exercised any such jurisdiction.

Acquittance by Simon Mosse, chaplain, co. Norfolk, to Philip de Albertis, of the society of the Albertines, merchants of Florence, for the sum of 40 marks borrowed by the said Philip and now repaid. He records that the said Philip, when borrowing the money, had given him a note (*cedula*) thereof and that he had lost it. *19 Oct. 1407*

Precept was given to Otho Brys, one of the mayor's serjeants, to bring before the Mayor and Aldermen a plaint pending in the Sheriffs' Court between John Niandeser, esquire, plaintiff, and John West, defendant. The serjeant brought the plaint, together with the plaintiff's declaration, in which he complained that the defendant had entered his house in the parish of St Andrew Holborn *vi et armis* on 1 Aug. 1406, and had looked everywhere through the house, seeking for the plaintiff in order to kill him, against the king's peace and to his damage £100. *17 Oct. 1407*

Afterwards on 20 Oct. the defendant appeared before the Mayor and Aldermen prepared to answer the plaintiff, but the latter made default. It was considered that the defendant go thence without a day.

Philip de Albertis came before the Mayor and Aldermen in the Inner Chamber of the Guildhall, according to the law merchant and custom of the city, and complained that whereas William Venour, merchant, bought from John Megre, merchant, 139½ cwt. 4 lbs. of tin, at 112 lbs. to the cwt., by Mark Marcat, broker, for the sum of £150, giving a bond for the money, and at the same time instructed the said John Megre to deliver the tin either to Mark Marcat or to some person nominated by him, and whereas the complainant bought the tin from William Venour for £125 11s 8d money paid down, the said John Megre refused to deliver the tin. *13 May 1407* Membr. 22 *b*

Thereupon, by virtue of this complaint (*queremonia*), the Mayor and Aldermen, according to the law merchant and the custom of the city, summoned John Megre before them and questioned him on oath. He admitted the facts and the non-delivery. Accordingly, after consultation, it was considered that the complainant recover the tin and that John Megre deliver it under penalty of the merchandise.[1]

[1] See above, p. 285, for an action of detinue, following on the respondent's failure to obey this order.

ROLL A 40

Rolls of Memoranda and Pleas of the time of Drew Barentyn, mayor, in the 10th year of Henry IV

Writ of *certiorari* to the mayor demanding that a return be made to Chancery of a confession made by John Luter, *leche*[1], Fleming, at the suit of John Clotes of Bemelond, with regard to certain jewels delivered to him under certain conditions by the said John Clotes. Dated at Westminster 15 Nov. 1408. Membr. 1 *15 Nov. 1408*

Return of Drew Barentyn, mayor, as follows: On 5 Nov. last, John Clotes and John Luter, *leche*, appeared before himself and the recorder. John Clotes complained that on 26 Sept. he had delivered to the defendant fifteen stones called "*serpentyns*[2]," of the value of 9 marks, a *table*[3] of gold of the value of 60s and a sword of the value of 6s 8d, which the defendant was to retain if he cured him of a disease called "*lepre*," but he had not cured him, to his damage £20. To this the defendant answered that it was true that John Clotes had come to him, but he had asked him to cure him of a disease in the face called "*salsefleume*[4]." He agreed to cure him so long as he was not leprous, and the plaintiff assured him that he was not leprous. Then the mayor asked the defendant whether the plaintiff was leprous or not at the time the goods were handed over. The defendant said he knew well that the plaintiff was leprous and told him so, though the plaintiff was willing to swear that he was not. Then the mayor told the defendant that he had taken the plaintiff's goods fraudulently, deceptively and injuriously. And afterwards the defendant said that though he had not cured the plaintiff of leprosy, he had taught him how to make balsam and other medicaments, and so he thought he might justly keep the goods.

[1] Leach, physician.
[2] A semi-precious stone of a dull green colour with markings similar to those of a serpent's skin.
[3] Tablet.
[4] *N.E.D.* gives *saucefleme* as the main form, from med. Lat. *salsum phlegma*. It was a facial inflammation supposed to be due to salt humour.

19 Nov. 1408 Nicholas Cok, son of Robert Cok, late citizen and glover, brought a plaint of intrusion against William FitzHughe and Ellen his wife touching his free tenement in the parish of All Hallows atte Wall.

Membr. 1 *b*
13 Nov. 1408 John Monk, carpenter, came before the Mayor and Aldermen and informed them that on 13 Sept. a certain Richard Byrlyngham, a monk of Westminster, had pledged in his name to John Fawne of London two silvergilt basins of the value of £10 and more for the sum of £6 repayable at the feast of All Hallows, and although he, John Monk, had offered the money to John Fawne a few days after the said feast, he refused to accept it or return the basins.

John Fawne, on being summoned and examined, admitted lending £6 to the monk on the basins, and said that since the money was not paid on the said feast, the basins became his own by the terms of the agreement, in witness of which agreement he had paid the monk one penny. No payment having been made, he sold them for £8 5s to a certain Walter Marwe, keeper of the Exchange, who sold them to a certain William Bysmar. The latter admitted buying them for £8 10s.

And because the said John Fawne [made no] plaint nor caused the basins to be valued, as he ought to have done by the custom of the city[1], and because a pledging of this kind with a penny was of no value, according to the custom of the city and sound conscience, even though the day of payment had passed, the Mayor and Aldermen asked the said William Bysmar for what he would sell the basins. He answered, not willingly for less than double their weight. Thereupon, since he had bought the basins properly and without fraud, they induced him to agree to accept 20s above what he had paid for them, and then, after all the circumstances had been weighed, it was considered that John Monk pay £6 and one penny to John Fawne, and that the latter pay William Bysmar the 45s which he had himself received in

[1] He ought to have brought an action of debt and claimed the basins as a foreign attachment. In the city this was the only method of obtaining legal possession of unredeemed pledges. Pawnbroking in the modern sense came into existence when the pledges after a given interval automatically became the possession of the lender.

profit from Walter Marwe, the 5s which the said Walter received in profit when he sold the basins to William, and in addition 20s to William in place of his profit. This was done and the basins were handed back to John Monk.

Bonds of William Crowmere, draper, and William Parys of Ludlow to William Staundon, William Symmes and William Pycard to settle lands and tenements of the value of 400 marks and to pay divers sums of money to William Hyde, son and heir of William Hyde, grocer, deceased, and Elizabeth his wife, daughter of William Parys, with remainder to their children, and failing children, to the heirs of the said William Hyde. *20 Jan. 1409*

Writ of *certiorari*, returnable in Chancery, as to whether Ralph de Monthermer (*de monte Hermerii*)[1], in his will enrolled in the Chamber of the Guildhall on 15 July 1325, had devised a tenement in the parish of St Dunstan to his wife Isabella de Hastynges for life with remainder to his sons Edward and Thomas in successive tail. Dated at Westminster 18 May 1409. Membr. 2 *18 May 1409*

Note that a return was made.

John Sawtre, prior of the house and church of St Laurence of Blakemore[2] co. Essex, brings a plaint of intrusion against John Tannere, chaplain, touching his free tenement in the parish of St Mary Vanchirche[3], London. *8 July 1409*

Bond of John Kelsey, William Bonauntre, Ralph Spayne, Thomas Wade, Robert Hebbe and William Bullok, tapicers, and John Port and Philip Tayllour, parishioners of St Denis Bakchirche, for their good behaviour towards the mistery of Cordwainers, and that none of them would in future collect money for a football (*pro pila pedali*)[4], or money called "*cok-* Membr. 2 *b* *4 March 1409*

[1] He married Joan, daughter of Edw. I and widow of Gilbert de Clare, earl of Gloucester and Hertford. He was summoned to parliament from 1299 to 1306 as earl of Gloucester and Hertford, but on the death of his wife in 1307 as "Ralph de Monthermer" only. For his will, see *Cal. of Wills*, I, p. 315. [2] Blackmore. [3] Fenchurch.

[4] In accordance with a proclamation about this time. Riley's *Memorials*, p. 571. Football and the throwing of sticks at tethered fowls were indulged in on the occasion of marriages.

sylver" for a cock, hen, capon, pullet or other bird or for any other use, and that they would not thrash (*trituret Anglice thresshe*) any hen or capon or any other bird in the streets and lanes of the city, under penalty of £20.

Note that this bond was annulled by Richard Merlawe during his mayoralty.

19 Aug. 1409 Thomas Lakenham, master of the hospital of St Bartholomew in Westsmethfeld, demands an assize of nuisance against John Watteford, prior of the house of St Bartholomew, touching his free tenement in the parish of St Sepulchre without Newgate.

Membr. 3 *b*
13 March 1409 Memorandum that, in the presence of Drew Barentyn, Mayor, and the Aldermen in the Chamber of the Guildhall, Robert Colney, draper, was examined on oath as to the number of statutes staple of Westminster[1] in which Richard Wiltshire of Heydon co. Essex, son of (John) Wiltshire, grocer, deceased, was bound to him. He answered four, of which one was executed in Chancery and the other three remained unexecuted, and that the latter were pledged for £10 to a certain William Hanyngfeld of co. Essex. When the mayor charged him on his oath to have the statutes produced in court without delay, he answered that it was impossible, as Hanyngfeld was then in Essex. However, evidence was given by credible persons that Hanyngfeld was in the city of London.

Membr. 4
7 May 1409 Richard Jardeville, one of the mayor's serjeants, was ordered to bring before the Mayor and Aldermen the plaint levied in the Sheriffs' Court between John Alleslee, draper, plaintiff, and Nicholas Walssh, draper, defendant, for a debt of £5 8s 9d.

In his count the plaintiff alleged that this money remained unpaid on an account made between them relating to certain woollen cloths. The defendant admitted a debt of 48s 10d,

[1] A statute was a bond of record. See Statute of Acton Burnel, 11 Edw. I, *Statutes of the Realm*, 1, pp. 53, 99. By the Ordinance of the Staple, bonds of this kind, with certain reservations, were allowed to be enrolled in staple towns, *ibid.* p. 337. As such, they were known as "statutes staple."

which he was ready to pay, but denied that he owed the balance of 59s 11d and offered to defend it by his law as a freeman of the city, according to the custom of the city. The plaintiff pleaded that he ought not to be admitted to his law, because it was immemorial custom in the city that if any person acknowledged himself to be debtor to another person in any sum before any alderman[1], and the creditor afterwards sued him for the amount, the debtor ought not to be admitted to his law, and the defendant had acknowledged that he was debtor of 59s 11d in the presence of William Crowmere, then and now alderman, which he was ready to verify.

The defendant denied that he had acknowledged owing 59s 11d and put himself on the record of William Crowmere, praying the court that the said William might be examined. The plaintiff did likewise. Thereupon William Crowmere said that the defendant made no such acknowledgment. Accordingly it was considered that as regards the sum of 59s 11d the plaintiff take nothing by his plaint, and that he recover the sum of 48s 10d, but without damages, because the defendant was ready to pay that amount.

Robert Steven, son of Laurence Steven of Great Jernmuth[2], was exonerated from his apprenticeship to William Butte, mercer, who was then in the Fleet prison and had ceased to instruct and provide for him. The master was summoned at his former dwelling-place and made four defaults. The

Membr. 4 *b*
18 March 1409

[1] No such custom is mentioned in any of the city books or rolls before this date. No doubt a recognisance of debt might be made before an alderman, as *locum tenens* of the mayor, and the mayor's clerk, when a bill of obligation was drawn up and sealed with the debtor's seal and the king's seal. *Statutes of the Realm*, I, pp. 53, 99. Rolls of such recognisances are preserved. The sheriffs could also take recognisances in their courts. *Munim. Gild. Lond.* I, p. 215. Recognisances were regarded as judgments in themselves and could be executed when the day of payment had passed. But even if an action had been sued, the plaintiff could produce his obligation or vouch the record, in either of which cases the defendant would be debarred from making his law. Possibly the plaintiff pleaded that the alderman was present when a verbal acknowledgment was made, and claimed that the evidence of one alderman was equal to that of the two ordinary witnesses, *pur forbarrer un homme de sa ley*. *Ibid.* p. 475. If so, there is no previous mention of this custom. The defendant willingly put himself on the evidence of the alderman and won his case.

[2] Yarmouth.

apprentice was then committed by the court to Richard Whityngton, mercer, to serve the remainder of his term.

Membr. 5
22 Dec. 1408

Writ of error demanding that the record and process of a plaint of trespass, levied in the court of Henry Pountfreit, sheriff, between John Burdon, *charietmaker*, and Richard Charlton, *pavyer*, and removed into the court of the Chamber of the Guildhall before the mayor, be brought before John Cokayn, William Haukeford, Robert Huls and Roger Horton, the king's justices assigned to examine the record and process and to correct the errors therein, if any, at the church of St Martin le Grand. Dated at Westminster 22 Dec. 1408.

Precept of the justices demanding the record and process at St Martin le Grand on 20 June. Dated at Westminster 13 Feb. 1409.

Return of Drew Barentyn, mayor, and Thomas Duke and William Norton, sheriffs, claiming the city custom of a respite of 40 days and the right of producing the record and process *oretenus* by the recorder.

Membr. 6
17 Aug. 1409

Francis Marini, merchant of Florence, in the name of the society of Francis, son of Sir Simon de Tornabonis[1], merchants of Florence, came into the Chamber and prayed that two writs of attorney, and two instruments and three open letters of the Priors of Florence, sealed with their seals, might be enrolled in the memoranda rolls of the city. The Mayor and Aldermen ordered the documents to be entered as follows:

4 March 1408

Writ of attorney testifying that Dominicus Cachynne of Florence, merchant, who by the king's licence was about to cross the seas, had appointed as his attorneys Peter Cambyn of Florence, merchant, and Francis Maryn of Florence, merchant. Dated at Westminster 4 March 1408.

27 June 1409

On 27 June 1409, according to the second indiction after the custom of the Florentines, it was certified in the Chancery of the lords Priors of the Arts and the Standard-bearer of Justice of the people and commune of Florence in

[1] *Nomine societatis Francisci domini Simonis de Tornabonis.*

the Residency Palace, in the presence of Jandonato Cecchi de Jandonatis, Gregorio Pieri Corbizini Fracassini, Ser Paulo Volte, notary, and other citizens of Florence, that Dominicus Cachynne, merchant of Florence, who during his stay in England had on 4 March 1407(8) appointed Peter Cambini and Francis Marini his attorneys in the king's Chancery, whereof he declared that there was an authentic record in the said Chancery, now appeared and revoked the above appointment of attorneys and declared himself not responsible for any future business carried out by the said Peter and Francis, and further requested Firenze, son of Pero Teci[1] of Florence, judge-ordinary and public notary, to write a public instrument concerning the said revocation, in accordance with which the said Firenze had written the present document and sealed it with his seal.

Certificate of the Priors of the Arts and the Standard-bearer of Justice that Firence Pieri Teci, who wrote the above instrument, was a public and authentic notary and that his documents were worthy of credit in public and private, within courts of justice and without. *28 June 1409*

Writ of attorney testifying that Peter Cambini, merchant of Florence, who by the king's licence was about to cross the seas, had appointed as his attorneys Francis Marini and Gerard Daniz, merchants of Florence. Dated at Westminster 18 Oct. 1408. *18 Oct. 1408*

On 27 June 1409 it was certified in the Chancery of the Priors of the Arts and the Standardbearer of Justice of the people and commune of Florence that Peter Cambini, who had appointed Francis Marini and Gerard Daniz his attorneys on 18 Oct. 1407[2], now appeared and revoked the appointment and requested Firenze, son of Piero Teci, to write an instrument to that effect. *27 June 1409* Membr. 6 *b*

Open letter of the Priors and Standardbearer of Justice to the same effect. Dated at Florence 28 June 1409. *28 June 1409*

[1] *Firenze, filius Peri Teci.*
[2] An error for 1408, see above.

Certificate of the same that Dominicus Chaccyni and Peter Cambini, who had been accustomed to carry on business in England from the kalends of June 1408 according to the first indiction after the custom of the Florentines, had not been since that date and were not now partners of Francis, son of Sir Simon de Cornabuonis (*sic*), citizen and merchant of Florence, and that from the same date there was no partnership (*societas*) between them, such partnership as previously existed having been terminated on that date. Dated at Florence 28 June 1409.

Membr. 7
6 Feb. 1409

Precept was given by the mayor to Richard Jardeville to bring before the Mayor and Aldermen a plaint pending in the Sheriffs' Court between Richard Crowlond, plaintiff, and Thomas Lamport, goldsmith, defendant.

The plaint set forth a claim of £36 16s 4d, which the plaintiff in his count declared to be due on an account made between the parties in the parish of St Mary Colchirche on 22 Feb. 1407 before Robert Upgate and John Cloos, the plaintiff's auditors, for arrears of a rent-charge (*pro censu domus*). To this the defendant had pleaded that on 6 March 1407, by mediation of John St Jermayn, renter, it was agreed between the parties that he should be exonerated from the arrears, and on this pleading he put himself on the country.

Afterwards, on 15 July 1409, the defendant appeared before the Mayor and Aldermen and, being examined on his oath according to the custom of the city upon the matter contained in the plaintiff's bill, said that he was in Calais at the time of the supposed account, and that neither Robert Upgate and John Cloos nor any others were appointed auditors by the plaintiff. The plaintiff was also examined and admitted that his claims were not stated in the account. Accordingly it was considered that he take nothing by his plaint.

26 June 1409

Writ to the mayor to proceed without delay in an assize of *freshforce*[1] without writ which he had summoned before

[1] Assizes of *novel disseisin*, or *freshforce*, were begun by a bill, making plaint of intrusion, brought into the Husting or to a Congregation of Mayor and Aldermen in the Chamber of the Guildhall. A copy of this bill was sent to the sheriffs, whose officer summoned the tenants on Wednesday to appear on the following Saturday before the two sheriffs

himself in the Chamber of the Guildhall, the assize having previously been before Thomas Duke and William Norton, sheriffs, in the king's court of the city, between John Bodelee and Elizabeth, widow of Thomas Welford, concerning three parts of a messuage in the parish of St Mary Somerset, which assize was being grievously delayed. Dated at Westminster 26 June 1409.

Return of the mayor that he had not taken the said assize before himself out of the Sheriffs' Court, but that it was still pending before the sheriffs.

William Crane, haberdasher, formerly servant in the art of Haberdashery to John Frenssh, goldsmith, came before the Mayor and Aldermen in the Chamber of the Guildhall and was examined on his oath on certain matters relating to an action of debt of £42 12s brought by William Yrby and John Corner, merchants, against the said John Frenssh and his wife Katherine, trading sole as a merchant, which action after being levied in the Sheriffs' Court was then pending before the Mayor and Aldermen. In answer to questions by the recorder he said that the goods mentioned in the action had not been bought by him for the use of John and Katherine, but for his own use, that those goods never came to the use of John and Katherine, that the latter knew nothing about the purchase, and that he had converted to his own use the goods and the money received for the same goods and had used them to pay his own debts. Membr. 7 *b* *8 Feb. 1409*

Writ to the mayor that whereas William Tiryngton, clerk, had surrendered at the Fleet prison after being put in exigent in the Husting and outlawed in an action before the justices at Westminster at the suit of Laurence Markeys, *fusycyan*, for having broken into the latter's house and carried away goods to the value of £40, with force and arms and against the peace, and whereas the king had pardoned the outlawry *22 Oct. 1409*

and coroner. The assize, or body of jurors, might be summoned to appear on the same day or some other Saturday, at the plaintiff's convenience. This court was not a true Sheriffs' Court, and the mayor had no power to call the action into the Mayor's Court, as supposed by Chancery. See *Munim. Gild. Lond.* (R.S.), I, pp. 195–7.

on condition that he submitted to justice, and whereas precept had been given to the sheriffs to summon the prosecutor and the said William had been mainprised for his appearance, certain malevolent persons had caused him to be arrested and detained in prison, as the king was informed, wherefore the mayor was commanded to bring him before the justices on 23 Oct. that he might keep his day and save his mainpernors harmless. Witness W. Thirnyng, 22 Oct. 1409.

Return of Drew Barantyn, mayor, that before the arrival of the writ the said William Tiryngton had been taken and detained in the king's prison at the suit of Laurence Markeys on a bill of trespass, which was pending in the king's court before the mayor; nevertheless the mayor would bring him as required.

Membr. 8
30 March 1409

Memorandum that on Saturday *in Ramispalmarum*[1] 1409 Salamon Oxney, John Palyng, Robert Halle and William Adys, then wardens of the art of the Goldsmiths, came before the Mayor, Aldermen and Sheriffs[2], and after reciting letters patent granted by assent of parliament, following on a petition made to King Edward III and his council in parliament in the first year of his reign, whereby it was granted that the Goldsmiths might choose from themselves good, lawful and sufficient men to inquire as to false work, to correct defects in the mistery and to set punishments upon offenders with the help of the mayor and sheriffs, and also letters patent of the sixteenth year of King Richard II, whereby it was granted that the Goldsmiths should be one perpetual commonalty, and that yearly they might choose four wardens to govern the mistery, and further letters patent of the present king given with the assent of the lords spiritual and temporal in his parliament in the fifth year of his reign, whereby he confirmed the grants of King Edward III, even though it might be that the concessions thus made had not been used, and granted that the Goldsmiths should have the scrutiny, survey, assay and government of all kinds of gold and silver work within the city and suburbs and in common fairs throughout the realm and might punish defects found there-

[1] Probably the eve of Palm Sunday is meant.
[2] Acting as justices of the peace.

in—the said wardens informed the Mayor, Aldermen and Sheriffs that divers persons of divers misteries of the city were working in gold and silver in shops and in private chambers in an evil and undue manner, in contempt of the king, to the intolerable damage of the whole people and to the shame and scandal of the art aforesaid, wherefore in accordance with the charters they prayed the mayor and sheriffs to assign two of their serjeants to accompany the wardens on their scrutiny and survey and to preserve the king's peace.

Thereupon the mayor and sheriffs assigned William Est, the mayor's serjeant, and Henry Roberd, the sheriffs' serjeant, and ordered them to arrest and lead to prison all those they should find by testimony of the wardens to be rebellious, contrariant or resisting in that part, and to report to the mayor and sheriffs what they had done and found. And the same day the serjeants and wardens entered the shop of a certain William Multon, cutler, in Fletestrete, and the wardens found there certain articles of silver, to wit, one buckle and one pendant, newly-worked, which they took for assay. And upon this William Multon with his servants left the shop and with force and arms and in contempt of the king rebelliously compelled the wardens to lay down the said articles, whereupon the serjeants by command of the wardens arrested William Multon and brought him before the Mayor, Aldermen and Sheriffs in the Guildhall, who after due consideration committed him to prison until *etc.*

Afterwards on 9 March the said William Multon, on the request of the good men of the art of Cutlers, was handed over under bail to Richard Pulle, cutler, to bring him before the Mayor and Aldermen where and when *etc.* Later, on Thursday 24 Oct. 1409, Richard Pulle was ordered to bring the said William on the Monday following to answer, and he, being charged and examined on oath, could not deny the record, nor the evidence of the wardens and the report of the serjeants that he had forced them to put back the silver articles. Accordingly it was considered that he be committed to prison to remain there until the Mayor and Aldermen should be better advised.

Membr. 9
11 Oct. 1409

Precept was given to bring before the Mayor and Aldermen a plaint pending in the Sheriffs' Court between Simon Copshep, draper, plaintiff, and Nicholas Plurio, *galeyman*, defendant, in a plea of debt of £90, in obedience to which the plaint was brought into court, together with a record of the proceedings, wherein it was contained that as the defendant was not free of the city nor to be found within it, order had been given to William Traynell, sheriffs' serjeant, to attach him by cloths of divers colours in the custody of John Dys, and that after the attachment the defendant had made three defaults at Foreign Courts before the sheriffs.

Afterwards on 12 Oct. the plaintiff made his declaration before the Mayor and Aldermen, in which he claimed £90 for woollen cloth sold to the defendant. The defendant made default on 16 Oct. Therefore it was considered that the plaintiff recover his debt and that the goods belonging to the defendant be appraised by good and lawful men of the city and delivered to the plaintiff. On 16 Oct. a valuation was made by John Claveryng, Thomas Symond, John Goldehauke and John Cake, drapers, and John Dryver and Godfrey Reynold, upholders, as follows:

145 *duszeins* of narrow cloth (*panni estreit*), *viz.* 56 of blanket, 32 of red, 14 of black, 15 of *blod*, 16 of russet, 5 of green, 4 of *medle*, 3 of *murree*, at 11s 6d the dozen; 2 chests, 2s and 20d; one chest called a "*cofyn*," 6d; one pair of gloves of *platys* and one *bokeler*, 12d; one *stantys*[1], one *glasse* and one *calamar*[2], 6d; one pair of tables[3], 6d; one *garnement* of Gascoign *shappe*[4] of striped *frise*, 2s; one *garnement* of *motle frise* doubled with black, 5s; 3 doublets, 2s; 3 caps (*capucia*) of divers colours, 12d; 3 pairs of old *hosyn*, 12d; 4 *shertys* and six pairs of drawers (*bracce*), 2s; 5 sacks and one *sarpuler*, 2s; one *arblast*[5], one *gyrdill*, 12 arrows and one *vice*[6], 4s; *cas puddynges*[7] and one *barell*, 4d; total, 25s 6d. Sum total, £84 13s.

The above goods were delivered to the plaintiff under

[1] *Sc.* standish, a pen-tray.
[2] Pen-case.
[3] Tablets, or a game-board.
[4] Shape.
[5] Cross-bow.
[6] A screw or winch for bending the cross-bow.
[7] Meaning uncertain. Cheese puddings?

mainprise to answer therefor if the defendant should come within a year and a day *etc.* Further it was agreed by the court on conscientious grounds[1] that the plaintiff should pay back to the defendant the sum of £10 received from him when the latter bought the cloth. Immediately afterwards the serjeant arrested that sum in the plaintiff's hands at the suit of Robert Twyer, draper, in a plea of debt of £26 19s 4d pending before the court.

Afterwards on 6 Nov. the said Simon Copshep produced in court a writ of *supersedeatis* directed to the Mayor and Aldermen reciting that, since the king had precedence of other creditors, the said Simon, who had in his hands £10 Membr. 9 *b*
of the goods of Nicholas Plureo, had been ordered in the court of Exchequer to pay to the king's collectors of custom and subsidy the sum of 115s 3d, which were due from the said Nicholas Plureo, merchant of Venice, for the *parva custuma*[2] and subsidy on goods brought into the port of London. The mayor was ordered to suspend all claims as regards that amount. Witness J. Cokayn at Westminster, 5 Nov. 1409.

Accordingly, since the said Simon had paid the king 115s 3d, it was considered that he pay the balance of the £10, *viz.* £4 4s 9d, to Robert Twyer.

[1] *Consultum fuit ulterius per Curiam per eorum conscienciam quod* etc.

[2] Originally a duty on foreign merchants established by the *Statutum de Nova Custuma* or *Carta Mercatoria* of 1303. *Munim. Gild. Lond.* (R.S.), II (1), p. 209. It was abolished by Edw. II in 1309 in the statute of Stamford as an experiment, *Rot. Parl.* I, p. 444 *a*, but subsequently revived. See Cunningham, *Growth of Eng. Industry and Commerce*, I, pp. 277–8, 291.

ROLL A 41

Rolls of Memoranda of the time of Thomas Knolles, mayor, in the 12th year of King Henry IV

Membr. 1
15 Nov. 1410

Recognisances by Robert Coventre, grocer, Alice his wife, *brasyere*[1], and John atte Wode, *brasyere*, of Oxford, of a debt of £80 payable to John Stapulford, grocer, and John Selman at the feast of St John the Baptist next coming, and of a debt of £100 payable to the same at Easter 1412.

Membr. 1 *b*
24 Nov. 1410

William Skrene brings a plaint of intrusion against Henry Talbot, John Syntawbyn, Richard Trevage, John Trelowny, James Treverbyn, John Keynys, Thomas Kelly, John Kylmynawt, William Derby, John Tredewey and John Lawer touching his free tenement in the parishes of St Olave in Silvyrstrete, St Alban in Wodestrete, St Mary Magdalene in Milkestrete and St Peter in Wodestrete.

23 Oct. 1410

Whereas there had been discord and litigation in the Sheriffs' Court and in the Mayor's Court between John Turvey, brewer, plaintiff, and Richard Wellom, defendant, both parties agreed to put themselves on the arbitration of George Crescy and Robert Queldryk, and entered into mutual bonds of £20 to abide by the award.

Afterwards on 11 Nov. the arbitrators reported that they had inspected all writings and evidences and had examined a register relating to costs and expenses, which had been put in by both parties, but they had afterwards discovered and learnt by the evidence of trustworthy persons that one folio of the register, containing expenses, costs and a full account between the parties, had been cunningly cut out and destroyed by the said John Turvey, wherefore on 9 Nov. they had given as a final award that the said John Turvey should be precluded from all actions and claims hitherto made, and that the defendant should be free of all further trouble and molestation, and that if either party refused the award he should pay the penalty of £20 to the party accepting it.

[1] *Sc. braseour*, a brewer.

Robert Hicheman, son of Thomas Hicheman, was exonerated from his apprenticeship to John Wellys, weaver, to whom he had been apprenticed for 13 years, his master having left the city and failed to provide for him. Membr. 2 *25 Oct. 1410*

Guy Hecheman, son of Thomas Hecheman of Rikmannesworthe, who had been apprenticed for 14 years to the same master, was similarly exonerated.

Edmund Kyng, son of Thomas Kyng, who had been apprenticed for 7 years, likewise exonerated. Membr. 2 *b*

John Ilshawe, son of William Ilshawe and Margaret his wife, who had been apprenticed for 11 years, likewise exonerated. Membr. 3 *4 Nov. 1410*

Margaret Olmestede, abbess of the house of Grace of the Blessed Mary of the order of St Clare without the Wall of London[1], brings a plaint of intrusion against Richard Morcok touching her free tenement in the parish of St Botulph without Aldgate. Membr. 2 *b* *22 Dec. 1410*

Writ of *certiorari* to the mayor. Whereas a plea of trespass was pending before the King[2] between John Judde, plaintiff, and John Saler, defendant, the action not yet having been pleaded to an issue, and whereas a certain Thomas Alfred, merchant, had lately affirmed a plaint of detinue of 1000 *degeon*[3] against the said John Saler in the Sheriffs' Court, which had been removed before the Mayor, the king demands information as to the said plaint and the time when it was levied and affirmed. Witness W. Gascoigne at Westminster, 7 Feb. 1411. Membr. 3 *b* *7 Feb. 1411*

Return of the mayor that there was no plaint of detinue as mentioned in the writ, but that a plaint of account on the receipt of 1000 "*degeoun made*," value 100s, levied in the Sheriffs' Court, had been removed before the Mayor and was

[1] See above, p. 286, n. 1.
[2] *Coram rege*, in King's Bench.
[3] *Sc. dudgeon*, short lengths of hard wood used for knife or dagger handles. Cf. Letter Book H, fo. 118, *qe nulles manches darbre forsque digeoun soyent colourez*. See *N.E.D.* for references as to dudgeon being of maple, wild-ash root and boxwood.

then pending unsettled. There was also an original bill concerning merchandise called "*a thowsand degeoun,*" value 4 marks, pending before the Mayor, arising out of a business transaction at the market-town of Burdeux[1], the pleadings of which had gone as far as a jury according to the law merchant and the custom of the city. This plaint was levied and affirmed on 9 Jan. 1411.

Membr. 4
12 March 1411

Writ of *corpus cum causa* demanding the body and the cause of the taking and detaining of Alice Messynger. Dated at Westminster 12 March 1411.

Return of the mayor and sheriffs that Alice Messynger, under the name of Alice Messanger, had been taken and detained in prison at the suit of William Boydell, *squyer*, by virtue of a plaint of detinue of a gold and diamond ring levied in the Sheriffs' Court and removed before the Mayor and Aldermen.

Membr. 4 *b*
7 April 1411

Robert Thorley, treasurer of Calais, came into court and acknowledged a writing, dated 5 April, whereby he constituted Thomas Vale, citizen of London, and John Lekeford his attorneys to receive from the collectors of the subsidy on wool, hides and woolfells in the port of London all moneys and securities accruing from three parts of the subsidy for a period of two years from Michaelmas in the preceding year.

2 May 1411

Memorandum that Alexander Albertis paid the sum of £48 2s 6d in court to Ralph Middelton, mercer, who was acting on behalf of Sir John Fuldon, chaplain, executor of the will of John Fawconer, late parson of the church of Little Cressyngham, this sum being due on an exchange of 300 ducats, the residue of £66 13s 4d, made on 2 Jan. 1408 by the said Ralph and Edmund Alderford, on behalf of John Fawconer, with Philip de Albertis, brother of the said Alexander. Thereupon Ralph Middelton acquitted the said Alexander and Philip and the society of the Albertines of all further claims, and John Fauntleroy and John Admund, mercers, undertook to save the society harmless as regards the above sum.

[1] Bordeaux.

Writ of error to the mayor, aldermen and sheriffs, demanding that the record and process of an action brought by Richard Reynowde, vintner, against William Hervy, *hurer*[1], for a debt of 20 marks 3s 4d before the Mayor and Aldermen, be produced before William Gascoigne, William Haukeford, Robert Tirwhyt and Robert Hull, the king's justices assigned to examine the same at the church of St Martin le Grand. Dated at Westminster 30 March 1411. Membr. 5 *30 March 1411*

John Reynowde, vintner, brought a bill before the Mayor and Aldermen against William Hervy, *hurer*, for non-payment of the sum of 20 marks 3s 4d, which he had agreed to pay on behalf of one Walter Tyd, taverner, who had bought from the plaintiff two pipes of red wine and one pipe of white wine in the parish of St Mary Wolnoth on 2 Aug. 1410. Membr. 5 *b* *23 Jan. 1411*

The defendant was summoned by John Upton, the mayor's serjeant, and appeared on 26 Jan. He denied having acted as surety for Walter Tyd in the purchase. The plaintiff then prayed, in accordance with the law merchant and the custom of the city, that William Wanstall, scrivener, and Henry Norfolk his servant, who were conversant with the facts, should be examined. The defendant likewise prayed that the matter should be examined "peremptorily," under penalty of condemnation.

On the following Saturday the said William and Henry were examined on oath and testified that the defendant became surety as alleged. Accordingly it was considered that the plaintiff recover his debt and damages 6s 8d against the defendant and his pledge, John Goodburghe, haberdasher, and execution against the same was granted.

Writ of *certiorari*, reciting that John Mapilton, junior, had recently before the King impleaded Robert Chestreford, cordwainer, and William Clay, currier, for having on 23 June 1407 broken into his house in the parish of St Bride and carried away timber to the value of £20, to which the defendants had pleaded that they had previously sued an assize of *freshforce* before the Sheriffs against the said John, John Mapilton, senior, clerk, Peter Mapilton, Robert Faucom, Membr. 6 *12 May 1411*

[1] A maker of *hures*, woolly caps.

John Kirkeby, Ellis Reyner and John Basset for having disseised them of five messuages in that parish and on 7 May they had received judgment that they recover the said five messuages, which they were prepared to prove by the record, and the said John Mapilton then said in replication that there was no such record. Accordingly the mayor is ordered to bring the record, if it exists, before the King on the octave of the Holy Trinity. Witness W. Gascoigne at Westminster, 12 May 1411.

Return of the mayor that it was contrary to the city's liberties to send any record out of the city except in "foreign warranties[1]" before the Mayor and Sheriffs[2], and in that case the record and process ought to be sent before the justices of the Common Bench and then returned to the city.

Membr. 5 *b* *9 Oct. 1411* Further writ of *certiorari*, reciting the above and noting that the record and process could not be sent outside the city. The mayor is ordered to send a transcript on 2 Nov. Witness W. Gascoigne at Westminster, 9 Oct. 1411.

Note that the transcript was sent as required.

Membr. 6 *22 Aug. 1411* Quitclaim from Guy, son of Simon Dosser, late saddler, to Henry Pountfreyt, saddler, brother and executor of the said Simon.

Membr. 6 *b* *10 Sept. 1411* Quitclaim from Thomas Wilmot, cutler, to William Barton, junior, late his apprentice. 1 Jan. 1410.

[1] A "foreign warranty" may be defined as follows: If a defendant in a plea relating to land in the city courts called to warrant his possession a non-citizen or foreigner, having no lands or chattels in the city whereby he might be distrained to appear, the record could be sent to Westminster before the justices of the Common Bench, who could there compel the attendance of the warrantor. The validity of the warranty having been tried, the action was returned to the city for further proceedings. This procedure was set up by the Statute of Gloucester, 6 Edw. I, c. 12. Liber Albus (*Munim. Gild. Lond.* (R.S.), 1, pp. 183–4, 198) explains the matter in reference to proprietary actions of land in the Husting on writs of right patent and in actions of *freshforce* before the sheriffs and coroner. But the same procedure took place in mixed actions relating to land, dower, waste, rents and services, *etc.* See Husting Rolls of Common Pleas, 8, m. 2; 10, m. 10; 11, m. 1; 13, m. 7 *b*; 19, m. 8; where the returns of the king's justices are enrolled.

[2] I.e. the Court of Husting.

Award of John Chadde, Richard Wellam, Thomas Kynton and John Swalowe, wardens of the mistery of Cutlers, enrolled by order of the mayor: *17 Sept. 1411*

Whereas Thomas Wilmot, cutler, had sold and alienated certain years of the apprenticeship of William Barton, junior, to William Barton, senior, glover, and had offended in other ways against the ordinances of the mistery, and had refused to be ruled and corrected by the wardens, whereof they had complained to the mayor, and whereas the said Thomas on being examined by the Mayor and Aldermen had prayed that he might accept the judgment of the wardens, they had made the following award: They award that he pay the sum of 6s 8d to the Chamber of the Guildhall, on account of the sale and alienation and the offences aforesaid, that he make a general acquittance to his late apprentice bearing date 1 Jan. 1410, and that, within eight days after the termination of the apprenticeship, at his own proper cost he cause the said William to be made free of the mistery of Cutlers. [*French*]

Membr. 7
18 July 1411

Bond of John Pottere, cordwainer, together with William atte Wode, goldsmith, John Champeneye, cordwainer, Walter Hydeman, shearman, and William Newham, cordwainer, to John Proffyt, chamberlain of the city, in £500 payable on 25 July, that the said John Pottere would appear before the Mayor and Aldermen when summoned, that he would observe and fulfil the decree and ordinance of the Mayor and Aldermen concerning himself, that he would keep the peace with John Martyn of Cornhill, William Doucet, Richard Shote and John Goodman, the present masters, and John Messyngham, John Yepeswyche, William Keneston and John Andrewe, late masters of the Cordwainers, and all the king's people, and all the piecers (*pictaciarios*) called "*cobelers*" dwelling in London, of whatsoever nation they might be, and that he would not interfere henceforth with any ordinance or regulation concerning the said mistery of Cordwainers[1].

[1] The dispute between the Cordwainers and Cobblers concerned the amount of new leather which a cobbler might apply to an old shoe. In 1409 the Cordwainers petitioned the king, who ordered an inquiry, the result of which is set out in Riley's *Memorials*, pp. 571–4. On 10 Dec. 1410 the Mayor, Aldermen and Sheriffs, in their capacity as guardians

The same day a similar bond was made by John Tebaud and George Benet, cordwainers, William Bray, fruiterer, John Sadeler, vintner, and John Yonge and John Wyghte, cordwainers.

Afterwards, since sufficient testimony was given before Thomas Fauconer, Mayor[1], and the Aldermen, both by late masters and by Richard Balman, John Baldewyn, John Chaumpeneys and Thomas atte Vanne, then masters of the Cordwainers, as to the good behaviour of John Potter and John Thebaud, and because the above bonds were not sufficient in law, and further because John Potter, John Thebaud and the others mentioned in the bonds had paid a fine of £3 to the Chamber to have the bonds annulled, therefore it was considered by the court, with the consent of the chamberlain, that the bonds should be annulled and withdrawn.

Membr. 8
15 June 1411

Robert Rykedon of co. Essex brought before the Mayor and Aldermen two letters[2] sent to Thomas Cogsale by John Haukwode, knight, in the following words:

8 Nov. (1392)

"Dere S' I grete you wel and do you to wytyn þ^{t} at the makyng of þis lettre I was in god poynt I thank god... I sende Johan Sampson bryngere of þis lettre to you enformed of certeyn thyngs quiche he schal tellyn you be mouthe Qwerfore I preye you þat ye levyn hym as my persone Wrytyn at Florence þe vii day of Novembre.

John Haukwode Chivaler."

20 Feb. 1393

"Dere trusty & welbiloved frend hertliche I grete you wel desiryng to heren god tidynges of youre welfare & preying you þ^{t} ye be helpyng & conseillyng to my welbiloved squyer Jankyn Sampson touchyng þ^{t} he hath to purseu for me atte þis tyme & nameliche for my sauf condutes & touchyng my will & my purpos I praye you þ^{t} ye wele yeve fei & credence

of the peace, gave judgment that a *pecyng* was a whole "quarter" of a shoe, which cobblers were entitled to apply to an old shoe, as against the contention of the Cordwainers that a *pecyng* was only part of a quarter. *Cal. of Letter Book I*, p. 96.

[1] Mayor, 1414–15.

[2] See *London Topographical Record*, XIII, pp. 10–15; and above, p. 257, n. 2. These are the earliest extant private letters written in English. R. L. Kingsford, *Prejudice and Promise*, pp. 22–3.

to the forsaid Jankyn Sampson of al that he wele seyen you by mouthe & also I preye you þ[t] ye wele speke to Hopky Rikyngdon & to Jankyn Serjaunt Robert Lyndeseye & alle myn other frendes þ[t] þei don as þe forseid Jankyn Sampson seyth to you touchyng my will Tristy frend þe holy gost have you in his kepyng writen at Florence þe xx day of Feverer þe yer of oure lord mccclxxxxiii."

The same 15 June the said Robert Rikedon brought before the same Mayor and Aldermen a copy of a certain indenture made between Thomas Coggesale and John Sampson, servant of the aforesaid John Haukwode, containing the following words: *15 June 1411*

"This endenture mad bitwen my maister Thomas Coggesale on that on half & me John Sampson on that other half witnesseth that my maister sire John Haukwode knyght bad me the forseid John Sampson seyen my credence to you Thomas Coggeshale in this wise: my maister sire John Haukwode greteth you wel & sendeth you to seyen that he purposeth hym for to comen in to Engelond. & I am comen to pursueu ii saufcondutes on for my maister & another my self & v men & v hors & therfor I wele hien me ayen to Galeys[1] therwilles that alle these lordes been there. & also my mayster sendeth you to seyen that yif he deye bifore his comyng hom that ye wolde knowe his will what he wolde were don with the londes & tenementz that been purchased to his bihufthe in Englond for he hath ordeyned for his doghtren in ytaille[2]. at ferste he wolde that the ledene halle with the avowesones of the cherches be sold. & ii prestes yfounded in the nonnerie of Hethyngham[3] to singen there in my maistre chapel & i prest in the parisshe chirche of Hethyngham Sibille. & also yif my lady Haukwode overlive my maister sire John Haukwode & kepe hire sole & come in to Engelond he preyeth you & alle the other feffetz ye wolde enfeffe here in lisstones[4] & ostages[5] in Hethyngham *20 April 1393*

[1] Calais? [2] Italy.

[3] Castle Hedingham and Sible Hedingham.

[4] Liston's. Probably not the manor but a house formerly belonging to the Essex family of that name.

[5] A house called the Hostage or Hostelage in which the priest of the chapelry of Sible Hedingham lived. Temple Leader and Marcotti, *Sir John Hawkwood*, p. 308.

to terme of here lyf: the reversioun to John Haukwode the sone of here in the tayle And the remenaunt to be kept in handis of the feffez til John my maistressone be of ful age. And at his ful age enfeffin hym ther in, that is to wetin to him and to his heires of his body getyn & for defaute of issue of his body. he wele that the forseide londes ben sold & do for his soule & for his frendes as yow thenketh best: And nameliche for the soules of hem that weren slayn for his love. And in the menetyme that my maistressone is withinne age that the profitez of the londes also be doon for my maistressoule & yif my maister come hom as I hope he shal than he wele ordeyne for hym self as hym liketh best. This is wretin by me forseid John Sampson atte the newe hall in boram[1] in Essex the xx^e^ day of April the yer of oure lord the kyng Richard xvi^e^."

12 Aug. 1411 Bond of Walter Jay, vintner, Walter Broun, dyer, and John Alfeld, draper, to Margaret Abelle, widow, in £52 that the said Walter Jay would not allege or show a protection or writ of the king to oust the Mayor's Court or Sheriffs' Court of their jurisdiction, so as to destroy a plaint of the said Margaret.

9 July 1411 Bond of William Trigillowe of co. Cornwall and John Megree, pewterers, and John Trigillowe and Henry Bedell, brewers, citizens of London, in £40 to John Profyt, chamberlain of the city, that the above William would keep in repair the lands, tenements and rents of John, son and heir of John Clophill, late of London, situate in the parish of St Botolph without Aldrichesgate, and render an annual account to the chamberlain of the profits received from the same, which lands *etc.* were extended as of an annual value of £10 3s 4d above all reprises, a third part of which profits belonged to Elizabeth, mother of the said orphan, by way of dower for her life, and further that he would pay to the chamberlain whatever remained of the profits, after expenses for repairs and moneys disbursed for the use of the orphan.

[1] Boreham.

ROLL A 42

Roll of Memoranda of the time of Robert Chichele, mayor of the city of London, in the 13th year of King Henry IV

Lease from Sir Robert Dukesworthe, master or warden of the new college of minor canons of St Paul's church, to Nicholas Ryngwode, bladesmith, and Emma his wife, for 20 years of a tenement in Diserlane[1], bounded on the east by a tenement of the minor canons in the occupation of Roger Westwode, on the west by Diserlane, on the south by a tenement of St Paul's church in the occupation of Sir William de Coloigne, canon, and on the north by the king's highway, at an annual rent of 4 marks, the tenants agreeing to keep the premises in repair, including the pavements, to cleanse a watercourse running through the lane from the Scoldynghous[2], to keep both ends of the lane closed with gates, keys and locks, not to remove any new buildings they might erect on the site, and not to sublet or assign the premises. Membr. 1 *14 Jan. (1412)*

Lease from Nicholas Whaddon, esquire, of co. Berks and Agnes his wife to William Gynore, *steynour*, for 20 years of a corner-shop with houses and solars built above it, and two other shops and solars on the south side, of which one was in the occupation of the lessee and the other late in the occupation of Thomas Meryng, clerk, the whole being situate outside Ludgate in the parish of St Martin, at an annual rent of 5 marks 4d. Dated 1 Feb. 1412. Membr. 1 *b* *4 Feb. 1412*

John Wolmer, cousin of William Serle, carpenter, who had been apprenticed to Richard Morcok, carpenter, by the said William, was exonerated from his indentures, because his master had left the city and failed to provide for him. *13 Jan. 1412*

Lease from Nicholas Whaddon, esquire, of co. Berks and Membr. 2 *4 Jan.* 1412[3]

[1] *Sc.* Dicereslane, otherwise called "the Rydye," in the parishes of St Nicholas Shambles and St Faith. See Harbin's *Dictionary of London.*

[2] Scalding-house, where pigs, geese, capons *etc.* were scalded, so as to remove hair and feathers.

[3] The date in the margin is that on which the deed was brought in to be enrolled. It was probably executed the previous Easter.

Agnes his wife to Richard Wellom, cutler, for 20 years of two shops outside Ludgate, which William Milward, late horner, held of the demise of Sir William Stratton, knight, and Ellen his wife, at an annual rent of 70s. Dated at London on Easterday the same year.

20 March 1412 John Multon, skinner, appeared before the mayor and John Penne, alderman, and acknowledged having received the sum of £100 due on a statute merchant from the late Sir Andrew Cavendissh, knight, of co. Suffolk, the said Sir Andrew having bound himself in £200 on 18 Oct. 1391 before John Hadeley, mayor of the Staple of Westminster, to pay the sum of £100 to the said John Multon on 18 April following.

26 March 1412 William Briggenorth, late apprentice of John Cosseham, mercer, acknowledged as his deed a public instrument, dated 24 March 1411, according to the fifth indiction and in the second year of Pope John XXIII, witnessing that, after a discussion with his late master in the church of St Lawrence Jewry, he had confessed that he had not acted as his attorney, factor or servant for seven years before last Christmas or at any time since, and immediately afterwards he had made a quitclaim to his master of all actions, real, personal and mixed, and had renounced all exceptions[1] and especially those of *doli mali* and *in hoc facto*, and all remedies and aids of civil and canon law and especially of the law[2] saying that general renunciations were of no validity except in so far as they preceded special renunciations. Witnesses, John Lane, alderman, Thomas Aleyn, Simon Bartelot, John Coventre, Richard Coventre, Richard Bures, John Middelton, Richard Herry, John Wareyn and Richard Awedre, mercers.

[1] *Renunciat dictus Willelmus omnibus et singulis excepcionibus et specialiter doli mali et in hoc facto dicto Willelmo erga prefatum Johannem competentibus.* An exception was not a direct negation of the plaintiff's story, but a suggestion that for one reason or another he had no right of action. For the *excepcio doli* see Pollock and Maitland, *Hist. Eng. Law*, II, p. 535. *In hoc facto* seems to be a similar exception, possibly the plea *non est factum meum, nient mon fet, ibid.* pp. 221, 224, or the *conditio sine causa seu injusta causa*. With this document compare that in *Archaeologia*, XXVIII, p. 227.

[2] *Juri dicenti.* This *jus* appears in the document of 1294 referred to above.

Certificates of Robert Northelod, clerk, of the diocese of Wells, public notary, procurator-general of the court of Canterbury, and of William Bray, clerk, of the diocese of Lincoln, public notary, who were present.

Writ demanding that William Sutton, clerk, and John Leek, *tawere*[1], who had been arrested and detained in prison, be brought before the king in person (*in propria persona nostra*) with the cause of their taking and detaining. Dated at Canterbury 6 April 1412. Membr. 2 *b* *6 April 1412*

Return of Robert Chichele, mayor, and Walter Cotton and John Reynewell, sheriffs, that William Sutton, clerk, and John Leek had been taken in the city and committed to prison on information that the former had written a paper in English, which the latter had affixed to the door of a garden in the parish of All Hallows Berkyng in Tower Ward, where on 24 Jan. certain unknown persons had broken down the earthen wall surrounding the garden, the writing on the paper being as follows:

"Here hath ben this nyght a cumpanye of trewe men by comen assent of alle this worshipfull Citee to warne yow with a litel stroke or more harme come to gader up your erbys[2] & trees or ellys it shal al be destried right as ye see for we wole have our grounde whos evyr be grucche it for we have yoven o stroke & more is for to come but yf ye with your ovne goode wylle amende it your selfe for this is not don of on or two but of many one & mo wil come of al the craftes of alle this worshipful Citee. & ther for thanke god that yo have no more harm at this tyme for thorughe þe counseille of viii men, iii score lefte to do more harme & yet þei seyne þei wole come ayen we wote never howe sone. & ther for it is the best be goddis ore[3] your ovne worship for to save: loke þ[t] noman pleyne[4] hym more but holde þ[t] he have."

By reason of the above, the said William and John had been detained until the mayor and sheriffs might take counsel as to their delivery.

[1] A tawyer, one who tawed or cured leather.
[2] Herbs. [3] Mercy. [4] Complain.

5 May 1412 Bond of Richard Newman, brewer, to Robert Bastewyk, vintner, in £20 to abide by the award of John Russell, Robert Blake, Thomas Heighelme and William Edward, salter, who had been chosen[1] by the jury between the parties, with the consent of the said Richard and Robert, to arbitrate on their differences.

22 Aug. 1412 Geo Bovy, merchant of Lucca, came into court and delivered to Thomas Aleyn, mercer, in part payment of money owed to him, an obligation dated 13 April 1412, in which a certain John Ikelyngdon, clerk, was bound to the said Geo in 244 marks.

Membr. 3

8 June 1412 Bond of John Mynne and John Tredewe, skinners, to William Grome and Thomas Sawyn, cheesemongers, in £13 7s 6d that the said John Mynne, or someone on his behalf, would produce before Aug. 1 letters under the authentic seal of the town of Bruges, proving that he or others in his name had already paid the above-mentioned sum to them.

21 Aug. 1412 Bond of John Sundyford of Camerwelle[2] co. Surrey to William Bourgchier, knight, in 50 marks, that two acquittances, which he had delivered in the presence of the mayor to a certain Walter Verney to be handed over to the said Sir William, were genuine acquittances made by Sir John Assheton, that he was the attorney of Sir John Assheton, and that neither the latter nor his executors would afterwards repudiate them.

The first acquittance, dated 24 June 1412, acknowledged receipt by Sir John de Assheton, knight, from Sir William Borugchier, knight, of the sum of 50 marks in part payment of 200 marks due to him on a recognisance, the money having been awarded to him in an arbitration concerning the manor of Rothewell, and paid by the hands of John Lopham.

Membr. 3 *b* The second acquittance, dated the same day, acknowledged receipt of the whole sum of 200 marks.

8 Sept. 1412 Bond of Stephen Turnebonis of Florence, attorney of Francis de Turnebonis and of the whole society of the same,

[1] *Per juratam inter partes predictas electam et triatam electi.*

[2] Camberwell.

and Philip de Albertis, merchant of Florence, in 100 marks, to John Reynewell, ironmonger, that they would exonerate him from any claims for £50 made against him by Henry Kaym, constable of the town of Sydingbourne[1]. This sum had been paid by Henry Kaym in the presence of Nicholas Bubbewyth, then keeper of the rolls of Chancery, to a certain Stephen Boche, attorney of the society of Turnebonis, John Reynewell being surety.

The same day a similar bond was made to save harmless the above-mentioned Philip de Albertis.

Bond of John Ballard, brewer, to Alexander de Albertis, to pay 10 marks, if authentic proof were brought before Easter either that Maurice Senain of Ireland was alive at the present date, or, if he were dead, that he or some one in his name before his death had received from the society of the Albertines the sum of 40 gold florins. *13 Sept. 1412*

William Furnesse of co. Lancaster, who had bound himself apprentice to John Carleton, goldsmith, by indentures enrolled at the Guildhall on 9 Nov. 1410 in a register (*papiro*) marked C, reported that his master had died and prayed the Mayor and Aldermen to assign him to some other good man of the same mistery to learn his trade and serve the remainder of his term. And as this was a reasonable petition and consonant with the custom of the city, the Mayor and Aldermen, with the consent of the said William Fournesse, assigned the said William Furneux[2] to William Randolph, goldsmith, on condition that, if his master or his master's executors testified to the chamberlain that he had served well and faithfully, he should become a freeman of the city. *3 Nov. 1412*

Membr. 4

Writ of *certiorari* demanding that information be sent to Chancery concerning the examination of Richard Fylongley, esquire, and John Broun in the presence of Thomas Knolles, late Mayor, the Recorder and the Aldermen of the City, with regard to an alleged release from the said Richard to the said John and other matters touching an action of account between them pending before the justices of the Bench; and *4 Oct. 1412*

[1] Sittingbourne co. Kent. [2] *Sic.*

further, concerning the evidence of Thomas Wodyngfeld, esquire, the king's serjeant-at-arms, taken before the Mayor, Aldermen and Recorder. Dated at Westminster 4 Oct. 1412.

Return of the mayor, Robert Chichele, as follows: The plaintiff Richard Fylongley and the defendant John Broun had appeared before the Mayor, Recorder and Aldermen on 16 Oct. 1411, in connection with the action pending before the justices of the Bench, when John Broun, being examined on oath, said that Richard Fylongley sealed a quitclaim and gave it to him in his house in the parish of St Dunstan, but he could not remember whether the person who wrote the quitclaim was cleric or lay, young or old, or where it was written or in whose presence, and that afterwards in his house he accounted with the said Richard every night and sometimes paid him a noble or two, more or less, and sent down fish, spices and other things by Richard's orders to his manor of Hertfeld[1] in payment of arrears, but he did not know the amount or value of them. Further, he said in examination that no one was present when these payments were made beyond Richard and himself, and that no other account was made. On the same day Thomas Wodyngfeld appeared before the Mayor, Aldermen and Recorder, and said that he had taken into his service a certain John, who had been servant of John Broun, and afterwards when they were in Gascony, this servant told him that John Broun had secretly applied Richard Fylongley's seal without his knowledge to the pendant of a large blank sheet of parchment, at a time when Richard was ill in Broun's house. When he, the witness, remarked that John Broun was much indebted to Richard Fylongley for the office of weighing and tronage in the city, the servant replied that John Broun had told him that the parchment was for a deed, in order that the king might be excluded from his debt. On the other hand John Broun swore expressly that at the time when Richard Fylongley was sick in his house he had no menservants at all but only women.

[1] Hartfield.

Memorandum that the Mayor and Aldermen called before themselves a plaint levied in the Sheriffs' Court by Thomas Coventry, *hurer*, against William Dylcok and John Dylcok as executors of the will of Robert Drayton, late of Coventry, barber, for a debt of £10. The said Thomas and John appeared on 8 July, when the plaintiff, being examined in the Inner Chamber as to the matter of the bill, said that the defendant had goods of the testator in administration and was well able to pay the debt. The defendant offered to pay the whole or as much as the plaintiff demanded, if it could be legally proved that he ever had or administered any goods, chattels or rents of the testator, and he offered to produce authentic letters under the seal of the city of Coventry. The plaintiff agreed to be precluded from his action, if he produced such letters. Membr. 5 *20 April 1412*

On July 19 the defendant brought letters proving that he never had any such goods in administration or received any profits or considerations (*avantagia*) from the lands and tenements of the testator. Therefore it was considered that the plaintiff be excluded *etc.*

Memorandum that Robert Broun, goldsmith, complained that great damage and injury was being done to his tenement and wharf near Fletebrigge in Fletestret by the raising of the pavement on the north side opposite the wharf, as the result of which the watercourse coming from the west, which ran down the middle of the street to the bridge, so flooded the wharf that he lost his profit from it. Accordingly on 16 Oct. the mayor and aldermen went to the tenement and wharf, and acting on the view and report of the sworn masters of the Masons and Carpenters of the city, gave orders that the pavements on either side of the street should be of the same height, and that neither of them should in future be so raised higher than the other as to prevent the water having a free course down the middle of the street to the drain[1] at Fletebrigge. Membr. 5 *b* *12 Oct. 1412*

Writ demanding that the mayor send before the King at Westminster a general release, dated 12 Nov. 1410, from *13 Oct. 1412*

[1] *In voragine.*

William Wardon, late abbot of the monastery of S[t] Mary of Graces by the Tower, to William Sampson, fishmonger. The writ recites that the present abbot, Roger, had brought an action against William Sampson for breaking into the close and buildings of the monastery during the time of the late abbot, and the defendant William had put in the release to exclude the abbot from his action, and the abbot had disputed the release. The document had been returned to William Sampson with orders to bring it again before the court on 6 Oct. last. But meanwhile William Sampson had produced the release in other proceedings in the Sheriffs' Court and deposited it there, and the document had been handed over by the sheriffs to the mayor, with the result that William Sampson had been unable to bring it before the King on 6 Oct., as he complained, wherefore the mayor is ordered to produce it on 15 Oct., in order that the action might be continued. Witness W. Gascoigne at Westminster, 13 Oct. 1412.

End of Rolls A 25—A 42

A LIST OF LESS USUAL WORDS IN THE TEXT

INDEX OF SUBJECTS

INDEX OF NAMES AND PLACES

For EU product safety concerns, contact us at Calle de José Abascal, 56–1°,
28003 Madrid, Spain or eugpsr@cambridge.org.

www.ingramcontent.com/pod-product-compliance
Ingram Content Group UK Ltd.
Pitfield, Milton Keynes, MK11 3LW, UK
UKHW051449290926
15471UKWH00008B/1101
* 9 7 8 1 1 0 7 4 6 3 9 7 4 *